British Merchant Ships
Sunk By U Boats
In
The 1914-1918 War

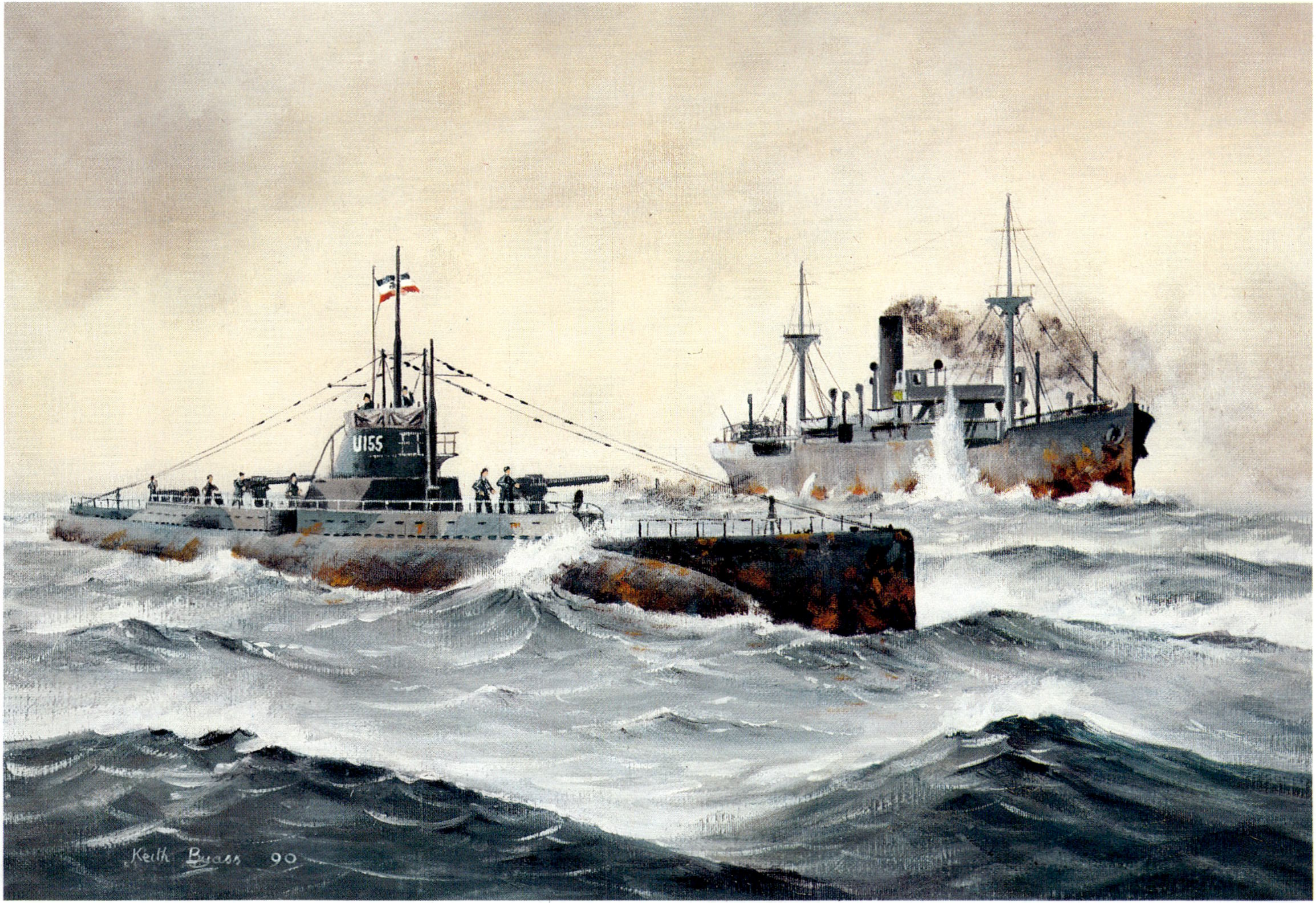
U155
Keith Byass 90

BRITISH MERCHANT SHIPS SUNK BY U BOATS IN THE 1914-1918 WAR

A. J. TENNENT

THE STARLING PRESS LTD.
PRINTERS
ROGERSTONE, NEWPORT, GWENT
1990

© A. J. Tennent, 1990

All rights reserved. No part of this publication may be reproduced, stored in a retrieval system, or transmitted in any form or by any means, electronic, mechanical, photocopying, recording or otherwise, without prior permission in writing from the Publisher.

First published in 1990

British Library Cataloguing Publication Data
Tennent, A. J. (Alan J.)
  British Merchant Ships sunk by U boats in the 1914-1918 War.
  I. British ships. Losses, 1914-1918
  I. Title
  940.45

ISBN 0 9516314 0 3

Published by A. J. Tennent, Chipstead, Kent, TN13 2RA

Printed by The Starling Press Limited, Rogerstone, Newport, Gwent. NP1 9FQ

This book is dedicated to the men of the Merchant Service who gave their lives during the 1914-1918 war.

INTRODUCTION

During the First World War over 2,500 British merchant ships, and auxiliaries on Admiralty service, were sunk by enemy action a total in excess of 8 million gross tons of shipping. Of these over 2000 ships were destroyed by U-boats.

This work contains the names of known ships that were lost through the action of Austro-Hungarian and German submarines.

Merchant ships under 500 gross tons, fishing vessels and sailing ships have been excluded from this work.

I have endeavoured to be as accurate as possible from the records that are available, however I should appreciate any additional information.

Chipstead,   A. J. Tennent
Kent.
March, 1990

ACKNOWLEDGEMENTS

In compiling this reference book I should like to thank the staff of the Guildhall Library, Lloyd's Register of Shipping, Information Section, Ministry of Defence, Naval Historical Branch for their help. My thanks to Duncan Haws for the profile drawings.

CONTENTS

British Merchant Ships' Sunk by U Boats in 1914-1918 War 9
Index of Ships' Names 241
Index of Places 253

BRITISH MERCHANT SHIPS SUNK BY U BOATS IN THE 1914-1918 WAR

ABERDEEN LIME CO. LTD—ABERDEEN

BALLOCHBUIE* 921 Grt. Blt. *1905
20.4.1917: Torpedoed and sunk in the North Sea 7 miles E. from May Island, Firth of Forth by the German submarine *UC 41* whilst on a voyage from Aberdeen to Sunderland in ballast. 3 lost including Master.

ABERDEEN STEAM NAVIGATION COMPANY—ABERDEEN

HOGARTH* 1231 Grt. Blt. *1892
7.6.1918: Torpedoed and sunk in the North Sea 10 miles S.½E. from Longstone, Farne Islands off the Northumberland coast by the German submarine *UB 107* whilst on a voyage from London to Aberdeen with general cargo. 26 lost including Master.

ADAM BROTHERS—LONDON

AULTON ex *Ardenza* ex *Melford* ex *Gipsy* **634 Grt. Blt. *1899***
23.3.1918: Torpedoed and sunk in the North Sea 9 miles S.E. by E.½E. from Berwick by the German submarine *UB 83* whilst on a voyage from Seaham Harbour to Aberdeen with a cargo of coal. 2 lost.

Adam S.S. Co. Ltd.

ASHMORE* 2519 Grt. Blt. *1899
12.9.1915: Struck a mine and sunk off the mouth of the River Thames 5 miles E.½E. from Kentish Knock Lightvessel laid by the German submarine *UC 3* whilst on a voyage from Rosario to Rotterdam with a cargo of maize. 4 lost.

ADAMS (ALLEN) & CO. LTD.—SOUTHAMPTON

WREATHIER* 852 Grt. Blt. *1897
3.12.1917: Torpedoed and sunk in the English Channel 1 mile W. from Prawle Point, 7 miles S.E. from Kingsbridge by the German submarine *UB 35* whilst on a voyage from Barry to Rouen with a cargo of coal. 3 lost.

LAVERNOCK* 2406 Grt. Blt. *1888
17.9.1918: Torpedoed and sunk in the Atlantic 5 miles S.W. from Trevose Head, 4½ miles W. of Padstow by the German submarine *UB 117* whilst on a voyage from Bilbao to Glasgow with a cargo of iron ore. 25 lost including Master.

ADAMS, D. & G. T.—NEWCASTLE UPON TYNE

Brand-Adams S.S. Co. Ltd.

ADAMS ex *Ethelburga* **2223 Grt. Blt. *1887***
17.10.1917: Torpedoed and sunk in the English Channel 6 miles S.E. by E. from the Lizard, 12 miles S. of Helston by the German submarine *U 62* whilst on a voyage from Tyne to St. Nazaire with a cargo of coal.

Canute S.S. Co. Ltd.

AMPLEGARTH 3707 Grt. Blt. 1910
10.5.1918: Struck a mine and sunk in the Strait of Dover 1 mile W.S.W. from Dover harbour laid by the German submarine *UC 71* whilst on a voyage from Tyne to St. Nazaire with a cargo of coal.

ADELAIDE S.S. CO. LTD—ADELAIDE

ECHUNGA 6285 Grt. Blt. 1907
5.9.1917: Torpedoed and sunk in the English Channel 40 miles N. by E. from Ushant by the German submarine *U 52* whilst on a voyage from Port Arthur, Texas to the United Kingdom with a cargo of fueloil. 9 lost.

WARILDA 7713 Grt. Blt. 1912
3.8.1918: Torpedoed and sunk in the English Channel 32 miles S.S.W. from Owers Lightvessel, 7 miles S.E. of Selsey Bill in position 50.11N 00.13W by the German submarine *UC 49* whilst on a voyage from Le Havre to Southampton. Lost whilst on Government service employed as a Hospital Ship.

ADMIRALTY, THE—LONDON

HUNTLY 1153 Grt. Blt. 1912
20.12.1915: Torpedoed and sunk in the English Channel off Boulogne by the German submarine *UB 10* whilst on a voyage from Portishead to Boulogne with a cargo of petrol. 2 lost.

VAN STIRUM 3284 Grt. Blt. 1915
25.12.1915: Captured and torpedoed in the St. George's Channel 8 miles S.S.W. from the Smalls off the coast of Pembrokeshire in position 51.55N 06.16W by the German submarine *U 24* whilst on a voyage from Rouen to Liverpool. 2 lost.

SALTA 7284 Grt. Blt. 1911
10.4.1917: Struck a mine and sunk in the English Channel ½ mile N. from Whistle Buoy, Le Havre laid by the German submarine *UC 26* whilst on a voyage from Southampton to Le Havre with a cargo of hospital stores. 79 lost. Lost whilst on Government service employed as a Hospital Ship.

DERBENT 3178 Grt. Blt. 1907
30.11.1917: Torpedoed and sunk in the Irish Sea 6 miles N.E. by E. from Lynas Point, Anglesey by the German submarine *U 96* whilst on a voyage from Liverpool to Queenstown (Cobh) with a cargo of fuel oil.

TITHONUS ex *Titania* 3463 Grt. Blt. 1908
28.3.1918: Torpedoed and sunk in the North Sea by the German submarine *UB 72*. Lost whilst on Government service employed as an Armed Boarding Steamer.

ALEXANDER & MAIR—GLASGOW

PALMGROVE ex *Radley* 3100 Grt. Blt. 1896
22.8.1915: Captured and sunk by gunfire in the Atlantic 46 miles W. by N. ½ N. from Bishop Rock, Scilly Isles in position 49.52N 07.40W by the German submarine *U 38* whilst on a voyage from Clyde to Porto-Vecchio with a cargo of coal.

PINEGROVE ex *Thornley* **2847 Grt. Blt. 1896**
11.12.1915: Struck a mine and sunk in the English Channel 8 miles W.½S. from Cape Gris Nez laid by the German submarine *UC 3* whilst on a voyage from Dunkirk to London in ballast. 2 lost.

MARGIT 2490 Grt. Blt. 1903
4.4.1917: Torpedoed and sunk 80 miles S.W.½W. from Cape Matapan, Greece in position 35.28N 21.24E by the German submarine *U 63* whilst on a voyage from Malta to—with cargo of coal.

MELANIE ex *Melanie Groedal* **2996 Grt. Blt. 1903**
16.6.1918: Torpedoed and sunk in the North Sea 2 miles E. from South Cheek, Robin Hood Bay, 5 miles S.E. of Whitby by the German submarine *UC 40* whilst on a voyage from Blyth to Blaye, River Gironde with a cargo of coal. 5 lost.

S.S. Elmgrove Co. Ltd.

ELMGROVE ex *Treasury* **3018 Grt. Blt. 1896**
29.5.1916: Captured and sunk by gunfire in the Mediterranean 96 miles N.E. from Algiers in position 34.00N 04.00E by the German submarine *U 39* whilst on a voyage from Toulon to Huelva in ballast.

MILLY ex *Ludwig Groedal* **2964 Grt. Blt. 1904**
6.9.1918: Torpedoed and sunk in the Atlantic 2¼ miles W.¾S. from Tintagel Head, 5 miles N.W. from Camelford in position 50.39N 05.15W by the German submarine *UB 87* whilst on a voyage from Brest to Barry Roads in ballast. 2 lost.

S.S. Mary Co. Ltd.

GISELLA ex *Gisella Groedal* **2502 Grt. Blt. 1904**
18.11.1917: Torpedoed and sunk in the St. George's Channel 2 miles S.W. by S. from Skokham Island off the coast of Pembrokeshire by the German submarine *UC 77* whilst on a voyage from Cardiff to—with a cargo of coal. 2 lost.

BIRCHGROVE ex *Dovedale* **2821 Grt. Blt. 1894**
2.12.1917: Torpedoed and sunk in the Bay of Biscay 10 miles W. by N.½N. from Ile de Groix near Lorient in position 47.38N 03.45W by the German submarine *U 84* whilst on a voyage from Penarth to Bordeaux with a cargo of coal. 1 lost.

ALEXANDER BROTHERS—NEWCASTLE UPON TYNE

BURNSTONE ex *Kilsyth* **2340 Grt. Blt. 1903**
19.3.1918: Torpedoed and sunk in the North Sea 4 miles N. from the Farne Islands by the German submarine *UB 62* whilst on a voyage from Immingham to—with a cargo of coal. 5 lost.

ALLAN, BLACK & COMPANY—SUNDERLAND

Albyn Line

THISTLEBAN 4117 Grt. Blt. 1910
23.12.1916: Struck a mine and was damaged in the Mediterranean 5 miles N.N.W. from Alexandria laid by the German submarine *U 73* whilst on a voyage from

Karachi to Hull with a cargo of rape seed, linseed and peas. Later beached but became a total loss.

THISTLEARD 4136 Grt. Blt. 1912
24.4.1917: Torpedoed and sunk in the Atlantic 135 miles W.N.W. from Tory Island off the coast of co. Donegal in position 55.10N 12.00W by the German submarine *U 82* whilst on a voyage from Tocopilla and Norfolk (Va) to Glasgow with a cargo of nitrate.

THISTLEDU 4026 Grt. Blt. 1901
18.6.1917: Torpedoed and sunk in the Atlantic 218 miles N.W.½W. from the Fastnet Rock 4 miles S.W. of Cape Clear, co. Cork in position 52.17N 15.18W by the German submarine *U 82* whilst on a voyage from Iquique and Newport News to Newport, Mon. with a cargo of nitrate. 4 lost.

ANCHOR LINE (HENDERSON BROTHERS) LIMITED—GLASGOW

PERUGIA 4348 Grt. Blt. 1901
3.12.1916: Torpedoed and sunk in the Mediterranean in the Gulf of Genoa in position 42.56N 07.56E by the German submarine *U 63*. Lost whilst on Government service employed as Special Service Ship. *Q1*.

CALEDONIA 9223 Grt. Blt. 1904
4.12.1916: Torpedoed and sunk in the Mediterranean 125 miles E. by S. from Malta in position 35.40N 17.05E by the German submarine *U 65* whilst on a voyage from Salonica to Marseilles with a cargo of mails. 1 lost, Master taken prisoner.

CALIFORNIA 8669 Grt. Blt. 1907
7.2.1917: Torpedoed and sunk in the Atlantic 38 miles W. by S. from the Fastnet Rock in position 51.10N 09.24W by the German submarine *U 85* whilst on a voyage from New York to Clyde with general cargo. 43 lost.

CAMERONIA 10963 Grt. Blt. 1911
15.4.1917: Torpedoed and sunk in the Mediterranean 150 miles E. from Malta by the German submarine *U 33* whilst on Government Service carrying troops and a cargo of Government stores. 11 lost.

TRANSYLVANIA 14315 Grt. Blt. 1914
4.5.1917: Torpedoed and sunk in the Mediterranean 2½ miles S. from Cape Vado, Gulf of Genoa in position 44.15N 08.30E by the German submarine *U 63* whilst on a voyage from Marseilles to Alexandria carrying troops and a cargo of Government stores. 12 lost including Master.

TUSCANIA 14348 Grt. Blt. 1914
5.2.1918: Torpedoed and sunk in the North Channel 7 miles N. from Rathlin Island off the coast of co. Antrim by the German submarine *UB 77* whilst on a voyage from New York to Liverpool carrying US troops and general cargo. 44 lost.

TIBERIA ex *Frimley* **4880 Grt. Blt. 1913**
26.2.1918: Torpedoed and sunk in the North Channel 1½ miles E. from Black Head, Belfast Lough by the German submarine *U 19* whilst on a voyage from Clyde to New York with general cargo.

ANGLO-AMERICAN OIL CO. LTD.—LONDON

MIMOSA 3466 Grt. Blt. 1905
4.9.1915: Captured and sunk by gunfire in the Atlantic 137 miles S.W. by W. from the Fastnet Rock in position 49.40N 12.00W by the German submarine *U 33* whilst on a voyage from New York to Belfast with a cargo of oil.

NARRAGANSETT 9196 Grt. Blt. 1903
16.3.1917: Torpedoed and sunk in the Atlantic off S.W. Ireland in position 50.12N 17.34W by the German submarine *U 44* whilst on a voyage from New York to London with a cargo of lubricating oil. 46 lost including Master.

CUYAHOGA 4586 Grt. Blt. 1914
5.7.1917: Torpedoed and sunk in the Atlantic 130 miles W.N.W. from Tory Island in position 55.12N 12.10W by the German submarine *U 57* whilst on a voyage from Liverpool to Philadelphia in ballast.

EARL OF ELGIN 4448 Grt. Blt. 1909
7.12.1917: Torpedoed and sunk 10 miles W.½S. from Caernarvon Bay Lightvessel, Anglesey by the German submarine *UC 75* whilst on a voyage from London to Dublin in ballast. 18 lost including Master.

ANGLO-BRETAGNE SHIPPING CO. LTD.—CARDIFF

JUTLAND ex *Green Jacket* 2824 Grt. Blt. 1898
19.11.1917: Torpedoed and sunk in the English Channel 18 miles N.E. by N. from Ushant by the German submarine *UC 79* whilst on a voyage from Bilbao to Middlesbrough with a cargo of iron ore. 26 lost including Master.

ANGLO-SAXON PETROLEUM CO. LTD.—LONDON

GOLDMOUTH 7446 Grt. Blt. 1903
31.3.1916: Captured and torpedoed in the Atlantic 60 miles W.N.W. from Ushant by the German submarine *U 44* whilst on a voyage from Tarakan to Falmouth with a cargo of fueloil. Master taken prisoner.

ELAX 3980 Grt. Blt. 1893
10.10.1916: Torpedoed and sunk in the Mediterranean 70 miles W.S.W. from Cape Matapan in position 35.54N 21.19E by the German submarine *UB 43* whilst on a voyage from Rangoon to Malta with a cargo of oil.

CONCH 5620 Grt. Blt. 1909
8.12.1916: Torpedoed and sunk in the English Channel 12 miles S. by W.½W. from Anvil Point, 10 miles S. of Poole in position 50.23N 02.02W by the German submarine *UB 23* whilst on a voyage from Calcutta and Rangoon to River Thames with a cargo of benzine. 28 lost including Master.

MUREX 3564 Grt. Blt. 1892
21.12.1916: Torpedoed and sunk in the Mediterranean 94 miles N.W. from Port Said in position 32.20N 31.00E by the German submarine *U 73* whilst on a voyage from Mudros, Aegean Sea to Port Said in ballast. 1 lost.

TELENA 4778 Grt. Blt. 1895
21.4.1917: Torpedoed and sunk in the Atlantic 170 miles W.N.W. from the Fastnet Rock in position 51.16N 14.00W by the German submarine *U 61* whilst on a voyage from Philadelphia to Queenstown with a cargo of benzine.

BULLMOUTH 4018 Grt. Blt. 1893
28.4.1917: Torpedoed and sunk in the Atlantic 125 miles N.W. by N. from Tory Island in position 56.30N 11.20W by the German submarine *U 58* whilst on a voyage from Clyde to Hampton Roads in ballast.

BULYSSES 6127 Grt. Blt. 1900
20.8.1917: Torpedoed and sunk in the Atlantic 145 miles W.N.W. from the Butt of Lewis, Hebrides in position 58.34N 10.50W by the German submarine *U 52* whilst on a voyage from the Firth of Forth to Port Arthur, Texas in ballast.

TROCAS 4129 Grt. Blt. 1893
19.1.1918: Torpedoed and sunk in the Aegean Sea 10 miles N.E. from Skyro Lighthouse by the German submarine *UC 23* whilst on a voyage from Abadan to Salonica with a cargo of oil. 24 lost.

ROMANY ex *Rossija* ex *Romany* 3983 Grt. Blt. 1902
27.4.1918: Torpedoed and sunk in the Mediterranean 47 miles S.W. by W. ¾W. from Cape Spartivento, Sicily in position 38.22N 08.00E by the German submarine *UB 48* whilst on a voyage from Marseilles to Port Said in ballast.

ARCA 4839 Grt. Blt. 1912
2.10.1918: Torpedoed and sunk in the Atlantic 40 miles N.W. by W. from Tory Island in position 55.45N 07.35W by the German submarine *U 118* whilst on a voyage from Philadelphia to Portishead with a cargo of benzine. 52 lost including Master.

ANTRIM IRON ORE CO. LTD.—BELFAST

GLENRAVEL 1092 Grt. Blt. 1906
8.8.1915: Captured and sunk with bombs in the North Sea 25 miles N. from Kinnard Head, N. of Fraserburgh by the German submarine *U 17* whilst on a voyage from Belfast to Leith with general cargo.

ASHDOWN, C. G.—LONDON

City of London Shipping & Trading Co. Ltd.

DALEGARTH 2265 Grt. Blt. 1889
30.5.1916: Captured and torpedoed in the Mediterranean 12 miles N.E. from Cape Corbelin, Algiers by the German submarine *U 39* whilst on a voyage from Limni to Clyde with a cargo of magnesite.

ASIATIC STEAM NAVIGATION CO. LTD.—LIVERPOOL

KOHINUR 2265 Grt. Blt. 1905
25.5.1917: Torpedoed and sunk in the Mediterranean 150 miles N. from Alexandria by the German submarine *U 38* whilst on a voyage from Salonica to Karachi in ballast. 37 lost including Master.

PASHA 5930 Grt. Blt. 1902
15.6.1917: Torpedoed and sunk in the Mediterranean in the S. entrance to the Strait of Messina in position 37.52N 15.27E by the German submarine *UC 38* whilst on a voyage from Karachi to Spezia with a cargo of grain. 3 lost.

BEGUM 4646 Grt. Blt. 1907
29.5.1918: Torpedoed and sunk in the Atlantic 270 miles W. by S. from Bishop Rock in position 47.30N 12.28W by the German submarine *U 90* whilst on a voyage from Cardiff to Santiago de Cuba in ballast. 15 lost.

PUNDIT 5917 Grt. Blt. 1902
9.6.1918: Torpedoed and sunk in the Mediterranean 85 miles W.N.W. from Alexandria by the German submarine *UB 105* whilst on a voyage from Tyne to Alexandria with a cargo of coal. 6 lost including Master.

SUBADAR 4911 Grt. Blt. 1912
27.7.1918: Torpedoed and sunk in the Atlantic 112 miles N. by W. from Cape da Roca, near Lisbon in position 40.26N 10.39W by the German submarine *U 43* whilst on a voyage from London to Salonica with a cargo of Government stores. 3 lost.

ASTON, E.—STOCKTON-ON-TEES

Field S.S. Co. Ltd.

LYNFIELD 3023 Grt. Blt. 1905
8.1.1917: Captured and sunk with bombs in the Mediterranean 32 miles S.E. by S. from Malta by the German submarine *U 35* whilst on a voyage from Cardiff to Alexandria with a cargo of coal. 1 lost, Master taken prisoner.

ATKINSON BROTHERS—NEWCASTLE UPON TYNE

WISBECH 1282 Grt. Blt. 1901
14.8.1917: Torpedoed and sunk in the Atlantic 12 miles N.E. from Trevose Head by the German submarine *UC 51* whilst on a voyage from Cardiff to St. Malo with a cargo of patent fuel and steel tyres. 2 lost.

ATKINSON, E. E. & PRICKETT—HULL

The Shipping Controller

HERDIS 1157 Grt. Blt. 1911
29.6.1918: Torpedoed and sunk in the North Sea 7 miles S.E. by S. from South Cheek, Robin Hood Bay in position 54.20N 02.00W by the German submarine *UB 40* whilst on a voyage from Tyne to Rouen with a cargo of coal.

ATKINSON, E. P. & SONS—GOOLE

The Shipping Controller

DJERV 1527 Grt. Blt. 1906
20.2.1918: Torpedoed and sunk in the Irish Sea 12 miles N.N.W. from the Skerries, a group of rocky islands off the N.W. coast of Anglesey by the German submarine *U 86* whilst on a voyage from Heysham to Newport, Mon. in ballast. 2 lost including Master.

OTIS TETRAX 996 Grt. BLT. 1916
20.8.1918: Torpedoed and sunk in the North Sea 28 miles S.¼E. from Flamborough Head probably by the German submarine *UB 112* whilst on a voyage from Methil to Rouen with a cargo of coal.

ATLANTIC TRANSPORT CO. LTD.—LONDON

MARQUETTE ex *Bordicea* **7057 Grt. Blt. 1898**
23.10.1915: Torpedoed and sunk in the Aegean Sea 36 miles from Salonica Bay by the German submarine *U 35* whilst on a voyage from Alexandria to Salonica with a cargo of Government stores and ammunition. 29 lost.

MINNEAPOLIS 13543 Grt. Blt. 1900
23.3.1916: Torpedoed and sunk in the Mediterranean 195 miles E.½N. from Malta in position 36.30N 18.22E by the German submarine *U 35* whilst on a voyage from Marseilles to Alexandria in ballast. 12 lost.

MINNEWASKA 14317 Grt. Blt. 1909
29.11.1916: Struck a mine and sunk in the Mediterranean in Suda Bay, Crete, laid by the German submarine *UC 23* whilst on a voyage from Alexandria to Malta in ballast.

MAINE ex *Sierra Blanca* **3616 Grt. Blt. 1905**
23.3.1917: Torpedoed and sunk in the English Channel 11 miles S.E. by E. from Start Point, 9½ miles S.S.W. of Dartmouth by the German submarine *UC 17* whilst on a voyage from London to Philadelphia.

MINNEHAHA 13714 Grt. Blt. 1900
7.9.1917: Torpedoed and sunk in the Atlantic 12 miles S.E. from the Fastnet Rock by the German submarine *U 48* whilst on a voyage from London to New York with general cargo. 43 lost.

MINNETONKA 13528 Grt. Blt. 1902
30.1.1918: Torpedoed and sunk in the Mediterranean 40 miles E.N.E. from Malta in position 36.12N 14.55E by the German submarine *U 64* whilst on a voyage from Port Said to Malta with a cargo of mails. 4 lost, 10 Officers taken prisoner.

MESABA ex *Winifreda* **6833 Grt. Blt. 1898**
1.9.1918: Torpedoed and sunk in the St. George's Channel 21 miles E.¼N. from the Tuskar Rock off S.E. coast of co. Wexford in position 52.17N 05.38W by the German submarine *UB 118* whilst on a voyage from Liverpool to Philadelphia in ballast. 20 lost including Master.

AUSTIN, ELLIOT & COMPANY—NEWCASTLE UPON TYNE

HUGUENOT 1032 Grt. Blt. 1892
20.10.1916: Struck a mine and sunk off the mouth of the River Thames 4 miles N.E.½E. from the Sunk Lightvessel laid by the German submarine *UC 11* whilst on a voyage from London to Tyne in ballast.

AUSTRALIAN STEAMSHIPS LIMITED—MELBOURNE

***ERA** 2379 Grt. Blt. 1888*
1.5.1918: Torpedoed and sunk in the Mediterranean 18 miles N.E. by E. from Cape Tenez, Algeria in position 36.45N 01.56E by the German submarine *UC 27* whilst on a voyage from Porto-Ferrajo to Glasgow with a cargo of ore. 12 lost.

AUSTRALASIAN UNITED STEAM NAVIGATION CO. LTD.—LONDON

***KYARRA** 6953 Grt. Blt. 1903*
26.5.1918: Torpedoed and sunk in the English Channel 2 miles S.S.E. from Anvil Point by the German submarine *UB 57* whilst on a voyage from London to Sydney, N.S.W. with general cargo. 6 lost.

AXARLIS, A. D.—LONDON

WARREN ex *Libuse* ex *Hornby Castle* **3709 Grt. Blt. 1899**
1.4.1917: Torpedoed and sunk in the Mediterranean 20 miles S.W. from Civitavecchia by the German submarine *UC 38* whilst on a voyage from Karachi to Civitavecchia and Spezia with a cargo of grain. 3 lost, Master taken prisoner.

BADCO, W.—CARDIFF

***POLVARTH** 3146 Grt. Blt. 1909*
20.12.1917: Torpedoed and sunk in the Atlantic 35 miles W. from Ushant in position 48.20N 06.00W by the German submarine *U 86* whilst on a voyage from Gibraltar to Swansea with a cargo of zinc oil, phosphates and naval stores. 2 lost.

BAIN, GARDNER & COMPANY—GLASGOW

KILWINNING ex *Londesborough* **3071 Grt. Blt. 1898**
24.8.1917: Torpedoed and sunk in the Mediterranean 94 miles E.S.E. from Malta in position 35.26N 16.30E by the Austro-Hungarian submarine *U 14* whilst on a voyage from Barry to Port Said with general cargo and coal.

BAIRD, JAMES LIMITED.—ST. JOHN'S, NEWFOUNDLAND

***ERIK** 583 Grt. Blt. 1865*
25.8.1918: Captured and sunk with bombs in the Atlantic 70 miles N.W. by W. from St. Pierre, Newfoundland by the German submarine *U 156* whilst on a voyage from St. John's, NFL to Sydney, (CB) in ballast.

BAIRD, J. W. & COMPANY—WEST HARTLEPOOL

MABEL BAIRD ex *Cockerill* **2500 Grt. Blt. 1901**
22.12.1917: Torpedoed and sunk in the English Channel 4 miles W.S.W. from the Lizard by the German submarine *UB 57* whilst on a voyage from Penarth to— with a cargo of coal. 5 lost.

BALLS, WILLIAM D. C. & SON—NORTH SHIELDS

***SOUTHGARTH** 2414 Grt. Blt. 1891*
29.5.1916: Captured and sunk with bombs in the Mediterranean 60 miles N.N.E.

from Algiers by the German submarine *U 39* whilst on a voyage from Marseilles to Benisaf in ballast.

BALLS, STANSFIELD—NORTH SHIELDS

Ville Steamship Ltd.

WESTVILLE 3207 Grt. Blt. 1913
31.12.1917: Torpedoed and sunk in the English Channel 5 miles W.S.W. from St. Catherine's Point, Isle of Wight by the German submarine *UB 35* whilst on voyage from Blyth to Blaye with a cargo of coal.

STEELVILLE 3649 Grt. Blt. 1915
3.1.1918: Torpedoed and sunk in the Mediterranean 20 miles N. from Cape Bon, Tunis in position 37.25N 11.00E by the German submarine *UB 50* whilst on a voyage from Barry to Malta with general cargo and coal.

BANNATYNE, J. & SONS LIMITED—LIMERICK

KEEPER ex *Kelpie* ***572 Grt. Blt. 1906***
10.6.1917: Torpedoed and sunk in the Irish Sea by the German submarine *UC 66* whilst on a voyage from Belfast to Limerick with a cargo of grain. 12 lost including Master.

BARNETT, DAVID P.—CARDIFF

Italian Export Shipping Co. Ltd.

BASUTA 2876 Grt. Blt. 1897
8.2.1918: Torpedoed and sunk in the English Channel 45 miles S.S.W. from the Lizard by the German submarine *U 53* whilst on a voyage from Newport, Mon. to Blaye with a cargo of coal. 1 lost.

BARNETT, J. & COMPANY—LIVERPOOL

La Plata S.S. Co. Ltd.

SHIMOSA 4221 Grt. Blt. 1902
31.7.1917: Torpedoed and sunk in the Atlantic 220 miles N.W. ½ W. from Eagle Island, 3 miles S.W. of Erris Head, co. Mayo in position 55.14N 15.05W by the German submarine *U 46* whilst on a voyage from Le Havre to Montreal in ballast. 17 lost including Master.

UGANDA 4315 Grt. Blt. 1905
8.3.1918: Torpedoed and sunk in the Mediterranean 32 miles N.E. ¾ N. from Linosa Island midway between Malta and Tunis in position 36.18N 13.15E by the Austro-Hungarian submarine *U 28* whilst on a voyage from Alexandria to London with a cargo of cotton. 1 lost.

BARR, CROMBIE & COMPANY—GLASGOW

GRYFEVALE 4437 Grt. Blt. 1906
21.10.1917: Chased in the Mediterranean by the German submarine *U 151* and ran ashore and was wrecked 10 miles N. from Cape Blanco, Majorca whilst on a voyage from Port Louis to Gibraltar with a cargo of sugar.

BARRIE, CHARLES & SONS—DUNDEE

DEN OF CROMBIE 4949 Grt. Blt. 1907
8.11.1915: Captured and sunk by gunfire in the Mediterranean 112 miles S. by W. from Cape Martello, Crete in position 33.10N 24.50E by the German submarine *U 35* whilst on a voyage from Bangkok to Lisbon and Oporto with general cargo.

BATHO, CHARLES A.—LONDON

SEMANTHA 2847 Grt. Blt. 1899
14.10.1917: Torpedoed and sunk in the Mediterranean 10 miles N.W. by N. from Cape St. John, Crete by the German submarine *UC 74* whilst on a voyage from Liverpool to—with a cargo of Government stores. 32 lost including Master.

BAZELEY, GEORGE & SONS, LIMITED—PENZANCE

COATH ex *Skerryvore* *975 Grt. Blt. 1882*
12.12.1916: Torpedoed and sunk in the English Channel off Beachy Head, 3 miles S.W. of Eastbourne by the German submarine *UB 38* whilst on a voyage from Le Havre to—. 16 lost including Master.

BEATLEY, T. G. & SON—LONDON

MADAME MIDAS ex *Duva* *1203 Grt. Blt. 1909*
23.3.1918: Torpedoed and sunk in the English Channel 38 miles S. by W. ¾ W. from the Lizard by the German submarine *UB 55* whilst on a voyage from Cardiff to La Rochelle, Bay of Biscay with a cargo of coal.

MADAME RENEE ex *Thordis* *509 Grt. Blt. 1904*
10.8.1918: Torpedoed and sunk in the North Sea 1 mile N.N.E. from Scarborough by the German submarine *UB 30* whilst on a voyage from London to Tyne with a cargo of copper pyrites. 10 lost.

BECKER & CO., LTD.—LONDON

Preston Steam Navigation Co. Ltd.

CHIC ex *Camperdown* *3037 Grt. Blt. 1914*
13.4.1916: Torpedoed and sunk in the Atlantic 45 miles S.W. from the Fastnet Rock by the German submarine *U 22* whilst on a voyage from Halifax, Nova Scotia to Manchester with a cargo of wood pulp. 9 lost including Master.

CHARTERHOUSE 3021 Grt. Blt. 1895
23.9.1916: Captured and sunk with bombs in the Mediterranean 26 miles E. by S. ½ S. from S.E. point of Formentera Island, Balearic Islands by the German submarine *U 35* whilst on a voyage from Toulon to Gibraltar in ballast. Master and 2 Gunners taken prisoner.

GEO 3048 Grt. Blt. 1915
29.1.1918: Torpedoed and sunk in the Mediterranean 6 miles N. by W. from Cape Peloro, Sicily by the German submarine *UC 53* whilst on a voyage from Naples to Tunis in ballast. 16 lost including Master.

BELL BROTHERS & COMPANY—GLASGOW

BELLUCIA 4368 Grt. Blt. 1909
7.7.1917: Torpedoed and sunk in the English Channel 2 miles S.S.E. from the Lizard in position 49.54N 05.08W by the German submarine *UB 31* whilst on a voyage from Montreal to London with a cargo of wheat and flour. 4 lost.

BELL, JAMES & COMPANY—HULL

Bell Lines, Ltd.

BELLBANK ex *Castle Bruce* ex *Kirby Bank* ex *Lustleigh* 3250 Grt. Blt. 1901
7.9.1918: Torpedoed and sunk in the Mediterranean 25 miles S.S.W. from Planier Island, Gulf of Lions in position 42.48N 05.08E by the German submarine *UC 67* whilst on a voyage from Algiers to Spezia with general cargo. 1 lost.

Keighley Shipping Co. Ltd.

IVYDENE 3541 Grt. Blt. 1901
17.3.1918: Torpedoed and sunk in the Mediterranean 36 miles N.N.E. from Cape Bougaroni, Tunis by the German submarine *UB 52* whilst on a voyage from Sfax and Bizerta to Gibraltar with a cargo of phosphates. 1 lost.

BELLVIEW ex *Breconshire* 3567 Grt. Blt. 1894
21.4.1918: Torpedoed and sunk in the Mediterranean 16 miles E.N.E. from Cape Bon by unknown submarine whilst on a voyage from Barry to Malta with general cargo and coal.

Neotsfield Shipping Co. Ltd.

NEOTSFIELD ex *Ada* 3821 Grt. Blt. 1906
14.9.1918: Torpedoed and sunk in the Irish Sea 1½ miles S. from Skulmartin Lighthouse, 9 miles S.E. from Donaghadee, co. Down by the German submarine *UB 64* whilst on a voyage from Clyde to Naples with a cargo of coal.

BELL, SYMONDSON & COMPANY—LONDON

Southdown S.S. Co. Ltd.

JEVINGTON 2747 Grt. Blt. 1905
23.1.1917: Torpedoed and sunk in the Atlantic 52 miles N.W.½W. from Cape Ortegal, near Ferrol in position 44.08N 09.00W by the German submarine *U 43* whilst on a voyage from Rosario to Rochefort, Bay of Biscay with a cargo of wheat.

LULLINGTON 2816 Grt. Blt. 1903
8.2.1917: Struck a mine and sunk in the English Channel 3 miles E. from Royal Sovereign Lightvessel, 10 miles S.W. of Hastings in position 50.42½N 00.33E laid by the German submarine *UC 47* whilst on a voyage from Blyth to Rouen with a cargo of coal.

RUSTINGTON 3071 Grt. Blt. 1909
25.7.1917: Torpedoed and sunk in the Atlantic 235 miles W. by S. from Ushant in position 46.26N 10.00W by the German submarine *U 54* whilst on a voyage from Aquilas to Cardiff with a cargo of iron ore.

BELLE AGENCY LIMITED—LIVERPOOL

BELLE OF FRANCE* 3876 Grt. Blt. *1905
1.2.1916: Torpedoed and sunk in the Mediterranean 126 miles N.W. by W. from Alexandria in position 32.30N 27.45E by the German submarine *U 21* whilst on a voyage from Karachi to Algiers with a cargo of grain. 19 lost.

BENNETT S.S. CO. LIMITED—GOOLE

AFRICA* 1038 Grt. Blt. *1903
16.9.1915: Struck a mine and sunk in the Downs 1½ miles off Kingsdown, 2½ miles S. of Deal laid by the German submarine *UC 6* whilst on a voyage from London to Boulogne with general cargo. 2 lost.

BURMA* 706 Grt. Blt. *1891
23.6.1916: Struck a mine and sunk in the North Sea 5 miles N. by E.½E. from Shipwash Lightvessel, 15 miles E. of Harwich, Essex laid by the German submarine *UC 6* whilst on a voyage from London to Goole in ballast. 7 lost.

MOPSA* 885 Grt. Blt. *1902
16.7.1916: Struck a mine and sunk in the North Sea 7 miles S. of Lowestoft laid by the German submarine *UC 1* whilst on a voyage from Goole to Boulogne with general cargo and coal.

BENTINCK-SMITH, W. F.—QUEBEC

Arctic S.S. Co. Ltd.

KWASIND* ex *Turret Bell* 2211 Grt. Blt. *1894
11.3.1917: Struck a mine and sunk in the North Sea off Southwold in position 52.08N 01.45E laid by the German submarine *UC 4* whilst on a voyage from Bilbao to Hartlepool with a cargo of iron ore. 12 lost.

BICKET & COMPANY—LIVERPOOL

Kyle Transport Co. Ltd.

COILA* 4135 Grt. Blt. *1911
14.12.1917: Torpedoed and sunk in the Mediterranean 3 miles S.E. from Canet Point, Valencia by the German submarine *U 64* whilst on a voyage from Clyde to Leghorn with a cargo of coal. 3 lost.

RIO PALLARESA* ex *Harcroft* ex *Incharran* 4043 Grt. Blt. *1904
29.7.1918: Torpedoed and sunk in the Mediterranean 62 miles E.N.E. from Malta by the German submarine *UC 25* whilst on a voyage from Alexandria to Hull. 2 lost.

BLACK, JOHN & COMPANY—GLASGOW

Glasgow S.S. Co. Ltd.

KELVINBANK* 4209 Grt. Blt. *1903
24.3.1916: Torpedoed and sunk in the English Channel in Le Havre Roads by the German submarine *UB 18* whilst on a voyage from Buenos Aires to Le Havre with a cargo of frozen meat and oats. 1 lost.

KELVINIA 5039 Grt. Blt. 1913
2.9.1916: Struck a mine and sunk in the Bristol Channel 9 miles S. by W. from Caldy Island laid by the German submarine *U 78* whilst on a voyage from Newport News to Clyde with general cargo.

KELVINHEAD 3063 Grt. Blt. 1905
27.3.1917: Struck a mine and sunk in the Irish Sea ¾ mile W.S.W. from Liverpool Bar Lightvessel laid by the German submarine *UC 65* whilst on a voyage from Clyde and Liverpool to Buenos Aires with general cargo.

KELVINBANK ex *Drumcliffe* **4072 Grt. Blt. 1905**
13.6.1917: Torpedoed and sunk in the Atlantic 100 miles N. from Cape Wrath in position 60.04N 05.40W by the German submarine *U 69* whilst on a voyage from Clyde to Archangel with general cargo. 16 lost including Master.

BLACKPOOL PASSENGER STEAM BOAT CO. LTD.—FLEETWOOD

QUEEN OF THE NORTH 594 Grt. Blt. 1895
20.7.1918: Struck a mine and sunk in the North Sea N.E. of Shipwash Lightvessel laid by the German submarine *UC 4*. Lost whilst on Government service employed as a Minesweeper.

BLACKWATER, A. F. & J. C.—GLASGOW

Cadeby S.S. Co. Ltd.

CADEBY 1130 Grt. Blt. 1892
27.5.1915: Captured and sunk by gunfire in the Atlantic 20 miles S.W. by S. from Wolf Rock, 8 miles S.W. of Land's End by the German submarine *U 41* whilst on a voyage from Oporto to Cardiff with a cargo of pitwood.

BLAND, M. H. & CO. LTD.—GIBRALTAR

Bland Line

GIBEL YEDID ex *Narova* **949 Grt. Blt. 1911**
13.7.1917: Captured and sunk with bombs in the Atlantic 150 miles W.¾N. from Ushant by the German submarine *U 48* whilst on a voyage from Newport, Mon. to Gibraltar.

GIBEL HANAM ex *Banbury* **647 Grt. Blt. 1895**
14.9.1918: Torpedoed and sunk in the English Channel off Abbotsbury by the German submarine *UB 103* whilst on a voyage from Swansea to France with a cargo of coal. 21 lost including Master.

BLOW, RICHARDS & COMPANY—CARDIFF

Whitehall Steam Navigation Co. Ltd.

WHITEHALL ex *Barnesmore* **3158 Grt. Blt. 1905**
29.7.1917: Torpedoed and sunk in the Atlantic 270 miles W. by N. from the Fastnet Rock in position 50.05N 16.28W by the German submarine *U 95* whilst on a voyage from Montreal to Ipswich with a cargo of wheat and flour. 1 lost.

WHITECOURT ex *Othello* **3680 Grt. Blt. 1905**
28.8.1917: Captured and sunk by gunfire in the Arctic 120 miles N.N.E. from North Cape by the German submarine *U 28* whilst on a voyage from Archangel to London.

The Shipping Controller

BAMSE ex *Thomas Coates* **1001 Grt. Blt. 1881**
2.10.1918: Torpedoed and sunk in the English Channel 5½ miles E.¾E. from the Lizard by the German submarine *UB 112* whilst on a voyage from Swansea to Falmouth with a cargo of patent fuel. 11 lost.

BLUE STAR LINE—LONDON

BRODMORE ex *Graf Muravjev* ex *Count Muravieff* ex *Rangatira* **4071 Grt. Blt. 1890**
27.2.1917: Torpedoed and sunk in the Mediterranean 70 miles N.W. by N. from Marsa Susa, Libya in position 33.50N 21.02E by the German submarine *UB 43* whilst on a voyage from Majunga to Marseilles with a cargo of frozen meat. Master taken prisoner.

BRODNESS ex *Banffshire* **5736 Grt. Blt. 1894**
31.3.1917: Torpedoed and sunk in the Mediterranean 5 miles W.N.W. from Anzio by the German submarine *UC 38* whilst on a voyage from Genoa to Port Said in ballast.

BRODSTONE ex *Indraghiri* **4927 Grt. Blt. 1896**
15.8.1917: Torpedoed and sunk in the Atlantic 95 miles W.¼S. from Ushant by the German submarine *UB 40* whilst on a voyage from Cardiff to Zarate with a cargo of coal. 5 lost.

BRODERICK ex *Lizanka* ex *Pakeha* **4321 Grt. Blt. 1890**
29.4.1918: Torpedoed and sunk in the English Channel 7 miles S.S.E. from Hastings by the German submarine *UB 57* whilst on a voyage from London to Puerto Cabello with a cargo of cattle.

BOMBAY & PERSIA STEAM NAVIGATION CO. LTD.—BOMBAY

ALAVI ex *William Storrs* **3627 Grt. Blt. 1893**
13.10.1917: Captured and sunk by gunfire in the Mediterranean 6 miles N.E. from Cape de Palos, near Cartagena by the German submarine *U 35* whilst on a voyage from Genoa to Cartagena in ballast. 13 lost.

BLEAMOOR 3755 Grt. Blt. 1902
27.11.1917: Torpedoed and sunk in the English Channel 4 miles S.S.E. from Berry Head, Tor Bay by the German submarine *UB 80* whilst on a voyage from Hull to Falmouth with a cargo of coal. 8 lost.

BOOKER BROTHERS, McCONNELL & CO. LTD.—LONDON

IMATAKA 1776 Grt. Blt. 1911
23.4.1917: Torpedoed and sunk in the Atlantic 15 miles S.S.W. from Daunts Rock,

off the coast of co. Cork by the German submarine *UC 47* whilst on a voyage from Demerara to Le Havre with a cargo of sugar, rum and frozen meat.

AMAKURA ex *Castillian Prince* *2316 Grt. Blt. 1893*
12.6.1917: Torpedoed and sunk in the Atlantic 80 miles N.W. ½ W. from Tory Island in position 56.10N 13.00W by the German submarine *U 94* whilst on a voyage from Liverpool to Demerara with general cargo. 2 lost.

BOOTH STEAMSHIP CO. LTD.—LIVERPOOL

ANTONY 6466 Grt. Blt. 1907
17.3.1917: Torpedoed and sunk in the St. George's Channel 19 miles W. by N. from Coningbeg Lightvessel, Saltee Islands, co. Wexford in position 51.56N 07.09W by the German submarine *UC 48* whilst on a voyage from Para to Liverpool with general cargo. 55 lost.

CRISPIN 3965 Grt. Blt. 1907
29.3.1917: Torpedoed and sunk in the Atlantic 14 miles S. from Hook Point, co. Wexford in position 51.54N 06.49W by the German submarine *U 57* whilst on a voyage from Newport News to Avonmouth with a consignment of horses. 8 lost.

LANFRANC 6287 Grt. Blt. 1907
17.4.1917: Torpedoed and sunk in the English Channel 42 miles N. ½ E. from Le Havre in position 50.11N 00.12E by the German submarine *UB 40* whilst on a voyage from Le Havre to Southampton carrying wounded troops. 5 lost. Lost whilst on Government service employed as a Hospital Ship.

OSWALD 5185 Grt. Blt. 1915
23.4.1917: Torpedoed and sunk in the Atlantic 200 miles S.W. from the Fastnet Rock in position 51.10N 14.15W by the German submarine *U 50* whilst on a voyage from Sabine to Liverpool with a cargo of sulphur. 1 lost.

HILARY 6329 Grt. Blt. 1908
25.5.1917: Torpedoed and sunk in the Atlantic W. of the Shetland Islands in position 60.33N 03.00W by the German submarine *U 88*. Lost whilst on Government service employed as an Armed Merchant Cruiser.

BONIFACE 3799 Grt. Blt. 1904
23.8.1917: Torpedoed and sunk in the Atlantic 7 miles N.E. by N. from Aran Island, Galway Bay, co. Clare by the German submarine *U 53* whilst on a voyage from New York to Glasgow with general cargo. 1 lost.

ORIGEN 3545 Grt. Blt. 1918
1.7.1918: Torpedoed and sunk in the Atlantic 115 miles W. ¼ S. from Ushant in position 47.28N 08.20W by the German submarine *U 86* whilst on a voyage from London to Oporto. 1 lost.

BOWRING, C. T.—LONDON

Bear Creek Oil & Shipping Co. Ltd.

CYMBELINE 4505 Grt. Blt. 1902
4.9.1915. Captured and torpedoed in the Atlantic 29 miles W. by S. from the Fastnet Rock by the German submarine *U 33* whilst on a voyage from Port Arthur, Texas to Dartmouth with a cargo of oil. 6 lost.

BEACON LIGHT 2768 Grt. Blt. 1890
19.2.1918: Torpedoed and sunk in the North Minch 15 miles S.E. from Butt of Lewis by the German submarine *U 91* whilst on a voyage from Liverpool to Scapa Flow with a cargo of oil. 33 lost including Master.

English & American Shipping Co. Ltd.

MORA 3047 Grt. Blt. 1899
8.9.1915: Captured and sunk by gunfire in the Bay of Biscay 68 miles W. by S. from Belle Ile near Lorient in position 46.50N 04.40W by the German submarine *U 20* whilst on a voyage from Santander to Newport, Mon. with a cargo of steel.

ZAFRA 3578 Grt. Blt. 1905
8.4.1916: Captured and sunk with bombs in the Mediterranean 44 miles N. from Oran by the German submarine *U 34* whilst on a voyage from Cardiff to Malta with a cargo of coal.

GAFSA 3922 Grt. Blt. 1906
16.6.1916: Captured and sunk by gunfire in the Mediterranean 80 miles S.W. by S. from Genoa by the German submarine *U 35* whilst on a voyage from Swansea to Genoa with a cargo of patent fuel and coal.

LORCA 4129 Grt. Blt. 1910
15.11.1916: Torpedoed and sunk in the Atlantic 200 miles W. from Ushant by the German submarine *U 49* whilst on a voyage from Gulfport and Norfolk (Va) to Cherbourg with a cargo of timber.

BRIKA 3549 Grt. Blt. 1908
14.3.1917: Torpedoed and sunk in the St. George's Channel 13 miles S.E. by S. from Coningbeg Lightvessel in position 51.55N 06.24W by the German submarine *UC 47* whilst on a voyage from Santiago de Cuba to Bristol with a cargo of sugar. 2 lost.

POLA 3061 Grt. Blt. 1898
18.3.1917: Torpedoed and sunk in the Atlantic 280 miles W.N.W. from Ushant in position 48.30N 12.00W by the German submarine *U 81* whilst on a voyage from Cardiff to Norfolk (Va) with a cargo of coal. 5 lost.

GAFSA ex *Dominion* 3974 Grt. Blt. 1902
28.3.1917: Torpedoed and sunk in the Atlantic 10 miles S.E.½S. from Kinsale Head, co. Cork in position 51.31N 08.18W by the German submarine *U 57* whilst on a voyage from Port Arthur, Texas to Queenstown (fo) with a cargo of fuel oil. 7 lost.

HUELVA 4867 Grt. Blt. 1915
23.7.1917: Torpedoed and sunk in the Atlantic 270 miles S.W. from the Fastnet Rock in position 47.15N. 12.28W. by the German submarine *U 54* whilst on a voyage from Newport, Mon. to Malta.

NOYA 4282 Grt. Blt. 1912
30.8.1917: Torpedoed and sunk in the English Channel 8 miles W.S.W. from the Lizard by the German submarine *U 62* whilst on a voyage from New Orleans to Falmouth with a cargo of barley and oil. 1 lost.

MURCIA 4871 Grt. Blt. 1915
2.11.1918: Torpedoed and sunk in the Mediterranean 12 miles N. from Port Said by the German submarine *UC 74* whilst on a voyage from Bussein to Marseilles with a cargo of gunny bags and rice. 1 lost.

Lobitos Oilfields Ltd.

EL ZORRO 5989 Grt. Blt. 1914
28.12.1915: Captured and torpedoed in the Atlantic 10 miles S. from Old Head of Kinsale, co. Cork by the German submarine *U 24* whilst on a voyage from Port Arthur, Texas to Dartmouth with a cargo of oil. 2 lost.

New York, Newfoundland & Halifax S.S. Co. Ltd.

STEPHANO 3449 Grt. Blt. 1911
8.10.1916: Captured and torpedoed in the Atlantic 2½ miles E.N.E. from Nantucket Lightvessel by the German submarine *U 53* whilst on a voyage from St. John's, NFL to New York with general cargo.

Oil Tank S.S. Co. Ltd.

SILVIA 5268 Grt. Blt. 1913
23.8.1915: Captured and sunk by gunfire in the Atlantic 47 miles W. from the Fastnet Rock in position 51.70N 10.46W by the German submarine *U 38* whilst on a voyage from Halifax, (NS) to Queenstown with a cargo of oil.

ROSALIND 6535 Grt. Blt. 1913
6.4.1917: Torpedoed and sunk in the Atlantic 180 miles W.N.W. from the Fastnet Rock in position 51.39N 14.20W by the German submarine *U 86* whilst on a voyage from Port Arthur, Texas and Norfolk (Va) to Queenstown with a cargo of oil. 2 lost.

BRADLEY, W. C. & SONS—HULL

JUPITER 2124 Grt. Blt. 1901
21.5.1917: Torpedoed and sunk in the English Channel 15 miles W. from Beachy Head in position 50.38N 00.05W by the German submarine *UB 40* whilst on a voyage from Dieppe to Manchester in ballast. 19 lost including Master.

BRIGHTMAN, H. A. & COMPANY—NEWCASTLE UPON TYNE

European Gas Co. Ltd.

NANTES 1580 Grt. Blt. 1917
7.5.1918: Torpedoed and sunk in the North Sea 83 miles E.S.E. from the Fair Isle by the German submarine *U 105* whilst on a voyage from Bergen to West Hartlepool with general cargo.

BRISTOL STEAM NAVIGATION CO. LTD.—BRISTOL

ARGO ex Moorhen 1720 Grt. Blt. 1882
8.2.1916: Struck a mine and sunk in the English Channel 4½ miles N.W. from Boulogne Pier laid by the German submarine *UC 3* whilst on a voyage from Boulogne to Dunkirk with a cargo of pitwood. 1 lost.

PLUTO 1266 Grt. Blt. 1897
10.4.1917: Torpedoed and sunk in the North Sea 32 miles S.E. by E. from Lowestoft in position 52.19N 02.34E by the German submarine *UB 20* whilst on a voyage from Rotterdam to Bristol with general cargo.

JUNO ex *Nigel 1384 Grt. Blt. 1882*
2.5.1917: Torpedoed and sunk in the English Channel 17 miles E. ¾ S. from Cape Barfleur, near Cherbourg in position 49.48N 00. 51W by the German submarine *UB 18* whilst on a voyage from Rouen to Cardiff in ballast. 1 lost.

BRITISH & IRISH STEAM PACKET CO. LTD.—LONDON

LADY OLIVE ex *Tees Trader 701 Grt. Blt. 1913*
19.2.1917: Sunk by gunfire in the English Channel N.W. of St. Malo in position 49.15N 02.34W by the German submarine *UC 18*. Lost whilst on Government service employed as a Special Service Ship.

LADY PATRICIA 1372 Grt. Blt. 1916
20.5.1917: Torpedoed and sunk in the Atlantic N.W. of Tory Island in position 55.00N 12.00W by the German submarine U 46. Master and Chief Engineer taken prisoner. Lost whilst on Government service employed as a Special Service Ship.

BRITISH & NORTH ATLANTIC STEAM NAVIGATION COMPANY— LIVERPOOL

Dominion Line

ENGLISHMAN ex *Sandusky* ex *Montezuma* ex *Ionia 5257 Grt. Blt. 1891*
24.3.1916: Captured and torpedoed in the Atlantic 30 miles N.E. from Malin Head, co. Donegal by the German submarine *U 43* whilst on a voyage from Avonmouth to Portland (Me) with general cargo. 10 lost.

BRITISH INDIA STEAM NAVIGATION CO. LTD.—LONDON

UMETA 5312 Grt. Blt. 1914
1.12.1915: Captured and sunk by gunfire in the Mediterranean 112 miles E.S.E. from Malta by the German submarine *U 33* whilst on a voyage from Port Said to Marseilles in ballast. 2 lost.

CHANTALA 4951 Grt. Blt. 1913
5.4.1916: Torpedoed and sunk in the Mediterranean 15 miles N. from Cape Bengut, Algeria by the German submarine *U 34* whilst on a voyage from Tees and London to Malta and Calcutta with general cargo. 9 lost.

GOLCONDA ex *Nulli Secundus* ex *Transpacific 5874 Grt. Blt. 1887*
3.6.1916: Struck a mine and sunk in the North Sea 5 miles S.E. by E. from Aldeburgh laid by the German submarine *UC 3* whilst on a voyage from Tees and London to Calcutta with general cargo. 19 lost.

MOMBASSA 4689 Grt. Blt. 1889
20.10.1916: Torpedoed and sunk in the Mediterranean 8 miles N.W. by N. from Cape Corbelin by the German submarine *U 39* whilst on a voyage from London to Zanzibar Island with general cargo. 1 lost.

ITONUS ex *Anglia **5340 Grt. Blt. 1898***
20.12.1916: Torpedoed and sunk in the Mediterranean 60 miles N.W. by W.½W. from Malta by the German submarine *U 38* whilst on a voyage from Marseilles to Sydney, NSW with cargo of tiles. 5 lost, Master taken prisoner.

MANTOLA 8253 Grt. Blt. 1916
8.2.1917: Torpedoed and sunk by gunfire in the Atlantic 143 miles W.S.W. from the Fastnet Rock in position 49.50N 12.20W by the German submarine *U 81* whilst on a voyage from London to Calcutta carrying passengers and general cargo. 7 lost.

BERBERA ex *Nidderdale **4352 Grt. Blt. 1905***
25.3.1917: Torpedoed and sunk in the Mediterranean 60 miles E. from Catania, Strait of Messina by the German submarine *U 64* whilst on a voyage from Bombay to Marseilles with a cargo of grain, cotton and manganese ore. 1 lost, 2nd Officer and 2 Cadets taken prisoner.

MASHOBRA 8173 Grt. Blt. 1914
15.4.1917: Torpedoed and sunk in the Mediterranean 140 miles S.W. from Cape Matapan in position 35.34N 20.40E by the Austro-Hungarian submarine *U 29* whilst on a voyage from Calcutta to London with general cargo. 8 lost, Master taken prisoner.

UMARIA 5317 Grt. Blt. 1914
26.5.1917: Captured and torpedoed in the Mediterranean 20 miles S.W. by S. from Policastro by the German submarine *U 65* whilst on a voyage from Calcutta to the United Kingdom with general cargo. 5 lost, Chief Engineer, 2nd Officer and 1 Cadet taken prisoner.

MONGARA 8205 Grt. Blt. 1914
3.2.1917: Torpedoed and sunk in the Mediterranean 1½ miles from Messina breakwater in position 38.10N 15.36E by the Austro-Hungarian submarine *U 28* whilst on a voyage from Sydney, NSW to London with general cargo.

MALDA 7896 Grt. Blt. 1913
25.8.1917: Torpedoed and sunk in the Atlantic 130 miles W.¼S. from Bishop Rock by the German submarine *U 70* whilst on a voyage from Boston, Mass. to London with general cargo. 64 lost

UMBALLA 5310 Grt. Blt. 1898
25.12.1917: Torpedoed and damaged in the Mediterranean 8 miles S.W. by W. from Cape Scala, Gulf of Policastro by the German submarine *UB 49* whilst on a voyage from Karachi to Naples with a cargo of barley. 15 lost. She was afterwards beached off Praia, Calabria and became a constructive total loss.

REWA 7305 Grt. Blt. 1906
4.1.1918: Torpedoed and sunk in the Bristol Channel 19 miles W.¼S. from Hartland Point in position 50.55N 04.49W by the German submarine *U 55* whilst on a voyage from Mudros to Avonmouth carrying 279 wounded officers and troops. 4 lost. Lost whilst on Government service employed as *Hospital Ship No. 5.*

NIRPURA 7640 Grt. Blt. 1916
16.4.1918: Torpedoed and sunk in the Atlantic 110 miles W.N.W. (true) from

Cape da Roca in position 39.00N 11.48W by the German submarine *U 155* whilst on a voyage from Bombay and Karachi to London with a cargo of peas and lentils.

MATIANA 5264 Grt. Blt. 1894
1.5.1918: Torpedoed and sunk in the Mediterranean on Keith Reef, Tunis while aground in position 37.15N 10.50E by the German submarine *UC 27* whilst on a voyage from Alexandria to London with a cargo of cottonseed and bales of cotton.

ITINDA 5203 Grt. Blt. 1900
10.5.1918: Torpedoed and sunk in the Mediterranean 40 miles N. from Marsa Susa in position 32.24N 21.48E by the Austro-Hungarian submarine *U 47* whilst on a voyage from Malta to Alexandria with a cargo of Government stores. 1 lost.

UGANDA 5431 Grt. Blt. 1898
27.5.1918: Torpedoed in the Mediterranean 90 miles N.E. by N.¾N. from Algiers in position 38.16N 03.30E by the German submarine *UB 49* and sank on the 29.5.1918 about 40 miles off Algiers whilst on a voyage from Genoa to Gibraltar in ballast.

SHIRALA 5306 Grt. Blt. 1901
2.7.1918: Torpedoed and sunk in the English Channel 4 miles N.E. by E.½E. from Owers Lightvessel by the German submarine *UB 57* whilst on a voyage from London to Bombay with general cargo. 8 lost.

SURADA 5324 Grt. Blt. 1902
2.11.1918: Torpedoed and sunk in the Mediterranean in the Port Said swept channel by the German submarine *UC 74* whilst on a voyage from Karachi to—. The last British merchant ship to be sunk by a German U boat in the First World War.

BRITISH TANKER CO. LTD.—LONDON

BRITISH VISCOUNT ex *Rock Light* 3287 Grt. Blt. 1889
23.2.1918: Torpedoed and sunk in the Irish Sea 12 miles N. by W.½W. from the Skerries, Anglesey by the German submarine *U 91* whilst on a voyage from Liverpool to Queenstown with a cargo of oil. 6 lost.

EUPION 3575 Grt. Blt. 1914
3.10.1918: Torpedoed and sunk in the Atlantic 10 miles W. from Loop Head, mouth of the River Shannon, co. Clare by the German submarine *UB 123* whilst on a voyage from Philadelphia to Limerick with a cargo of oil. 11 lost.

BROCKLEBANK, T. & J. LIMITED—LIVERPOOL

Anchor-Brocklebank Line

ISTRAR 4582 Grt. Blt. 1896
2.12.1916: Torpedoed and sunk in the Mediterranean 120 miles N.N.W.½W. from Alexandria in position 33.00N 28.40E by the German submarine *U 39* whilst on a voyage from Liverpool to Calcutta with general cargo and coal. 1 lost, Chief Engineer taken prisoner.

MALAKAND 7653 Grt. Blt. 1905
20.4.1917: Captured and torpedoed in the Atlantic 145 miles W.½W. from Bishop Rock in position 49.20N 10.00W by the German submarine *U 84* whilst on a voyage from Calcutta to Dundee with general cargo. 1 lost.

IRAN 6250 Grt. Blt. 1896
7.8.1917: Torpedoed and sunk in the Atlantic 200 miles E.S.E. from Santa Maria, Azores by the German submarine *U 155* whilst on a voyage from Calcutta to London and Middlesbrough with general cargo.

ASSYRIA 6370 Grt. Blt. 1900
26.8.1917: Torpedoed and sunk in the Atlantic 34 miles N.W. by N.½N. from Tory Island in position 55.40N 09.00W by the German submarine *UB 61* whilst on a voyage from Clyde to New York with general cargo.

MAIZAR 7293 Grt. Blt. 1917
30.1.1918: Torpedoed and sunk by gunfire in the Mediterranean 38 miles N. by W.½W. from Cape Ferrat, Algeria in position 36.32N 01.00W by the German submarine *U 34* whilst on a voyage from Clyde and Liverpool to Calcutta with general cargo.

BENGALI ex *Montgomeryshire* ex *Bengali* 5684 Grt. Blt. 1901
8.4.1918: Torpedoed and sunk in the Mediterranean 14 miles N. from Alexandria by the German submarine *UC 34* whilst on a voyage from Tobruk to Alexandria and Calcutta in ballast.

Well Line, Ltd.

CAMBERWELL 4078 Grt. Blt. 1903
18.5.1917: Struck a mine and sunk in the English Channel 6 miles S.E. by S. from Dunnose Head, Isle of Wight in position 50.35N 01.03W laid by the German submarine *UC 36* whilst on a voyage from Tees and London to Calcutta with general cargo. 7 lost.

BROWN, JENKINSON & COMPANY—LONDON

Hackensack S.S. Co. Ltd.

STEPHANOTIS ex *Hackensack* 4060 Grt. Blt. 1904
25.4.1917: Torpedoed and sunk in the Atlantic 180 miles N.W. by W. from the Fastnet Rock in position 51.40N 14.23W by the German submarine *U 82* whilst on a voyage from Cienfuegos and Halifax (NS) to Queenstown with a cargo of sugar. 6 lost.

BRUCE, JOHN P.—DUNDEE

ANGUS 3619 Grt. Blt. 1904
11.4.1916: Captured and sunk by gunfire in the Mediterranean 76 miles E. by N. from Valencia in position 39.57N 01.08E by the German submarine *U 34* whilst on a voyage from Calcutta to Barcelona and Bilbao with a cargo of cotton and jute.

BRYS & GLYSEN LIMITED—LONDON

YZER ex *Cayo Manzan* 3538 Grt. Blt. 1904
20.7.1916: Captured and torpedoed in the Mediterranean 56 miles N.W.½N. from

Algiers by the German submarine *U 39* whilst on a voyage from Cette to Gibraltar in ballast. 1 lost.

BELGIER 4588 Grt. Blt. 1914
23.2.1917: Captured and sunk by gunfire in the Bay of Biscay 30 miles W. from Belle Ile in position 47.32N 03.58W by the German submarine *UC 17* whilst on a voyage from New York and Norfolk (Va) to Le Havre with a cargo of munitions.

CHORLEY 3828 Grt. Blt. 1901
22.3.1917: Torpedoed and sunk in the English Channel 25 miles E. by S. from Start Point in position 50.14N 03.02W by the German submarine *UC 48* whilst on a voyage from Norfolk (Va) to Le Havre with general cargo.

PATAGONIER ex *Lincluden* **3832 Grt. Blt. 1910**
14.4.1917: Captured and sunk by gunfire in the Atlantic 135 miles W. from Gibraltar in position 36.00N 09.00W by the German submarine *U 35* whilst on a voyage from Gibraltar to Kingston (Ja) in ballast. Master taken prisoner.

CAYO BONITO ex *Caledonier* ex *Cayo Bonito* **3427 Grt. Blt. 1901**
11.10.1917: Torpedoed and sunk in the Mediterranean 4 miles E.N.E. from Savona, Gulf of Genoa by the German submarine *UC 35* whilst on voyage from Swansea to Leghorn with a cargo of patent fuel. 6 lost.

Anglier S.S. Co. Ltd.

APOLLO 3774 Grt. Blt. 1905
9.10.1915: Captured and sunk by gunfire in the Mediterranean 63 miles S. from Gavdo Island, Crete in position 33.44N 24.40E by the German submarine *U 39* whilst on a voyage from Cardiff to Port Said with a cargo of coal and two lighters.

TOWERGATE 3697 Grt. Blt. 1906
16.4.1917: Captured and torpedoed in the Atlantic 250 miles N.W. by W. from the Fastnet Rock in position 52.10N 16.16W by the German submarine *U 43* whilst on a voyage from Galveston to Liverpool with a cargo of cotton, lard and beef.

Lloyd Royal (Gt. Britain) Ltd.

PERSIER ex *Daventry* **3874 Grt. Blt. 1910**
10.12.1917: Torpedoed and sunk in the Mediterranean 50 miles E. from Cape Spartivento, Italy in position 37.53N 17.09E by the German submarine *U 35* whilst on a voyage from Cardiff to Taranto with general cargo and coal. 1 lost.

GALLIER 4592 Grt. Blt. 1914
2.1.1918: Torpedoed and sunk in the Atlantic 7 miles E.N.E. from Wolf Rock by the German submarine *U 95* whilst on a voyage from Le Havre to Barry in ballast.

AUSTRALIER ex *Aldersgate* **3687 Grt. Blt. 1906**
29.4.1918: Torpedoed and sunk in the English Channel 6 miles S.W. by S. from Dungeness Lighthouse, 3¾ miles S.E. of Lydd by the German submarine *UB 57* whilst on a voyage from Bilbao to Middlesbrough with a cargo of iron ore. 5 lost.

BULLARD, KING & COMPANY—LONDON

Natal Line

***UMVOTI** 2616 Grt. Blt. 1896*
8.4.1917: Torpedoed and sunk in the Atlantic 200 miles N.W. by W. from Ushant in position 48.48N 10.15W by the German submarine *U 55* whilst on a voyage from Cape Town to London with general cargo. 4 lost, Master and 1 Gunner taken prisoner.

BURDICK & COOK—LONDON

***BURCOMBE** 3516 Grt. Blt. 1913*
1.12.1916: Torpedoed and sunk in the Mediterranean 100 miles S.E. by E. from Malta in position 35.20N 16.23E by the German submarine *UC 22* whilst on a voyage from Karachi to Hull with a cargo of grain. 2 lost.

***CLARA** 2425 Grt. Blt. 1898*
28.12.1917: Torpedoed and sunk in the English Channel 1½ miles S.S.W. from Rundle Stone, Mount's Bay by the German submarine *UB 57* whilst on a voyage from Rouen to Barry Roads in ballast.

***LYDIE** 2559 Grt. Blt. 1899*
9.2.1918: Torpedoed and sunk in the English Channel 1 mile E. by S. from the Manacle Rocks, 7½ miles S. of Falmouth by the German submarine *U 53* whilst on a voyage from Cardiff to Brest with a cargo of coal. 2 lost.

***ETHEL** 2336 Grt. Blt. 1898*
16.9.1918: Torpedoed and sunk in the English Channel 8 miles S.E. from Berry Head by the German submarine *UB 104* whilst on a voyage from Rouen to Barry Roads in ballast.

Buresk S.S. Co. Ltd.

***BURESK** 3673 Grt. Blt. 1914*
5.11.1915: Torpedoed and sunk in the Mediterranean 30 miles N. by W. from Cape Bengut in position 37.23N 03.40E by the German submarine *U 38* whilst on a voyage from Malta to Barry Roads in ballast.

BURKILL, A. R. & SONS—SHANGHAI

***ARAB** ex M. S. Dollar ex Stanley Dollar ex Toppi Maru ex M. S. Dollar ex Arab 4191 Grt. Blt. 1890*
7.1.1918: Torpedoed and sunk in the Mediterranean 18 miles N. by E. from Cape Serrat, Tunis by the German submarine *UB 50* whilst on a voyage from Cardiff to Messina with a cargo of coal. 21 lost.

BURNETT & COMPANY—NEWCASTLE UPON TYNE

Burnett S.S. Co. Ltd.

***HORDEN** 1434 Grt. Blt. 1906*
20.9.1915: Struck a mine and sunk in the North Sea ½ mile E. from Aldeburgh Napes Buoy laid by the German submarine *UC 6* whilst on a voyage from London to Hartlepool in ballast.

BURNHOPE 1941 Grt. Blt. 1907
14.12.1916: Struck a mine and sunk in the North Sea in Hartlepool Bay laid by the German submarine *UC 32* whilst on a voyage from Hartlepool to London with a cargo of coal. 1 lost (Master).

BIRTLEY 1438 Grt. Blt. 1906
5.1.1918: Torpedoed and sunk in the North Sea 8 miles N. from Flamborough Head by the German submarine *UB 38* whilst on a voyage from Dunkirk to Tyne in ballast. 18 lost including Master.

TOWNELEY 2476 Grt. Blt. 1910
31.1.1918: Torpedoed and sunk in the Atlantic 18 miles N.E.¼E. from Trevose Head in position 50.48N 04.48W by the German submarine *U 46* whilst on a voyage from Devonport to Barry Roads in ballast. 6 lost including Master.

WALLSEND 2697 Grt. Blt. 1917
14.8.1918: Torpedoed and sunk in the North Sea 1 mile S.E. from South Cheek, Robin Hood Bay by the German submarine *UB 104* whilst on a voyage from Hartlepool to London with a cargo of coal.

HEBBURN 1938 Grt. Blt. 1908
25.9.1918: Torpedoed and sunk in the Atlantic 14 miles S. from Mine Head, 5 miles S.W. to the entrance of Dungarvan harbour, co. Waterford by the German submarine *UB 91* whilst on a voyage from Barry to—with a cargo of coal. 6 lost.

BURNS, G. & T. LIMITED—GLASGOW

REDBREAST 1313 Grt. Blt. 1908
15.7.1917: Torpedoed and sunk in the Aegean Sea by the German submarine *UC 38*. Lost whilst on Government service employed as *Fleet Messenger No. 26.*

ERMINE 1777 Grt. Blt. 1912
2.8.1917: Struck a mine and sunk in the Aegean Sea laid by the German submarine *UC 23* whilst on a voyage from Saros to Mudros. Lost whilst on Government service employed as *Fleet Messenger No. 25.*

SETTER 956 Grt. Blt. 1906
13.9.1918: Torpedoed and sunk in the North Channel 6 miles N.W. by N. from Corsewall Point, 9 miles N.W. from Stranraer by the German submarine *UB 64* whilst on a voyage from Manchester to Clyde with general cargo. 9 lost including Master.

BURRELL & SON.—GLASGOW

STRATHCARRON 4347 Grt. Blt. 1912
8.6.1915: Torpedoed and sunk in the Bristol Channel 60 miles W. from Lundy Island in position 51.50N 06.10W by the German submarine *U 35* whilst on a voyage from Barry to—with a cargo of coal.

STRATHNAIRN 4336 Grt. Blt. 1906
15.6.1915: Torpedoed and sunk in St. George's Channel 25 miles N. by E. from Bishop and Clerks, 2 miles W. of Ramsey Island by the German submarine

U 22 whilst on a voyage from Penarth to Archangel with a cargo of coal. 21 lost including Master.

STRATHTAY 4428 Grt. Blt. 1906
6.9.1916: Captured and torpedoed in the English Channel 4 miles N. from Pointe de Pontusval, near Ushant by the German submarine *UB 39* whilst on a voyage from New York to Le Havre with general cargo.

STRATHDENE 4321 Grt. Blt. 1909
8.10.1916: Captured and torpedoed in the Atlantic 20 miles S.E. from Nantucket Lightvessel by the German submarine *U 53* whilst on a voyage from New York to Bordeaux with general cargo.

STRATHALBYN 4331 Grt. Blt. 1909
10.12.1916: Struck a mine and sunk in the English Channel 2 miles N.E. from Cherbourg breakwater in position 49.41N 01.37W laid by the German submarine *UC 26* whilst on a voyage from New York to Le Havre with general cargo.

CAIRNS, DAVID LIMITED—LEITH

SILVERTON ex *Lincolnshire* 2682 Grt. Blt. 1891
13.7.1916: Captured and torpedoed in the Mediterranean 14 miles N.E. from Canai Rocks, Tunis by the German submarine *U 39* whilst on a voyage from Cardiff to Gibraltar and Alexandria with a cargo of coal.

CAIRNS, NOBLE & CO. LTD.—NEWCASTLE UPON TYNE

Cairn Line of Steamships Ltd.

CAIRNTORR 3588 Grt. Blt. 1904
21.3.1915: Torpedoed and sunk in the English Channel 7 miles S. from Beachy Head by the German submarine *U 34* whilst on a voyage from Tyne to Genoa with a cargo of coal.

IONA 3344 Grt. Blt. 1892
3.6.1915: Captured and torpedoed in the North Sea 22 miles S.S.E. from Fair Isle in position 59.13N 01.12W by the German submarine *U 19* whilst on a voyage from Tees to Montreal with general cargo.

CAIRNGOWAN 4017 Grt. Blt. 1911
20.4.1916: Captured and sunk by gunfire in the Atlantic 55 miles W. by N. from the Fastnet Rock by the German submarine *U 69* whilst on a voyage from Liverpool to Newport News.

CAIRNDHU 4109 Grt. Blt. 1911
16.4.1917: Torpedoed and sunk in the English Channel 25 miles W. from Beachy Head by the German submarine *UB 40* whilst on a voyage from Tyne to Gibraltar with a cargo of coal. 11 lost.

FREMONA 3028 Grt. Blt. 1887
31.7.1917: Torpedoed and sunk in the Atlantic 10 miles N. by W. from Ile de Bas near Ushant in position 48.55N 04.11W by the German submarine *UC 47* whilst on a voyage from Montreal to Leith with a cargo of grain and lumber. 11 lost.

CAIRNROSS 4016 Grt. Blt. 1913
28.5.1918: Torpedoed and sunk in the Atlantic 110 miles N.N.W. (true) from Flores, Azores by the German submarine *U 62* whilst on a voyage from Tyne to Buenos Aires with a cargo of coal.

The Shipping Controller

GEORGIOS ANTIPPA ex *Elpiniki* ex *Prins Wilhelm III 1960 Grt. Blt. 1890*
28.11.1917: Torpedoed and sunk in the North Sea 6 miles S. from Withernsea Lighthouse, 4 miles N.E. of Partington by unknown German submarine whilst on a voyage from Sunderland to Rouen with a cargo of coal.

BORG ex *Hampton 2111 Grt. Blt. 1888*
10.6.1918: Torpedoed and sunk in the English Channel 20 miles S.W. by S. from the Lizard in position 49.37N 05.70W by the German submarine *UB 103* whilst on a voyage from Bilbao to Jarrow with a cargo of iron ore. 24 lost including Master.

CALEDONIAN STEAM PACKET CO. LTD.—GLASGOW

DUCHESS OF HAMILTON 553 Grt. Blt. 1890
29.11.1915: Struck a mine and sunk off the mouth of the River Thames near Galloper Lightvessel in position 51.47N 01.40E laid by the German submarine *UC 3*. Lost whilst on Government service employed as a Minesweeper.

CALVERT, ALFRED—GOOLE

Maude S.S. Co. Ltd.

MAUDE LARSSEN ex *Wilhelm Behrens 1222 Grt. Blt. 1897*
27.11.1916: Captured and sunk with bombs in the Mediterranean 22 miles W.S.W. from Marittimo Island by the German submarine *U 63* whilst on a voyage from Bagnoli to Seville in ballast.

CAMPBELL, P. and A. LIMITED—SHOREHAM

BRIGHTON QUEEN 553 Grt. Blt. 1897
6.10.1915: Struck a mine and sunk in the English Channel off Nieuport near Ostend laid by the German submarine *UC 5*. Lost whilst on Government service employed as a Minesweeper.

CANADA STEAMSHIP LINES, LIMITED—MONTREAL

EMPRESS OF MIDLAND 2224 Grt. Blt. 1907
27.3.1916: Struck a mine and sunk off the mouth of the River Thames 9 miles S. from Kentish Knock Lightvessel in position 51.31N 01.43E laid by the German submarine *UC 1* whilst on a voyage from Tyne to Rouen with a cargo of coal.

DUNDEE 2290 Grt. Blt. 1906
31.1.1917: Torpedoed and sunk in the Atlantic 10 miles N. by W. from St. Ives Head in position 50.22N 05.36W by the German submarine *U 55* whilst on a voyage from London to Swansea in ballast. 1 lost.

STRATHCONA 1881 Grt. Blt. 1900
13.4.1917: Captured and sunk in the Atlantic with bombs 145 miles W.N.W. from Ronaldsay, Orkney Islands in position 59.35N 05.49W by the German submarine *U 78* whilst on a voyage from Tyne to Marseilles with a cargo of coal. 9 lost, Master, Chief Engineer and 3rd Engineer taken prisoner.

NEEPAWAH 1799 Grt. Blt. 1903
22.4.1917: Captured and sunk with bombs in the Atlantic 120 miles W. from Bishop Rock in position 49.10N 09.20W by the German submarine *U 53* whilst on a voyage from Huelva to Rouen with a cargo of iron pyrites.

C. A. JACQUES 2105 Grt. Blt. 1909
1.5.1917: Torpedoed and sunk in the English Channel 26 miles W.S.W. from Boulogne in position 50.27N 01.40E by the German submarine *UB 18* whilst on a voyage from Rouen to Tyne in ballast. 3 lost.

D. A. GORDON 2301 Grt. Blt. 1910
11.12.1917: Torpedoed and sunk in the Mediterranean 1¼ miles E.S.E. from Cabo de las Huertas near Alicante in position 38.22N 00.19W by the German submarine *U 64* whilst on a voyage from Marseilles to Melilla in ballast. 1 lost.

ARMONIA ex *Santiago* ex *Weimar* ex *Armonia* **5226 Grt. Blt. 1891**
15.3.1918: Torpedoed and sunk in the Mediterranean 38 miles S.E. by S. ¼S. from Ile de Porquerolles near Toulon in position 42.33N 06.46E by the German submarine *UC 67* whilst on a voyage from Genoa to New York in ballast. 7 lost.

TRINIDAD 2592 Grt. Blt. 1884
22.3.1918: Torpedoed and sunk in the St. George's Channel 12 miles E. from Codling Bank Lightvessel by the German submarine *U 101* whilst on a voyage from Le Havre to Liverpool with a cargo of onions. 39 lost including Master.

TAGONA 2004 Grt. Blt. 1908
16.5.1918: Torpedoed and sunk in the Atlantic 5 miles W.S.W. from Trevose Head by the German submarine *U 55* whilst on a voyage from Bilbao to Clyde with a cargo of iron ore. 8 lost including Master.

ACADIAN 2305 Grt. Blt. 1908
16.9.1918: Torpedoed and sunk in the Atlantic 11 miles S.W. by W. from Trevose Head by the German submarine *UB 117* whilst on a voyage from Bilbao to Ayr with a cargo of iron ore. 25 lost including Master.

Richelieu & Ontario Division

MIDLAND QUEEN 1993 Grt. Blt. 1901
4.8.1915: Captured and sunk by gunfire in the Atlantic 70 miles S.W. by W. from the Fastnet Rock by the German submarine *U 28* whilst on a voyage from Sydney, (CB) to Newport, Mon. with a cargo of steel goods.

CANADIAN NORTHERN STEAMSHIPS LIMITED—TORONTO

ROYAL EDWARD ex *Cairo* **11117 Grt. Blt. 1908**
13.8.1915: Torpedoed and sunk in the Aegean Sea 6 miles W. from Kandeliusa in position 36.31N 25.51E by the German submarine *UB 14* whilst on a voyage from Avonmouth and Alexandria to Mudros with a cargo of Government stores.

132 lost including Master. Lost whilst on Government service employed as a troopship.

CANADIAN PACIFIC OCEAN SERVICES LIMITED—MONTREAL

Allan Line S.S. Co. Ltd.

HESPERIAN 10920 Grt. Blt. 1908
4.9.1915: Torpedoed and sunk in the Atlantic 85 miles S.W. by S. from the Fastnet Rock by the German submarine *U 20* whilst on a voyage from Liverpool to Montreal with general cargo. 32 lost.

CARTHAGINIAN 4444 Grt. Blt. 1884
14.6.1917: Struck a mine and sunk in the Atlantic 2½ miles N.W. from Inishtrahull Lighthouse 9 miles N.E. of Malin Head, co. Donegal laid by the German submarine *U 79* whilst on a voyage from Clyde to Montreal with general cargo.

IONIAN 8268 Grt. Blt. 1901
20.10.1917: Struck a mine and sunk in the St. George's Channel 2 miles W. from St. Govan's Head in position 51.35N 04.59W by the German submarine *UC 51* whilst on a voyage from Milford Haven to Plymouth in ballast. 7 lost.

CALGARIAN 12515 Grt. Blt. 1914
1.3.1918: Torpedoed and sunk in the North Channel off Rathlin Island by the German submarine *U 19*. Lost whilst on Government service employed as an Armed Merchant Cruiser.

POMERANIAN ex *Grecian Monarch 4241 Grt. Blt. 1882*
15.4.1918: Torpedoed and sunk in the English Channel 9 miles N.W. by W. ½ W. from Portland Bill by the German submarine *UC 77* whilst on a voyage from London to St. John, NB. 55 lost including Master.

Canadian Pacific Railway Ocean Lines.

MINIOTA ex *Hackness 6422 Grt. Blt. 1914*
31.8.1917: Torpedoed and sunk in the English Channel 30 miles S.E.½E. from Start Point in position 49.50N 03.00W by the German submarine *U 19* whilst on a voyage from Montreal to Portland with general cargo. 3 lost.

LAKE MICHIGAN 9288 Grt. Blt. 1902
16.4.1918: Torpedoed and sunk in the Atlantic 93 miles N. by W. from Eagle Island in position 55.30N 11.52W by the German submarine *U 100* whilst on a voyage from Clyde to St. John, NB. with general cargo. 1 lost, Master.

MEDORA ex *Frankmount 5135 Grt. Blt. 1912*
2.5.1918: Torpedoed and sunk in the North Channel 11 miles W.S.W. from Mull of Galloway by the German submarine *U 86* whilst on a voyage from Liverpool to Montreal with general cargo. Master, Wireless Operator and 1 Gunner taken prisoner.

MILWAUKEE 7323 Grt. Blt. 1897
31.8.1918: Torpedoed and sunk in the Atlantic 260 miles S.W. from the Fastnet Rock in position 47.22N 12.14W by the German submarine *U 105* whilst on a voyage from London to Montreal with general cargo. 1 lost.

MISSANABIE 12469 Grt. Blt. 1914
9.9.1918: Torpedoed and sunk in the Atlantic 52 miles S. by E. ½E. from Daunts Rock by the German submarine *UB 87* whilst on a voyage from Liverpool to New York in ballast. 45 lost.

MONTFORT 6578 Grt. Blt. 1899
1.10.1918: Torpedoed and sunk in the Atlantic 170 miles W. by S. ¾S. from Bishop Rock by the German submarine *U 55* whilst on a voyage from London to Montreal with general cargo. 5 lost.

CAPEL & CO., (NEWCASTLE & HULL) LIMITED—NEWCASTLE UPON TYNE

LOWMOUNT ex *Orkla* **2070 Grt. Blt. 1888**
7.5.1917: Struck a mine and sunk in the English Channel 4 miles N. from Owers Lightvessel laid by the German submarine *UC 70* whilst on a voyage from Bilbao to Stockton-on-Tees with a cargo of iron ore. 5 lost.

BRUNHILDA 2296 Grt. Blt. 1901
11.7.1917: Torpedoed and sunk in the English Channel 7 miles S. from Start Point by the German submarine *UB 31* whilst on a voyage from Bona to Sunderland with a cargo of aluminium earth and esparto grass.

CAIRNSTRATH ex *Felbridge* **2128 Grt. Blt. 1888**
4.8.1917: Torpedoed and sunk in the Bay of Biscay 6 miles S.S.W. from Ile du Pilier near St. Nazaire by the German submarine *UC 71* whilst on a voyage from Bilbao to Tyne with a cargo of iron ore. 22 lost including Master.

HARTBURN 2367 Grt. Blt. 1900
15.10.1917: Struck a mine and sunk in the English Channel 10 miles S. from Anvil Point laid by the German submarine *UC 62* whilst on a voyage from Manchester to St. Helens Roads with a cargo of hay and trucks. 3 lost.

AXMINSTER 1905 Grt. Blt. 1881
13.11.1917: Struck a mine and sunk in the North Sea off Pakefield Gat near Lowestoft in position 52.26N 01.48E laid by the German submarine *UC 4* whilst on a voyage from Blyth to Dieppe with a cargo of coal. 3 lost.

CAPPER, ALEXANDER & CO. LTD.—LONDON

MIDDLETON 2506 Grt. Blt. 1895
30.11.1915: Captured and sunk by gunfire in the Mediterranean 75 miles S.W. by W. from Gavdo Island in position 33.58N 22.56E by the German submarine *U 39* whilst on a voyage from Mudros to Alexandria with a cargo of sandbags. 4 lost.

Alexander Shipping Co. Ltd.

ISLE OF HASTINGS 1575 Grt. Blt. 1885
5.10.1916: Captured and sunk with bombs in the Atlantic 10 miles S. by W. from Ushant by the German submarine *UC 26* whilst on a voyage from Fray Bentos to London with a cargo of tinned meat.

LEDBURY ex *Obi* ***3046 Grt. Blt. 1892***
26.3.1917: Torpedoed and sunk in the Mediterranean 90 miles N. by E. from Benghazi by the German submarine *UB 43* whilst on a voyage from Karachi to Italy with a cargo of maize, barley and peas. 3 lost.

WESTBURY ex *Gogovale* ***3097 Grt. Blt. 1904***
31.8.1917: Torpedoed and sunk in the Atlantic 8 miles S.S.E. from the Fastnet Rock by the German submarine *U 48* whilst on a voyage from Barry to Halifax, (NS) with a cargo of coal.

LORLE 2686 Grt. Blt. 1896
11.6.1918: Torpedoed and sunk in the English Channel 12 miles S.S.W. from the Lizard in position 49.47N 05.14W by the German submarine *UB 103* whilst on a voyage from Bilbao to Heysham with a cargo of iron ore. 19 lost including Master.

CARE & EIDMAN LIMITED—CARDIFF

TARPEIA ex *Earl of Durham* ex *Stock Force* ***538 Grt. Blt. 1905***
11.5.1917: Captured and sunk with bombs in the English Channel 9 miles N. from Port en Bessin, near Caen in position 49.30N 00.49W by the German submarine *UB 18* whilst on a voyage from Alderney to Treport with a cargo of stone.

CARMICHAEL, J. W. & CO. LIMITED—ST. JOHN'S, NEWFOUNDLAND

Pontiac S.S. Co. Ltd.

PONTIAC 3345 Grt. Blt. 1903
28.4.1917: Torpedoed and sunk in the Mediterranean 70 miles N. by E. from Marsa Susa in position 34.45N 22.60E by the German submarine *UC 74* whilst on a voyage from Karachi to Italy with a cargo of maize, peas and barley. 1 lost, Master, Chief Engineer and two Gunners taken prisoner.

CARR, L. S. & COMPANY—NEWCASTLE UPON TYNE

The Shipping Controller

AUDAX 975 Grt. Blt. 1903
6.9.1918: Torpedoed and sunk in the North Sea 6½ miles E. by N. from North Cheek, Robin Hood Bay in position 54.29N 00.21W by the German submarine *UB 80* whilst on a voyage from Rouen to Tyne in ballast. 3 lost.

CARRON & COMPANY—FALKIRK

AVON 1574 Grt. Blt. 1897
9.4.1916: Struck a mine and sunk off the mouth of the River Thames 2½ miles S.E. by S. from the Tongue Lightvessel laid by the German submarine *UC 7* whilst on voyage from London to Leith with general cargo. 2 lost.

FORTH 1159 Grt. Blt. 1886
9.12.1916: Struck a mine and sunk in the North Sea 4 miles S.W. from Shipwash Lightvessel laid by the German submarine *UC 11* whilst on a voyage from London to Leith with general cargo.

***THAMES** 1327 Grt. Blt. 1887*

26.5.1918: Torpedoed and sunk in the North Sea 6 miles S.E. by E. from Seaham Harbour by the German submarine *UC 17* whilst on a voyage from London to Leith with general cargo. 4 lost including Master.

CASPER, E. A. EDGAR & COMPANY—WEST HARTLEPOOL

Minnie S.S. Co. Ltd.

***SPIRAL** 1342 Grt. Blt. 1906*

5.8.1916: Captured and sunk with bombs in the English Channel 40 miles W.S.W. from St. Catherine's Point by the German submarine *UB 18* whilst on a voyage from Tyne to Bordeaux with a cargo of coal.

CAYZER, IRVINE & CO. LTD—GLASGOW

Clan Line

***CLAN MACALISTER** 4835 Grt. Blt. 1903*

6.11.1915: Captured and torpedoed in the Mediterranean 120 miles S. by E. from Cape Martello in position 33.10N 25.50E by the German submarine *U 35* whilst on a voyage from Liverpool to Calcutta with general cargo.

***CLAN MACLEOD** 4796 Grt. Blt. 1903*

1.12.1915: Captured and sunk by gunfire in the Mediterranean 100 miles E.S.E. from Malta by the German submarine *U 33* whilst on a voyage from Chittagong to London with general cargo. 2 lost.

***CLAN MACFARLANE** 4823 Grt. Blt. 1898*

30.12.1915: Torpedoed and sunk in the Mediterranean 66 miles S.E. by S. from Cape Martello in position 34.50N 25.55E by the German submarine *U 38* whilst on a voyage from Glasgow and Liverpool to Bombay with general cargo. 52 lost including Master.

***CLAN CAMPBELL** 5897 Grt. Blt. 1914*

3.4.1916: Torpedoed and sunk in the Mediterranean 29 miles S.E. from Cape Bon by the German submarine *U 39* whilst on a voyage from Tuticorn to London with a cargo of cotton and foodstuff.

***CLAN LESLIE** 3937 Grt. Blt. 1902*

4.11.1916: Torpedoed and sunk in the Mediterranean 200 miles E.½S. from Malta in position 35.56N 18.37E by the German submarine *UB 43* whilst on a voyage from Bombay to London with general cargo. 3 lost.

***CLAN SHAW** 3943 Grt. Blt. 1902*

23.1.1917: Struck a mine and was damaged in the Firth of Tay laid by the German submarine *UC 29* and was beached 8 miles N.E. from St. Andrew's and became a wreck whilst on a voyage from Calcutta via London to Dundee with a cargo of jute. 2 lost.

***CLAN FARQUHAR** 5858 Grt. Blt. 1899*

26.2.1917: Torpedoed and sunk in the Mediterranean 80 miles E. from Benghazi in position 33.30N 20.50E by the German submarine *UB 43* whilst on a voyage from Calcutta and Bombay to London with a cargo of cotton, jute and tea. 49 lost, 2nd Engineer taken prisoner.

CLAN MACMILLAN 4525 Grt. Blt. 1901
23.3.1917: Torpedoed and sunk in the English Channel 10 miles W. from Beachy Head in position 50.41N 00.01W by the German submarine *UB 39* whilst on a voyage from Chittagong via London to Glasgow with a cargo of coir matting.

CLAN MURRAY 4835 Grt. Blt. 1897
29.5.1917: Torpedoed and sunk in the Atlantic 40 miles W. by S. from the Fastnet Rock in position 50.57N 10.12W by the German submarine *UC 55* whilst on a voyage from Port Pirie to Belfast with a cargo of wheat. 64 lost including Master, 3rd Officer and 3rd Engineer taken prisoner.

CLAN ALPINE 3587 Grt. Blt. 1899
10.6.1917: Torpedoed and sunk in the North Sea 40 miles N. by E. ½E. from Muckle Flugga by the German submarine *U 60* whilst on a voyage from Tyne to Archangel. 8 lost.

CLAN DAVIDSON 6486 Grt. Blt. 1912
24.6.1917: Torpedoed and sunk in the Atlantic 130 miles S.W. by W. ¼W. from the Scilly Isles in position 48.16N 08.36W by the German submarine *UC 17* whilst on a voyage from Sydney, NSW to London with general cargo including maize and butter. 12 lost.

CLAN FERGUSON 4808 Grt. Blt. 1898
7.9.1917: Torpedoed and sunk in the Atlantic 15 miles N.W. from Cape Spartel in position 35.50N 06.10W by the German submarine *UB 49* whilst on a voyage from Glasgow to Alexandria and Bombay with a cargo of coal. 10 lost.

CLAN MACCORQUODALE 6517 Grt. Blt. 1913
17.11.1917: Torpedoed and sunk in the Mediterranean 165 miles N.W. by N. from Alexandria in position 33.26N 27.52E by the German submarine *UB 51* whilst on a voyage from Chittagong to London with general cargo.

CLAN CAMERON 3595 Grt. Blt. 1900
22.12.1917: Torpedoed and sunk in the English Channel 23 miles S.W. by S. ½S. from Portland Bill by the German submarine *UB 58* whilst on a voyage from Chittagong to London and Dundee with a cargo of tea and jute.

CLAN MACPHERSON 4779 Grt. Blt. 1905
4.3.1918: Torpedoed and sunk in the Mediterranean 24 miles N. from Cape Serrat by the German submarine *UC 27* whilst on a voyage from Malta and Bizerta to Colon with a cargo of Government stores. 18 lost.

CLAN MACDOUGALL 4710 Grt. Blt. 1904
15.3.1918: Torpedoed and sunk in the Mediterranean 60 miles S.E. by E. ½E. from Cape Carbonara by the German submarine *UB 49* whilst on a voyage from Naples to Bizerta in ballast. 33 lost including Master.

CLAN FORBES 3946 Grt. Blt. 1903
9.6.1918: Torpedoed and sunk in the Mediterranean 115 miles W.N.W. from

Alexandria in position 31.55N 27.50E by the German submarine *UB 105* whilst on a voyage from Newport, Mon. to Port Said with a cargo of coal. 2 lost.

CLAN MACNAB 4675 Grt. Blt. 1905
4.8.1918: Torpedoed and sunk in the Atlantic 14 miles N.N.W. from Pendeen Lighthouse in position 50.20N 05.55W by the German submarine *U 113* whilst on a voyage from Plymouth to Clyde in ballast. 22 lost including Master.

CLAN MACNEIL 3939 Grt. Blt. 1903
6.8.1918: Torpedoed and sunk in the Mediterranean 10 miles N. from Alexandria by the German submarine *UC 34* whilst on a voyage from Karachi to Marseilles with a cargo of grain and onions.

CLAN MACVEY 5815 Grt. Blt. 1918
8.8.1918: Torpedoed and sunk in the English Channel ½ mile S.E. from Anvil Point by the German submarine *UB 57* whilst on her maiden voyage from Newcastle to Port Said with a cargo of coal. 7 lost.

CHADWICK, J. & SONS—LIVERPOOL

Astral Shipping Co. Ltd.

DRUMCREE 4052 Grt. Blt. 1905
18.5.1915: Torpedoed and sunk in the Atlantic 11 miles N. by E. from Trevose Head by the German submarine *U 27* whilst on a voyage from Barry to Port Arthur, Texas in ballast.

The Shipping Controller

WAR FIRTH 3112 Grt. Blt. 1918
4.9.1918: Torpedoed and sunk in the English Channel 33 miles S.¾W. from the Lizard by the German submarine *U 53* whilst on a voyage from Bilbao to Glasgow with a cargo of iron ore. 11 lost.

CHAMBERS, JAMES & COMPANY—LIVERPOOL

Lancashire Shipping Co. Ltd.

KENDAL CASTLE 3885 Grt. Blt. 1910
15.9.1918: Torpedoed and sunk in the English Channel 4 miles S.E. from Berry Head by the German submarine *UB 103* whilst on a voyage from Le Havre to Cardiff in ballast. 18 lost including Master.

The Shipping Controller

WAR PATROL 2045 Grt. Blt. 1917
10.8.1917: Struck a mine and sunk in the Bay of Biscay 1 mile from Pointe de Penmarch near Lorient laid by the German submarine *UC 69* whilst on a voyage from Barry to—with a cargo of coal. 13 lost including Master.

CHAPMAN, R. & SONS—NEWCASTLE UPON TYNE

CARLTON 5265 Grt. Blt. 1905
29.5.1918: Torpedoed and sunk in the Atlantic 270 miles W. by S. from the Bishop

Rock by the German submarine *U 90* whilst on a voyage from Cardiff to Chile in ballast.

CHARLTON, McALLUM & CO. LTD—NEWCASTLE UPON TYNE

Charlton S.S. Co. Ltd.

HOLLINSIDE ex *Robert Coverdale 2862 Grt. Blt. 1905*
3.2.1917: Torpedoed and sunk in the Atlantic 115 miles W.S.W. from the Fastnet Rock by the German submarine *U 43* whilst on a voyage from Sunderland to Marseilles with a cargo of coal. 1 lost, Master taken prisoner.

HURSTSIDE ex *Portreath 3149 Grt. Blt. 1907*
4.7.1917: Torpedoed and sunk in the Atlantic 108 miles N.N.E.½E. from Cape Wrath in position 60.25N 04.38W by the German submarine *UC 54* whilst on a voyage from Barry to Archangel with a cargo of coal.

HEATHERSIDE *2767 Grt. Blt. 1909*
25.8.1917: Torpedoed and sunk in the Bay of Biscay by the German submarine *U 93* whilst on a voyage from Milford Haven to Malta with a cargo of coal. 27 lost including Master.

Hopeside S.S. Co. Ltd.

LINCAIRN *3638 Grt. Blt. 1904*
27.5.1916: Struck a mine and sunk in the North Sea 8 miles N. by E. from Shipwash Lightvessel in position 52.08N 01.42E laid by the German submarine *UC 10* whilst on a voyage from Tyne to Gibraltar with a cargo of coal.

The Shipping Controller

WAR SWALLOW *5216 Grt. Blt. 1918*
16.7.1918: Torpedoed and sunk in the Mediterranean 72 miles S.W. by S.½S. from Malta in position 34.35N 15.00E by the German submarine *UB 50* whilst on a voyage from Tyne to Port Said with a cargo of coal. 7 lost.

CHELLEW, R. B.—TRURO

CORNUBIA *1736 Grt. Blt. 1889*
9.9.1915: Captured and sunk by gunfire in the Mediterranean 75 miles S.E. by S. from Cartagena in position 36.46N 00.15E by the German submarine *U 39* whilst on a voyage from Alexandria and Cartagena to Clyde with a cargo of beans.

DUCHESS OF CORNWALL *1706 Grt. Blt. 1889*
11.4.1917: Torpedoed and sunk in the English Channel 5 miles N. from Cape Barfleur by the German submarine *UC 26* whilst on a voyage from London to Le Havre. 23 lost including Master.

PENHALE *3712 Grt. Blt. 1911*
18.5.1917: Torpedoed and sunk in the Atlantic 72 miles N.W. by N.½N. from Tearaght Island, co. Kerry in position 52.48N 12.15W by the German submarine *U 46* whilst on a voyage from Jucaro and Halifax, (NS) to Queenstown with a cargo of sugar. 1 lost, Master taken prisoner.

PENVEARN 3710 Grt. Blt. 1906
1.3.1918: Torpedoed and sunk in the Irish Sea 15 miles N.½W. from South Stack Rock, Holyhead Island, Anglesey by the German submarine *U 105* whilst on a voyage from Barrow to Barry Roads in ballast. 21 lost.

PENHALLOW 4318 Grt. 1913
13.6.1918: Torpedoed and sunk in the Mediterranean 52 miles N. by W. from Cape Caxine, Algeria by the German submarine *UB 48* whilst on a voyage from Buenos Aires to Italy with a cargo of grain.

CHINA NAVIGATION CO. LTD.—LONDON

KALGAN 1862 Grt. Blt. 1895
6.3.1918: Torpedoed and sunk in the Mediterranean 33 miles S.W.½W. from Yafa, Syria by the German submarine *UB 53*.

YOCHOW 2127 Grt. Blt. 1901
20.3.1918: Torpedoed and sunk in the Mediterranean 54 miles N.¾E. from Port Said by the German submarine *U 33* whilst on a voyage from Suez to—in ballast. 50 lost including Master.

SZECHEUN 1862 Grt. Blt. 1895
10.5.1918: Torpedoed and sunk in the Mediterranean 60 miles N. by E.½E. from Port Said by the German submarine *UB 51* whilst on a voyage from Famagusta to Port Said with a cargo of firewood. 9 lost.

ANHUI 2209 Grt. Blt. 1903
13.8.1918: Torpedoed and sunk in the Mediterranean 2 miles S.E. from Cape Greco, Cyprus in position 35.04N 34.08E by the Austro-Hungarian submarine *U 27* whilst on a voyage from Famagusta to Port Said carrying passengers and general cargo. 4 lost.

CHITHAM, GEORGE & COMPANY—CARDIFF

Ogmore S.S. (1899) Co. Ltd.

FALCON 2244 Grt. Blt. 1916
24.2.1917: Captured and sunk by gunfire in the Atlantic 190 miles W.N.W. from the Fastnet Rock in position 52.40N 14.45W by the German submarine *U 50* whilst on a voyage from Newport, Mon. to Marseilles with a cargo of coal.

CITY OF CORK STEAM PACKET CO. LTD.—CORK

LISMORE 1305 Grt. Blt. 1905
12.4.1917: Torpedoed and sunk in the English Channel 22 miles N.W. by N.½N. from Le Havre in position 49.48N 00.19W by the German submarine *UB 38* whilst on a voyage from Rouen to Portishead in ballast. 5 lost.

BANDON 1456 Grt. Blt. 1910
13.4.1917: Torpedoed and sunk in the Atlantic 2½ miles S.W. from Mine Head in position 51.56N 07.36W by the German submarine *UC 33* whilst on a voyage from Liverpool to Cork with general cargo. 28 lost.

ARDMORE 1304 Grt. Blt. 1909
13.11.1917: Torpedoed and sunk in the St. George's Channel 13 miles W.S.W. from Coningbeg Lightvessel by the German submarine *U 95* whilst on a voyage from London to Cork with general cargo. 19 lost.

KENMARE 1330 Grt. Blt. 1895
2.3.1918: Torpedoed and sunk in the Irish Sea 25 miles N.W. from the Skerries, Anglesey by the German submarine *U 104* whilst on a voyage from Liverpool to Cork with general cargo. 29 lost including Master.

INNISCARRA 1412 Grt. Blt. 1903
12.5.1918: Torpedoed and sunk in the Atlantic 10 miles S.E. ½ E. from Ballycottin Island, co. Cork by the German submarine *U 86* whilst on a voyage from Fishguard to Cork with general cargo. 28 lost.

INNISFALLEN 1405 Grt. Blt. 1896
23.5.1918: Torpedoed and sunk in the Irish Sea 16 miles E.¾N. from Kish Lightvessel, co. Wicklow in position 53.26N 05.21W by the German submarine *UB 64* whilst on a voyage from Liverpool to Cork with general cargo. 10 lost.

The Shipping Controller

POLJAMES ex *James J. Dickson* **856 Grt. Blt. 1872**
2.10.1918: Torpedoed and sunk in the English Channel 6 miles S. from the Lizard by the German submarine *UB 112* whilst on a voyage from Newport, Mon. to— with Admiralty cargo. 13 lost.

CITY OF DUBLIN STEAM PACKET CO. LTD.—DUBLIN

CONNAUGHT 2646 Grt. Blt. 1897
3.3.1917: Torpedoed and sunk in the English Channel 29 miles S. by W.½W. from Owers Lightvessel in position 50.08N 00.45W by the German submarine *U 48* whilst on a voyage from Le Havre to Southampton. 3 lost.

CORK 1232 Grt. Blt. 1899
26.1.1918: Torpedoed and sunk in the Irish Sea 9 miles N.E. from Lynas Point by the German submarine *U 103* whilst on a voyage from Dublin to Liverpool carrying passengers and general cargo. 12 lost.

LEINSTER 2646 Grt. Blt. 1897
10.10.1918: Torpedoed and sunk in the Irish Sea 7 miles E.S.E. from Kish Lightvessel by the German submarine *UB 123* whilst on a voyage from Dublin to Holyhead carrying passengers. 176 lost including Master.

CLARK & SERVICE—GLASGOW

TELA 7226 Grt. Blt. 1916
2.5.1917: Torpedoed and sunk in the English Channel 16 miles N.E.½E. from Cape Barfleur in position 49.50N 00.50W by the German submarine *UB 18* whilst on a voyage from Le Havre to Cardiff in ballast.

SAN ANDRES 3314 Grt. Blt. 1918
2.9.1918: Torpedoed and sunk in the Mediterranean 40 miles N. by W. from Port

Said by the German submarine *U 65* whilst on a voyage from Salonica to Port Said in ballast.

Crossburn S.S. Co. Ltd.

LEONATUS* ex *Scarsdale* *2099 Grt. Blt. 1903
12.12.1917: Torpedoed and sunk in the North Sea 2 miles E. by S. from Kirkabister Lighthouse, Shetland Islands by the German submarine *UC 40* whilst on a voyage from Swansea to Lerwick with a cargo of coal.

CLYDE SHIPPING CO. LTD.—GLASGOW

TOWARD 1218 Grt. Blt. 1899
31.10.1915: Struck a mine and sunk in the Downs off South Foreland, 3 miles N.E. of Dover laid by the German submarine *UC 6* whilst on a voyage from London to Belfast with general cargo.

ARANMORE 1050 Grt. Blt. 1906
21.3.1916: Captured and torpedoed in the Atlantic 24 miles E.N.E. from Eagle Island by the German submarine *U 43* whilst on a voyage from Limerick to Clyde with general cargo.

BEACHY 4718 Grt. Blt. 1909
18.6.1916: Captured and torpedoed in the Mediterranean 98 miles N.E. by E. from Port Mahon, Minorca by the German submarine *U 35* whilst on a voyage from Calcutta and Marseilles to Hull with general cargo and manganese ore.

SKERRIES 4278 Grt. Blt. 1906
4.11.1916: Struck a mine and sunk in the Irish Sea 15 miles N.N.W. from the Skerries, Anglesey in position 53.45N 04.18W laid by the German submarine *U 80* whilst on a voyage from Barrow to Barry in ballast.

WARNER 1273 Grt. Blt. 1911
13.3.1917: Torpedoed and sunk in the Atlantic off S.W. Ireland in position 52.30N 11.00W by the German submarine *U 61*. Lost whilst on Government service employed as Special Service Ship—*Q 27*. 1 Officer, Wireless Operator and 4 Seamen taken prisoner.

SPITHEAD 4697 Grt. Blt. 1899
6.4.1917: Torpedoed and sunk in the Mediterranean 12 miles N. by W. from Damietta Light, Egypt in position 31.44N 31.46E by the German submarine *UC 34* whilst on a voyage from Alexandria to Rangoon in ballast. 1 lost, Master and Chief Engineer taken prisoner.

KISH 4928 Grt. Blt. 1902
17.4.1917: Torpedoed and sunk in the Atlantic 160 miles N.W. by W. from the Fastnet Rock in position 51.40N 14.28W by the German submarine *U 67* whilst on a voyage from Iquique to Newport, Mon. with a cargo of nitrate. 6 lost.

GARMOYLE 1229 Grt. Blt. 1896
10.7.1917: Torpedoed and sunk in the Atlantic 14 miles S.E. from Mine Head in position 51.49N 06.52W by the German submarine *U 57* whilst on a voyage from Cork to Clyde with general cargo. 20 lost including Master.

POLANNA ex *Anna Woermann* ex *Antonina* **2345 Grt. Blt. 1893**
6.8.1917: Torpedoed and sunk in the North Sea 3 miles E. from Whitby by the German submarine *UC 40* whilst on a voyage from Tyne to Dunkirk with a cargo of coal. 2 lost.

TUSKAR 1159 Grt. Blt. 1890
6.9.1917: Struck a mine and sunk in the Atlantic 3 miles W. from Eagle Island laid by the German submarine *U 80* whilst on a voyage from Clyde to Limerick with general cargo. 10 lost.

HURST 4718 Grt. Blt. 1910
3.10.1917: Torpedoed and sunk in the St. George's Channel 2¼ miles W. by N. from Skokham Island by the German submarine *U 96* whilst on a voyage from Chile to Newport, Mon. with a cargo of nitrate.

KALIBIA 4930 Grt. Blt. 1902
30.11.1917: Torpedoed and sunk in the English Channel 29 miles S.W. from the Lizard in position 49.31N 05.32W by the German submarine *UB 80* whilst on a voyage from Norfolk (Va) to Bordeaux with a cargo of steel billets. 25 lost.

COPELAND 1184 Grt. Blt. 1894
3.12.1917: Torpedoed and sunk in the St. George's Channel 5 miles S.S.W. from the Tuskar Rock by the German submarine *U 57* whilst on a voyage from Clyde to Cork with general cargo. 12 lost.

FORMBY 1282 Grt. Blt. 1914
15.12.1917: Torpedoed and sunk in Caernarvon Bay by the German submarine *U 62* whilst on a voyage from Liverpool to Waterford with general cargo. 15 lost including Master.

CONINGBEG ex *Clodagh* **1279 Grt. Blt. 1904**
17.12.1917: Torpedoed and sunk in the Irish Sea by the German submarine *U 62* whilst on a voyage from Liverpool to Waterford with general cargo. 15 lost including Master.

The Shipping Controller

POLWELL ex *Syra* ex *Deutsche Kaiser* ex *Northumbria* **2013 Grt. Blt. 1888**
5.6.1918: Torpedoed and sunk in the Irish Sea 6 miles E. by S. ½S. from Rockabill Lighthouse, 5 miles N.E. of Skerries, co. Dublin by the German submarine *U 96* whilst on a voyage from Troon to—with a cargo of coal.

COAST LINES LIMITED—LIVERPOOL

WESTERN COAST 1394 Grt. Blt. 1916
17.11.1917: Torpedoed and sunk in the English Channel 10 miles W.S.W. from the Eddystone Lighthouse, 14 miles S.W. of Plymouth by the German submarine *UB 40* whilst on a voyage from Portsmouth to Barry Roads in ballast. 17 lost.

NORFOLK COAST 782 Grt. Blt. 1910
18.6.1918: Torpedoed and sunk in the North Sea 23 miles S.E. from Flamborough Head in position 54.00N 00.34E by the German submarine *UB 30* whilst on a voyage from Rouen to Tyne in ballast. 8 lost.

COATES, HENRY—NEWCASTLE UPON TYNE

Broomhill Collieries Ltd.

BROOMHILL 1392 Grt. Blt. 1909
10.5.1917: Captured and sunk with bombs in the English Channel 9 miles S.W. from Portland Bill in position 50.25N 02.32W by the German submarine *UC 61* whilst on a voyage from Penarth to Sheerness with a cargo of coal. 2 lost.

AXWELL 1442 Grt. Blt. 1909
13.11.1917: Torpedoed and sunk in the English Channel 3 miles W.S.W. from Owers Lightvessel by the German submarine *UB 56* whilst on a voyage from Warkworth to Rouen with a cargo of coal. 2 lost.

COCHRANE, HENRY. A.—SUNDERLAND

F. STOBART 801 Grt. Blt. 1895
11.8.1916: Struck a mine and sunk in the North Sea ½ mile N. from North Aldeburgh Napes Buoy laid by the German submarine *UC 1* whilst on a voyage from Goole to Jersey with a cargo of coal. 4 lost.

COCKERLINE, W. H. & COMPANY—HULL

BRITANNIC 3487 Grt. Blt. 1904
30.7.1916: Captured and sunk in the Mediterranean by gunfire 20 miles E.S.E. from Cape Bon by the German submarine *U 35* whilst on a voyage from Tyne to Alexandria with a cargo of coal.

CAMBRIC 3403 Grt. Blt. 1906
31.10.1917: Torpedoed and sunk in the Mediterranean 14 miles W. from Cape Shershel, Algeria by the German submarine *U 35* whilst on a voyage from Tunis to the United Kingdom with a cargo of iron ore. 24 lost including Master.

COCKROFT, C.—LONDON

Fenay S.S. Co. Ltd.

FENAY BRIDGE 3838 Grt. Blt. 1910
24.3.1916: Captured and torpedoed in the Atlantic 54 miles W. from Bishop Rock in position 49.32N 07.43W by the German submarine *U 70* whilst on a voyage from Philadelphia to Hull with a cargo of wheat.

FENAY LODGE 3223 Grt. Blt. 1904
6.3.1917: Torpedoed and sunk in the Atlantic 250 miles N.W. by W. ½ W. from the Fastnet Rock in position 51.42N 16.11W by the German submarine *U 44* whilst on a voyage from Mobile to Cherbourg with a cargo of pit props. 4 lost including Master.

COCKS, S. J.—DUNDALK

Dundalk & Newry Steam Packet Co. Ltd.

DUNDALK 794 Grt. Blt. 1899
14.10.1918: Torpedoed and sunk in the Irish Sea 5 miles N.N.W. from the Skerries,

Anglesey by the German submarines *UB 123* and *U 90* whilst on a voyage from Liverpool to Dundalk with general cargo. 21 lost including Master.

COLONIAL COAL & SHIPPING CO. LTD.—LONDON

***BRIGITTA* ex *Tennyson* 2084 Grt. Blt. 1894**
4.12.1917: Struck a mine and sunk in the English Channel 6 miles S.W. from the Nab Lighthouse laid by the German submarine *UC 63* whilst on a voyage from Barry to Dieppe with a cargo of coal. 2 lost.

COMMON BROTHERS—NEWCASTLE UPON TYNE

Hindustan Steam Shipping Co. Ltd.

***LARISTAN* 3675 Grt. Blt. 1910**
4.9.1916: Captured and torpedoed in the Mediterranean 30 miles W. from Gozo Island in position 36.00N 13.00E by the German submarine *U 38* whilst on a voyage from Karachi to Hull with a cargo of wheat and barley. Master taken prisoner.

***HINDUSTAN* 3692 Grt. Blt. 1912**
21.3.1917: Torpedoed and sunk in the Atlantic 150 miles W.N.W. from the Fastnet Rock in position 51.25N 13.30W by the German submarine *U 46* whilst on a voyage from Newport News and Halifax, (NS) to Queenstown with a cargo of timber. 2 lost.

***KURDISTAN* 3720 Grt. Blt. 1914**
20.9.1917: Torpedoed and sunk in the Mediterranean 27 miles E.S.E. from Pantellaria Island in position 35.45N 06.40W by the German submarine *U 32* whilst on a voyage from Blyth to Alexandria with a cargo of coal.

COMMONWEALTH AND DOMINION LINE LIMITED—LONDON

***MARERE* 6443 Grt. Blt. 1902**
18.1.1916: Captured and sunk by gunfire in the Mediterranean 36 miles E. from Malta in position 35.51N 19.70E by the German submarine *U 35* whilst on a voyage from Fremantle to Mudros and Gibraltar with general cargo.

***PORT NICHOLSON* ex *Makarini* 8418 Grt. Blt. 1912**
15.1.1917: Struck a mine and sunk in the English Channel 15 miles W.½N. from Dunkirk in position 51.02N 01.58E laid by the German submarine *UC 1* whilst on a voyage from Sydney, NSW to Dunkirk and London with general cargo and meat. 2 lost.

***PORT ADELAIDE* ex *Indrapura* 8181 Grt. Blt. 1911**
3.2.1917: Torpedoed and sunk in the Atlantic 180 miles S.W. from the Fastnet Rock in position 48.49N 11.40W by the German submarine *U 81* whilst on a voyage from London to Sydney, NSW. Master taken prisoner.

***PORT CURTIS* 4710 Grt. Blt. 1910**
7.8.1917: Captured and sunk by bombs in the Bay of Biscay 70 miles W. from Pointe de Penmarch in position 47.30N 06.00W by the German submarine *UC 71* whilst on a voyage from Bahia Blanca to Brest with a cargo of oats.

PORT CAMPBELL ex *Star of Scotland* **6230 Grt. Blt. 1904**
7.4.1918: Torpedoed and sunk in the Atlantic 115 miles W.S.W. from Bishop Rock by the German submarine *U 53* whilst on a voyage from London to New York.

PORT HARDY ex *Nerehana* **6533 Grt. Blt. 1907**
6.7.1918: Torpedoed and sunk in the Atlantic 78 miles W. by N. from Cape Spartel by the German submarine *U 91* whilst on a voyage from Buenos Aires to Genoa with a cargo of frozen meat. 7 lost.

COMMONWEALTH GOVERNMENT LINE OF STEAMERS—LONDON

MOORINA ex *Thuringen* **4994 Grt. Blt. 1906**
7.11.1915: Captured and sunk by gunfire in the Mediterranean 105 miles S. from Cape Martello in position 33.10N 25.10E by the German submarine *U 35* whilst on a voyage from Bombay to Marseilles with a cargo of Government stores.

AUSTRALDALE ex *Strathendrick* **4379 Grt. Blt. 1907**
19.10.1917: Torpedoed and sunk in the Atlantic 165 miles N.W. by N. ¾N. from Cape Villano, near Corunna in position 45.24N 11.32W by the German submarine *U 22* whilst on a voyage from Barry to Gibraltar with a cargo of coal. 27 lost.

AUSTRALBUSH ex *Strathgarry* **4398 Grt. Blt. 1907**
13.11.1917: Torpedoed and sunk in the English Channel 7 miles E. ½N. from the Eddystone Lighthouse by the German submarine *UC 31* whilst on a voyage from Le Havre to Barry in ballast. 2 lost.

COMMONWEALTH GOVERNMENT OF AUSTRALIA—MELBOURNE

CONARGO ex *Altona* **4312 Grt. Blt. 1902**
31.3.1918: Torpedoed and sunk in the Irish Sea 12 miles W. by N. from Calf of Man, S.W. of the Isle of Man by the German submarine *U 96* whilst on a voyage from Liverpool to—. 9 lost.

BARUNGA ex *Sumatra* **7484 Grt. Blt. 1913**
15.7.1918: Torpedoed and sunk in the Atlantic 150 miles W. by S. ½S. from Bishop Rock in position 49.00N 10.00W by the German submarine *U 108* whilst on a voyage from London to Australia via Cape of Good Hope carrying wounded Australian troops.

CONSTANTINE, JOSEPH—MIDDLESBROUGH

LOCHWOOD 2042 Grt. Blt. 1900
2.4.1915: Captured and torpedoed in the English Channel 25 miles S.W. from Start Point by the German submarine *U 24* whilst on a voyage from Barry to— with a cargo of coal.

THORPWOOD 3184 Grt. Blt. 1912
8.10.1915: Captured and sunk by gunfire in the Mediterranean 122 miles S. from Cape Martello by the German submarine *U 39* whilst on a voyage from Tyne to Malta with a cargo of coal.

CEDARWOOD 654 Grt. Blt. 1907
12.2.1916: Struck a mine and sunk in the North Sea 2½ miles E. from Aldeburgh

Napes laid by the German submarine *UC 4* whilst on a voyage from Middlesbrough to Fécamp with a cargo of pig iron. 6 lost.

COPSEWOOD 599 Grt. Blt. 1908
27.12.1916: Captured and torpedoed in the English Channel 34 miles S. by W. ¾ W. from the Lizard in position 49.19N 05.49W by the German submarine *U 79* whilst on a voyage from Bordeaux to Middlesbrough with a cargo of pitwood.

BROOKWOOD 3093 Grt. Blt. 1904
10.1.1917: Captured and sunk by gunfire in the Atlantic 210 miles N. by W. from Cape Finisterre, near Corunna in position 45.50N 11.50W by the German submarine *U 79* whilst on a voyage from Penarth to Port Said with a cargo of coal. 2 lost.

TOFTWOOD 3082 Grt. Blt. 1906
13.1.1917: Torpedoed and sunk in the English Channel 24 miles N. ½ W. from Sept Iles, near Roscoff in position 49.15N 03.43W by the German submarine *UC 18* whilst on a voyage from New York to Le Havre with general cargo.

WARLEY PICKERING 4196 Grt. Blt. 1912
5.2.1917: Torpedoed and sunk in the Atlantic 46 miles W. by N. from the Fastnet Rock in position 51.18N 10.45W by the German submarine *U 60* whilst on a voyage from Sagunto to Middlesbrough with a cargo of iron ore.

QUEENSWOOD 2710 Grt. Blt. 1897
16.2.1917: Captured and sunk by gunfire in the Bristol Channel 6 miles S.W. from Hartland Point in position 50.56N 04.38W by the German submarine *UC 65* whilst on a voyage from Rouen to Port Talbot in ballast. 3 lost.

BILSWOOD 3097 Grt. Blt. 1915
12.3.1917: Struck a mine and sunk in the Mediterranean 8 miles N.W. from Alexandria laid by the German submarine *U 73* whilst on a voyage from Malta to Alexandria.

MAPLEWOOD 3239 Grt. Blt. 1915
7.4.1917: Captured and torpedoed in the Mediterranean 47 miles S.W. from Cape Sperone, Sardinia by the German submarine *U 35* whilst on a voyage from La Goulette to West Hartlepool with a cargo of iron ore. Master taken prisoner.

MORDENWOOD 3125 Grt. Blt. 1910
19.5.1917: Torpedoed and sunk in the Mediterranean 90 miles S.E. by S. ½ S. from Cape Matapan in position 35.02N 22.05E by the Austro-Hungarian submarine *U 29*. 21 lost, Master taken prisoner.

GOODWOOD 3086 Grt. Blt. 1900
21.8.1917: Torpedoed and sunk in the Mediterranean 28 miles N.W. by W. from Cape Bon by the German submarine *UC 67* whilst on a voyage from Naples to Tunis in ballast.

BIRCHWOOD 2756 Grt. Blt. 1910
3.1.1918: Torpedoed and sunk in the St. George's Channel 25 miles E. from the Blackwater Lightvessel, 10 miles S.E. of Enniscorthy, co. Wexford by the German submarine *U 61* whilst on a voyage from Clyde to Devonport with a cargo of coal.

The Shipping Controller

***STRYN** ex Louise 2143 Grt. Blt. 1901*
10.6.1918: Torpedoed and sunk in the English Channel 5 miles E. from Berry Head by the German submarine *UB 80* whilst on a voyage from Rouen to Barry in ballast. 8 lost.

***KUL** ex Garonne 1095 Grt. Blt. 1900*
12.6.1918: Torpedoed and sunk in the Atlantic 3½ miles N.E.¼N. from Wolf Rock by the German submarine *UB 103* whilst on a voyage from Swansea to Rouen with a cargo of coal. 4 lost.

COOK, JOHN & SON—ABERDEEN

***GLEN TANAR** 817 Grt. Blt. 1909*
3.5.1917: Struck a mine and sunk in the North Sea 1 mile N.E. from Girdle Ness near Aberdeen laid by the German submarine *UC 77* whilst on a voyage from Seaham Harbour to Aberdeen with a cargo of coal.

COOMBES, MARSHALL & CO. LTD.—MIDDLESBROUGH

***GREATHAM** ex Bussorah 2338 Grt. Blt. 1890*
22.1.1918: Torpedoed and sunk in the English Channel 3 miles S.E. from Dartmouth by the German submarine *UB 31* whilst on a voyage from Grimsby to Blaye with a cargo of coal. 7 lost.

CORFIELD, W. R.—CARDIFF

Cardiff S.S. Co. Ltd.

***WINDERMERE** 2292 Grt. Blt. 1904*
27.6.1916: Captured and scuttled in the Mediterranean 58 miles S.S.E. from Port Mahon in position 39.50N 05.00E by the German submarine *U 35* whilst on a voyage from Tyne to Savona with a cargo of coal. 12 lost including Master.

CORK STEAM SHIP CO. LTD.—CORK

***BITTERN** 1797 Grt. Blt. 1912*
20.8.1915: Captured and sunk by gunfire in the English Channel 50 miles N.W. from Ushant in position 48.53N 06.18W by the German submarine *U 38* whilst on a voyage from Clyde to Leghorn with general cargo and coal.

***MERGANSER** 1905 Grt. Blt. 1908*
20.11.1915: Captured and sunk by gunfire in the Mediterranean 40 miles W.N.W. from Gozo Island by the German submarine *U 33* whilst on a voyage from Clyde to Alexandria with general cargo and coal.

***TRINGA** 2154 Grt. Blt. 1913*
26.11.1915: Captured and sunk by gunfire in the Mediterranean 30 miles N.E. by N. from Galita Island, Tunis by the German submarine *U 33* whilst on a voyage from Malta to Gibraltar. 3 lost.

DOTTEREL** 1596 Grt. Blt. **1904
29.11.1915: Struck a mine and sunk in the English Channel 4¾ miles N. by E. from Boulogne Pier laid by the German submarine *UC 5* whilst on a voyage from Manchester and Liverpool to Dunkirk with general cargo. 5 lost.

FULMAR** 1270 Grt. Blt. **1902
24.3.1916: Struck a mine and sunk off the mouth of the River Thames 8 miles S.W. of the Kentish Knock Lightvessel laid by the German submarine *UC 7* whilst on a voyage from Rotterdam to—with general cargo. Master lost.

RALLAS** 1752 Grt. Blt. **1915
27.9.1916: Captured and sunk by gunfire in the Mediterranean 45 miles N.E. by N. from Dragonera Island, Balearic Islands by the German submarine *U 35* whilst on a voyage from Clyde to Palermo with general cargo and coal. Master taken prisoner.

VANELLUS** 1797 Grt. Blt. **1912
1.10.1916: Struck a mine and sunk in the English Channel in Le Havre Roads laid by the German submarine *UC 26* whilst on a voyage from Portishead to Rouen with a cargo of oil. 3 lost.

KITTIWAKE** 1866 Grt. Blt. **1906
9.4.1917: Torpedoed and sunk in the North Sea 25 miles N.W. from the Maas Lightvessel at the mouth of the River Maas in position 52.15N 03.18E by the German submarine *UB 31* whilst on a voyage from Liverpool to Rotterdam with general cargo. 7 lost.

DAFILA** 1754 Grt. Blt. **1917
21.7.1917: Torpedoed and sunk in the Atlantic 85 miles W. by S.¼S. from the Fastnet Rock in position 50.16N 12.18W by the German submarine *U 45* whilst on a voyage from Valencia to Liverpool with a cargo of iron ore and onions. 2 lost.

CLANGULA** 1754 Grt. Blt. **1917
19.11.1917: Torpedoed and sunk in the Bristol Channel 4 miles S.W.¾W. from Hartland Point by the German submarine *UC 77* whilst on a voyage from Liverpool to Rotterdam with general cargo. 15 lost including Master.

SERULA** 1388 Grt. Blt. **1905
16.9.1918: Torpedoed and sunk in the St. George's Channel 13½ miles N.E.½N. from Strumble Head, 5 miles N.W. of Fishguard by the German submarine *UB 64* whilst on a voyage from Manchester to Rouen with general cargo. 17 lost including Master.

CORMACK, JAMES & COMPANY—LEITH

KENNETT** 1679 Grt. Blt. **1889
22.9.1916: Torpedoed and sunk in the Gulf of Finland by the German submarine *U 19* whilst on a voyage from Petrograd to Reval in ballast. Master lost.

BRANTINGHAM** 2617 Grt. Blt. **1897
4.10.1916: Torpedoed and sunk in the Arctic by the German submarine *U 46* whilst on a voyage from Archangel to Leith with general cargo. 24 lost including Master.

PETUNIA 1749 Grt. Blt. 1889
8.5.1917: Torpedoed and sunk in the Atlantic 45 miles W. from Bishop Rock in position 49.26N 08.36W by the German submarine *U 49* whilst on a voyage from Bathurst to Leith with a cargo of groundnuts. 2 lost, Master and 2 Gunners taken prisoner.

NORTH SEA 1711 Grt. Blt. 1899
31.10.1017: Torpedoed and sunk in the English Channel 2½ miles S.W. by S. from Prawle Point by the German submarine *UC 65* whilst on a voyage from Hartlepool to Pauillac with a cargo of coal. 1 lost.

ENNISMORE 1499 Grt. Blt. 1880
29.12.1917: Torpedoed and sunk in the North Sea 20 miles E. of Peterhead by the German submarine *UC 58* whilst on a voyage from Tyne to Christiania (Oslo) with a cargo of coal. 10 lost.

MOIDART 1303 Grt. Blt. 1878
9.6.1918: Torpedoed and sunk in the English Channel 7 miles S.E.½E. from Lyme Regis by the German submarine *UC 77* whilst on a voyage from Barry to— with a cargo of coal. 15 lost.

The Shipping Controller

HILDA LEA 1328 Grt. Blt. 1916
23.12.1917: Torpedoed and sunk in the English Channel 24 miles S. by E. from St. Catherine's Point by the German submarine *UB 35* whilst on a voyage from Blyth to Rouen with a cargo of coal. 1 lost.

CORPORATION OF TRINITY HOUSE, THE—LONDON

IRENE 543 Grt. Blt. 1890
9.11.1915: Struck a mine and sunk in the mouth of the River Thames 1½ miles E.S.E. from the Tongue Lightvessel laid by the German submarine *UC 1* whilst on a voyage from Harwich to London in ballast. 21 lost including Master.

ALERT 777 Grt. Blt. 1911
15.4.1917: Struck a mine and sunk in the Strait of Dover off Dover laid by unknown German submarine whilst on a voyage from London to Dover. 11 lost.

CORY COLLIERS LIMITED (WILLIAM CORY)—LONDON

HADLEY 1777 Grt. Blt. 1901
27.12.1915: Struck a mine and sunk in the North Sea 3 miles S.E.½E. from Shipwash Lightvessel laid by the German submarine *UC 3* whilst on a voyage from Tyne to London with a cargo of coal.

DENEWOOD 1221 Grt. Blt. 1905
26.5.1916: Struck a mine and sunk in the North Sea off Aldeburgh laid by the German submarine *UC 3* whilst on a voyage from Tyne to London with a cargo of coal.

BRENTWOOD 1192 Grt. Blt. 1904
12.1.1917: Struck a mine and sunk in the North Sea 4 miles E.N.E. from Whitby

laid by the German submarine *UC 43* whilst on a voyage from London to Tyne in ballast. 2 lost.

HURSTWOOD 1229 Grt. Blt. 1906
5.2.1917: Torpedoed and sunk in the North Sea 6 miles N.E. from Whitby in position 54.35N 00.35W by the German submarine *UB 34* whilst on a voyage from London to Tyne in ballast. 4 lost.

HARBERTON 1443 Grt. Blt. 1894
30.3.1917: Probably struck a mine and sunk in the North Sea laid by the German submarine *UC 31* whilst on a voyage from Blyth to London with a cargo of coal. 15 lost including Master.

SIR FRANCIS 1991 Grt. Blt. 1910
7.6.1917: Torpedoed and sunk in the North Sea 2 miles N.E. from Scarborough in position 54.19N 00.22W by the German submarine *UB 21* whilst on a voyage from London to Tyne in ballast. 10 lost including Master.

VERNON 982 Grt. Blt. 1878
31.8.1917: Torpedoed and sunk in the North Sea 22 miles S.E. by S. from Spurn Point by the German submarine *UB 30* whilst on a voyage from Seaham Harbour to London with a cargo of coal. Master lost.

HARROW 1777 Grt. Blt. 1900
8.9.1917: Torpedoed and sunk in the North Sea 4 miles S.E. from Whitby by the German submarine *UB 41* whilst on a voyage from Granton to London with a cargo of coal. 2 lost.

OCEAN 1442 Grt. Blt. 1894
23.11.1917: Torpedoed and sunk in the North Sea 4 miles E. by N. from Hartlepool by the German submarine *UB 21* whilst on a voyage from Granton to London with a cargo of coal.

HIGHGATE 1780 Grt. Blt. 1899
5.12.1917: Torpedoed and sunk in the North Sea 2½ miles E. from South Cheek, Robin Hood Bay by the German submarine *UB 75* whilst on a voyage from Tyne to London with a cargo of coal.

CORSHAM 2760 Grt. Blt. 1918
8.3.1918: Torpedoed and sunk in the North Sea 6 miles E.S.E. from the entrance to River Tees by the German submarine *UC 40* whilst on a voyage from London to Tyne in ballast. 9 lost.

CRAYFORD 1209 Grt. Blt. 1911
13.3.1918: Torpedoed and sunk in the North Sea 110 miles W. by S. from Skudesnes probably by the German submarine *U 46* whilst on a voyage from Tyne and Methil to Christiania with a cargo of coke. 1 lost.

LADY CORY WRIGHT 2516 Grt. Blt. 1906
26.3.1918: Torpedoed and sunk in the English Channel 14 miles S.S.W. from the Lizard by the German submarine *UC 17* whilst on a voyage from Malta to—. 39 lost including Master. Lost whilst on Government service employed as a Mine Carrier.

CORY, JOHN & SONS LIMITED—CARDIFF

British Steam Shipping Co. Ltd.

ROTHESAY 2007 Grt. Blt. 1891
5.3.1916: Captured and torpedoed in the Atlantic 30 miles S.W. from Bishop Rock by the German submarine *U 32* whilst on a voyage from Seville to Troon with a cargo of iron ore.

RUABON 2004 Grt. Blt. 1891
2.5.1916: Captured and torpedoed in the Atlantic 160 miles W. by S.½S. from Ushant by the German submarine *U 20* whilst on a voyage from Seville to Troon with a cargo of iron ore.

RUPERRA 4232 Grt. Blt. 1904
20.6.1917: Torpedoed and sunk in the Mediterranean 50 miles E. by S. from Pantellaria Island in position 36.44N 13.60E by the German submarine *UC 27* whilst on a voyage from Port Sudan to London with general cargo.

RAMILLIES 2935 Grt. Blt. 1892
21.7.1917: Captured and sunk by gunfire in the Atlantic 120 miles W.N.W. from Tory Island in position 55.24N 11.08W by the German submarine *U 58* whilst on a voyage from Troon to Huelva with a cargo of coal.

NORHILDA 1175 Grt. Blt. 1910
21.8.1917: Torpedoed and sunk in the North Sea 5 miles S.E. from Scarborough in position 54.15N 00.10W by the German submarine *UC 17* whilst on a voyage from Harwich to Tyne in ballast. 1 lost.

CHARING CROSS 2534 Grt. Blt. 1892
1.7.1918: Torpedoed and sunk in the North Sea 4 miles E. by N. from Flamborough Head by the German submarine *UB 40* whilst on a voyage from Tyne to—with a cargo of coal.

New Restormel S.S. Co. Ltd.

RESTORMEL 2118 Grt. Blt. 1901
19.8.1915: Captured and torpedoed in the Atlantic 28 miles N.N.W. from Bishop Rock by the German submarine *U 38* whilst on a voyage from Seville to Clyde with a cargo of iron ore.

New Ross S.S. Co. Ltd.

ROSS 2666 Grt. Blt. 1907
22.4.1916: Captured and torpedoed in the Atlantic 108 miles W. by N. from Bishop Rock in position 48.75N 08.05W by the German submarine *U 19* whilst on a voyage from Seville to Clyde with a cargo of iron ore.

New Ruperra S.S. Co. Ltd.

ROSALIE 4243 Grt. Blt. 1914
10.8.1915: Torpedoed and sunk in the North Sea 3 miles off Blakeney Buoy by the German submarine *UB 10* whilst on a voyage from Tyne to San Francisco.

Seville & United Kingdom Carrying Co. Ltd.

CRAIGSTON 2617 Grt. Blt. 1911
4.10.1915: Captured and sunk by gunfire in the Mediterranean 35 miles W. from Ovo Island, Crete by the German submarine *U 33* whilst on a voyage from Cardiff to Mudros with a cargo of coal.

ADAMTON 2304 Grt. Blt. 1904
8.4.1916: Captured and sunk by gunfire in the Atlantic 15 miles S. from Skerryvore Lighthouse, 10 miles S.W. from Tiree Island by the German submarine *U 22* whilst on a voyage from Scapa Flow to Barry Roads in ballast. 1 lost.

ROSALIE 4237 Grt. Blt. 1915
20.2.1917: Torpedoed and sunk in the Mediterranean 8 miles E. from Jidjelli, Algeria by the German submarine *U 39* whilst on a voyage from New York to Salonica. 21 lost including Master.

KILMAHO 2155 Grt. Blt. 1898
17.5.1917: Torpedoed and sunk in the English Channel 10 miles W.N.W. from the Lizard in position 49.58N 05.28W by the German submarine *UB 20* whilst on a voyage from Cardiff to Dunkirk with a cargo of railway material. 21 lost including Master.

ROSEMOUNT 3044 Grt. Blt. 1905
6.8.1917: Captured and torpedoed in the North Sea 45 miles N.E. by N. ½N. from Muckle Flugga by the German submarine *U 101* whilst on a voyage from Archangel to Lerwick with a cargo of wood. 1 lost.

KILDONAN 2118 Grt. Blt. 1898
29.9.1917: Torpedoed and sunk in the Atlantic 2 miles N.N.W. from Pendeen Lighthouse near St. Just, Cornwall by the German submarine *UB 35* whilst on a voyage from Santander to Ardrossan with a cargo of iron ore. 14 lost including Master.

COTTS, MITCHELL & CO., LTD.—LONDON

Sun Shipping Co. Ltd.

JULIA PARK 2900 Grt. Blt. 1894
30.5.1916: Captured and torpedoed in the Mediterranean 10 miles N. from Cape Carbon, Algeria by the German submarine *U 34* whilst on a voyage from Liverpool to Alexandria with a cargo of coal.

LORD CHARLEMONT ex *Ormiston 3209 Grt. Blt. 1886*
19.4.1918: Torpedoed and sunk in the Mediterranean 22 miles N. from Alboran Island, Morocco by the German submarine *U 34* whilst on a voyage from Spezia to Gibraltar in ballast. 8 lost.

COULL, JOHN & SONS—NEWCASTLE UPON TYNE

Port S.S. Co. Ltd.

FAIRPORT 3838 Grt. Blt. 1906
15.4.1916: Captured and torpedoed in the Atlantic 31 miles N. by W. from Bishop

Rock in position 50.18N 06.52W by the German submarine *U 69* whilst on a voyage from Rosario to Manchester with a cargo of wheat.

COUPLAND, W. & COMPANY—NEWCASTLE UPON TYNE

AISLABY ex *Ethelgonda* **2692 Grt. Blt. *1891***
27.12.1916: Captured and sunk with bombs in the Bay of Biscay 10 miles N.E. from Estaca Point near Ferrol in position 43.51N 07.28W by the German submarine *U 46* whilst on a voyage from Lisbon to Bilbao in ballast.

CYRENE* 2904 Grt. Blt. *1888
5.4.1918: Torpedoed and sunk in Caernarvon Bay 15 miles N. from Bardsey Island by the German submarine *UC 31* whilst on a voyage from Tyne to Blaye with a cargo of coal. 24 lost including Master.

Amaryllis Shipping Co. Ltd.

EMPRESS ex *Cadiz* ex *Empress* **2914 Grt. Blt. *1893***
31.7.1917: Struck a mine and sunk in the North Sea 4½ miles E. by S.½S. from Withernsea Lighthouse in position 53.45N 00.08E laid by the German submarine *UC 63* whilst on a voyage from Tyne to Southend with a cargo of coal. 5 lost.

The Shipping Controller

ATLAS* 989 Grt. Blt. *1904
13.11.1917: Torpedoed and sunk in the English Channel 5 miles S.E. from Owers Lightvessel by the German submarine *UB 56* whilst on a voyage from Warkworth to Rouen with a cargo of coal.

HERCULES* 1295 Grt. Blt. *1909
30.12.1917: Torpedoed and sunk in the North Sea 3 miles E.N.E. from Whitby in position 54.32N 00.39W by the German submarine *UB 21* whilst on a voyage from Tyne to Newhaven with a cargo of coal. 12 lost including Master.

LOFOTEN* 942 Grt. Blt. *1913
3.2.1918: Torpedoed and sunk in the English Channel 7 miles S.E. by E. from Start Point by the German submarine *UB 59* whilst on a voyage from Clyde to Le Havre with general cargo. 17 lost.

COWPER, R. C.—ABERDEEN

Aberdeen, Newcastle & Hull Steam Co. Ltd.

NORWOOD* 798 Grt. Blt. *1895
11.2.1917: Torpedoed and sunk in the North Sea by the German submarine *UC 29* whilst on a voyage from Middlesbrough to Aberdeen with general cargo. 18 lost including Master.

CRAIG, H. & COMPANY—BELFAST

AILSA CRAIG* 601 Grt. Blt. *1906
15.4.1918: Torpedoed and sunk in the English Channel 13 miles W. by N. from Portland Bill by the German submarine *UB 80* whilst on a voyage from Cardiff to Granville with a cargo of coal.

M. J. CRAIG 691 Grt. Blt. 1898
13.9.1918: Torpedoed and sunk in the Irish Sea 7 miles N.E.½E. from Black Head, Belfast Lough by the German submarine *UB 64* whilst on a voyage from Ayr to Belfast with a cargo of coal. 4 lost.

CRASS, J. & COMPANY—NEWCASTLE UPON TYNE

SERAPIS 1932 Grt. Blt. 1877
26.6.1917: Torpedoed and sunk in the Atlantic 106 miles N.N.W.½W. from Tory Island in position 56.20N 10.45W by the German submarine *U 79* whilst on a voyage from Clyde to Marseilles with a cargo of coal. 19 lost, Master and Chief Engineer taken prisoner.

KINGSDYKE ex *Orestes 1710 Grt. Blt. 1888*
17.1.1918: Torpedoed and sunk in the English Channel 20 miles N.E.¾E. from Cape Barfleur by the German submarine *UB 80* whilst on a voyage from Rouen to Cardiff in ballast. 16 lost including Master.

Lowlands Steam Shipping Co. Ltd.

LOWLANDS 1789 Grt. Blt. 1888
18.3.1916: Struck a mine and sunk in the Downs 8 miles N.E. by E. from North Foreland, 2½ miles S.E. of Margate, Kent laid by the German submarine *UC 7* whilst on a voyage from Hull to—with a cargo of timber.

LOWDALE ex *Cairndon* ex *Phoenix 2260 Grt. Blt. 1893*
20.4.1917: Captured and sunk by gunfire in the Atlantic 90 miles W. by N. from Gibraltar by the German submarine *U 35* whilst on a voyage from Tyne to Tunis with a cargo of coal.

NORTHVILLE 2472 Grt. Blt. 1897
17.2.1918: Torpedoed and sunk in the English Channel 3½ miles S.E. by E. from Berry Head in position 50.23N 03.24W by the German submarine *UB 33* whilst on a voyage from Newport, Mon. to Dieppe with a cargo of coal.

LOWTYNE ex *Slingsby 3231 Grt. Blt. 1892*
10.6.1918: Torpedoed and sunk in the North Sea 3½ miles E.S.E. from Whitby by the German submarine *UB 34* whilst on a voyage from Tyne to—with a cargo of coal. 3 lost.

CRAVOS, CHARLES & COMPANY—CARDIFF

Ampleforth S.S. Co. Ltd.

AMPLEFORTH 3873 Grt. Blt. 1914
21.5.1917: Torpedoed and sunk in the Mediterranean 15 miles W.S.W. from Gozo Island by the German submarine *U 65* whilst on a voyage from Cardiff to Alexandria with a cargo of coal and aeroplanes. 4 lost.

CROWFOOT, C. J.—LONDON

F. MATARAZZO ex *Ennisbrook 2823 Grt. Blt. 1906*
15.11.1916: Torpedoed and sunk in the Mediterranean 26 miles E.N.E. from Linosa

Island in position 35.50N 13.20E by the German submarine *U 64* whilst on a voyage from Cardiff to—with a cargo of coal.

CUNARD STEAM SHIPPING CO., LTD.—LIVERPOOL

LUSITANIA 30396 Grt. Blt. 1907
7.5.1915: Torpedoed and sunk in the Atlantic 15 miles S. from Old Head of Kinsale by the German submarine *U 20* whilst on a voyage from New York to Liverpool carrying passengers and general cargo. 1198 lost.

CARIA ex *Clematis 3032 Grt. Blt. 1900*
6.11.1915: Captured and sunk by gunfire in the Mediterranean 120 miles S. by E. from Cape Martello in position 33.14N 25.47E by the German submarine *U 35* whilst on a voyage from Liverpool to Alexandria in ballast.

VERIA 3229 Grt. Blt. 1899
7.12.1915: Captured and sunk with bombs in the Mediterranean 24 miles N.W. by W. from Alexandria by the German submarine *U 39* whilst on a voyage from Patras to Alexandria in ballast.

FRANCONIA 18510 Grt. Blt. 1911
4.10.1916: Torpedoed and sunk in the Mediterranean 195 miles E.½S. from Malta in position 35.56N 18.30E by the German submarine *UB 47* whilst on a voyage from Alexandria to Marseilles. 12 lost.

ALAUNIA 13405 Grt. Blt. 1913
19.10.1916: Struck a mine and sunk in the English Channel 2 miles S. from the Royal Sovereign Lightvessel laid by the German submarine *UC 16* whilst on a voyage from New York to London with general cargo. 2 lost.

IVERNIA 14278 Grt. Blt. 1900
1.1.1917: Torpedoed and sunk in the Mediterranean 58 miles S. by E.½E. from Cape Matapan by the German submarine *UB 47* whilst carrying troops to Alexandria. 121 lost.

LYCIA ex *Oceano 2715 Grt. Blt. 1896*
11.2.1917: Captured and sunk with bombs in the St. George's Channel 20 miles N.E. by N. from South Bishop Lighthouse, 5½ miles S.W. from St. David's Head in position 52.12N 05.27W by the German submarine *UC 65* whilst on a voyage from Genoa and Bougie to Swansea and Liverpool with general cargo.

LACONIA 18099 Grt. Blt. 1912
25.2.1917: Torpedoed and sunk in the Atlantic 160 miles N.W. by W. from the Fastnet Rock in position 52.00N 13.40W by the German submarine *U 50* whilst on a voyage from New York to Liverpool carrying passengers, general cargo and mails. 12 lost.

FOLIA ex *Principello* ex *Principe Di Piemonte 6705 Grt. Blt. 1907*
11.3.1917: Torpedoed and sunk in the Atlantic 4 miles E.S.E. from Ram Head, co. Waterford in position 51.51N 07.41W by the German submarine *U 53* whilst on a voyage from New York to Avonmouth with general cargo. 7 lost.

THRACIA ex *Orono 2891 Grt. Blt. 1898*
27.3.1917: Torpedoed and sunk in the Bay of Biscay 12 miles N. from Belle Ile

in position 47.32N 03.19W by the German submarine *UC 69* whilst on a voyage from Bilbao to Ardrossan with a cargo of iron ore. 36 lost including Master.

FELTRIA ex *Uranium* ex *Avoca* ex *Atlanta* ex *Avoca* ex *San Fernando* ex *Avoca* **5254 Grt. Blt. 1891**
5.5.1917: Torpedoed and sunk in the Atlantic 8 miles S.E. from Mine Head in position 51.56N 07.24W by the German submarine *UC 48* whilst on a voyage from New York to Avonmouth with general cargo. 45 lost including Master.

ULTONIA 10402 Grt. Blt. 1898
27.6.1917: Torpedoed and sunk in the Atlantic 190 miles S.W. from the Fastnet Rock in position 48.25N 11.23W by the German submarine *U 53* whilst on a voyage from New York to London with general cargo. 1 lost.

VOLODIA ex *Den of Ogil* **5689 Grt. Blt. 1913**
21.8.1917: Torpedoed and sunk in the Atlantic 285 miles W.¼S. from Ushant in position 46.30N 11.30W by the German submarine *U 93* whilst on a voyage from Montreal to London. 10 lost.

VINOVIA ex *Anglo Bolivian* **7046 Grt. Blt. 1896**
19.12.1917: Torpedoed and sunk in the Atlantic 8 miles S. from Wolf Rock by the German submarine *U 105* whilst on a voyage from New York to London with general cargo. 9 lost.

ANDANIA 13405 Grt. Blt. 1913
27.1.1918: Torpedoed and sunk in the North Channel 2 miles N.N.E. from Rathlin Island by the German submarine *U 46* whilst on a voyage from Liverpool to New York carrying passengers and general cargo. 7 lost.

AURANIA 13936 Grt. Blt. 1917
4.2.1918: Torpedoed and damaged in the Atlantic 15 miles N.½W. from Inishtrahull by the German submarine *UB 67* whilst on a voyage from Liverpool to New York in ballast. Taken in tow but stranded near Tobermory, Isle of Mull and was wrecked. 8 lost.

AUSONIA ex *Tortona* **8133 Grt. Blt. 1909**
30.5.1918: Torpedoed and sunk in the Atlantic 620 miles W. by S.¾S. (true) from the Fastnet Rock in position 47.59N 23.42W by the German submarine *U 62* whilst on a voyage from Liverpool to New York in ballast. 44 lost.

VANDALIA ex *Anglo California* **7333 Grt. Blt. 1912**
9.6.1918: Torpedoed and sunk in the St. George's Channel 18 miles W.N.W. from the Smalls in position 51.44N 06.10W by the German submarine *U 96* whilst on a voyage from Liverpool to Montreal in ballast.

CARPATHIA 13603 Grt. Blt. 1903
17.7.1918: Torpedoed and sunk in the Atlantic 170 miles W. by N. from Bishop Rock by the German submarine *U 55* whilst on a voyage from Liverpool to Boston, Mass. carrying passengers. 5 lost.

FLAVIA ex *Campanello* ex *Campania* ex *British Empire* **9291 Grt. Blt. 1902**
24.8.1918: Torpedoed and sunk in the Atlantic 30 miles N.W. by W. from Tory

Island in position 55.23N 09.40W by the German submarine *U 107* whilst on a voyage from Montreal to Avonmouth with general cargo and a consignment of horses. 1 lost.

The Shipping Controller

WAR BARON 6240 Grt. Blt. 1917
5.1.1918: Torpedoed and sunk in the Atlantic 8 miles N.E. from Godrevy Lighthouse, St. Ives Bay by the German submarine *U 55* whilst on a voyage from Southampton to Barry Roads in ballast. 2 lost.

WAR MONARCH 7887 Grt. Blt. 1917
14.2.1918: Torpedoed and sunk in the English Channel 11 miles E. from the Royal Sovereign Lightvessel in position 50.46N 00.43E by the German submarine *UB 57* whilst on a voyage from Hull to Italy with a cargo of coal.

DWINSK ex *C. F. Tietgen* ex *Rotterdam* 8173 Grt. Blt. 1897
18.6.1918: Torpedoed and sunk in the Atlantic 400 miles N.E. by N.¾N. (true) from Bermuda in position 39.10N 63.10W by the German submarine *U 151* whilst on a voyage from Brest to Newport News carrying troops and munitions. 24 lost.

CURRIE, DONALD & COMPANY—LONDON

Liverpool & Hamburg S.S. Co. Ltd.

RHINELAND 1501 Grt. Blt. 1903
11.11.1915: Struck a mine and sunk in the North Sea 6½ miles S.E.½S. from Southwold laid by the German submarine *UC 3* whilst on a voyage from Tees to Nantes with a cargo of steel bars. 20 lost including Master.

GREENLAND 1753 Grt. Blt. 1908
14.2.1917: Captured and sunk with bombs in St. George's Channel 20 miles S.W. from Bardsey Island in position 52.30N 05.05W by the German submarine *UC 65* whilst on a voyage from Fleetwood to Cherbourg with a cargo of Government stores.

ICELAND 1501 Grt. Blt. 1903
3.7.1917: Torpedoed and sunk in the Atlantic 10 miles S.W. from Galley Head, near Rosscarbery Bay, co. Cork by the German submarine *U 88* whilst on a voyage from Valencia to Clyde with general cargo and fruit. 2 lost.

CURRIE, JAMES & COMPANY—LEITH

Leith, Hull and Hamburg Steam Packet Co.

SAVONA 1180 Grt. Blt. 1881
1.9.1915: Struck a mine and sunk in the North Sea ½ mile from Shipwash Lightvessel laid by the German submarine *UC 7* whilst on a voyage from Oran to Leith with a cargo of esparto grass and lead. 3 lost.

SARDINIA 1119 Grt. Blt. 1895
15.6.1916: Captured and sunk by gunfire in the Mediterranean 38 miles W.¼N. from Gorgona Island, near Leghorn by the German submarine *U 35* whilst on a voyage from Genoa to London with general cargo.

RONA *1312 Grt. Blt. 1884*
18.6.1916: Captured and sunk by gunfire in the Mediterranean 212 miles S.W. by S. from Capo delle Mele, Gulf of Genoa by the German submarine *U 35* whilst on a voyage from Genoa to Lisbon with general cargo.

DRESDEN *807 Grt. Blt. 1865*
23.9.1916: Captured and sunk with bombs in the English Channel 41 miles S. by E.¼E. from the Nab Lighthouse by the German submarine *UB 37* whilst on a voyage from Tyne to Rouen with a cargo of coke.

BERNICIA *957 Grt. Blt. 1912*
13.11.1916: Captured and sunk with bombs in the English Channel 20 miles S.S.E. from Beachy Head by the German submarine *UB 38* whilst on a voyage from Rouen to London in ballast.

SCALPA *1010 Grt. Blt. 1902*
18.4.1917: Torpedoed and sunk in the Atlantic 150 miles N.W. by W. from the Fastnet Rock in position 52.05N 13.26W by the German submarine *U 53* whilst on a voyage from Marseilles to Liverpool with a cargo of oranges and onions.

LUXEMBOURG *1417 Grt. Blt. 1910*
11.9.1917: Struck a mine and sunk in the Atlantic 3½ miles N.N.E. from Pendeen Lighthouse laid by the German submarine *UC 51* whilst on a voyage from Le Havre to Newport, Mon. with a cargo of Government stores.

BRITANNIA ex *Earl of Aberdeen* *765 Grt. Blt. 1889*
19.10.1917: Torpedoed and sunk in the English Channel off Portland Bill by the German submarine *UC 75* whilst on a voyage from Middlesbrough to St. Malo with a cargo of pig iron. 22 lost including Master.

MINORCA *1145 Grt. Blt. 1892*
11.12.1917: Torpedoed and sunk in the Mediterranean 2 to 3 miles from Cabo de las Huertas by the German submarine *U 64* whilst on a voyage from Genoa to Cartagena in ballast. 15 lost including Master.

WARSAW *608 Grt. Blt. 1864*
20.12.1917: Torpedoed and sunk in the English Channel 4 miles S.E. by E. from Start Point by the German submarine *UB 31* whilst on a voyage from St. Malo to Liverpool in ballast. 17 lost including Master.

ALSTER *964 Grt. Blt. 1909*
14.1.1918: Torpedoed and sunk in the North Sea 5 miles E.S.E. from Noss Head, 3½ miles N.E. of Wick by the German submarine *UB 62* whilst on a voyage from Bergen to Hull with a cargo of dried fish.

BIRKHALL *4541 Grt. Blt. 1900*
23.1.1918: Torpedoed and sunk in the Mediterranean 4 miles S.E. from Cape Doro, Greece by the German submarine *UC 23* whilst on a voyage from Salonica to Alexandria with a cargo of Government stores. 2 lost including Master.

WESTPHALIA *1467 Grt. Blt. 1913*
11.2.1918: Torpedoed and sunk in the Irish Sea N. of Dublin by the German

submarine *U 97*. Lost whilst on Government service employed as a Special Service Ship.

ELBA 1081 Grt. Blt. *1899*
28.4.1918: Torpedoed and sunk in the Atlantic 6 miles N.W. by N. from Pendeen Lighthouse by the German submarine *UB 103* whilst on a voyage from Cardiff to—. 10 lost.

THORSA 1319 Grt. Blt. *1884*
2.5.1918: Torpedoed and sunk in the Atlantic 3 miles N.N.W. from Pendeen Lighthouse by the German submarine *UB 103* whilst on a voyage from Le Havre to Liverpool with general cargo.

DALGLIESH R. S.—NEWCASTLE UPON TYNE

SJAELLAND ex *Libau* ex *Sjaelland* **1405 Grt. Blt. *1872***
25.3.1917: Captured and sunk by gunfire in the English Channel 18 miles E. by N. from Start Point by the German submarine *UC 66* whilst on a voyage from Le Havre to Barry Roads in ballast. Master lost.

Dalgliesh Steam Shipping Co. Ltd.

KENILWORTH ex *Ras Elba* **2735 Grt. Blt. *1895***
24.4.1917: Struck a mine and sunk in the Atlantic 3½ miles S.W. by S. from St. Mathieu Point, Finisterre laid by the German submarine *UC 36* whilst on a voyage from Cardiff to La Pallice with a cargo of patent fuel and benzine.

HAWORTH 4456 Grt. Blt. *1912*
17.7.1917: Torpedoed and sunk in the Atlantic 94 miles W. from the Fastnet Rock in position 50.47N 55.00W by the German submarine *U 45* whilst on a voyage from Philadelphia to Avonmouth with a cargo of wheat.

WENTWORTH 3828 Grt. Blt. *1913*
2.9.1917: Torpedoed and sunk in the Bay of Biscay 36 miles W.¼S. from Belle Ile in position 47.50N 04.40W by the German submarine *U 52* whilst on a voyage from New York to La Pallice with general cargo including agricultural machinery. 1 lost, Master and 2 Gunners taken prisoner.

PLAWSWORTH 4724 Grt. Blt. *1917*
13.7.1918: Torpedoed and sunk in the Atlantic 105 miles W. by N. from Bishop Rock in position 49.36N 09.10W by the German submarine *U 60* whilst on a voyage from Newport, Mon. to Genoa with a cargo of coal. 1 lost.

The Shipping Controller

AGNETE 1127 Grt. Blt. *1894*
24.4.1918: Torpedoed and sunk in the English Channel 4 miles S. by W. from Start Point probably by the German submarine *UB 40* whilst on a voyage from Newport, Mon. to Rouen with a cargo of coal. 12 lost including Master.

DAVIDSON, J. & A. LIMITED—ABERDEEN

BALLOGIE ex *Antwerpen* ex *Bull* ex *Mittelweg* **1207 Grt. Blt. 1889**
9.11.1917: Torpedoed and sunk in the North Sea 1½ miles N.E. from Filey by the German submarine *UC 47* whilst on a voyage from Middlesbrough to Dunkirk with a cargo of slag. 13 lost including Master.

DAWSON, FREDERICK LIMITED—NEWCASTLE UPON TYNE

Dawson S.S. Co. Ltd.

MARION DAWSON ex *Fenmore* **2300 Grt. Blt. 1894**
15.2.1917: Captured and sunk with bombs in the Bay of Biscay 8 miles S.S.W. from Ile d'Oleron near Rochefort in position 46.03N 01.33W by the German submarine *UC 21* whilst on a voyage from Huelva to La Pallice with a cargo of iron ore.

***MELDON* 2514 Grt. Blt. 1902**
3.3.1917: Struck a mine and sunk in the Firth of Lorne laid by the German submarine *U 78* whilst on a voyage from Cardiff to—with a cargo of coal.

DE MATTOS, HAROLD—CARDIFF

***FORNEBO* 4259 Grt. Blt. 1906**
17.6.1917: Torpedoed and sunk in the Atlantic 4 miles N. from Cape Wrath by the German submarine *U 78* whilst on a voyage from Port Arthur, Texas to the United Kingdom with a cargo of fuel oil.

DENABY & CADEBY MAIN COLLIERIES LIMITED—LONDON

***EDLINGTON* 3864 Grt. Blt. 1913**
23.9.1918: Torpedoed and sunk in the Mediterranean 70 miles E. by S. from Cape Passaro, Sicily by the German submarine *UC 54* whilst on a voyage from Taranto to Malta with a cargo of Naval stores.

DENHOLM, J. & J. LIMITED—GLASGOW

The Denholm Line of Steamers Ltd.

***HAZELPARK* 1964 Grt. Blt. 1916**
20.3.1917: Torpedoed and sunk in the English Channel 3 miles S. by E. from Start Point in position 50.11N 03.35W by the German submarine *UC 66* whilst on a voyage from Tyne to La Rochelle with a cargo of coal.

***BEECHPARK* 4763 Grt. Blt. 1917**
3.8.1917: Torpedoed and sunk in the Atlantic 4 miles S. from St. Mary's, Scilly Isles by the German submarine *UC 75* whilst on a voyage from Tyne to Port Said with a cargo of coal.

***HEATHPARK* 2205 Grt. Blt. 1916**
5.10.1918: Torpedoed and sunk in the Bay of Biscay by the German submarine *U 91* whilst on a voyage from Bilbao to Maryport with a cargo of iron ore. 25 lost.

DICKIE, A.—ST. JOHN'S, NEWFOUNDLAND

Colchester S.S. Co. Ltd.

***BRIARDENE* 2701 Grt. Blt. 1882**
1.12.1916: Captured and sunk with bombs in the Atlantic 12½ miles S.E. by S. from Bishop Rock in position 49.45N 06.11W by the German submarine *UC 19* whilst on a voyage from New York to London with general cargo.

DIXON, T. & SONS LIMITED—BELFAST

***ALLANTON* 4253 Grt. Blt. 1901**
3.1.1918: Torpedoed and sunk in the Mediterranean 20 miles N. from Cape Bon by the German submarine *UB 50* whilst on a voyage from Hull to Malta with a cargo of coal.

Irish Shipowners' Co. Ltd. (Lord Line)

***LORD ROBERTS* 4166 Grt. Blt. 1901**
21.6.1917: Captured and sunk by gunfire in the Atlantic 270 miles N. W. by N. from the Fastnet Rock in position 53.38N 15.58W by the German submarine *U 62* whilst on a voyage from Montreal to Belfast with a cargo of wheat and flour.

The Shipping Controller

***WAR CLOVER* 5174 Grt. Blt. 1917**
19.10.1917: Torpedoed and sunk in the Mediterranean 25 miles E. by N. ¾N. from Pantellaria in position 37.00N 12.35E by the German submarine *U 64* whilst on a voyage from Barry to Malta with a cargo of coal. 14 lost.

DODD, GEORGE—LONDON

Buenos Ayres & Pacific Railway Co. Ltd.

***DON DIEGO* 3632 Grt. Blt. 1906**
21.5.1917: Captured and sunk by gunfire in the Mediterranean 40 miles E. by S. from Linosa Island in position 35.50N 13.40E by the German submarine *U 65* whilst on a voyage from Swansea to Alexandria with a cargo of Government stores. 5 lost.

***DON ARTURO* 3680 Grt. Blt. 1906**
28.6.1917: Torpedoed and sunk in the Atlantic 90 miles W.S.W. from Scilly Isles by the German submarine *UC 62* whilst on a voyage from Algiers and Oran to Tees in ballast. 34 lost including Master.

***DON EMILIO* 3651 Grt. Blt. 1906**
1.7.1917: Torpedoed and sunk in the North Sea 10 miles N.W. by W. from Esha Ness Lighthouse, W. Northmavine, Shetland Islands in position 60.33N 02.08W by the German submarine *U 80* whilst on a voyage from Barry to Yukanski (Archangel) with a cargo of coal. 1 lost.

DONALDSON BROTHERS LIMITED—GLASGOW

Anchor Donaldson Ltd.

ATHENIA 8668 Grt. Blt. 1904
16.8.1917: Torpedoed and sunk in the Atlantic 7 miles N. from Inishtrahull by the German submarine *U 53* whilst on a voyage from Montreal to Glasgow with general cargo. 15 lost.

The Donaldson Line Ltd

INDRANI 3640 Grt. Blt. 1888
27.6.1915: Captured and torpedoed in the St. George's Channel 36 miles S.W. of Tuskar Rock by the German submarine *U 24* whilst on a voyage from Glasgow to Montreal with general cargo.

CABOTIA ex *Ontarian* *4309 Grt. Blt. 1900*
20.10.1916: Captured and sunk by gunfire in the Atlantic 120 miles W.N.W. from Tory Island in position 55.16N 11.16W by the German submarine *U 69* whilst on a voyage from Montreal to Manchester with a cargo of wood pulp and a consignment of horses. 32 lost including Master.

MARINA 5204 Grt. Blt. 1900
28.10.1916: Torpedoed and sunk in the Atlantic 30 miles W. from the Fastnet Rock by the German submarine *U 55* whilst on a voyage from Glasgow to Baltimore with a part cargo of whisky. 18 lost.

TRITONIA ex *Borderdale* ex *Gulistan* *4445 Grt. Blt. 1905*
27.2.1917: Torpedoed and sunk in the Atlantic 20 miles N.W. by W. from Tearaght Island in position 52.13N 11.26W by the German submarine *U 49* whilst on a voyage from St. John, NB and Halifax, (NS) to Glasgow with general cargo and a consignment of horses. 2 lost.

PARTHENIA 5160 Grt. Blt. 1901
6.6.1917: Torpedoed and sunk in the Atlantic 140 miles W. by N. from Bishop Rock by the German submarine *U 69* whilst on a voyage from New York to London with a cargo of oats and steel. 3 lost.

The Anglo Newfoundland Development Co. Ltd.

ARGALIA ex *Swanley* *4641 Grt. Blt. 1903*
6.8.1917: Torpedoed and sunk in the Atlantic 81 miles N.W.¾W. from Tory Island in position 55.35N 10.35W by the German submarine *U 94* whilst on a voyage from Baltimore to Glasgow with general cargo and a consignment of horses. 3 lost.

DOUGHTY, H. & COMPANY—WEST HARTLEPOOL

Doughty Shipping Co. Ltd.

MOHACSFIELD 3678 Grt. Blt. 1910
7.1.1917: Captured and sunk by gunfire in the Mediterranean 40 miles S.E. by E.½E. from Malta by the German submarine *U 35* whilst on a voyage from Cette to—with a cargo of hay. 3 lost, Master taken prisoner.

WATHFIELD 3012 Grt. Blt. 1905
21.2.1917: Torpedoed and sunk in the Mediterranean 15 miles N. from Cape

Carbon by the German submarine *U 39* whilst on a voyage from Limni to Malta with a cargo of magnesite. 18 lost including Master.

MUIRFIELD 3086 Grt. Blt. 1907
12.7.1917: Torpedoed and sunk in the Atlantic 350 miles N.W. from the Fastnet Rock in position 50.30N 18.30W by the German submarine *U 49* whilst on a voyage from Portland, Oregon to Dublin with a cargo of wheat. 2 lost, Chief Officer and Wireless operator taken prisoner.

FIRFIELD 4029 Grt. Blt. 1915
16.7.1917: Torpedoed and sunk in the Mediterranean 10 miles N.W. from Cape Papas, Greece in position 37.42N 25.47E by the German submarine *UC 38* whilst on a voyage from Salonica to Port Said in ballast.

DOWNING, E. C.—CARDIFF

Strath S.S. Co. Ltd.

HELMSMUIR 4111 Grt. Blt. 1913
3.12.1915: Captured and torpedoed in the Mediterranean 66 miles S. by E. from Gavdo Island by the German submarine *U 39* whilst on a voyage from Port Louis to—with a cargo of sugar.

DRUGHORN, J. F. LIMITED—LONDON

DYKLAND 4291 Grt. Blt. 1914
23.4.1917: Torpedoed and sunk in the Atlantic 200 miles W.N.W. from the Fastnet Rock in position 51.04N 14.06W by the German submarine *U 50* whilst on a voyage from Halifax, (NS) to Falmouth with a cargo of timber.

ENGLAND 3798 Grt. Blt. 1906
23.5.1917: Captured and sunk by gunfire in the Mediterranean 40 miles S. by E. from Cape Bon in position 36.20N 11.15E by the German submarine *U 65* whilst on a voyage from Cardiff and Bizerta to Malta with a cargo of coal. 3 lost including Master.

The Noreuro Traders Ltd.

MIDLAND 4247 Grt. Blt. 1913
20.10.1916: Captured and sunk with bombs in the English Channel 60 miles E. by N.½N. from Ushant in position 48.55N 03.46W by the German submarine *UB 39* whilst on a voyage from Melbourne and Cape Town to Le Havre with a cargo of wheat.

DUFF, T. L. & COMPANY—GLASGOW

CHERBURY 3220 Grt. Blt. 1911
29.4.1915: Captured and sunk with bombs in the Atlantic 27 miles W.N.W. from Eagle Island by the German submarine *U 30* whilst on a voyage from Barry to Cromarty with a cargo of coal.

DUNCAN, J. T. & COMPANY—CARDIFF

MAYWOOD 1188 Grt. Blt. 1901
30.9.1916: Struck a mine and sunk in the English Channel 1 mile W. from Whistle

Buoy, Le Havre laid by the German submarine *UC 26* whilst on a voyage from Newport, Mon. to Le Havre with a cargo of coal and coke.

ETHEL DUNCAN 2510 Grt. Blt. 1912
18.10.1916: Captured and torpedoed in the Atlantic 40 miles W.N.W. from Noup Head, Orkney Islands in position 59.25N 04.36W by the German submarine *U 20* whilst on a voyage from Cardiff to—with a cargo of coal.

DUNLOP, T. & SONS—GLASGOW
The Dunlop Steam Ship Co. Ltd.

QUEEN EUGENIE 4359 Grt. Blt. 1909
25.3.1917: Torpedoed and sunk in the Mediterranean 23 miles N.N.E. from Cani Rocks by the German submarine *UC 67* whilst on a voyage from New York to Calcutta with general cargo. 35 lost including Master, 1 Apprentice and 1 Gunner taken prisoner.

QUEEN MARY 5658 Grt. Blt. 1915
16.4.1917: Torpedoed and sunk in the Atlantic 180 miles N.W. by W. from the Fastnet Rock in position 51.48N 14.52W by the German submarine *U 60* whilst on a voyage from New York to Le Havre with general cargo. 9 lost.

QUEEN ADELAIDE 4965 Grt. Blt. 1911
18.6.1917: Torpedoed and sunk in the Atlantic 13 miles N.N.E. from St. Kilda Island, Outer Herbrides in position 58.40N 08.35W by the German submarine *U 70* whilst on a voyage from Montreal to Leith with a cargo of wheat. 3 lost.

QUEEN AMELIA 4278 Grt. Blt. 1905
17.9.1917: Captured and torpedoed in the North Sea 19 miles N.N.E. from Muckle Flugga, North Unst, Shetland Islands by the German submarines *U 95* and *UB 62* whilst on a voyage from Archangel to Dundee with a cargo of flax.

DUNDEE, PERTH & LONDON SHIPPING CO. LTD.—DUNDEE

DUNDEE 2187 Grt. Blt. 1911
2.9.1917: Torpedoed and sunk in the Atlantic S.W. of the Scilly Isles by the German submarine *UC 49*. Lost whilst on Government service employed as an Armed Boarding Steamer.

GOWRIE 1031 Grt. Blt. 1909
10.10.1917: Torpedoed and sunk in the English Channel 14 miles N.E. from Cherbourg by the German submarine *U 53* whilst on a voyage from Newhaven to Cherbourg with general cargo and mails.

LONDON 1706 Grt. Blt. 1892
23.6.1918: Torpedoed and sunk in the North Sea 4 miles E. by S. from Whitby by the German submarine *UB 88* whilst on a voyage from Methil to London with a cargo of jute and coal.

EAGLE OIL TRANSPORTATION CO. LTD.—LONDON

SAN HILARIO 10157 Grt. Blt. 1913
20.4.1917: Captured and torpedoed in the Atlantic 270 miles W. by N. from the Fastnet Rock in position 50.55N 16.28W by the German submarine *U 43* whilst on a voyage from Puerto Mexico, Gulf of Mexico to Queenstown with a cargo of petroleum. Master taken prisoner.

SAN URBANO 6458 Grt. Blt. 1913
1.5.1917: Torpedoed and sunk in the Atlantic 180 miles N.W. by W. from the Fastnet Rock in position 52.00N 14.20W by the German submarine *U 81* whilst on a voyage from Puerto Mexico to London with a cargo of naphtha. 4 lost.

SAN ONOFRE 9717 Grt. Blt. 1914
12.5.1917: Torpedoed and sunk in the Atlantic 64 miles N.W. ½N. from the Skelligs Rocks, 7 miles W. of Bolus Head, co. Kerry in position 52.26N 14.40W by the German submarine *U 48* whilst on a voyage from Puerto Mexico to London with a cargo of fueloil. 1 lost.

SANTA AMALIA ex *Drumlanrig* **4309 Grt. Blt. 1906**
28.12.1917: Torpedoed and sunk in the Atlantic 30 miles N. by E. ½E. from Malin Head in position 55.36N 07.38W by the German submarine *U 19* whilst on a voyage from Manchester to Puerto Mexico in ballast. 43 lost including Master.

EASTON, GRIEG & COMPANY—GLASGOW

S.S. Glenfruin Co. Ltd.

GLENFRUIN 3097 Grt. Blt. 1904
29.1.1918: Torpedoed and sunk in the Irish Sea N.W. of Holyhead probably by the German submarine *UC 31* whilst on a voyage from Seriphos to Ardrossan with a cargo of iron ore. 32 lost.

EDGAR, J. & CO., LIMITED—LIVERPOOL

Wirral Transport Co. Ltd.

WIRRAL 4207 Grt. Blt. 1911
12.5.1917: Torpedoed and sunk in the North Sea 23 miles N.W. from Utvaer Island in position 61.12N 03.47E by the German submarine *U 19* whilst on a voyage from London to Archangel with a cargo of munitions. 1 lost.

EDWARDS, SONS & COMPANY—CARDIFF

Western Counties Shipping Co. Ltd.

SOUTHINA ex *Southfield* ex *Mariston* **3506 Grt. Blt. 1899**
7.7.1917: Torpedoed and sunk in the Mediterranean 6 miles W.N.W. from Cape Sigli, Algeria by the German submarine *UC 67* whilst on a voyage from Cardiff and Oran to—with a cargo of Government stores and coal. 1 lost.

EDYE & COMPANY—LONDON

Palmerston S.S. Co. Ltd.

SAN BERNARDO ex *Bellasco 3803 Grt. Blt. 1896*
10.8.1916: Captured and sunk with bombs in the North Sea 17 miles S.E. from Longstone in position 55.30N 01.00W by the German submarine *UB 19* whilst on a voyage from Tyssedal to Tyne in ballast.

ELDER, DEMPSTER & CO. LTD.—LIVERPOOL

IKBAL 5434 Grt. Blt. 1894
29.4.1917: Torpedoed and sunk in the Atlantic 200 miles W. by S. from Bishop Rock in position 48.43N 12.35W by the German submarine *U 93* whilst on a voyage from St. John, NB to Falmouth with a cargo of ammunition. Master and 2 Gunners taken prisoner.

African S.S. Co.—London

ILARO 2799 Grt. Blt. 1895
23.10.1915: Struck a mine and sunk in the Strait of Dover 4 miles E. from Dungeness laid by the German submarine *UC 5* whilst on a voyage from West Africa to Hull with general cargo. 1 lost.

ABURI 3730 Grt. Blt. 1906
17.4.1917: Torpedoed and sunk in the Atlantic 125 miles N.W. from Tory Island in position 56.15N 11.30W by the German submarine *U 61* whilst on a voyage from Liverpool to Dakar. 25 lost.

ABOSSO 7782 Grt. Blt. 1912
25.4.1917: Torpedoed and sunk in the Atlantic 180 miles W. by N. from the Fastnet Rock in position 57.10N 14.58W by the German submarine *U 43* whilst on a voyage from Bathurst to Liverpool with general cargo. 65 lost.

TARQUAH 3859 Grt. Blt. 1902
7.7.1917: Torpedoed and sunk in the Atlantic 10 miles S.W. from Bull Rock, 3 miles W. from Dursey Island, co. Cork in position 51.29N 10.25W by the German submarine *U 57* whilst on a voyage from Sierra Leone to Liverpool with general cargo.

KARINA 4222 Grt. Blt. 1905
1.8.1917: Torpedoed and sunk in the Atlantic 17 miles S.S.W.½W. from Hook Point by the German submarine *UC 75* whilst on a voyage from Sierra Leone to Liverpool with a cargo of palm oil and kernels. 11 lost.

APAPA 7832 Grt. Blt. 1914
28.11.1917: Torpedoed and sunk in the Irish Sea 3 miles N. by E. from Lynas Point in position 53.26N 04.18W by the German submarine *U 96* whilst on a voyage from West Africa to Liverpool with general cargo. 77 lost.

ASABA 972 Grt. Blt. 1900
6.12.1917: Torpedoed and sunk in the English Channel 2 miles W.S.W. from the Lizard by the German submarine *UC 17* whilst on a voyage from Newport, Mon. to Le Havre with Admiralty cargo. 16 lost including Master.

AGBERI 4821 Grt. Blt. 1905
25.12.1917: Torpedoed and sunk in the St. George's Channel 18 miles N.W. ½ N. from Bardsey Island by the German submarine *U 87* whilst on a voyage from Dakar to Liverpool with general cargo.

British & African Steam Navigation Co. Ltd.

BONNY 2702 Grt. Blt. 1891
17.8.1915: Captured and sunk by gunfire in the St. George's Channel 16 miles S. by E. from Tuskar Rock by the German submarine *U 38* whilst on a voyage from Marseilles to Liverpool in ballast.

ADANSI 2644 Grt. Blt. 1901
6.5.1917: Torpedoed and sunk in the Atlantic 80 miles W. ½ N. from the Fastnet Rock in position 50.40N 11.05W by the German submarine *U 21* whilst on a voyage from West Africa to Liverpool with general cargo.

BATHURST 2821 Grt. Blt. 1893
30.5.1917: Captured and torpedoed in the Atlantic 90 miles W. from Bishop Rock in position 49.23N 08.43W by the German submarine *U 87* whilst on a voyage from West Africa to Hull with a cargo of mahogany and palm kernels.

ADDAH 4397 Grt. Blt. 1905
15.6.1917: Torpedoed and sunk in the Bay of Biscay 35 miles S.W. from Pointe de Penmarch in position 47.24N 05.00W by the German submarine *UC 69* whilst on a voyage from Montreal to Cherbourg with general cargo. 9 lost.

ELELE 6557 Grt. Blt. 1913
18.6.1917: Torpedoed and sunk in the Atlantic 300 miles N.W. ¾ W. from the Fastnet Rock in position 52.20N 17.30W by the German submarine *U 24* whilst on a voyage from Boston, Mass. to Liverpool with a cargo of wheat and munitions.

OBUASI ex *Christopher* **4416 Grt. Blt. 1910**
8.7.1917: Torpedoed and sunk in the Atlantic 290 miles N.W. by W. ¼ W. from the Fastnet Rock in position 52.26N 17.41W by the German submarine *U 49* whilst on a voyage from Dakar to Liverpool with general cargo. 2 lost, Master and 1 Gunner taken prisoner.

TAMELE 3932 Grt. Blt. 1910
16.7.1917: Torpedoed and sunk in the Atlantic 65 miles W. by S. from the Fastnet Rock by the German submarine *U 87* whilst on a voyage from West Africa to Liverpool with general cargo. 1 lost.

ELOBY 6545 Grt. Blt. 1913
19.7.1917: Torpedoed and sunk in the Mediterranean 75 miles S.E. by E. from Malta in position 35.11N 15.38E by the German submarine *U 38*. 56 lost including Master.

SAPELE 4366 Grt. Blt. 1904
26.10.1917: Torpedoed and sunk in the Atlantic 100 miles N.W. from Tory Island in position 55.56N 11.00W by the German submarine *U 104* whilst on a voyage from Liverpool and Clyde to West Africa with general cargo. 3 lost.

HARTLEY 1150 Grt. Blt. 1903
26.1.1918: Torpedoed and sunk in the North Sea 2 miles N.E. from Skinningrove by the German submarine *UB 34* whilst on a voyage from Boulogne to Tyne in ballast.

BOMA 2694 Grt. Blt. 1889
11.6.1918: Torpedoed and sunk in the English Channel 10 miles S.W.¾W. from Beer Head by the German submarine *UB 80* whilst on a voyage from Belfast to St. Helena Island with general cargo.

Elder Line

FALABA 4806 Grt. Blt. 1906
28.3.1915: Captured and torpedoed in the St. George's Channel 38 miles W. from the Smalls by the German submarine *U 28* whilst on a voyage from Liverpool to West Africa. 104 lost including Master.

ETHIOPE ex *Coaling* **3794 Grt. Blt. 1906**
28.5.1915: Captured and torpedoed in the English Channel 40 miles S.W. by S. from Start Point in position 49.39N 04.16W by the German submarine *U 41* whilst on a voyage from Hull and London to Calabar with general cargo.

ANDONI 3188 Grt. Blt. 1898
8.1.1917: Torpedoed and sunk in the Mediterranean 46 miles S.E. from Malta in position 35.19N 15.07E by the German submarine *U 35* whilst on a voyage from Karachi to London. 3 lost.

MEMNON ex *Plassey* **3203 Grt. Blt. 1890**
12.3.1917: Torpedoed and sunk in the English Channel 20 miles S.W. from Portland Bill in position 50.15N 02.48W by the German submarine *UC 66* whilst on a voyage from Dakar to Hull with general cargo. 6 lost.

GOLD COAST ex *Hans Woermann* **4255 Grt. Blt. 1900**
19.4.1917: Torpedoed and sunk in the Atlantic 14 miles S. from Mine Head in position 51.46N 07.28W by the German submarine *UC 47* whilst on a voyage from Dakar to Liverpool with general cargo.

AKASSA 3919 Grt. Blt. 1910
13.8.1917: Torpedoed and sunk in the Atlantic 8 miles S.E. from Galley Head by the German submarine *UC 33* whilst on a voyage from Liverpool to West Africa with general cargo and passengers. 7 lost.

BADAGRI 2956 Grt. Blt. 1907
13.7.1918: Torpedoed and sunk in the Atlantic 425 miles W.N.W. from Cape St. Vincent, Cape Verde Islands by the German submarine *U 91* in position 37.30N 17.50W whilst on a voyage from Liverpool to Sierra Leone with general cargo, £25,000 in gold, silver and other coins and munitions. Master taken prisoner.

Imperial Direct Line Ltd.

BENITO ex *Falls of Nith* **4712 Grt. Blt. 1907**
26.12.1917: Torpedoed and sunk in the English Channel 9 miles S. from Dodman

Point, 8½ miles S. of St. Austell, Cornwall by the German submarine *UB 57* whilst on a voyage from Tyne to—with a cargo of coal.

The Shipping Controller

ESTRELLA ex *Sanwarine 1740 Grt. Blt. 1912*
5.3.1918: Struck a mine and sunk in the North Sea 5 miles S.½W from Shipwash Lightvessel laid by the German submarine *UC 4* whilst on a voyage from Le Havre to Tyne in ballast. 20 lost.

HUNSDON ex *Arnfried 2899 Grt. Blt. 1911*
18.10.1918: Torpedoed and sunk in the Irish Sea 1 mile S. from Strangford Light Buoy, co. Down by the German submarine *UB 92* whilst on a voyage from Le Havre to Belfast in ballast. 1 lost.

ELDERS & FYFFES LIMITED—LIVERPOOL

BAYANO 5948 Grt. Blt. 1913
11.3.1915: Torpedoed and sunk in the North Channel 3 miles off Corsewall Point by the German submarine *U 27*. Lost whilst on Government service employed as an Armed Merchant Cruiser.

ZENT 3890 Grt. Blt. 1905
5.4.1916: Torpedoed and sunk in the Atlantic 28 miles W. by S.½S. from the Fastnet Rock by the German submarine *U 66* whilst on a voyage from Garston to Santa Marta in ballast. 49 lost.

CAVINA 6539 Grt. Blt. 1915
1.6.1917: Torpedoed and sunk in the Atlantic 45 miles W. by S. from the Fastnet Rock in position 50.56N 10.35W by the German submarine *U 88* whilst on a voyage from Santa Marta to Avonmouth with a cargo of bananas and logwood.

MIAMI 3762 Grt. Blt. 1904
22.6.1917: Torpedoed and sunk in the Atlantic 11 miles E.S.E. from the Fastnet Rock in position 51.21N 09.19W by the German submarine *UC 51* whilst on a voyage from New York to Manchester with general cargo.

MANISTEE 3869 Grt. Blt. 1904
26.6.1917: Torpedoed and sunk in the Atlantic 86 miles W.S.W. from Bishop Rock in position 49.00N 07.54W by the German submarine *U 62* whilst on a voyage from New York to London with general cargo. 5 lost.

CHIRRIPO 4050 Grt. Blt. 1906
28.12.1917: Struck a mine and sunk in the Irish Sea ½ mile from Black Head, Belfast Lough laid by the German submarine *UC 75* whilst on a voyage from Liverpool to Kingston, (Ja). with general cargo.

CHAGRES 5288 Grt. Blt. 1912
10.3.1918: Torpedoed and sunk in the Mediterranean 62 miles N. by E.¾E. from Cape Drepano, Crete by the German submarine *UC 74* whilst on a voyage from Port Said to Salonica with a cargo of Government stores. 1 lost.

PATIA 6103 Grt. Blt. 1913
13.6.1918: Torpedoed and sunk in the Bristol Channel by the German submarine *UC 49*. Lost whilst on Government service employed as an Armed Merchant Cruiser.

TORTUGUERO 4175 Grt. Blt. 1900
26.6.1918: Torpedoed and sunk in the Atlantic 205 miles N.W.¼N. from Eagle Island in position 55.50N 15.30W by the German submarine *U 156* whilst on a voyage from Liverpool to Kingston, (Ja) in ballast. 12 lost.

REVENTAZON 4050 Grt. Blt. 1906
5.10.1918: Torpedoed and sunk in the Aegean Sea 14 miles W. by S. from Kassandra Point, Gulf of Salonica by the German submarine *UC 23* whilst on a voyage from Salonica to Port Said in ballast. 15 lost including Master.

ELLERMAN & BUCKNALL STEAM SHIP CO. LTD.—LONDON

ARABIAN ex *Bloemfontein 2744 Grt. Blt. 1892*
2.10.1915: Captured and sunk by gunfire in the Mediterranean 15 miles W.½S. from Cerigo Island, Greece by the German submarine *U 33* whilst on a voyage from London and Malta to Salonica with a cargo of general stores.

KASENGA 4652 Grt. Blt. 1907
1.4.1917: Torpedoed and sunk in the Mediterranean 2 miles from Hormigas, Cape de Palos by unknown submarine whilst on a voyage from Newport News to Marseilles with general cargo.

KARONGA 4665 Grt. Blt. 1907
28.4.1917: Torpedoed and sunk in the Mediterranean in the Strait of Messina by the German submarine *U 63* whilst on a voyage from Newport, Mon. to Bombay with general cargo. 18 lost, Master taken prisoner.

KIOTO 6182 Grt. Blt. 1910
11.7.1917: Torpedoed and sunk in the Atlantic 20 miles S.W. from the Fastnet Rock in position 51.07N 09.51W by the German submarine *U 87* whilst on a voyage from New York to Manchester with general cargo.

KAREMA ex *Ranza 5263 Grt. Blt. 1894*
25.11.1917: Torpedoed and sunk in the Mediterranean 33 miles S.E. by E. from Cabo de Gata, near Almeria in position 36.30N 01.32W by the German submarine *U 39* whilst on a voyage from Bombay to Liverpool with general cargo. 3 lost.

SALDANHA 4594 Grt. Blt. 1912
19.3.1918: Torpedoed and sunk in the Mediterranean 95 miles N. from Algiers in position 38.19N 02.39E by the German submarine *UB 52* whilst on a voyage from Alexandria to Avonmouth with general cargo. 6 lost.

KAFUE 6044 Grt. Blt. 1913
30.4.1918: Torpedoed and sunk in the North Channel 11 miles S.W. from Mull of Galloway by the German submarine *U 86* whilst on a voyage from Clyde to Calcutta with general cargo. 1 lost.

KEELUNG 6672 Grt. Blt. 1914
27.6.1918: Torpedoed and sunk in the Atlantic 110 miles W.¾S. from Ushant in position 47.48N 07.24W by the German submarine *U 53* whilst on a voyage from London to Montreal in ballast. 6 lost.

ELLERMAN LINES, LIMITED—LIVERPOOL

City Line, Ltd.

CITY OF LUCKNOW ex *Guyana 3669 Grt. Blt. 1896*
30.4.1916: Torpedoed and sunk in the Mediterranean 60 miles E. from Malta by the German submarine *U 21* whilst on a voyage from Alexandria to Liverpool with a cargo of onions.

CITY OF PARIS 9191 Grt. Blt. 1907
4.4.1917: Torpedoed and sunk in the Mediterranean 46 miles S. by E. from Cap d'Antibes, near Nice in position 42.07N 07.56E by the German submarine *UC 35* whilst on a voyage from Karachi to Marseilles carrying passengers and general cargo. 122 lost.

CITY OF PERTH 3427 Grt. Blt. 1890
11.6.1917: Torpedoed and sunk in the Atlantic 195 miles S.S.W. from the Fastnet Rock in position 48.60N 10.30W by the German submarine *U 70* whilst on a voyage from Alexandria to London with general cargo. 8 lost.

CITY OF CAMBRIDGE 3788 Grt. Blt. 1882
3.7.1917: Torpedoed and sunk in the Mediterranean 10 miles N.W. from Jidelli by the German submarine *UC 67* whilst on a voyage from Alexandria to Liverpool with general cargo.

CITY OF GLASGOW 6457 Grt. Blt. 1906
1.9.1918: Torpedoed and sunk in the St. George's Channel 21 miles E.¼N. from Tuskar Rock in position 52.17N 05.38W by the German submarine *UB 118* whilst on a voyage from Manchester to Montreal in ballast. 12 lost.

Hall Line, Ltd.

LANGTON HALL 4437 Grt. Blt. 1905
30.11.1915: Captured and sunk by gunfire in the Mediterranean 112 miles E.S.E. from Malta in position 35.30N 16.50E by the German submarine *U 33* whilst on a voyage from Calcutta to New York with general cargo.

CITY OF BIRMINGHAM 7498 Grt. Blt. 1911
27.11.1916: Torpedoed and sunk in the Mediterranean 90 miles S.E. from Malta in position 36.10N 16.00E by the German submarine *U 32* whilst on a voyage from Liverpool to Karachi carrying passengers and general cargo. 4 lost.

LOCKSLEY HALL ex *Prome 3635 Grt. Blt. 1893*
12.5.1917: Torpedoed and sunk in the Mediterranean 30 miles S.E. by S. from Malta in position 35.23N 14.56E by the German submarine *U 32* whilst on a voyage from Madras to London with general cargo. 6 lost.

***CITY OF CORINTH** 5870 Grt. Blt. 1913*
21.5.1917: Torpedoed and sunk in the English Channel 12 miles S.W. from the Lizard in position 49.54N 05.30W by the German submarine *UB 31* whilst on a voyage from Singapore to London with general cargo.

***CITY OF BARODA** 5032 Grt. Blt. 1911*
4.6.1917: Torpedoed and sunk in the Atlantic 90 miles N.W.½N. from Tory Island in position 56.00N 10.20W by the German submarine *UC 53* whilst on a voyage from Liverpool to Calcutta with general cargo. 6 lost.

***MELFORD HALL** 6339 Grt. Blt. 1911*
22.6.1917: Torpedoed and sunk in the Atlantic 95 miles N. by W.¾W. from Tory Island by the German submarine *U 100* whilst on a voyage from Liverpool to Bombay with general cargo.

***ANATOLIA** 3847 Grt. Blt. 1898*
25.6.1917: Struck a mine and sunk in the Mediterranean 1½ miles off Genoa laid by the German submarine *UC 35* whilst on a voyage from Liverpool to Genoa with general cargo.

***CITY OF FLORENCE** 5399 Grt. Blt. 1914*
20.7.1917: Torpedoed and sunk in the Atlantic 188 miles W.¾N. from Ushant in position 47.45N 09.45W by the German submarine *UC 17* whilst on a voyage from Cuddalore to Falmouth with general cargo.

***ADALIA** 3847 Grt. Blt. 1899*
29.7.1917: Captured and sunk by gunfire in the North Sea 53 miles N.E. from Muckle Flugga in position 61.38N on the Meridian by the German submarine *U 94* whilst on a voyage from Archangel to London with a cargo of timber. 1 lost.

***RYDAL HALL** 3314 Grt. Blt. 1889*
1.12.1917: Torpedoed and sunk in the English Channel 14 miles E. by S. from Royal Sovereign Lightvessel by the German submarine *UC 75* whilst on a voyage from Calcutta to Dunkirk with general cargo. 23 lost.

***CITY OF LUCKNOW** 8293 Grt. Blt. 1917*
21.12.1917: Torpedoed and sunk in the Mediterranean 50 miles N.E. by N.½N. from Cani Rocks in position 38.10N 10.30E by the German submarine *UB 50* whilst on a voyage from Clyde to Calcutta with general cargo.

***SANDON HALL** 5134 Grt. Blt. 1906*
1.1.1918: Torpedoed and sunk in the Mediterranean 22 miles N.N.E. from Linosa Island in position 36.15N 13.00E by the Austro-Hungarian submarine *U 40* whilst on a voyage from Bussorah to London with a cargo of dates and linseed oil.

***MERTON HALL** ex *Knight Templar* 4327 Grt. Blt. 1889*
11.2.1918: Torpedoed and sunk in the English Channel 30 miles N. by W. from Ushant by the German submarine *U 53* whilst on a voyage from New York to La Pallice with a cargo of steel. 57 lost including Master.

***DENBIGH HALL** 4943 Grt. Blt. 1906*
18.5.1918: Torpedoed and sunk in the Atlantic 90 miles W.S.W. from Bishop Rock

by the German submarine *U 55* whilst on a voyage from Buenos Aires to the United Kingdom with a cargo of wheat.

BRANKSOME HALL ex *Glenavon* ex *Branksome Hall* **4262 Grt. Blt. 1904**
14.7.1918: Torpedoed and sunk in the Mediterranean 68 miles N.W. by W. from Marsa Susa by the German submarine *UB 105* whilst on a voyage from Newport, Mon. to Port Said with a cargo of coal.

CITY OF ADELAIDE 8389 Grt. Blt. 1917
11.8.1918: Torpedoed and sunk in the Mediterranean 60 miles E.N.E. from Malta by the German submarine *U 63* whilst on a voyage from Rangoon to Liverpool with general cargo including rice. 4 lost.

CITY OF BRISBANE 7138 Grt. Blt. 1918
13.8.1918: Torpedoed and sunk in the English Channel 1½ miles S.S.W. from Newhaven by the German submarine *UB 57* whilst on a voyage from London to Buenos Aires in ballast.

Papayanni Line

ANDALUSIAN 2349 Grt. Blt. 1911
12.3.1915: Captured and scuttled in the Atlantic 25 miles W.N.W. from Bishop Rock in position 49.08N 07.00W by the German submarine *U 29* whilst on a voyage from Liverpool to Patras with general cargo.

FLAMINIAN 3500 Grt. Blt. 1914
29.3.1915: Captured and sunk by gunfire in the Atlantic 50 miles S.W. by W. from Scilly Isles in position 49.08N 07.00W by the German submarine *U 28* whilst on a voyage from Clyde to Port Natal with general cargo.

DOURO ex *Congella* **1604 Grt. Blt. 1881**
5.9.1915: Captured and sunk by gunfire in the Atlantic 79 miles S.W. by W. from Bishop Rock in position 48.55N 07.48W by the German submarine *U 20* whilst on a voyage from Oporto to Liverpool with general cargo.

ALGERIAN ex *Flintshire* **3837 Grt. Blt. 1896**
12.1.1916: Struck a mine and sunk in the English Channel 2½ miles S.W. from the Needles Lighthouse, Isle of Wight laid by the German submarine *UC 5* whilst on a voyage from Cowes to Avonmouth in ballast.

FAVONIAN ex *Alnwick* **3049 Grt. Blt. 1894**
4.8.1916: Captured and sunk in the Mediterranean 24 miles S.W. from Planier Island by the German submarine *U 35* whilst on a voyage from Tellicherri and Marseilles to London and Tees with general cargo.

TAGUS 937 Grt. Blt. 1898
6.9.1916: Captured and sunk with bombs in the English Channel 35 miles N.E. by E. ½E. from Ushant by the German submarine *UB 39* whilst on a voyage from Oporto to London with general cargo.

LESBIAN 2555 Grt. Blt. 1915
5.1.1917: Captured and sunk by gunfire in the Mediterranean 125 miles E. by S.

from Malta in position 35.48N 17.06E by the German submarine *U 35* whilst on a voyage from Calicut to London and Tees with general cargo. Master taken prisoner.

BRITANNIA 3129 Grt. Blt. 1885
2.4.1917: Torpedoed and sunk in the Mediterranean 22 miles W.N.W. from Pantellaria Island in position 36.35N 11.28E by the German submarine *U 65* whilst on a voyage from Alexandria to Liverpool with general cargo. Master and Wireless Operator taken prisoner.

CASTILIAN ex *Umbilo* ***1923 Grt. Blt. 1890***
18.4.1917: Torpedoed and sunk in the Atlantic 110 miles N.W. by N. from Tory Island in position 56.20N 10.45W by the German submarine *U 61* whilst on a voyage from Liverpool to Genoa with general cargo. 10 lost.

MARDINIAN 3322 Grt. Blt. 1913
19.5.1917: Torpedoed and sunk in the Mediterranean 4 miles S. by W. from Tabarka Island, Algeria by the German submarine *U 34* whilst on a voyage from Calicut to London with general cargo.

LISBON 1203 Grt. Blt. 1910
30.5.1917: Struck a mine and sunk in the English Channel 5 miles S. from Royal Sovereign Lightvessel laid by the German submarine *UC 62* whilst on a voyage from Newhaven to Boulogne with general cargo. 1 lost.

FABIAN 2248 Grt. Blt. 1881
20.9.1917: Torpedoed and sunk in the Atlantic 30 miles W.½N. from Cape Spartel in position 35.45N 06.40W by the German submarine *UB 50* whilst on a voyage from Almeria to Liverpool with general cargo. 3 lost.

ESTRELLANO 1161 Grt. Blt. 1910
31.10.1917: Torpedoed and sunk in the Bay of Biscay 14 miles W. by N.½N. from Ile du Pilier in position 47.40N 02.42W by the German submarine *UC 71* whilst on a voyage from Oporto to London with general cargo. 3 lost.

BORDER KNIGHT 3724 Grt. Blt. 1899
4.11.1917: Torpedoed and sunk in the English Channel 1½ miles E.S.E. from the Lizard by the German submarine *UC 17* whilst on a voyage from London to Barry in ballast. 1 lost.

PALMELLA 1352 Grt. Blt. 1913
22.8.1918: Torpedoed and sunk in the Irish Sea 25 miles N.W.½W. from South Stack Rock by the German submarine *UB 92* whilst on a voyage from Liverpool to Lisbon with general cargo. 28 lost including Master.

Westcott & Laurance Lines, Ltd.

BULGARIAN ex *Clan Macintyre* ***2515 Grt. Blt. 1891***
20.1.1917: Torpedoed and sunk in the Atlantic S.W. of Ireland by the German submarine *U 84* whilst on a voyage from Cartagena to Garston with a cargo of iron ore. 14 lost including Master.

JOSHUA NICHOLSON 1853 Grt. Blt. 1880
18.3.1917: Torpedoed and sunk in the Atlantic off the Wolf Rock in position 49.37N 06.37W by the German submarine *U 70* whilst on a voyage from London to Alexandria with general cargo. 26 lost including Master.

Wilson Line, Ltd.—Hull

TRURO 836 Grt. Blt. 1898
6.5.1915: Captured and torpedoed in the North Sea 85 miles E.N.E. from St. Abb's Head, 4 miles N.W. of Eyemouth by the German submarine *U 39* whilst on a voyage from Christiania to Grimsby with a cargo of wood.

GUIDO 2093 Grt. Blt. 1913
8.7.1915: Captured and torpedoed in the North Sea 27 miles N.E. ¼ N. from Rattray Head, 7½ miles N.W. of Peterhead in position 58.03N 01.28W by the German submarine *U 25* whilst on a voyage from Hull to Archangel with general cargo.

GRODNO 1955 Grt. Blt. 1912
12.8.1915: Captured and torpedoed in the Atlantic 98 miles N.W. from Lofoten Islands in position 68.55N 09.08E by the German submarine *U 22* whilst on a voyage from Hull to Archangel with general cargo.

SERBINO 2205 Grt. Blt. 1913
16.8.1915: Torpedoed and sunk in the Baltic off Worms Lighthouse by the German submarine *U 9* whilst on a voyage from Riga to Petrograd with a cargo of iron goods and machinery.

URBINO 6651 Grt. Blt. 1915
24.9.1915: Captured and sunk by gunfire in the Atlantic 67 miles S.W. by W. from Bishop Rock by the German submarine *U 41* whilst on a voyage from New York to Hull with general cargo.

SALERNO 2017 Grt. Blt. 1912
14.10.1915: Struck a mine and sunk in the mouth of the River Thames 2½ miles S. from Long Sand Lightvessel in position 51.45N 01.42E laid by the German submarine *UC 3* whilst on a voyage from Hull to Marseilles, Naples and Genoa with general cargo.

COLENSO 3861 Grt. Blt. 1900
30.11.1915: Captured and sunk by gunfire in the Mediterranean 95 miles E.S.E. from Malta by the German submarine *U 33* whilst on a voyage from Tees and Hull to Bombay with general cargo. 1 lost.

DIDO 4769 Grt. Blt. 1896
26.2.1916: Struck a mine and sunk in the North Sea 4 miles N.N.E. from Spurn Lightvessel laid by the German submarine *UC 7* whilst on a voyage from Tees and Hull to India with general cargo. 28 lost including Master.

TEANO 1907 Grt. Blt. 1913
29.6.1916: Captured and scuttled in the Mediterranean 24 miles N.W. by N. from Marittimo Island in position 38.15N 11.45E by the German submarine *U 35* whilst on a voyage from Hull to Naples with general cargo and coal.

CALYPSO 2876 Grt. Blt. *1904*
11.7.1916: Torpedoed and sunk in the Skagerrak off Lindesnes by the German submarine *U 53* whilst on a voyage from London to Christiania with general cargo. 30 lost including Master.

AARO 2603 Grt. Blt. *1909*
1.8.1916: Torpedoed and sunk in the North Sea by the German submarine *U 20* whilst on a voyage from Hull to Christiania with general cargo. 3 lost and remainder of crew taken prisoner.

THURSO 1244 Grt. Blt. *1909*
27.9.1916: Captured and sunk by gunfire in the North Sea 60 miles N.E. by E. from Rattray Head by the German submarine *U 44* whilst on a voyage from Archangel to Hull with a cargo of timber. Master and Chief Engineer taken prisoner.

SPERO 1132 Grt. Blt. *1896*
2.11.1916: Captured and torpedoed in the North Sea 95 miles W.S.W. from Helliso Lighthouse in position 59.43N 01.52E by the German submarine *U 69* whilst on a voyage from Drontheim and Bergen to Hull with general cargo.

VASCO 1914 Grt. Blt. *1895*
16.11.1916: Struck a mine and sunk in the English Channel 10 miles W. by S. from Beachy Head in position 50.43N 00.02W laid by the German submarine *UC 16* whilst on a voyage from Hull to Naples with general cargo. 17 lost including Master.

CANNIZARO 6133 Grt. Blt. *1914*
28.3.1917: Torpedoed and sunk in the Atlantic 145 miles S.S.W. from the Fastnet Rock in position 49.00N 10.00W by the German submarine *U 24* whilst on a voyage from New York to Hull with general cargo and Government stores.

SALMO 1721 Grt. Blt. *1900*
7.4.1917: Torpedoed and sunk in the Atlantic 210 miles N.W. from the Fastnet Rock in position 52.30N 14.40W by the German submarine *U 60* whilst on a voyage from Oporto to Liverpool with general cargo. 2 lost.

TORO 3066 Grt. Blt. *1904*
12.4.1917: Torpedoed and sunk in the Atlantic 200 miles W.N.W. from Ushant in position 48.30N 10.00W by the German submarine *U 55* whilst on a voyage from Alexandria to Hull with general cargo. 14 lost, Master and 1 Gunner taken prisoner.

ZARA 1331 Grt. Blt. *1897*
13.4.1917: Torpedoed and sunk in the North Sea 90 miles W.¾W. from Helliso Island in position 60.08N 01.52E by the German submarine *U 30* whilst on a voyage from London to Drontheim in ballast. 27 lost.

RINALDO 4321 Grt. Blt. *1908*
18.4.1917: Torpedoed and sunk in the Mediterranean 18 miles W. by N. from Cape Shershel by the German submarine *U 32* whilst on a voyage from Tees and Hull to Bombay with general cargo.

***TYCHO** 3216 Grt. Blt. 1904*
20.5.1917: Torpedoed and sunk in the English Channel 16 miles W.½S. from Beachy Head by the German submarine *UB 40* whilst on a voyage from Bombay to Hull with general cargo. 15 lost including Master.

***OSWEGO** 5793 Grt. Blt. 1916*
29.5.1917: Torpedoed and sunk in the Atlantic 175 miles W.½S. from Bishop Rock in position 48.44N 10.15W by the German submarine *U 86* whilst on a voyage from New York to Hull with general cargo.

***BUFFALO** 4106 Grt. Blt. 1907*
19.6.1917: Torpedoed and sunk in the Atlantic 80 miles N.W. by N.½N. from Cape Wrath in position 59.34N 07.30W by the German submarine *U 70* whilst on a voyage from Hull to New York with general cargo.

***KELSO** 1292 Grt. Blt. 1909*
19.6.1917: Torpedoed and sunk in the Atlantic 33 miles W.S.W. from Bishop Rock by the German submarine *UC 75* whilst on a voyage from Lisbon to London with general cargo.

***CATTARO** 2908 Grt. Blt. 1912*
26.9.1917: Torpedoed and sunk in the Atlantic 130 miles W.S.W. from Bishop Rock in position 48.50N 07.47W by the German submarine *U 62* whilst on a voyage from Palermo to Hull with general cargo.

***TORCELLO** 2929 Grt. Blt. 1912*
15.7.1917: Torpedoed and sunk in the Atlantic 160 miles S.W. by W. from Bishop Rock by the German submarine *U 48* whilst on a voyage from Palermo and Oran to Hull with general cargo. 1 lost.

***OSLO** 2296 Grt. Blt. 1906*
21.8.1917: Torpedoed and sunk in the North Sea 15 miles E. by N. from Out Skerries, Shetland Islands by the German submarine *U 87* whilst on a voyage from Drontheim to Liverpool with a cargo of copper ore. 3 lost.

***HIDALGO** 4271 Grt. Blt. 1908*
28.8.1917: Torpedoed and sunk in the Arctic 120 miles N.E.½N. from North Cape by the German submarine *U 28* whilst on a voyage from Manchester to Archangel with general cargo including munitions. 15 lost.

***ERATO** 2041 Grt. Blt. 1911*
1.9.1917: Struck a mine and sunk in the English Channel 4 miles S.E. from the Lizard laid by the German submarine *UC 69* whilst on a voyage from Dunkirk to Barry Roads in ballast.

***COLORADO** 7165 Grt., Blt. 1914*
20.10.1917: Torpedoed and sunk in the English Channel 1½ miles E. from Start Point by the German submarine *UB 31* whilst on a voyage from Hull to Alexandria with a cargo of coal. 4 lost.

***CARLO** 3040 Grt. Blt. 1913*
13.11.1917: Torpedoed and sunk in the St. George's Channel 7 miles S. by W.

from Coningbeg Lightvessel by the German submarine *U 95* whilst on a voyage from Lisbon to Liverpool with general cargo. 2 lost.

KYNO 3034 Grt. Blt. 1913
16.11.1917: Torpedoed and sunk in the Mediterranean 9 miles N. by E. ¾E. from Cape Shershel by the German submarine *U 63* whilst on a voyage from Hull to Alexandria with general cargo. 5 lost.

CAVALLO 2086 Grt. Blt. 1913
1.2.1918: Torpedoed and sunk in the Atlantic 6 miles N.W. from Trevose Head by the German submarine *U 46* whilst on a voyage from Swansea to Odde with a cargo of coal and tinplates. 3 lost.

JAFFA 1383 Grt. Blt. 1897
2.2.1918: Torpedoed and sunk in the English Channel 3 miles E. by S. from Owers Lightvessel by the German submarine *UB 30* whilst on a voyage from Boulogne to Southampton in ballast. 10 lost.

POLO 2915 Grt. Blt. 1913
12.2.1918: Torpedoed and sunk in the English Channel 6 miles S.E. by E. from St. Catherine's Point by the German submarine *UB 57* whilst on a voyage from Hull to Alexandria with general cargo and coal. 3 lost.

ROMEO 1730 Grt. Blt. 1881
3.3.1918: Torpedoed and sunk in the North Channel 7 miles S. from Mull of Galloway by the German submarine *U 102* whilst on a voyage from—to Liverpool in ballast. 29 lost including Master.

DESTRO 859 Grt. Blt. 1914
25.3.1918: Torpedoed and sunk in the North Channel 5 miles S.W. from Mull of Galloway in position 54.34N 04.45W by the German submarine *U 96* whilst on a voyage from Namsos to Manchester with a cargo of umber (iron and manganese) and ferro-chrome ore.

UMBA ex *Utgard* ex *Imgard* ex *Adelheird Menzell* **2042 Grt. Blt. 1903**
30.4.1918: Torpedoed and sunk in the English Channel 1 mile S. from Royal Sovereign Lightvessel by the German submarine *UB 57* whilst on a voyage from Dunkirk to Barry Roads in ballast. 20 lost including Master.

MONTEBELLO 4324 Grt. Blt. 1911
21.6.1918: Torpedoed and sunk in the Atlantic 320 miles W.½N. from Ushant by the German submarine *U 100* whilst on a voyage from London to Hampton Roads. 41 lost including Master.

CHICAGO 7709 Grt. Blt. 1917
8.7.1918: Torpedoed and sunk in the North Sea 4 miles N.E. from Flamborough Head by the German submarine *UB 107* whilst on a voyage from Tyne to Gibraltar with a cargo of coal. 3 lost.

The Shipping Controller

BIRUTA ex *Marpressessa 1732 Grt. Blt. 1899*
6.8.1918: Torpedoed and sunk in the English Channel 8 miles N.W.¾W. from Calais by unknown German submarine whilst on a voyage from Calais to Barry Roads in ballast. 12 lost including Master.

ELLIS & McHARDY—ABERDEEN

SPRAY ex *Firsby* ex *Denaby 1072 Grt. Blt. 1891*
14.4.1917: Torpedoed and sunk in the North Sea 3½ miles N.E. from Tyne Pier by the German submarine *UC 31* whilst on a voyage from Aberdeen to Sunderland in ballast.

ELVIDGE & MORGAN—CARDIFF

Scarisbrick S.S. Co. Ltd.

MONKSTONE *3097 Grt. Blt. 1909*
25.7.1917: Torpedoed and sunk in the Atlantic 240 miles W. from Scilly Islands by the German submarine *U 82* whilst on a voyage from Tyne to Gibraltar with a cargo of coal. 1 lost.

DAYBREAK *3238 Grt. Blt. 1911*
24.12.1917: Torpedoed and sunk in the Irish Sea 1 mile E. from South Rock Lightvessel, 5 miles N.E. of Ballyquintin, co. Down by the German submarine *U 87* whilst on a voyage from Huelva to Clyde with a cargo of pyrites. 21 lost including Master.

EMBIRICOS, M.—LONDON

Byron S.S. Co. Ltd.

REMEMBRANCE *3660 Grt. Blt. 1910*
14.8.1916: Torpedoed and sunk in the Aegean Sea N. of Paros Island by the German submarine *U 38*. Lost whilst on Government service employed as a Special Service Ship.

BOLDWELL ex *Voorburg 3118 Grt. Blt. 1901*
27.5.1917: Torpedoed and sunk in the Mediterranean 35 miles N.E. from Linosa Island in position 36.12N 13.24E by the German submarine *UC 20* whilst on a voyage from Tyne to Alexandria with a cargo of coal. 3 lost.

EMLYN-JONES & CO. LTD.—CARDIFF

Emlyn Line, Ltd.

EMLYNVERNE ex *Eleanor 544 Grt. Blt. 1894*
25.11.1916: Captured and sunk in the English Channel 30 miles N.W. by N. from Cape d'Antifer, near Fécamp in position 49.57N 00.30W by the German submarine *UB 18* whilst on a voyage from Treport to Swansea in ballast.

EMPRESS TRANSPORTATION CO. OF MIDLAND, LIMITED—MIDLAND, ONTARIO

EMPRESS OF FORT WILLIAM ex *Mount Stephen* **2181 Grt. Blt. 1908**
27.2.1916: Struck a mine and sunk in the Strait of Dover 2 miles S. from Dover Pier laid by the German submarine *UC 6* whilst on a voyage from Tyne to Dunkirk with a cargo of coal.

ENGLISH & COMPANY—MIDDLESBROUGH

***CASTLETON* 2395 Grt. Blt. 1891**
12.7.1917: Captured and sunk by gunfire in the Atlantic 60 miles S.S.W. from Bishop Rock by the German submarine *U 87* whilst on a voyage from La Goulette to Middlesbrough with a cargo of iron ore.

The Shipping Controller

SKARAAS ex *Karmo* ex *Lesley* ex *Deer Hill* **1625 Grt. Blt. 1882**
23.5.1918: Torpedoed and sunk in the English Channel 1 mile S.W. from Black Head, 6 miles N.E. of the Lizard probably by the German submarine *UB 31* whilst on a voyage from Barry to Fécamp with Admiralty cargo. 19 lost.

ERICSSON, A. F.—NEWCASTLE UPON TYNE

***MONITORIA* 1904 Grt. Blt. 1909**
21.10.1915: Struck a mine and sunk off the mouth of the River Thames 1¾ miles N. by E¾E. from Sunk Head Buoy in position 51.47N 01.31E laid by the German submarine *UC 6* whilst on a voyage from Humber to London with a cargo of coal.

***WILLINGTONIA* 3228 Grt. Blt. 1918**
25.8.1918: Torpedoed and sunk in the Mediterranean 13 miles S.W. by W. from Marittimo Island in position 37.49N 11.10E by the German submarine *UC 27* whilst on a voyage from Barry to Corfu with a cargo of coal. 4 lost.

ESPLEN, SIR JOHN. K. B. E.—LIVERPOOL

***HERON BRIDGE* 2422 Grt. Blt. 1918**
16.5.1918: Torpedoed and sunk in the Atlantic 320 miles E. by N.(true) from San Miguel, Azores in position 38.49N 18.26W by the German submarine *U 62* whilst on a voyage from Penarth to Dakar with a cargo of coal. 1 lost.

EVANS (PALIN) & CO. LTD.—CARDIFF

Beaver Shipping Co. Ltd.

***KINGSWAY* 3647 Grt. Blt. 1907**
27.11.1915: Captured and sunk by gunfire in the Mediterranean 20 miles E.S.E. from Cape Bon by the German submarine *U 33* whilst on a voyage from Malta to Huelva in ballast.

ASTORIA ex *Elvaston* ex *Heathburn* **4262 Grt. Blt. 1901**
9.10.1916: Torpedoed and sunk in the Arctic 120 miles N.W. by W. from Vardo by the German submarine *U 46* whilst on a voyage from Philadelphia to Archangel with general cargo. 17 lost.

EVERETT & NEWBIGIN—NEWCASTLE UPON TYNE

The Admiralty

ERNA BOLT 1731 Grt. Blt. 1908
9.6.1915: Torpedoed and sunk at the mouth of the River Thames ½ mile N.E. by E. from Sunk Lightvessel by the German submarine *UC 11* whilst on a voyage from Tyne to London with a cargo of coal.

TERGESTEA 4308 Grt. Blt. 1911
13.2.1916: Struck a mine and sunk in the North Sea 8 miles E. by S. from Aldeburgh laid by the German submarine *UC 4* whilst on a voyage from Tyne to London with a cargo of coal.

SABBIA 2802 Grt. Blt. 1908
20.4.1916: Struck a mine and sunk in the North Sea 7 miles S.E. by S. from May Island in position 56.07N 02.18W laid by the German submarine *U 74* whilst on a voyage from Burntisland to London with a cargo of coal.

HANNA LARSEN ex *Robert Koppen* ex *Mulheim* ex *Friderun* ex *Hedwig Menzel* **1311 Grt. Blt. 1903**
8.2.1917: Captured and sunk with bombs in the North Sea 20 miles E.¾N. from Spurn Point in position 53.42N 00.39E by the German submarine *UC 39* whilst on a voyage from London to Tyne in ballast. 1 lost, Master and 1 Officer taken prisoner.

MARIE LEONHARDT ex *Anhalt* ex *Wilhelm Oelssner* **1466 Grt. Blt. 1902**
14.2.1917: Struck a mine and sunk at the mouth of the River Thames 2¼ miles E.½N. from Sunk Lightvessel in position 51.53N 01.40E laid by the German submarine *UC 11* whilst on a voyage from Hartlepool to London with a cargo of coal. 5 lost.

WEGA 839 Grt. Blt. 1885
14.6.1917: Torpedoed and sunk in the English Channel 20 miles W. by S. from Royal Sovereign Lightvessel laid by the German submarine *UC 71* whilst on a voyage from Hartlepool to Cowes with a cargo of coal. 5 lost.

BREMA ex *Mecklenburg* **1537 Grt. Blt. 1904**
19.8.1917: Torpedoed and sunk in the North Sea 7½ miles S.½E. from Flamborough Head by the German submarine *UC 17* whilst on a voyage from Sunderland to London with a cargo of coal.

HORNSUND 3646 Grt. Blt. 1913
23.9.1917: Torpedoed and sunk in the North Sea 2½ miles E.S.E. from Scarborough by the German submarine *UC 71* whilst on a voyage from Tyne to London with a cargo of coal. 1 lost.

GEMMA ex *Konigsan* **1385 Grt. Blt. 1904**
19.10.1917: Torpedoed and sunk in the North Sea 5 miles N. by W. from Flamborough Head by the German submarine *UB 21* whilst on a voyage from Blyth to London with a cargo of coal. 4 lost.

OSTPREUSSEN 1779 Grt. Blt. 1901
25.11.1917: Struck a mine and sunk in the North Sea 1½ miles E. from Shipwash

Lightvessel laid by the German submarine *UC 11* whilst on a voyage from Sunderland to London with a cargo of coal. 1 lost.

POLLEON ex *Leonora 1155 Grt. Blt. 1915*
22.3.1918: Torpedoed and sunk in the North Sea 3 miles E.N.E. from the entrance to River Tyne by the German submarine *UB 78* whilst on a voyage from Blyth to Tyne with a cargo of coal. 4 lost.

HERCULES *1095 Grt. Blt. 1881*
25.3.1918: Torpedoed and sunk in the North Sea 4 miles N.N.W. from Flamborough Head by the German submarine *UB 21* whilst on a voyage from London to Tyne in ballast. 1 lost.

DENEBOLA *1481 Grt. Blt. 1899*
17.8.1918: Torpedoed and sunk in the Atlantic 2 miles N. by W. from Gurnards Head, 5½ miles S.W. of St. Ives by unknown German submarine whilst on a voyage from Swansea to Rouen with a cargo of coal. 2 lost.

EZARD, H. W. & C. M.—GOOLE

Yorkshire Coal & Steam Shipping Co. Ltd.

LISETTE *895 Grt. Blt. 1899*
13.3.1918: Torpedoed and sunk in the North Sea 8 miles N.E. by N. from Shipwash Lightvessel by the German submarine *UB 16* whilst on a voyage from Goole to Honfleur with a cargo of coal. 1 lost.

The Shipping Controller

DUX *1349 Grt. Blt. 1904*
8.5.1918: Torpedoed and sunk in the Atlantic 7 miles N.W. from Godrevy Lighthouse by the German submarine *U 54* whilst on a voyage from Swansea to La Rochelle with a cargo of coal.

PRUNELLE ex *Asbjorn* ex *Selsbane* ex *Saturnus 579 Grt. Blt. 1874*
22.8.1918: Torpedoed and sunk in the North Sea 2 miles S.E. from Blyth by the German submarine *UB 112* whilst on a voyage from London to Dundee with a cargo of jute. 12 lost including Master.

FARRAR, GROVES & CO. LTD.—LONDON

POLPEDN ex *Thor 1510 Grt. Blt. 1902*
14.11.1916: Torpedoed and sunk in the English Channel 20 miles S. from Littlehampton by the German submarine *UB 38* whilst on a voyage from Dunkirk to Ayr in ballast.

POLAR PRINCE ex *Kawak* ex *Oberon* ex *Persia* ex *Ingeborg* ex *Goldenfels 3611 Grt. Blt. 1895*
18.9.1917: Torpedoed and sunk in the Atlantic 8 miles W. by S. from Cape Spartel in position 35.50N 05.00W by the German submarine *UB 50* whilst on a voyage from Milford Haven to Gibraltar with a cargo of coal. Master taken prisoner.

POLESLEY ex *Istria* ex *Den of Crombie* **4221 Grt. Blt. 1905**
22.9.1918: Torpedoed and sunk in the Atlantic 1 mile N. from Pendeen Lighthouse by the German submarine *UB 88* whilst on a voyage from Cardiff to France with a cargo of coal. 43 lost including Master.

Fargrove Steam Navigation Co. Ltd.
FARN 4393 Grt. Blt. 1910
19.11.1917: Torpedoed and sunk in the English Channel 5 miles E. by N. from Start Point by the German submarine *UB 31* whilst on a voyage from London to Salonica with general cargo.

The Shipping Controller
HUNSBRIDGE ex *Haidar Pascha* ex *Hornfels* **3424 Grt. Blt. 1912**
7.9.1917: Torpedoed and sunk in the Atlantic 60 miles S.W. by W.¾W. from Cape Spartel in position 35.10N 06.50W by the German submarine *UB 49* whilst on a voyage from Swansea to Gibraltar with a cargo of stores and coal. 2 lost.

FEDERAL STEAM NAVIGATION CO. LTD.—LONDON

MIDDLESEX ex *Knight Bachelor* **7265 Grt. Blt. 1914**
16.5.1917: Torpedoed and sunk in the Atlantic 150 miles N.W. from Tory Island in position 56.03N 12.30W by the German submarine *U 30* whilst on a voyage from Manchester to Australia with general cargo.

SOMERSET 7163 Grt. Blt. 1903
26.7.1917: Torpedoed and sunk in the Atlantic 230 miles W. by S.½S. from Ushant in position 46.09N 09.32W by the German submarine *U 54* whilst on a voyage from Buenos Aires to Le Havre with a cargo of meat.

The Shipping Controller
TASMAN 5028 Grt. Blt. 1912
16.9.1918: Torpedoed and sunk in the Atlantic 220 miles N. by W.¼W. from Cape Villano by the German submarine *U 46* whilst on a voyage from London to Calcutta with general cargo. 14 lost including Master.

FEDERATED COAL & SHIPPING CO. LTD—CARDIFF

HARPALUS 1445 Grt. Blt. 1895
2.12.1916: Captured and sunk with bombs in the Atlantic 34 miles S.S.W. from Galley Head in position 50.56N 08.58W by the German submarine *UB 23* whilst on a voyage from Penarth to Nantes with a cargo of coal.

FENWICK, J. & SON.—LONDON

ETAL MANOR 1875 Grt. Blt. 1916
19.9.1917: Torpedoed and sunk in the Atlantic 7 miles S. by W. from Hook Point by the German submarine *UC 48* whilst on a voyage from Barry to Queenstown with a cargo of coal. 6 lost including Master.

FERNIE, H. & SONS—LIVERPOOL

Liverpool Shipping Co. Ltd.

FLORAZAN 4658 Grt. Blt. 1913
11.3.1915: Torpedoed and sunk in the Atlantic 53 miles N.E.½E. from Longships Lighthouse by the German submarine *U 20* whilst on a voyage from Le Havre to Liverpool in ballast. 1 lost.

RAMAZAN 3477 Grt. Blt. 1905
19.9.1915: Captured and sunk by gunfire in the Mediterranean 55 miles S.W. from Cerigotto Island by the German submarine *U 35* whilst on a voyage from—to Salonica with a cargo of Government war stores. 1 lost.

MORAZAN 3486 Grt. Blt. 1905
11.11.1916: Captured and torpedoed in the Atlantic 145 miles S.W. by W. from Ushant in position 46.41N 07.39W by the German submarine *U 50* whilst on a voyage from Calcutta to Dundee with a cargo of jute and manganese ore. Master taken prisoner.

FERRIER & REES, LIMITED—CARDIFF

***STATHE* ex *Tregenna* 2623 Grt. Blt. 1892**
26.9.1916: Captured and sunk by gunfire in the Mediterranean 50 miles E. by S. from Barcelona in position 41.25N 03.20E by the German submarine *U 35* whilst on a voyage from Penarth to Leghorn with a cargo of coal.

FISHER, ALIMONDA & CO. LTD.—LONDON

***SECONDO* ex *Columbia* 3912 Grt. Blt. 1904**
27.9.1916: Torpedoed and sunk in the Mediterranean 40 miles N.N.E. from Dragonera Island by the German submarine *U 35* whilst on a voyage from Clyde to Genoa with a cargo of coal.

National S.S. Co. Ltd.

GLENCLIFFE 3673 Grt. Blt. 1910
12.4.1917: Torpedoed and sunk in the Mediterranean 2¼ miles S.E. from Tabarka Island by the German submarine *U 52* whilst on a voyage from Clyde to Genoa with general cargo and coal. 1 lost, Chief Engineer and 2 Gunners taken prisoner.

Rome S.S. Co. Ltd.

STRATHALLAN 4404 Grt. Blt. 1907
2.9.1916: Captured and sunk by gunfire in the Mediterranean 20 miles N.E. from Philippeville, Algeria in position 37.10N 07.10E by the German submarine *U 38* whilst on a voyage from Augusta to Barry Roads in ballast. Master taken prisoner.

NORMANTON 3862 Grt. Blt. 1912
1.10.1917: Torpedoed and sunk in the Atlantic 115 miles W.½N. from Cape Spartel in position 35.26N 08.15W by the German submarine *U 39* whilst on a voyage from Barry to Savona in ballast.

CONSOLS ex *Shira 3756 Grt. Blt. 1906*
9.12.1917: Torpedoed and sunk in the Mediterranean 40 miles N.W.½N. from Cape Bon by the German submarine *UB 48* whilst on a voyage from Malta to Bizerta in ballast. 3 lost.

QUEEN ex *Springburn 4956 Grt. Blt. 1907*
28.6.1918: Torpedoed and sunk in the Atlantic 130 miles N.½W. from Cape Villano in position 44.25N 10.25W by the German submarine *U 53* whilst on a voyage from Cardiff to Spezia with general cargo and coal. 20 lost including Master.

The Admiralty

HUNTSVALE ex *Barenfels 5398 Grt. Blt. 1898*
4.11.1916: Torpedoed and sunk in the Mediterranean 200 miles E. from Malta by the German submarine *UB 43* whilst on a voyage from Salonica to Algiers in ballast. 7 lost including Master.

FISHER, RENWICK & COMPANY—NEWCASTLE UPON TYNE

Ella Sayer S.S. Co. Ltd.

SPRINGHILL ex *Porthcawl 1507 Grt. Blt. 1904*
24.8.1917: Struck a mine and sunk in the North Sea 4 miles N. by E¾E. from Scarborough laid by the German submarine *UB 21* whilst on a voyage from Hartlepool to London with a cargo of coal. 5 lost.

NEWMINSTER ABBEY 3114 Grt. Blt. 1917
2.2.1918: Torpedoed and sunk in the Mediterranean 44 miles E. by N.½N. from Cape Creus, Gulf of Lions by the German submarine *UB 48* whilst on a voyage from Genoa to Huelva in ballast.

ELLA SAYER 2549 Grt. Blt. 1898
30.4.1918: Torpedoed and sunk in the English Channel 15 miles E. by N. from Royal Sovereign Lightvessel in position 50.49N 00.48E by the German submarine *UB 57* whilst on a voyage from Penarth to Dunkirk with a cargo of coal. 2 lost.

Fisher, Renwick—Manchester, London Steamers Ltd.

HALBERDIER 1049 Grt. Blt. 1915
6.1.1918: Torpedoed and sunk in the St. George's Channel 27 miles W. by N. from Bardsey Island by the German submarine *U 61* whilst on a voyage from Manchester to London with general cargo. 5 lost.

The Shipping Controller

EROS 1122 Grt. Blt. 1900
17.9.1918: Torpedoed and sunk in the North Sea 2 miles N.E. by N. from Filey Brigg, 9½ miles S.E. of Scarborough by the German submarine *UB 113* whilst on a voyage from Tyne to Rouen with a cargo of coal. 7 lost including Master.

FORSTER, J. J. & C. M.—NEWCASTLE UPON TYNE

Newcastle Steam Ship Co. Ltd

NEWCASTLE 3403 Grt. Blt. 1899
10.10.1915: Struck a mine and sunk in the Strait of Dover 4 miles S.W. from Folkestone Pier laid by the German submarine *UC 5* whilst on a voyage from Port Louis to London with general cargo.

NEWBURN 3554 Grt. Blt. 1904
7.8.1916: Captured and torpedoed in the Mediterranean 34 miles N. by E.¾E. from Dragonera Island by the German submarine *U 35* whilst on a voyage from Cardiff to Marseilles with a cargo of coal.

NEWLYN 4019 Grt. Blt. 1913
2.8.1917: Torpedoed and sunk in the English Channel 2 miles S. from Prawle Point by the German submarine *UB 31* whilst on a voyage from Tyne to Genoa with a cargo of coal. 4 lost.

NEWHOLM 3399 Grt. Blt. 1899
8.9.1917: Struck a mine and sunk in the English Channel 1 mile S. from Start Point laid by the German submarine *UC 31* whilst on a voyage from Bilbao to Middlesbrough with a cargo of iron ore. 20 lost.

FOSTER, HAIN & READ—LONDON

The Shipping Controller

ANTWERPEN 1637 Grt. Blt. 1887
18.11.1917: Torpedoed and damaged in the English Channel 2 miles S.S.W. from Rundle Stone Buoy by the German submarine *UC 77* whilst on a voyage from Barry to Rouen with a cargo of coal. She was beached but declared a total loss.

FRANCE, W. FENWICK & CO. LTD.—LONDON

WYCHWOOD 1985 Grt. Blt. 1907
28.3.1917: Torpedoed and sunk in the St. George's Channel 4 miles S.S.W. from South Arklow Lightvessel at the mouth of the River Ovoca, co. Wicklow in position 52.40N 05.55W by the German submarine *UC 65* whilst on a voyage from Barry to Scapa Flow with a cargo of coal. 3 lost.

LADYWOOD 2314 Grt. Blt. 1910
1.5.1917: Captured and sunk with bombs in the Atlantic 15 miles S.W. from Wolf Rock in position 49.52N 05.59W by the German submarine *UB 38* whilst on a voyage from Port Nolloth to Swansea with a cargo of copper ore.

ARNEWOOD 2259 Grt. Blt. 1916
13.12.1917: Struck a mine and sunk in the Sound of Sleat 4 miles E.S.E. from Sleat Point, Isle of Skye laid by the German submarine *U 78* whilst on a voyage from Barry to—with a cargo of coal.

PINEWOOD 2219 Grt. Blt. 1914
17.2.1918: Captured and sunk by gunfire in the Atlantic 15 miles S. from Mine

Head by the German submarine *U 86* whilst on a voyage from Cardiff to Queenstown with a cargo of timber and coal. 2 lost.

DALEWOOD 2420 Grt. Blt. 1911
26.2.1918: Torpedoed and sunk in the Irish Sea 10 miles S.W. from Isle of Man by the German submarine *U 105* whilst on a voyage from Cardiff to Scapa Flow with a cargo of coal. 19 lost including Master.

The Shipping Controller

WAR TUNE 2045 Grt. Blt. 1917
9.12.1917: Torpedoed and sunk in the English Channel 1½ miles S.S.E. from Black Head by the German submarine *U 53* whilst on a voyage from Barry to—with a cargo of coal. 1 lost.

WAR SONG 2535 Grt. Blt. 1917
15.1.1918: Captured and sunk by gunfire in the Bay of Biscay 12 miles W. from Ile de Sein near Brest by the German submarine *U 84* whilst on a voyage from Bilbao to Brest with a cargo of iron ore. 16 lost including Master.

ANNA SOFIE ex *Theologos S. Anargyros* ex *Vera* ***2577 Grt. Blt. 1896***
23.7.1918: Torpedoed and sunk in the Atlantic 4 miles W. from Trevose Head by the German submarine *U 55* whilst on a voyage from Rouen to Barry Roads in ballast. 1 lost.

FREEAR & DIX—SUNDERLAND

The Shipping Controller

GAUPEN ex *Oddfried* ex *Regent* ex *Stord* ***622 Grt. Blt. 1900***
12.3.1918: Struck a mine and sunk in the Downs 5 miles S.E. by E.¼E. from North Foreland Lighthouse laid by unknown German submarine whilst on a voyage from Tyne to Le Havre with a cargo of coal.

FRISKEN, MILLER & COMPANY—GLASGOW

Alban S.S. Co. Ltd.

NEWSTEAD 2836 Grt. Blt. 1894
3.3.1917: Torpedoed and sunk in the Atlantic 150 miles W.N.W. from the Fastnet Rock in position 52.02N 13.24W by the German submarine *U 49* whilst on a voyage from Barry to Naples with a cargo of coal. 15 lost.

FURNESS, WITHY & CO. LTD.—LONDON

SOUTH POINT 3837 Grt. Blt. 1912
27.3.1915: Captured and torpedoed in the Bristol Channel 60 miles W. of Lundy Island by the German submarine *U 28* whilst on a voyage from Cardiff to Philadelphia with a cargo of china clay.

MOBILE 1905 Grt. Blt. 1914
28.4.1915: Captured and sunk with bombs in the Atlantic 25 miles N.W. of Butt of Lewis by the German submarine *U 30* whilst on a voyage from Barry to—with a cargo of coal.

QUEEN WILHELMINA 3590 Grt. Blt. 1898
8.5.1915: Torpedoed and damaged in the North Sea 20 miles S. by E. from Longstone by the German submarine *U 9* whilst on a voyage from Leith to Fowey in ballast. She was beached at Bondicar, 1½ miles S.S.E. of Amble and became a total loss.

TUNISIANA ex Balaclava 4220 Grt. Blt. 1906
23.6.1915: Torpedoed and damaged off Lowestoft by the German submarine *UB 16* whilst on a voyage from Montreal to Hull with a cargo of grain. She was beached at Barnard Sands and became a total loss.

SHENANDOAH 3886 Grt. Blt. 1893
14.4.1916: Struck a mine and sunk in the Strait of Dover 1½ miles W. from Folkestone Gate laid by the German submarine *UC 6* whilst on a voyage from St. John (NB) and Halifax (NS) to London with general cargo. 2 lost.

PARISIANA ex Argentine Transport 4763 Grt. Blt. 1911
23.4.1916: Captured and torpedoed in the Atlantic 82 miles W.½S. from Ushant in position 47.55N 07.00W by the German submarine *U 19* whilst on a voyage from London to Newport News with a cargo of manure and Fuller's earth.

RAPPAHANNOCK 3871 Grt. Blt. 1893
26.10.1916: Captured and torpedoed in the Atlantic 70 miles from Scilly Isles by the German submarine *U 69* whilst on a voyage from Halifax (NS) to London with a cargo of grain, deals and general goods. 37 lost including Master.

TABASCO 2987 Grt. Blt. 1895
26.1.1917: Captured and torpedoed in the Atlantic 55 miles W.N.W. from the Skelligs in position 51.50N 12.00W by the German submarine *U 45* whilst on a voyage from Halifax (NS) to Liverpool with general cargo.

EAVESTONE 1858 Grt. Blt. 1912
3.2.1917: Captured and sunk by gunfire in the Atlantic 95 miles W. from the Fastnet Rock in position 51.00N 12.00W by the German submarine *U 45* whilst on a voyage from Barry to Gibraltar with a cargo of coal. 5 lost including Master.

ANNAPOLIS ex Lord Lonsdale 4567 Grt. Blt. 1911
19.4.1917: Torpedoed and damaged in the Atlantic 74 miles N.W.½N. from Eagle Island in position 54.55N 11.45W by the German submarine *U 61* on the following day she was sunk by *U 69* with a coup de grâce. She was on a voyage from Halifax, (NS) to London with general cargo.

EGYPTIANA ex Sandown 3818 Grt. Blt. 1905
9.6.1917: Torpedoed and sunk in the Atlantic 120 miles W.S.W. from Scilly Isles by the German submarine *U 70* whilst on a voyage from London to Halifax, (NS) with a part cargo.

ROTA 2171 Grt. Blt. 1915
22.7.1917: Torpedoed and sunk in the English Channel 7 miles E. by S. from Berry Head by the German submarine *UB 40* whilst on a voyage from Benisaf to Middlesbrough with cargo of iron ore. 5 lost including Master.

ROANOKE ex *Clan Macinnes* ex *Roanoke* **4803 Grt. Blt. 1907**
12.8.1917: Captured and sunk with bombs in the Atlantic 100 miles W.N.W. from the Butt of Lewis in position 58.39N 09.08W by the German submarine *UB 48* whilst on a voyage from Leith to Philadelphia with general cargo. Master taken prisoner.

DURANGO 3008 Grt. Blt. 1895
26.8.1917: Captured and sunk by gunfire in the Atlantic 50 miles N.W. from Barra Head, Outer Hebrides in position 57.08N 08.55W by the German submarine *U 53* whilst on a voyage from Liverpool to St. John's, NFL and Halifax (NS) with general cargo.

BEDALE 2116 Grt. Blt. 1914
6.10.1917: Torpedoed and sunk in the Atlantic 25 miles S.E. by S. from Mine Head by the German submarine *U 96* whilst on a voyage from Cardiff to Berehaven with a cargo of stores and coal. 3 lost.

CHARLESTON 1866 Grt. Blt. 1908
12.12.1917: Captured and sunk with bombs in the St. George's Channel 30 miles W. from the Smalls by the German submarine *UB 65* whilst on a voyage from Cardiff to Berehaven with a cargo of coal. 2 Gunners taken prisoner.

MAXTON ex *Start Point* **5094 Grt. Blt. 1912**
28.12.1917: Torpedoed and sunk in the Atlantic 28 miles N.¼W. from Malin Head by the German submarine *U 19* whilst on a voyage from Clyde to Philadelphia with general cargo. 1 lost.

CRESSWELL 2829 Grt. Blt. 1917
5.2.1918: Torpedoed and sunk in the Irish Sea 18 miles E. by N.¼N. from Kish Lightvessel in position 53.29N 05.30W by the German submarine *U 46* whilst on a voyage from Clyde to Gibraltar with a cargo of coal.

BEAUMARIS 2372 Grt. Blt. 1917
7.2.1918: Torpedoed and damaged in the Atlantic 2½ miles N. by W. from the Longships by the German submarine *U 53* whilst on a voyage from Cardiff to St. Nazaire with a cargo of coal. She was beached at Whitesand Bay and became a total wreck.

WHORLTON 1469 Grt. Blt. 1907
12.1.1918: Torpedoed and sunk in the English Channel near Owers Lightvessel in position 50.34N 00.45W by the German submarine *UB 30* whilst on a voyage from Dunkirk to Southampton.

CASTLE EDEN 1949 Grt. Blt. 1914
4.3.1918: Torpedoed and sunk in the Atlantic 4 miles S.S.E. from Inishtrahull Lighthouse by the German submarine *U 110* whilst on a voyage from Clyde to Lough Swilly with general cargo and coal. 1 lost.

ALLENDALE 2153 Grt. Blt. 1917
27.3.1918: Torpedoed and sunk in the English Channel 52 miles S. by W. from the Lizard in position 49.50N 05.50W by the German submarine *U 101* whilst on a voyage from Ardrossan to Bordeaux with a cargo of coal. 1 lost.

CONWAY 4003 Grt. Blt. 1900
30.4.1918: Torpedoed and sunk in the Mediterranean 38 miles S.½E. from Cape de Palos in position 37.10N 00.28W by the German submarine *UB 105* whilst on a voyage from Genoa to Almeria in ballast.

WESTWOOD 1968 Grt. Blt. 1907
3.10.1918: Torpedoed and sunk in the English Channel 5 miles S.W.½W. from the Lizard by the German submarine *UB 112* whilst on a voyage from Barry to Le Havre with a cargo of coal. 1 lost.

Argentine Cargo Line, Ltd.

EL ARGENTINO 6809 Grt. Blt. 1907
26.5.1916: Struck a mine and sunk in the North Sea 7 miles S.E. by S. from Southwold laid by the German submarine *UC 1* whilst on a voyage from Hull and London to Buenos Aires in ballast.

LA BLANCA 7479 Grt. Blt. 1906
23.11.1917: Torpedoed and sunk in the English Channel 10 miles S.S.E. from Berry Head by the German submarine *U 96* whilst on a voyage from Buenos Aires to Le Havre with general cargo and meat. 2 lost.

British & Argentine Steam Navigation Co. Ltd.

LA NEGRA 8312 Grt. Blt. 1913
3.9.1917: Torpedoed and sunk in the English Channel 50 miles S.S.W. from Start Point in position 49.29N 03.53W by the German submarine *UC 50* whilst on a voyage from Buenos Aires to the United Kingdom with a cargo of frozen meat. 4 lost.

Furness Houlder Argentine Lines, Ltd.

CONDESA 8557 Grt. Blt. 1916
7.7.1917: Torpedoed and sunk in the Atlantic 105 miles W. from Bishop Rock in position 49.23N 09.00W by the German submarine *U 84* whilst on her maiden voyage from Buenos Aires to Falmouth with a cargo of frozen meat.

Gulf Line, Ltd.

TURINO ex *Westoe Hall* 4241 Grt. Blt. 1914
4.2.1917: Torpedoed and sunk in the Atlantic 174 miles W. from the Fastnet Rock in position 50.25N 13.50W by the German submarine *U 43* whilst on a voyage from Norfolk (Va) to Liverpool with general cargo. 4 lost.

ORTONA 5524 Grt. Blt. 1916
21.6.1917: Torpedoed and sunk in the Atlantic 140 miles S.S.W. from the Fastnet Rock in position 49.10N 09.51W by the German submarine *U 50* whilst on a voyage from Philadelphia to London with general cargo. 1 lost.

LUGANO 3810 Grt. Blt. 1917
2.10.1917: Struck a mine and sunk in the Irish Sea 2 miles S.W. from Bull Point, co. Antrim laid by the German submarine *U 79* whilst on a voyage from Newport News to Liverpool with general cargo.

RAPALLO 3811 Grt. Blt. 1917
13.1.1918: Torpedoed and sunk in the Mediterranean 1½ miles S. from Cape Peloro in position 38.05N 15.34N by the Austro-Hungarian submarine *U 28* whilst on a voyage from Taranto to Messina in ballast. 1 lost.

Johnston Line, Ltd.
LARCHMORE 4355 Grt. Blt. 1912
3.7.1915: Captured and sunk by gunfire in the Atlantic 70 miles S.W.½S. from Wolf Rock in position 48.54N 06.28W by the German submarine *U 39* whilst on a voyage from Cardiff to Bombay with a cargo of coal.

ROWANMORE 10320 Grt. Blt. 1900
26.10.1916: Captured and torpedoed in the Atlantic 128 miles W.N.W. from the Fastnet Rock in position 51.30N 12.58W by the German submarine *U 57* whilst on a voyage from Baltimore to Liverpool with a cargo of copper, cotton, maize and oil. Master taken prisoner.

VEDAMORE 6330 Grt. Blt. 1896
7.2.1917: Torpedoed and sunk in the Atlantic 20 miles W. from the Fastnet Rock in position 51.17N 10.03W by the German submarine *U 85* whilst on a voyage from Baltimore to Liverpool with general cargo. 23 lost.

SWANMORE 6373 Grt. Blt. 1913
25.4.1917: Torpedoed and sunk by gunfire in the Atlantic 230 miles W.N.W. from the Fastnet Rock in position 51.11N 15.37W by the German submarines *U 50*, *U 43* and *U 93* whilst on a voyage from Baltimore to Liverpool with a cargo of ordnance. 11 lost.

DROMORE 4398 Grt. Blt. 1913
27.4.1917: Torpedoed and sunk in the Atlantic 140 miles N.W. by N. from Tory Island in position 56.30N 11.40W by the German submarine *U 58* whilst on a voyage from Liverpool to Baltimore with general cargo.

JESSMORE 3911 Grt. Blt. 1911
13.5.1917: Torpedoed and sunk in the Atlantic 180 miles W.N.W. from the Fastnet Rock in position 51.18N 14.20W by the German submarine *U 48* whilst on a voyage from Baltimore to Manchester with general cargo.

QUERNMORE 7302 Grt. Blt. 1898
31.7.1917: Torpedoed and sunk in the Atlantic 160 miles W. by N.¾N. from Tory Island by the German submarine *U 82* whilst on a voyage from Liverpool to Baltimore with general cargo. 1 lost.

INCEMOOR 3060 Grt. Blt. 1898
20.8.1917: Torpedoed and sunk in the Mediterranean 52 miles S.E. by S.½E. from Pantellaria Island in position 36.27N 13.02E by the German submarine *U 38* whilst on a voyage from Malta to Toulon in ballast. 1 lost.

SYCAMORE 6550 Grt. Blt. 1917
25.8.1917: Torpedoed and sunk in the Atlantic 125 miles N.W. from Tory Island by the German submarine *UB 61* whilst on a voyage from Baltimore to Liverpool with general cargo including cotton and copper. 11 lost.

KENMORE 3919 Grt. Blt. 1912
26.8.1917: Torpedoed and sunk in the Atlantic 30 miles N. from Inishtrahull by the German submarine *U 53* whilst on a voyage from Liverpool to Boston, Mass. with general cargo. 5 lost.

FOYLEMORE 3831 Grt. Blt. 1911
16.12.1917: Torpedoed and sunk in the English Channel 22 miles E.½S. from the Lizard by the German submarine *UB 55* whilst on a voyage from Calais to Manchester in ballast.

BARROWMORE 3832 Grt. Blt. 1911
19.2.1918: Torpedoed and sunk in the Atlantic 53 miles N.W. by W.¼W. from Bishop Rock in position 49.58N 07.54W by the German submarine *U 94* whilst on a voyage from Huelva to Port Talbot with a cargo of copper ore and precipitate. 25 lost including Master.

GORSEMORE 3079 Grt. Blt. 1899
22.9.1918: Torpedoed and sunk in the Mediterranean 44 miles S.E.½E. from Cape Colonne, Gulf of Taranto in position 38.40N 18.00E by the German submarine *UC 53* whilst on a voyage from Barry to Taranto with a cargo of coal.

Neptune Steam Navigation Co. Ltd.

SNOWDON RANGE ex Den of Kelly ex Dalhanna 4662 Grt. Blt. 1906
28.3.1917: Torpedoed and sunk in the St. George's Channel 25 miles W. of Bardsey Island in position 52.36N 05.34W by the German submarine *UC 65* whilst on a voyage from Philadelpia to Liverpool with a cargo of wheat and foodstuffs. 4 lost.

CHEVIOT RANGE 3691 Grt. Blt. 1914
21.2.1918: Captured and sunk by gunfire in the English Channel 25 miles S. from the Lizard by the German submarine *U 102* whilst on a voyage from Tuticorn to the United Kingdom with general cargo. 27 lost including Master.

LOWTHER RANGE 3926 Grt. Blt. 1906
20.4.1918: Torpedoed and sunk in the Irish Sea 20 miles W. by N.½N. from South Stack Rock probably by the German submarine *U 91* whilst on a voyage from Cartagena to Clyde with a cargo of iron ore.

Norfolk & North American Steam Ship Co. Ltd.

EAGLE POINT 5222 Grt. Blt. 1900
28.3.1916: Captured and torpedoed in the Atlantic 100 miles W.N.W. from Bishop Rock by the German submarine *U 70* whilst on a voyage from St. John (NB) to Le Havre with a cargo of hay and oats.

WEST POINT 3847 Grt. Blt. 1912
8.10.1916: Captured and sunk with bombs in the Atlantic 46 miles S.E. by E. from the Nantucket Lightvessel in position 40.25N 69.00W by the German submarine *U 53* whilst on a voyage from London to Newport News with general cargo.

CROWN POINT 5218 Grt. Blt. 1900
6.2.1917: Torpedoed and sunk in the Atlantic 55 miles W. of the Scilly Isles in position 50.06N 07.46W by the German submarine *U 83* whilst on a voyage from

London to Philadelphia with general cargo and chalk. 7 lost, Master and 1 Engineer Officer taken prisoner.

EAST POINT 5234 Grt. Blt. *1901*
9.3.1917: Torpedoed and sunk in the English Channel 9 miles E. by S.½S. from Eddystone Lighthouse in position 50.11N 04.02W by the German submarine *U 48* whilst on a voyage from London to Philadelphia with general cargo.

SOUTH POINT ex *Albert Hall* **4258 Grt. Blt. *1914***
12.6.1917: Torpedoed and sunk in the Atlantic 30 miles S.W.½S. from Bishop Rock by the German submarine *UB 32* whilst on a voyage from London to Newport News in ballast.

Prince Line, Ltd.

SAILOR PRINCE 3144 Grt. Blt. *1901*
2.10.1915: Captured and sunk by gunfire in the Mediterranean 56 miles S.E. by S. from Cape Sidero, Crete by the German submarine *U 39* whilst on a voyage from Cyprus to Leith with a cargo of locust beans. 2 lost.

ORANGE PRINCE ex *Wye* ex *Strathmore* **3583 Grt. Blt. *1894***
15.11.1915: Torpedoed and sunk in the Mediterranean 85 miles S.W. by W. from Gavdo Island in position 34.00N 22.40E by the German submarine *U 34* whilst on a voyage from Avonmouth and Alexandria to Mudros with general cargo. 3 lost.

SWEDISH PRINCE ex *Howick Hall* **3712 Grt. Blt. *1896***
17.8.1916: Captured and sunk by gunfire in the Mediterranean 12 miles N.W. by W. from Pantellaria Island in position 36.54N 11.42E by the German submarine *U 35* whilst on a voyage from Salonica to Bizerta in ballast. 1 lost, Master, Chief Engineer and 1 Gunner taken prisoner.

WELSH PRINCE 4934 Grt. Blt. *1903*
13.10.1916: Torpedoed and sunk in the Mediterranean 33 miles S.W. from Cape Matapan in position 36.00N 32.50E by the German submarine *UB 43* whilst on a voyage from Calcutta to Dundee with general cargo. 2 lost.

CORSICAN PRINCE ex *Briardale* **2776 Grt. Blt. *1900***
7.2.1917: Torpedoed and sunk in the North Sea 3 miles E. from Whitby in position 54.30N 00.31W by the German submarine *UB 34* whilst on a voyage from Dundee to Dunkirk with a cargo of timber. 1 lost.

JAPANESE PRINCE 4876 Grt. Blt. *1911*
10.2.1917: Torpedoed and sunk in the Atlantic 24 miles S.W. from Bishop Rock in position 49.36N 06.46W by the German submarine *UC 47* whilst on a voyage from Newport News to Southampton with general cargo.

TROJAN PRINCE 3196 Grt. Blt. *1896*
23.2.1917: Torpedoed and sunk in the Mediterranean 5 miles N.W. from Cape Shershel in position 36.39N 02.70E by the German submarine *U 39* whilst on a voyage from London to Alexandria with general cargo. 2 lost.

STUART PRINCE ex *Hutton* **3597 Grt. Blt. 1899**
22.3.1917: Torpedoed and sunk in the St. George's Channel 85 miles N. by W. from Broad Haven, co. Mayo in position 55.28N 11.20W by the German submarine *U 66* whilst on a voyage from Manchester and Belfast to Alexandria with general cargo. 20 lost including Master.

EGYPTIAN PRINCE 3117 Grt. Blt. 1902
12.5.1917: Captured and sunk with bombs in the Mediterranean 240 miles S.S.E. of Malta by the German submarine *U 38* whilst on a voyage from Alexandria to Manchester with general cargo.

AFRICAN PRINCE 4916 Grt. Blt. 1903
21.7.1917: Torpedoed and sunk in the Atlantic 60 miles N.N.W. from Tory Island in position 56.00N 09.30W by the German submarine *U 66* whilst on a voyage from Liverpool to Newport News with a cargo of china clay.

BELGIAN PRINCE ex *Hungarian Prince* ex *Mohawk* **4765 Grt. Blt. 1901**
31.7.1917: Torpedoed and sunk in the Atlantic 175 miles N.W. by W. from Tory Island by the German submarine *U 55* whilst on a voyage from Liverpool to Newport News with a cargo of blue clay. 39 lost, Master taken prisoner.

EASTERN PRINCE 2885 Grt. Blt. 1910
30.8.1917: Torpedoed and sunk in the English Channel 30 miles S.¾W. from the Eddystone Lighthouse in position 49.41N 04.12W by the German submarine *U 62* whilst on a voyage from Philadelphia to London with general cargo. 5 lost.

HIGHLAND PRINCE ex *Matteawan* **3390 Grt. Blt. 1901**
11.4.1918: Torpedoed and sunk in the Mediterranean 36 miles N.E.¼E. from Cape Bon in position 37.32N 11.32E by the German submarine *UB 50* whilst on a voyage from Alexandria to London with a cargo of cotton and cotton seed. 3 lost.

ASIATIC PRINCE 2887 Grt. Blt. 1910
30.5.1918: Torpedoed and sunk in the Mediterranean 190 miles E. by S.½S. from Malta in position 35.13N 18.24E by the German submarine *U 63* whilst on a voyage from Bona to Salonica with a cargo of straw.

Rio Cape Line, Ltd.

GLENCARRON 5117 Grt. Blt. 1917
19.2.1918: Torpedoed and sunk in the English Channel 47 miles S. by E.½E. from the Lizard in position 49.20N 04.57W by the German submarine *U 82* whilst on a voyage from Philadelphia to London with general cargo.

GLENLEE 4915 Grt. Blt. 1917
9.8.1918: Torpedoed and sunk in the English Channel 4 miles E. by N. from Owers Lightvessel by the German submarine *UB 57* whilst on a voyage from Clyde to Dunkirk with a cargo of Government stores. 1 lost.

White Diamond Steam Ship Co. Ltd.

SAGAMORE 5197 Grt. Blt. 1892
3.3.1917: Torpedoed and sunk in the English Channel 150 miles W. from the

Fastnet Rock in position 51.50N 14.00W by the German submarine *U 49* whilst on a voyage from Boston, Mass. to Liverpool with general cargo. 52 lost including Master.

BAY STATE 6583 Grt. Blt. 1915
10.6.1917: Torpedoed and sunk in the Atlantic 250 miles N.W. from the Fastnet Rock in position 53.00N 16.09W by the German submarine *U 66* whilst on a voyage from Boston, Mass. to Liverpool with general cargo.

The Shipping Controller
WAR KNIGHT ex *Southerner* **7951 Grt. Blt. 1917**
24.3.1918: In collision with American steamer *O. B. Jennings* 10289/17, she later struck a mine laid by *UC 17* near the Needles Lighthouse and subsequently beached at Freshwater Bay. The cargo of ammunition exploded and she broke up. 32 lost including Master.

HUNTSLAND ex *Erymanthos* **2871 Grt. Blt. 1911**
6.6.1918: Torpedoed and sunk in the English Channel 23 miles N. by W. from Le Havre in position 49.50N 00.10W by the German submarine *UC 77* whilst on a voyage from Le Havre to Portsmouth in ballast.

WAR COUNCIL 5875 Grt. Blt. 1917
16.10.1918: Torpedoed and sunk in the Mediterranean 85 miles W.S.W. from Cape Matapan in position 35.44N 21.00E by the German submarine *U 63* whilst on a voyage from Barry to Port Said with a cargo of coal.

GAFF, JOHN & COMPANY—GLASGOW

MALINCHE 1868 Grt. Blt. 1906
29.11.1915: Captured and torpedoed in the Mediterranean 50 miles E. from Malta by the German submarine *U 33* whilst on a voyage from Piraeus to New York with general cargo.

GALBRAITH, PEMBROKE & CO. LTD.—LONDON

SOWWELL ex *Kenley* **3781 Grt. Blt. 1900**
19.4.1917: Torpedoed and sunk in the Atlantic 170 miles W.½S. from Gibraltar by the German submarine *U 35* whilst on a voyage from Sagunto to Clyde with a cargo of iron ore. 21 lost including Master.

Austin Friars Steam Ship Co. Ltd.
GLENALMOND 2888 Grt. Blt. 1902
9.4.1916: Captured and torpedoed in the English Channel 27 miles N. from Ushant by the German submarine *U 66* whilst on a voyage from Bilbao to Clyde with a cargo of iron ore.

REPTON 2881 Grt. Blt. 1894
7.5.1917: Torpedoed and sunk in the Mediterranean 45 miles S.S.E. from Cape Matapan by the German submarine *UB 43* whilst on a voyage from Hull and Malta to Mudros with a cargo of coal. 3 lost.

GARDINER, JAMES & COMPANY—GLASGOW

Caledonia S.S. Co. Ltd.

GLENARTNEY 5201 Grt. Blt. 1911
18.3.1915: Torpedoed and sunk in the English Channel 4 miles S. from Royal Sovereign Lightvessel by the German submarine *U 34* whilst on a voyage from Bangkok to London and Liverpool with a cargo of rice and rice meal. 1 lost.

Western S.S. Co. Ltd.

GLENLEE 4140 Grt. Blt. 1904
29.5.1915: Captured and torpedoed in the Atlantic 67 miles S.S.W. from Wolf Rock by the German submarine *U 41* whilst on a voyage from Barry to Aden with a cargo of coal.

ORONSAY 3761 Grt. Blt. 1900
28.12.1916: Torpedoed and sunk in the Mediterranean 48 miles S.E. from Malta by the German submarine *UC 22* whilst on a voyage from Calcutta to Dundee with a cargo of jute and manganese ore. Master taken prisoner.

GLENCLUNY 4812 Grt. Blt. 1909
27.4.1917: Torpedoed and sunk in the Mediterranean 4 miles N.W. from Cape Sigli in position 36.58N 04.42E by the German submarine *UC 67* whilst on a voyage from Bombay to Hull with general cargo. 4 lost.

GARDINER, ROBERT. S.—NEWCASTLE UPON TYNE

Rodney S.S. Co. Ltd.

ALICE MARIE 2210 Grt. Blt. 1915
20.12.1917: Torpedoed and sunk in the English Channel 6 miles E.N.E. from Start Point by the German submarine *UB 31* whilst on a voyage from Tyne to Rochefort with a cargo of coal.

ROSE MARIE 2220 Grt. Blt. 1916
5.1.1918: Torpedoed and sunk in the St. George's Channel 13 miles S.E. from North Arklow Lightvessel by the German submarine *U 61* whilst on a voyage from Scapa Flow to Barry Roads in ballast. 1 lost.

GARTHWAITE, SIR WILLIAM, BART.—GLASGOW

GARTHCLYDE 2124 Grt. Blt. 1917
15.10.1917: Torpedoed and sunk in the English Channel 12 miles W.¼S. from the Lizard by the German submarine *UC 79* whilst on a voyage from Clyde to Bordeaux with a cargo of coal.

GARTHWAITE 5690 Grt. Blt. 1917
13.12.1917: Torpedoed and sunk in the North Sea 4 miles E. from Whitby by the German submarine *UB 22* whilst on a voyage from Tyne to New York in ballast. 14 lost including Master.

GAS LIGHT & COKE COMPANY—LONDON

FULGENS 2512 Grt. Blt. 1912
1.8.1915: Torpedoed and sunk in the North Sea 1 mile off Palling by the German submarine *UB 10* whilst on a voyage from Hartlepool to London with a cargo of coal.

IGNIS ex *Dorothea* 2042 Grt. Blt. 1903
8.12.1915: Struck a mine and sunk in the North Sea 5½ miles N.E. from Aldeburgh laid by the German submarine *UC 7* whilst on a voyage from Tyne to London with a cargo of gas coal.

LANTERNA ex *Carn Brea* 1685 Grt. Blt. 1882
6.10.1916: Struck a mine and sunk in the North Sea 2½ miles N.E.½E. from Cromer laid by the German submarine *UC 1* whilst on a voyage from Tyne to London with a cargo of coal.

FIRELIGHT ex *Rookwood* 1143 Grt. Blt. 1896
1.5.1917: Torpedoed and sunk in the North Sea 1¾ miles E. from North Tyne Pier in position 55.01N 01.21W by the German submarine *UC 29* whilst on a voyage from Tyne to London with a cargo of coal.

LANTHORN ex *Magnus Mail* 2299 Grt. Blt. 1889
22.5.1917: Captured and sunk with bombs in the North Sea 3 miles E. from Whitby in position 54.30N 00.29W by the German submarine *UB 41* whilst on a voyage from London to Tyne in ballast.

GLOW ex *Monkwood* 1141 Grt. Blt. 1900
22.7.1917: Torpedoed and sunk in the North Sea 4 miles S.E. by E. from South Cheek, Robin Hood Bay in position 54.23N 00.23W by the German submarine *UB 21* whilst on a voyage from Tyne to London with a cargo of coal. 1 lost.

ARDENS ex *Universal* 1274 Grt. Blt. 1878
18.8.1917: Torpedoed and sunk in the North Sea 2 miles E. from Filey Brigg by the German submarine *UC 16* whilst on a voyage from Tyne to London with a cargo of gas coal. 1 lost.

PHARE ex *Grovelea* ex *Lady Furness* 1282 Grt. Blt. 1906
31.10.1917: Torpedoed and sunk in the North Sea 2½ miles N.½E. from Scarborough by the German submarine *UB 35* whilst on a voyage from Tyne to London with a cargo of coal. 14 lost.

SUNTRAP ex *Sherwood* 1353 Grt. Blt. 1904
7.11.1917: Torpedoed and sunk in the North Sea 2½ miles E. from South Cheek, Robin Hood Bay by the German submarine *UB 22* whilst on a voyage from Tyne to London with a cargo of coal.

LAMPADA ex *Snilesworth* 2220 Grt. Blt. 1889
8.12.1917: Torpedoed and sunk in the North Sea 3 miles N. from Whitby by the German submarine *UB 75* whilst on a voyage from Tyne to London with a cargo of coal. 5 lost.

COALGAS ex *George Allen **2257 Grt. Blt. 1890***
5.3.1918: Struck a mine and sunk in the North Sea 5 miles S. by W. from Shipwash Lightvessel laid by the German submarine *UC 4* whilst on a voyage from London to Tyne in ballast.

GELLATLY, HANKEY & CO. LTD.—LONDON

Moguel Steam Ship Co. Ltd.

GHAZEE 5084 Grt. Blt. 1904
4.2.1917: Torpedoed and sunk in the Atlantic 2 miles S.S.W. from Galley Head in position 51.30N 08.55W by the German submarine *U 60* whilst on a voyage from Cardiff to Port Sudan with a cargo of coal.

The Shipping Controller

CONSTANTIA 772 Grt. Blt. 1890
8.5.1918: Torpedoed and sunk in the North Sea 2 miles E. from South Cheek, Robin Hood Bay by the German submarine *UB 21* whilst on a voyage from Tyne to—with a cargo of coal. 3 lost.

SIRIUS 1005 Grt. Blt. 1884
29.6.1918: Torpedoed and sunk in the Atlantic 1½ miles W. by S. from the Longship Lighthouse by unknown German submarine whilst on a voyage from Penarth to—with a cargo of coal.

GENERAL STEAM NAVIGATION CO. LTD.—LONDON

ORIOLE 1489 Grt. Blt. 1914
30.1.1915: Torpedoed and sunk in the English Channel by the German submarine *U 20* whilst on a voyage from London to Le Havre with general cargo. 21 lost including Master.

LEEUWARDEN 990 Grt. Blt. 1903
17.3.1915: Captured and sunk by gunfire in the North Sea 4 miles W. by N. ½N. from Maas Lightvessel by the German submarine *U 28* whilst on a voyage from London to Harlingen in ballast.

PTARMIGAN 784 Grt. Blt. 1891
15.4.1915: Torpedoed and sunk in the North Sea 6 miles W. by N. from North Hinder Lightvessel by the German submarine *UB 5* whilst on a voyage from Rotterdam to London with general cargo. 8 lost.

GRONINGEN 988 Grt. Blt. 1902
23.9.1915: Struck a mine and sunk off the mouth of the River Thames 1½ miles N. by E. from Sunk Head Buoy laid by the German submarine *UC 6* whilst on a voyage from Harlingen to London with general cargo. 1 lost.

BALGOWNIE 1061 Grt. Blt. 1880
6.2.1916: Struck a mine and sunk off the mouth of the River Thames 1¾ miles E.S.E. from Sunk Head Buoy laid by the German submarine *UC 7* whilst on a voyage from London to Leith with general cargo. 1 lost.

FAUVETTE 2644 Grt. Blt. 1912
9.3.1916: Struck a mine and sunk in the Downs off North Foreland in position 51.24N 01.29E laid by the German submarine *UC 7* whilst on a voyage from Girgenti to London. Lost whilst on Government service employed as an Armed Boarding Steamer.

VESUVIO ex *Czar* **1391 Grt. Blt. 1879**
6.4.1916: Struck a mine and sunk in the English Channel 6 miles E. from Owers Lightvessel laid by the German submarine *UB 29* whilst on a voyage from Messina to London with general cargo. 7 lost including Master.

HALCYON 1319 Grt. Blt. 1915
7.4.1916: Struck a mine and sunk in the Strait of Dover 3½ miles S.W. by S. from Folkestone Pier laid by the German submarine *UC 6* whilst on a voyage from Bordeaux to London with general cargo.

TEAL 766 Grt. Blt. 1876
29.4.1916: Captured and torpedoed in the North Sea 2 miles E. from Seaham Harbour by the German submarine *UB 27* whilst on a voyage from Leith to London.

GANNET 1127 Grt. Blt. 1879
7.7.1916: Struck a mine and sunk in the North Sea 5 miles E.N.E. from Shipwash Lightvessel laid by the German submarine *UC 6* whilst on a voyage from Rotterdam to London with general cargo. 8 lost.

SHELDRAKE ex *Kelvingrove* **2697 Grt. Blt. 1894**
8.11.1916: Captured and sunk by gunfire in the Mediterranean 20 miles W.S.W. from Marittimo Island by the German submarine *U 34* whilst on a voyage from Naples to London in ballast. Master and Chief Engineer taken prisoner.

HIRONDELLE 1648 Grt. Blt. 1890
25.4.1917: Torpedoed and sunk in the Bay of Biscay 13 miles S. by E. from Belle Ile by the German submarine *UC 36* whilst on a voyage from London to Bordeaux with general cargo.

ORTOLAN 1727 Grt. Blt. 1902
14.6.1917: Torpedoed and sunk in the Atlantic 100 miles W.S.W. from Bishop Rock in position 48.00N 10.00W by the German submarine *U 82* whilst on a voyage from Genoa to London with general cargo. 3 lost.

HERON 885 Grt. Blt. 1889
30.9.1917: Torpedoed and sunk in the Bay of Biscay 500 miles W. of Belle Ile by the German submarine *U 90* whilst on a voyage from Tyne to Oporto with a cargo of coal. 22 lost including Master.

DRAKE ex *Wildrake* ex *Drake* **2267 Grt. Blt. 1908**
30.9.1917: Captured and sunk by gunfire in the Atlantic 340 miles W. from Ushant in position 46.30N 10.33W by the German submarine *U 90* whilst on a voyage from London to Genoa with general cargo and explosives. Master taken prisoner.

LAPWING 1192 Grt. Blt. 1911
11.11.1917: Struck a mine and sunk in the North Sea 9 miles S.E. from Southwold laid by the German submarine *UC 4* whilst on a voyage from Rotterdam to London with general cargo.

GRIVE 2037 Grt. Blt. 1905
8.12.1917: Torpedoed and sunk in the North Sea off Lerwick by the German submarine *UC 40*. Lost whilst on Government service employed as an Armed Boarding Steamer.

PHILOMEL 3050 Grt. Blt. 1917
16.9.1918: Torpedoed and sunk in the Bay of Biscay 12 miles S.E. by E. from Iles de Glenan, near Lorient by the German submarine *UB 88* whilst on a voyage from London to Brest and Bordeaux with general cargo.

GIBBS & COMPANY—CARDIFF

SOUTH WALES 3668 Grt. Blt. 1906
24.6.1917: Torpedoed and sunk in the Atlantic 128 miles W. from Bishop Rock by the German submarine *U 62* whilst on a voyage from Bassein and Cape Town to London with a cargo of rice. 2 lost.

EAST WALES 4321 Grt. Blt. 1915
14.10.1917: Captured and sunk by gunfire in the Atlantic 8 miles S. by W. ½ W. from Daunts Rock by the German submarine *U 57* whilst on a voyage from Newport, Mon. to—in ballast. 3 lost.

WEST WALES 4336 Grt. Blt. 1912
21.1.1918: Torpedoed and sunk in the Mediterranean 140 miles S.E. ¾ S. from Malta in position 34.00N 16.50E by the Austro-Hungarian submarine *U 28* whilst on a voyage from Barry to Alexandria with a cargo of coal. 2 lost.

GIBSON, GEORGE & CO. LTD.—LEITH

DURWARD 1301 Grt. Blt. 1895
21.1.1915: Captured and sunk with bombs in the North Sea 22 miles N.W. from Maas Lightvessel by the German submarine *U 19* whilst on a voyage from Leith to Rotterdam with general cargo.

NIGEL 1400 Grt. Blt. 1903
12.11.1915: Struck a mine and sunk in the English Channel off Boulogne laid by the German submarine *UC 6* whilst on a voyage from Newhaven to Boulogne with a cargo of Government stores. 5 lost.

TRAQUAIR 1067 Grt. Blt. 1915
12.1.1916: Struck a mine and sunk in the Strait of Dover 1 mile S.W. from Admiralty Pier, Dover laid by the German submarine *UC 6* whilst on a voyage from Leith to Dunkirk with a cargo of coal.

ASTROLOGER 912 Grt. Blt. 1890
26.6.1916: Struck a mine and sunk in the North Sea 5 miles S.S.E. from Lowestoft laid by the German submarine *UC 1* whilst on a voyage from Leith to Dunkirk with general cargo and coal. 11 lost including Master.

MASCOTTE 1097 Grt. Blt. 1885
3.9.1916: Struck a mine and sunk in the North Sea 6½ miles S.E. from Southwold in position 52.15N 01.50E laid by the German submarine *UC 6* whilst on a voyage from Rotterdam to Leith with general cargo. 1 lost.

PEVERIL 1459 Grt. Blt. 1904
6.11.1917: Torpedoed and sunk in the Atlantic W. of the Strait of Gibraltar by the German submarine *U 63*. Lost whilst on Government service employed as Special Service Ship—Q Ship *Puma*.

GILLESPIE & NICOL—GLASGOW

BARNTON 1858 Grt. Blt. 1904
24.4.1917: Torpedoed and sunk in the Bay of Biscay 40 miles W. by S. from Chassiron Point near Rochefort in position 45.40N 02.12W by the German submarine *UC 21* whilst on a voyage from Bilbao to Tyne with a cargo of iron ore. 14 lost.

GLADSTONE & COMPANY—MIDDLESBROUGH

CALLIOPE 3829 Grt. Blt. 1901
5.4.1917: Torpedoed and sunk in the Mediterranean 35 miles S.W. from Ustica Island, N. of Sicily by the German submarine *U 65* whilst on a voyage from Barry to Malta with a cargo of coal. 6 lost including Master. 1st and 2nd Officers and 3rd Engineer taken prisoner.

GLEN & COMPANY—GLASGOW

Clydesdale Shipowners Co. Ltd.

ABOUKIR 3660 Grt. Blt. 1906
3.2.1918: Captured and sunk by gunfire in the Mediterranean 20 miles E. by S. from Cape Creus in position 42.20N 03.40E by the German submarine *UB 48* whilst on a voyage from Genoa to Montevideo in ballast. Master taken prisoner.

Glasgow Shipowners Co. Ltd.

TRAFALGAR 4572 Grt. Blt. 1911
23.8.1915: Captured and sunk with bombs in the Atlantic 54 miles S.W. by W. from the Fastnet Rock by the German submarine *U 38* whilst on a voyage from Mejillones to Clyde with a cargo of nitrate.

GIBRALTAR 3803 Grt. Blt. 1902
12.9.1917: Torpedoed and sunk in the Mediterranean 100 miles S.E.½S. from Cape Creus in position 41.17N 05.50E by the German submarine *UC 27* whilst on a voyage from Karachi to Marseilles with general cargo. 4 lost.

Scandinavian Shipping Co. Ltd.

KNARSDALE ex Herman Menzell ex Dunav 1641 Grt. Blt. 1896
21.12.1915: Struck a mine and sunk in the North Sea 2¾ miles E. by S. from Orfordness laid by the German submarine *UC 7* whilst on a voyage from Blyth to Sheerness with a cargo of coal. 1 lost.

THELMA 1002 Grt. Blt. 1903
26.9.1916: Captured and torpedoed in the North Sea 24 miles E. from the Fair Isle by the German submarine *U 20* whilst on a voyage from Clyde to Gothenburg with general cargo and coal.

GLOVER BROTHERS—LONDON

Shakespear Shipping Co. Ltd.

OVID 4159 Grt. Blt. 1902
25.11.1917: Torpedoed and sunk in the Mediterranean 65 miles N.E.½E. from Suda Bay by the German submarine *UC 74* whilst on a voyage from Bombay to a Mediterranean port with Admiralty cargo. 2 lost.

The Shipping Controller

ACHAIA 2733 Grt. Blt. 1907
7.9.1916: Struck a mine and sunk in the Mediterranean 300 yards E.N.E. from the entrance to Oran harbour in position 36.00N 00.50E laid by the German submarine *U 72* whilst on a voyage from Karachi to Cardiff with a cargo of wheat.

GLYNN, JOHN & SONS LIMITED—LIVERPOOL

Atlantic & Eastern S.S. Co. Ltd.

COSTELLO ex *Baron Kelvin 1591 Grt. Blt. 1903*
3.8.1915: Captured and sunk by gunfire in the Atlantic 95 miles W. by S. from Bishop Rock in position 49.02N 08.30W by the German submarine *U 28* whilst on a voyage from Liverpool to Genoa with general cargo. 1 lost.

TORINO 1850 Grt. Blt. 1895
29.10.1916: Captured and torpedoed in the Atlantic 70 miles W.½N. from Cape Trafalgar near Cadiz in position 36.00N 07.40W by the German submarine *U 63* whilst on a voyage from Genoa to Liverpool with general cargo. 1 lost.

PONTIAC 1698 Grt. Blt. 1879
21.4.1917: Torpedoed and sunk in the Atlantic 56 miles S.W.½S. from the Fastnet Rock in position 50.30N 10.00W by the German submarine *U 53* whilst on a voyage from Liverpool to Genoa with general cargo. 2 lost.

SCHOLAR 1635 Grt. Blt. 1886
18.5.1918: Torpedoed and sunk in the Atlantic 90 miles W. by S.¾S. from Bishop Rock by the German submarine *U 55* whilst on a voyage from Leghorn to Liverpool with general cargo. 2 lost.

GOOD, JOHN & SONS LIMITED—HULL

The Shipping Controller

TYRHAUG ex *Kjeld 1483 Grt. Blt. 1906*
21.3.1918: Torpedoed and sunk in the Atlantic 10 miles N.E. from Pendeen Lighthouse by the German submarine *UB 103* whilst on a voyage from Belfast to Falmouth with a cargo of potatoes, hay and wood. 2 lost.

GORDON, R. & COMPANY—LONDON

Gordon S.S. Co. Ltd.

WINLATON 3270 Grt. Blt. 1912
23.8.1917: Torpedoed and sunk in the Atlantic 25 miles W. from Cape Spartel in position 35.40N 06.25W by the German submarine *UB 48* whilst on a voyage from Barry to Gibraltar with a cargo of naval stores and coal. 2 lost, Master taken prisoner.

Unison S.S. Co. Ltd.

KARMA 3710 Grt. Blt. 1904
20.7.1916: Captured and sunk by gunfire in the Mediterranean 68 miles N.N.W. from Algiers by the German submarine *U 39* whilst on a voyage from Tyne to Porto-Ferrajo with a cargo of coal.

KARIBA 3697 Grt. Blt. 1904
13.4.1917: Torpedoed and sunk in the Atlantic 260 miles W.N.W. from Ushant in position 48.30N 11.28W by the German submarine *UC 27* whilst on a voyage from Java and Dakar to Falmouth with a cargo of sugar. 13 lost.

KARUMA 2995 Grt. Blt. 1910
27.4.1917: Torpedoed and sunk in the Mediterranean 5 miles N. from Cape Sigli by the German submarine *UC 67* whilst on a voyage from Malta to the United Kingdom with a cargo of Admiralty stores. 2 lost.

GOULD, J. C. & CO. (STEAMSHIP MANAGERS) LIMITED—CARDIFF

Dulcia S.S. Co. Ltd.

GRELDON ex Dartmouth 3322 Grt. Blt. 1903
8.10.1917: Torpedoed and sunk in the St. George's Channel 7 miles E.N.E. from North Arklow Lightvessel by the German submarine *U 96* whilst on a voyage from Birkenhead to Italy with a cargo of coal. 28 lost.

GRELHAME ex Tyninghame 3740 Grt. Blt. 1909
30.8.1917: Torpedoed and sunk in the English Channel 4 miles S.W. from Start Point by the German submarine *U 62* whilst on a voyage from Cuba to Le Havre with a cargo of sugar.

GRELTORIA 5143 Grt. Blt. 1917
27.9.1917: Torpedoed and sunk in the North Sea 3 miles N.W. by N.½N. from Flamborough Head by the German submarine *UB 34* whilst on a voyage from Tyne to Naples with a cargo of coal.

Haenton Steam Shipping Co. Ltd.

GRELEEN ex Ballater ex Blairmore 2286 Grt. Blt. 1894
22.9.1917: Torpedoed and sunk in the English Channel 7 miles E. by N. from Berry Head by the German submarine *UB 40* whilst on a voyage from Bilbao to Middlesbrough with a cargo of iron ore. 19 lost including Master.

PENISTONE 4139 Grt. Blt. 1913
1.8.1918: Torpedoed and sunk in the Atlantic 145 miles S.W. ½S. from Nantucket Island by the German submarine *U 156* whilst on a voyage from New York to Bordeaux with general cargo. 1 lost.

GOW, HARRISON & COMPANY—GLASGOW

VELLORE 4926 Grt. Blt. 1907
25.3.1917: Torpedoed and sunk in the Mediterranean 21 miles N.W. by N. from Alexandria in position 31.28N 29.37E by the German submarine *U 63* whilst on a voyage from Glasgow to Alexandria with a cargo of coal. Master and Chief Engineer taken prisoner.

VALETTA 5871 Grt. Blt. 1913
8.7.1917: Torpedoed and sunk in the Atlantic 118 miles N.W. ¾W. from the Fastnet Rock in position 51.49N 12.22W by the German submarine *U 87* whilst on a voyage from Montreal to Dublin with a cargo of flour and wheat.

VIENNA 4170 Grt. Blt. 1899
11.9.1917: Torpedoed and sunk in the Atlantic 340 miles W. ½N. from Ushant in position 46.59N 13.05W by the German submarine *U 49* whilst on a voyage from Brest to New York with a cargo of rags. 25 lost, Master taken prisoner.

VENETIA 3596 Grt. Blt. 1898
9.12.1917: Torpedoed and sunk in the North Sea 3 miles N.N.W. from Whitby Rock buoy in position 54.32N 00.39W by the German submarine *UB 75* whilst on a voyage from Tyne to—with a cargo of coal.

VOLNAY 4610 Grt. Blt. 1910
14.12.1917: Struck a mine and sunk in the English Channel 2 miles E. by S. from Manacle Rocks laid by the German submarine *UC 64* whilst on a voyage from Montreal to Plymouth with Admiralty cargo.

VIMEIRA 5884 Grt. Blt. 1914
12.5.1918: Torpedoed and sunk in the Mediterranean 16 miles W.S.W. from Lampedusa Island midway between Malta and Tunis in position 35.23N 12.19E by the German submarine *UC 54* whilst on a voyage from Tyne to Bizerta and Alexandria with a cargo of coal and coke.

GRAHAM, CHARLES—HULL

Roberts & Cooper Ltd.

BRIERLEY HILL ex Nanta **1168 Grt. Blt. 1903**
1.11.1916: Captured and torpedoed in the North Sea 18 miles W.N.W. from Helliso Lighthouse by the German submarine *U 30* whilst on a voyage from Halmstad to Hull with a cargo of pit props.

LUCY ANDERSON 1073 Grt. Blt. 1904
12.3.1917: Captured and sunk by gunfire in the North Sea 55 miles E.S.E. from Noss Head in position 58.27N 01.18W by the German submarine *UC 44* whilst on a voyage from Hartlepool to Gothenburg with a cargo of coal.

GRAHAMS & COMPANY—LONDON

The Admiralty

WARTENFELS 4511 Grt. Blt. 1903
5.2.1917: Torpedoed and sunk in the Atlantic 120 miles S.W. from the Fastnet Rock in position 50.10N 11.59W by the German submarine *U 81* whilst on a voyage from Barry to Alexandria with a cargo of Government stores. 2 lost, Master taken prisoner.

HUNSTANTON ex *Werdenfels* **4504 Grt. Blt. 1903**
4.4.1917: Torpedoed and sunk in the Atlantic 36 miles W. from Scilly Isles in position 49.50N 07.40W by the German submarine *UC 30* whilst on a voyage from Geelong to London with a cargo of wheat.

PAGENTURM 5000 Grt. Blt. 1909
16.5.1917: Torpedoed and sunk in the English Channel 16 miles W. from Beachy Head in position 50.40N 00.10W by the German submarine *UB 40* whilst on a voyage from London to Barry with a part general cargo. 4 lost.

PERLA 5355 Grt. Blt. 1912
10.6.1917: Captured and torpedoed in the Arctic 130 miles N.¾W. from Cape Teriberski, Murmansk in position 71.23N 35.26E by the German submarine *U 28* whilst on a voyage from Genoa to Archangel with a cargo of automobiles and coal. 1 lost.

GREAT CENTRAL RAILWAY COMPANY—GRIMSBY

LEICESTER 1001 Grt. Blt. 1891
12.2.1916: Struck a mine and sunk in the Strait of Dover 2½ miles S.E. by E. from Folkestone Pier laid by the German submarine *UC 6* whilst on a voyage from Portsmouth to Cromarty with general cargo. 17 lost.

CHESTERFIELD 1013 Grt. Blt. 1913
18.5.1918: Torpedoed and sunk in the Mediterranean 42 miles N.E. by E.½E. from Malta by the German submarine *UC 52*. Lost whilst on Government service employed as Fleet Messenger *No. 64*.

GREAT EASTERN RAILWAY COMPANY—LONDON

CLACTON 820 Grt. Blt. 1904
3.8.1916: Torpedoed and sunk in the Aegean Sea off Kavalla Bay by the German submarine *U 73*. Lost whilst on Government service employed as a Minesweeper.

COPENHAGEN 2570 Grt. Blt. 1907
5.3.1917: Torpedoed and sunk in the North Sea 8 miles E.½N. from North Hinder Lightvessel by the German submarine *UC 61* whilst on a voyage from Harwich to Hook of Holland carrying passengers. 6 lost.

NEWMARKET 833 Grt. Blt. 1907
17.7.1917: Torpedoed and sunk in the Aegean Sea S. off Nikaria Island by the German submarine *UC 38*. Lost whilst on Government service employed as a Minesweeper.

LOUVAIN ex *Dresden 1830 Grt. Blt. 1897*
20.1.1918: Torpedoed and sunk in the Aegean Sea in the Kelos Strait by the German submarine *UC 22*. Lost whilst on Government service employed as an Armed Boarding Steamer.

GREAT LAKES TRANSPORTATION CO. LTD.—MIDLAND, ONTARIO

GLENFOYLE 1680 Grt. Blt. 1913
18.9.1917: Torpedoed and sunk in the Atlantic off S.W. Ireland by the German submarine *U 43*. Lost whilst on Government service employed as a Special Service Ship.

GREENHALGH, HAROLD R.—LIVERPOOL

Bromport S.S. Co. Ltd.

DELAMERE 1525 Grt. Blt. 1915
30.4.1917: Torpedoed and sunk in the Atlantic 110 miles W. by N. from the Fastnet Rock in position 51.40N 13.00W by the German submarine *U 70* whilst on a voyage from West Africa to Liverpool with general cargo. 10 lost.

ESKMERE 2293 Grt. Blt. 1916
13.10.1917: Torpedoed and sunk in the Irish Sea 15 miles W.N.W. from South Stack Rock by the German submarine *UC 75* whilst on a voyage from Belfast to Barry in ballast. 20 lost including Master.

REDESMERE 2123 Grt. Blt. 1911
28.10.1917: Torpedoed and sunk in the English Channel 6 miles W.S.W. from St. Catherine's Point by the German submarine *UB 40* whilst on a voyage from Barry to Southampton with a cargo of coal. 19 lost.

COLEMERE 2120 Grt. Blt. 1915
22.12.1917: Torpedoed and sunk in the St. George's Channel 35 miles W. from the Smalls by the German submarine *U 105* whilst on a voyage from Penarth to Sierra Leone with general cargo. 4 lost.

GREENLEES, J. & COMPANY—GLASGOW

Netherton Shipping Co. Ltd.

NETHERLEE 4227 Grt. Blt. 1907
10.2.1917: Torpedoed and sunk in the Atlantic 92 miles W.½S. from the Fastnet Rock in position 50.44N 11.45W by the German submarine *U 81* whilst on a voyage from Philadelphia to Dunkirk with general cargo. 2 lost.

GREY, EDWARD & COMPANY—LIVERPOOL

VIRGINIA 4279 Grt. Blt. 1901
16.7.1916: Captured and torpedoed in the Mediterranean 42 miles S.W. by W. from Cape Matapan by the German submarine *UB 45* whilst on a voyage from Torrevieja to Calcutta with a cargo of salt. 2 lost.

GRIFFITHS, T. H. & CO. (DEPOTS) LIMITED—CARDIFF

Reid S.S. Co. Ltd.

MERSARIO* 3847 Grt. Blt. *1906
1.10.1917: Torpedoed and sunk in the Atlantic 86 miles W. by N. from Cape Spartel by the German submarine *U 39* whilst on a voyage from Barry to Italy with a cargo of coal. 3 lost.

GRIFFITHS, LEWIS & COMPANY—CARDIFF

Griffiths Lewis Steam Navigation Co. Ltd.

ECCLESIA* 3714 Grt. Blt. *1904
14.7.1916: Captured and sunk by gunfire in the Mediterranean 11 miles N.W. from Cape Bougaroni by the German submarine *U 39* whilst on a voyage from Norfolk. (Va) to Taranto with a cargo of coal.

SIDMOUTH* 4045 Grt. Blt. *1903
24.10.1916: Captured and torpedoed in the Atlantic 22 miles S. from Wolf Rock by the German submarine *UB 29* whilst on a voyage from Cardiff to Spezia with a cargo of coal.

GUERET. L. LIMITED—CARDIFF

PARKMILL* 1316 Grt. Blt. *1909
10.9.1917: Torpedoed and sunk in the North Sea 1¼ miles from Kirkabister Lighthouse by the German submarine *UC 40* whilst on a voyage from Tyne to Harstad with a cargo of coal.

GUINNESS, ARTHUR & SONS CO. LTD.—DUBLIN

W. M. BARKLEY* 569 Grt. Blt. *1898
12.10.1917: Torpedoed and sunk in the Irish Sea 7 miles E. from Kish Lightvessel by the German submarine *UC 75* whilst on a voyage from Dublin to Liverpool with a cargo of stout. 4 lost including Master.

GUTHE BROTHERS LIMITED—WEST HARTLEPOOL

Wiltonhall S.S. Co. Ltd.

WILTONHALL* ex *Knockwell* ex *Montauk* 3387 Grt. Blt. *1901
16.7.1916: Captured and sunk with bombs in the Mediterranean 65 miles N.W. from Algiers in position 37.54N 00.50E by the German submarine *U 39* whilst on a voyage from Bombay to Hull with general cargo.

RYTONHALL* ex *Saint Helena* 4203 Grt. Blt. *1905
2.9.1917: Captured and torpedoed in the Atlantic 105 miles W.½S. from Ushant in position 47.45N 07.28W by the German submarine *UC 69* whilst on a voyage from Montreal to Falmouth with a cargo of wheat and flour.

HAIN, EDWARD & SON—ST. IVES

KALLUNDBORG* ex *Denewell* 1590 Grt. Blt. *1898
5.6.1917: Captured and sunk with bombs in the Mediterranean 80 miles S.S.W.

from Toulon by the German submarine *U 64* whilst on a voyage from Genoa to Bougie in ballast. 1 lost.

Hain Steamship Co. Ltd.

TRENEGLOS 3886 Grt. Blt. 1906
14.11.1915: Torpedoed and sunk in the Mediterranean 70 miles W.S.W. from Gavdo Island by the German submarine *U 34* whilst on a voyage from Port Louis to the United Kingdom with a cargo of sugar. 3 lost.

TREMATON 4198 Grt. Blt. 1914
20.1.1916: Captured and sunk by gunfire in the Mediterranean 180 miles E. by S. from Malta in position 35.24N 18.09E by the German submarine *U 35* whilst on a voyage from Karachi to the United Kingdom with a cargo of grain.

TREGANTLE 3091 Grt. Blt. 1903
22.4.1916: Torpedoed and sunk in the North Sea 1½ miles E.S.E. from Corton Lightvessel, 3 miles N. of Lowestoft by the German submarine *UB 16* whilst on a voyage from Galveston to Hull with a cargo of wheat.

TREVARRACK 4199 Grt. Blt. 1914
16.11.1916: Captured and sunk by gunfire in the English Channel 25 miles W.½N. from Les Hanois, Guernsey in position 49.40N 03.48W by the German submarine *UC 18* whilst on a voyage from Buenos Aires to Hull with a cargo of maize.

TREMEADOW 3653 Grt. Blt. 1905
19.1.1917: Captured and sunk by gunfire in the English Channel 5 miles N.E.¾N. from Ushant in position 49.30N 04.50W by the German submarine *UC 21* whilst on a voyage from Buenos Aires to Hull with a cargo of maize.

TREVEAN 3081 Grt. Blt. 1902
22.1.1917: Captured and sunk with bombs in the Atlantic 240 miles S.W. by W. from the Fastnet Rock in position 48.00N 13.00W by the German submarine *U 57* whilst on a voyage from Benisaf to Tyne with a cargo of iron ore. Master and 2 Gunners taken prisoner.

TREVOSE 3112 Grt. Blt. 1896
18.3.1917: Torpedoed and sunk in the Atlantic 230 miles W. by N.½N. from Ushant in position 48.40N 11.29W by the German submarine *U 81* whilst on a voyage from Tyne to Italy with a cargo of coal. 2 lost.

TREFUSIS 2642 Grt. Blt. 1893
7.4.1917: Captured and sunk with bombs in the Mediterranean 30 miles S.E. from Cape Pula, Sardinia by the German submarine *U 65* whilst on a voyage from Cardiff to Alexandria with a cargo of coal. Master, Chief Officer and Chief Engineer taken prisoner.

TREMORVAH 3654 Grt. Blt. 1905
11.4.1917: Captured and sunk by gunfire in the Mediterranean 70 miles N.N.W. from Cape Bougaroni in position 38.50N 05.45E by the German submarine *U 65* whilst on a voyage from Malta to Gibraltar in ballast. Master, Chief Engineer and 2 Gunners taken prisoner.

TREKIEVE 3087 Grt. Blt. 1898
18.4.1917: Torpedoed and sunk in the Atlantic 100 miles W. from Gibraltar in position 35.00N 09.45W by the German submarine *U 35* whilst on a voyage from Cardiff to Genoa with a cargo of coal. 3 lost, Master taken prisoner.

TRELISSICK 4168 Grt. Blt. 1909
15.7.1917: Torpedoed and sunk in the Atlantic 80 miles S.W. by W.¼W. from Ushant in position 47.28N 06.28W by the German submarine *UC 72* whilst on a voyage from Boston. Mass. to Bordeaux with a cargo of oats and steel. Master and 2 Gunners taken prisoner.

TRELYON 3099 Grt. Blt. 1898
20.7.1917: Struck a mine and damaged in the North Sea 3 miles N. from Scarborough in position 54.18N 00.20W laid by the German submarine *UB 21* whilst on a voyage from Archangel to Methil and London with a cargo of timber. She went ashore, afterwards refloated and beached at White Nab, Scarborough but became a total loss.

TRELOSKE 3071 Grt. Blt. 1902
29.8.1917: Torpedoed and sunk in the Atlantic 145 miles N. by W.¾W. from Cape Finisterre in position 44.50N 11.20W by the German submarine *U 93* whilst on a voyage from Barry to Spezia with general cargo and coal. 1 lost.

TREVERBYN 4163 Grt. Blt. 1910
3.9.1917: Struck a mine and sunk in the Inner Hebrides 2 miles E.S.E. from Ushinish Lighthouse, South Uist, Outer Hebrides laid by the German submarine *U 75* whilst on a voyage from Narvik to Manchester with a cargo of iron ore. 27 lost including Master.

TREGENNA 5772 Grt. Blt. 1917
26.12.1917: Torpedoed and sunk in the English Channel 9 miles S. from Dodman Point by the German submarine *UB 57* whilst on her maiden voyage from Tyne to Gibraltar with a cargo of coal.

TREVEAL 4160 Grt. Blt. 1909
4.2.1918: Torpedoed and sunk in the Irish Sea off the Skerries, Anglesey by the German submarine *U 53* whilst on a voyage from Algiers to Barrow with a cargo of iron ore. 33 lost including Master.

Mercantile Steam Ship Co. Ltd.—London

DART 3207 Grt. Blt. 1898
14.6.1917: Torpedoed and sunk in the Atlantic 6 miles S.S.W. from Ballycottin Lighthouse by the German submarine *UC 47* whilst on a voyage from Huelva to Garston with a cargo of pyrites. 4 lost.

GANGES 4177 Grt. Blt. 1902
30.7.1917: Torpedoed and sunk in the Atlantic 8 miles S.W. from Cape Spartel by the German submarine *U 39* whilst on a voyage from Barry to Spezia with a cargo of coal. 1 lost.

NESS 3050 Grt. Blt. 1896
25.10.1917: Captured and sunk by gunfire in the Mediterranean 10 miles S.E. from

Cabo de Gata by the German submarine *U 64* whilst on a voyage from Sfax to Gibraltar with a cargo of phosphates. 2 lost.

AYR 3050 Grt. Blt. 1894
8.3.1918: Torpedoed and sunk in the Mediterranean 31 miles N.½W. from Linosa Island in position 36.23N 13.45E by the Austro-Hungarian submarine *U 28* whilst on a voyage from Alexandria to Bizerta with a cargo of lead and cotton.

HALDIN & CO. LTD.—LONDON

Court Line

ILVINGTON COURT ex *Dalebank* **4217 Grt. Blt. 1911**
6.12.1917: Torpedoed and sunk in the Mediterranean 8 miles N.W. by W. from Cape Shershel in position 36.43N 02.06E by the German submarine *U 34* whilst on a voyage from Barry to Malta with a cargo of coal. 8 lost.

HALL BROTHERS—NEWCASTLE UPON TYNE

Hall Brothers Steamship Co. Ltd.

DIADEM 3752 Grt. Blt. 1906
23.2.1916: Captured and sunk by gunfire in the Mediterranean 56 miles S.E. by S. from Ile de Porquerolles by the German submarine *U 38* whilst on a voyage from Marseilles to Port Said in ballast.

TRIDENT 3129 Grt. Blt. 1902
7.8.1916: Captured and torpedoed in the Mediterranean 34 miles N. by E.¾E. from Dragonera Island by the German submarine *U 35* whilst on a voyage from Penarth to Leghorn with a cargo of coal.

BRETWALDA 4037 Grt. Blt. 1911
13.12.1916: Torpedoed and sunk in the Mediterranean 220 miles E. by S. from Malta in position 35.30N 19.05E by the German submarine *UB 43* whilst on a voyage from Calcutta to Boulogne with a cargo of jute.

CILURNUM ex *Bishopsgate* **3126 Grt. Blt. 1902**
19.4.1917: Torpedoed and sunk in the Bay of Biscay 5 miles S.W. from Pointe de Penmarch in position 47.45N 04.30W by the German submarine *UC 21* whilst on a voyage from Cardiff to La Pallice with a cargo of coal. 1 lost.

DIADEM 4307 Grt. Blt. 1916
21.4.1917: Torpedoed and sunk in the Atlantic 200 miles S.W. by W. from the Fastnet Rock in position 48.37N 12.40W by the German submarine *U 50* whilst on a voyage from Bassein and Dakar to London with a cargo of rice.

PEERLESS 3112 Grt. Blt. 1898
4.9.1917: Torpedoed and sunk in the Atlantic 60 miles S.W. from Bishop Rock by the German submarine *U 52* whilst on a voyage from Lisbon to Manchester with a cargo of ore and cork. 2 lost, Master and 2 Gunners taken prisoner.

HALL, JOHN JNR. & CO. LTD.—LONDON

LUSITANIA 1834 Grt. Blt. 1903
17.11.1915: Struck a mine and sunk in the Strait of Dover 1 mile E. from Folkestone Gate laid by the German submarine *UC 5* whilst on a voyage from London to Cadiz with general cargo.

BRITANNIA 1814 Grt. Blt. 1902
8.12.1916: Torpedoed and sunk in the Atlantic 70 miles W. by S. from Cape Sines, near Sines in position 37.18N 10.29W by the German submarine *U 38* whilst on a voyage from London to Gibraltar with a cargo of Government stores and munitions. 2 lost, Master taken prisoner.

GALICIA ex *Tervoe* ex *Jabiru* **1400 Grt. Blt. 1899**
10.6.1917: Torpedoed and sunk in the Atlantic 140 miles S.W. by S.½S. from the Fastnet Rock in position 48.55N 10.00W by the German submarine *U 70* whilst on a voyage from Malaga to London with general cargo. 4 lost.

PENINSULA ex *Doris* ex *Prudent* **1384 Grt. Blt. 1877**
25.7.1917: Torpedoed and sunk in the Atlantic 235 miles S.W. from the Fastnet Rock in position 48.00N 11.10W by the German submarine *U 46* whilst on a voyage from London to Lisbon with general cargo. 1 lost.

HALLETT, N. & COMPANY—LONDON

Wing S.S. Co. Ltd.

SWIFT WINGS ex *Watermouth* **4465 Grt. Blt. 1911**
1.9.1916: Torpedoed and sunk in the Mediterranean 18 miles E. from Cape Bengut by the German submarine *U 38* whilst on a voyage from Cardiff to Malta with a cargo of coal and petrol. 2 lost, Master taken prisoner.

HANSEN BROTHERS LIMITED—CARDIFF

PENYLAN ex *Okehampton* **3875 Grt. Blt. 1906**
19.10.1916: Torpedoed and sunk in the Mediterranean 5 miles W. by N. from Cape Bourgaroni in position 37.07N 06.26E by the German submarine *U 39* whilst on a voyage from Newport, Mon. to Malta with a cargo of coal.

ROSE LEA 2830 Grt. Blt. 1902
14.3.1917: Torpedoed and sunk in the Atlantic 230 miles W. from Bishop Rock in position 48.45N 12.08W by the German submarine *U 62* whilst on a voyage from Cardiff to Malta with a cargo of coal.

TREDEGAR HALL 3764 Grt. Blt. 1906
23.10.1917: Torpedoed and sunk in the North Sea 4½ miles E.S.E. from Flamborough Head by the German submarine *UB 57* whilst on a voyage from Melilla to Middlesbrough with a cargo of iron ore. 3 lost.

WINDSOR HALL 3693 Grt. Blt. 1910
17.1.1918: Torpedoed and sunk in the Mediterranean 45 miles N.W. from Alexandria by the German submarine *UB 66* whilst on a voyage from Karachi to Marseilles with a cargo of grain. 27 lost, Master taken prisoner.

WELBECK HALL 5643 Grt. Blt. 1914
22.4.1918: Torpedoed and sunk in the Mediterranean 75 miles N.E. by N. from Port Said by the German submarine *UB 53* whilst on a voyage from Piraeus to Port Said in ballast. 4 lost.

Hansen Shipping Co. Ltd.

HOLGATE 2604 Grt. Blt. 1896
27.3.1917: Torpedoed and sunk in the Atlantic 10 miles N.W. from the Skelligs in position 51.43N 10.48W by the German submarine *U 57* whilst on a voyage from Almeria to Barrow with a cargo of iron ore. Master taken prisoner.

BLAGDON 1996 Grt. Blt. 1893
9.8.1917: Torpedoed and sunk in the North Sea 75 miles E. by S. from Muckle Flugga by the German submarine *U 100* whilst on a voyage from Lerwick to Bergen and Archangel with a cargo of herrings. 12 lost including Master.

Standish Hall S.S. Co. Ltd.

STANDISH HALL 3996 Grt. Blt. 1912
4.2.1918: Torpedoed and sunk in the Mediterranean 38 miles W. by N. from Alexandria by the German submarine *U 33* whilst on a voyage from Bizerta to Alexandria with general cargo.

HARDIE, JOHN & COMPANY—GLASGOW

Clutha Shipping Co. Ltd.

JOHN HARDIE 4372 Grt. Blt. 1906
6.9.1915: Captured and sunk by gunfire in the Atlantic 98 miles W. by S. from Cape Finisterre in position 42.10N 11.15W by the German submarine *U 33* whilst on a voyage from Java to Clyde with a cargo of sugar.

CALDERGROVE 4327 Grt. Blt. 1909
6.3.1917: Torpedoed and sunk in the Atlantic 200 miles W.N.W. from the Fastnet Rock in position 51.30N 14.51W by the German submarine *U 44* whilst on a voyage from Havana to Queenstown with a cargo of sugar. 19 lost including Master.

HARLAND, G. B. & COMPANY—WEST HARTLEPOOL

ANTIGUA 2876 Grt. Blt. 1903
14.7.1916: Captured and sunk with bombs in the Mediterranean 20 miles E. by N. from Jidjelli in position 36.57N 06.11E by the German submarine *U 39* whilst on a voyage from La Goulette to Middlesbrough with a cargo of iron ore.

ROMSDALEN 2548 Grt. Blt. 1895
17.2.1917: Torpedoed and sunk in the English Channel 10 miles S.W. from Portland Bill in position 50.22N 02.35W by the German submarine *U 84* whilst on a voyage from Swansea to Calais with a cargo of patent fuel.

GREENBANK 3881 Grt. Blt. 1905
3.6.1917: Captured and torpedoed in the Mediterranean 12 miles N. from Cape Falcon, Algeria in position 36.00N 00.50W by the German submarine *U 33* whilst on a voyage from Cardiff to Alexandria with a cargo of coal. 1 lost.

HARPER, H. G. & COMPANY—CARDIFF

CANFORD CHINE ex *Malfen* **2398 Grt. Blt. 1903**
24.6.1916: Captured and sunk by gunfire in the Mediterranean 5 miles from Calella, near Barcelona by the German submarine *U 35* whilst on a voyage from Marseilles to Porman in ballast.

Branksome Chine S.S. Co. Ltd.

BRANKSOME CHINE ex *Anna* **2026 Grt. Blt. 1899**
23.2.1915: Torpedoed and sunk in the English Channel 6 miles E. by S. ¾ S. from Beachy Head by the German submarine *U 8* whilst on a voyage from Grimsby Roads to Portsmouth with a cargo of coal.

HARRIS BROTHERS & COMPANY—SWANSEA

ALACRITY 1080 Grt. Blt. 1883
31.3.1916: Struck a mine and sunk in the North Sea off Lowestoft laid by the German submarine *UC 5* whilst on a voyage from Le Havre to Seaham Harbour in ballast. 14 lost including Master.

STAMFORDHAM 921 Grt. Blt. 1898
4.8.1916: Captured and sunk by gunfire in the North Sea 8 miles S. from Longstone by the German submarine *UB 39* whilst on a voyage from Kirkwall, Orkney Islands to Seaham Harbour in ballast.

GLYNYMEL ex *Maria Regier* ex *Abchurch* ex *Balear* **1394 Grt. Blt. 1890**
12.3.1917: Captured and torpedoed in the English Channel 23 miles S. by W. from St. Catherine's Point in position 50.12N 01.11W by the German submarine *UC 66* whilst on a voyage from Le Havre to Swansea in ballast. 1 lost.

LONGBENTON 924 Grt. Blt. 1898
27.6.1917: Torpedoed and sunk in the North Sea 12 miles S. by W. from Flamborough Head in position 53.55N 00.03W by the German submarine *UC 63* whilst on a voyage from Tyne to Devonport with a cargo of coal.

SONNIE 2642 Grt. Blt. 1917
11.8.1917: Torpedoed and sunk in the English Channel 5 miles N.W. from Le Four Lighthouse, near Ushant in position 48.34N 04.55W by the German submarine *UC 77* whilst on a voyage from Bilbao to Port Talbot with a cargo of iron ore. 11 lost.

LLWYNGWAIR 1304 Grt. Blt. 1913
26.4.1918: Torpedoed and sunk in the North Sea 5 miles S.S.E. from Seaham Harbour by the German submarine *UC 64* whilst on a voyage from Dunkirk to Tyne in ballast. 8 lost including Master.

HARRIS & DIXON LIMITED—LONDON

Century Shipping Co. Ltd.

SARAGOSSA 3541 Grt. Blt. 1916
8.6.1917: Torpedoed and sunk in the Atlantic 178 miles N.W. from the Fastnet

Rock in position 52.23N 14.12W by the German submarine *U 69* whilst on a voyage from Cuba and Halifax, (NS) to Queenstown with a cargo of sugar.

HAREWOOD 4150 Grt. Blt. 1913
13.4.1918: Captured and sunk by gunfire in the Atlantic 380 miles W. by S.(true) from Lisbon by the German submarine *U 155* whilst on a voyage from New York to Gibraltar with general cargo. 2 lost including Master.

HARRISON, J. & C. LIMITED—LONDON

HARPALION 5867 Grt. Blt. 1910
24.2.1915: Torpedoed and damaged in the English Channel 6½ miles W. from Royal Sovereign Lightvessel by the German submarine *U 8* and sunk on the 26.2.1915—40 miles off Cape d'Antifer whilst on a voyage from London to Newport News in ballast. 3 lost.

HARPALYCE 5940 Grt. Blt. 1911
10.4.1915: Torpedoed and sunk in the North Sea 7 miles E. by S. from North Hinder Lightvessel by the German submarine *UB 4* whilst on a voyage from Rotterdam to Tyne in ballast. 15 lost including Master.

HARMATRIS 6387 Grt. Blt. 1912
8.3.1916: Torpedoed and sunk in the English Channel ¼ mile N.E. by N. from Boulogne breakwater by the German submarine *UB 18* whilst on a voyage from St. John (NB) to Le Havre and Boulogne with a cargo of oats and hay. 4 lost.

HARFLETE 4814 Grt. Blt. 1913
26.4.1917: Captured by gunfire and torpedoed in the Atlantic 200 miles N.W. by W. from the Fastnet Rock in position 51.54N 14.48W by the German submarine *U 70* whilst on a voyage from Cienfuegos to Queenstown with a cargo of sugar. 1 lost.

HARMATTAN 4792 Grt. Blt. 1911
5.5.1917: Struck a mine and sunk in the Mediterranean 30 miles off Cape Bon laid by the German submarine *UC 37* whilst on a voyage from Avonmouth and Gibraltar to—with a part cargo of Government stores. 36 lost including Master.

HARPAGUS 5866 Grt. Blt. 1910
9.5.1917: Torpedoed and sunk in the Mediterranean 62 miles S.W. from Planier Island by the German submarine *U 34* whilst on a voyage from New York to Marseilles with general cargo. 3 lost, Master and Chief Engineer taken prisoner.

HARBURY 4572 Grt. Blt. 1913
9.6.1917: Torpedoed and sunk in the Atlantic 170 miles W.½N. from Ushant in position 47.47N 09.16W by the German submarine *U 70* whilst on a voyage from Buenos Aires to Cherbourg with a cargo of oats and maize. 12 lost including Master.

HARPATHIAN 4588 Grt. Blt. 1913
5.6.1918: Torpedoed and sunk in the Atlantic 80 miles off Cape Henry, Virginia by the German submarine *U 151* whilst on a voyage from Plymouth to Newport News in ballast.

HARRISON, JOHN. LIMITED—LONDON

CATERHAM ex *Burndyke* ex *Indian Prince* **1777 Grt. Blt. 1886**
13.11.1916: Captured and sunk with bombs in the English Channel 15 miles S.S.E. from Beachy Head by the German submarine *UB 38* whilst on a voyage from Rouen to Tyne in ballast.

HARRISON, SONS & CO. LTD.—CARDIFF

Town Line (London) Ltd.

ENNISTOWN ex *Eimstad* **689 Grt. Blt. 1908**
24.3.1917: Captured and sunk with bombs in the St. George's Channel 10 miles S.E. from South Arklow Lightvessel by the German submarine *UC 65* whilst on a voyage from Dublin to Cardiff in ballast.

BUTETOWN ex *Karanja* **1829 Grt. Blt. 1907**
29.1.1918: Torpedoed and sunk in the English Channel 1½ miles S. from Dodman Point by the German submarine *UB 40* whilst on a voyage from Clyde to Portsmouth with a cargo of coal. 2 lost.

HARRISON, THOMAS & JAMES—LIVERPOOL

Charente S.S. Co. Ltd.

CANDIDATE 5858 Grt. Blt. 1906
6.5.1915: Captured and torpedoed in the St. George's Channel 13 miles S. by E.¼E. from Coningbeg Lightvessel by the German submarine *U 20* whilst on a voyage from Liverpool to Kingston (Ja) with general cargo.

CENTURION 5495 Grt. Blt. 1908
6.5.1915: Torpedoed and sunk in the St. George's Channel 20 miles S. from Coningbeg Lightvessel by the German submarine *U 20* whilst on a voyage from Liverpool to South Africa with general cargo.

GLADIATOR 3359 Grt. Blt. 1904
18.8.1915: Captured and sunk by gunfire in the Atlantic 68 miles N. by W. from Bishop Rock by the German submarine *U 27* whilst on a voyage from Liverpool and Cardiff to Pernambuco with general cargo.

DICTATOR 4116 Grt. Blt. 1891
5.9.1915: Captured and sunk by gunfire in the Atlantic 135 miles S. by W. from the Fastnet Rock in position 49.09N 08.58W by the German submarine *U 20* whilst on a voyage from Pernambuco to Liverpool with general cargo.

CHANCELLOR ex *St. Cuthbert* **4586 Grt. Blt. 1895**
23.9.1915: Captured and sunk by gunfire in the Atlantic 86 miles S. by E. from the Fastnet Rock in position 50.08N 08.17W by the German submarine *U 41* whilst on a voyage from Liverpool to New Orleans with general cargo.

COMMODORE 5858 Grt. Blt. 1906
2.12.1915: Captured and sunk with bombs in the Mediterranean 160 miles E.S.E. from Malta in position 35.10N 17.39E by the German submarine *U 33* whilst on a voyage from Salonica to Marseilles in ballast. 1 lost.

***COUNSELLOR** 4958 Grt. Blt. 1903*
14.9.1916: Struck a mine and sunk in the Atlantic 5 miles W.½S. from Galley Head in position 51.28N 09.03W laid by the German submarine *U 79* whilst on a voyage from San Francisco and Colon to Liverpool with a cargo of barley and timber.

***STATESMAN** 6153 Grt. Blt. 1895*
3.11.1916: Torpedoed and sunk in the Mediterranean 200 miles E. from Malta in position 36.00N 18.30E by the German submarine *UB 43* whilst on a voyage from Liverpool to Calcutta with general cargo. 6 lost.

***ARTIST** 3570 Grt. Blt. 1909*
27.1.1917: Torpedoed and sunk in the St. George's Channel 58 miles W.½S. from the Smalls in position 51.20N 07.00W by the German submarine *U 55* whilst on a voyage from Newport, Mon. to Alexandria with a cargo of coal. 35 lost including Master.

***HUNTSMAN** 7460 Grt. Blt. 1904*
25.2.1917: Torpedoed and sunk in the Atlantic 180 miles N.W. by W. from the Fastnet Rock in position 52.04N 12.02W by the German submarine *U 50* whilst on a voyage from Liverpool to Calcutta with general cargo. 2 lost.

***SCULPTOR** 3846 Grt. Blt. 1911*
18.4.1917: Torpedoed and sunk in the Atlantic 120 miles N.W. by W. from the Fastnet Rock in position 52.00N 13.00W by the German submarine *U 53* whilst on a voyage from New Orleans to Liverpool with general cargo. 1 lost.

***COMEDIAN** 4889 Grt. Blt. 1903*
29.4.1917: Torpedoed and sunk in the Atlantic 200 miles W. by S. from Bishop Rock in position 48.06N 10.45W by the German submarine *U 93* whilst on a voyage from St. John (NB) to Falmouth with a cargo of Government stores. 3 lost, 1 Gunner taken prisoner.

***BARRISTER** 3679 Grt. Blt. 1915*
11.5.1917: Torpedoed and sunk in the Atlantic 7 miles S.W. from Mine Head in position 51.48N 07.46W by the German submarine *U 49* whilst on a voyage from Pernambuco to Liverpool with general cargo.

***ORATOR** 3563 Grt. Blt. 1905*
8.6.1917: Torpedoed and sunk in the Atlantic 84 miles W.N.W. from the Fastnet Rock by the German submarine *U 96* whilst on a voyage from Pernambuco to Liverpool with general cargo. 5 lost.

***MATADOR** 3642 Grt. Blt. 1904*
3.7.1917: Torpedoed and sunk in the Atlantic 115 miles W. by N.½N. from the Fastnet Rock in position 51.16N 12.25W by the German submarine *UC 31* whilst on a voyage from New Orleans to Liverpool with general cargo. 2 lost.

***SPECTATOR** 3808 Grt. Blt. 1914*
19.8.1917: Torpedoed and sunk in the Atlantic 11 miles S.E. from Galley Head by the German submarine *UC 33* whilst on a voyage from Zanzibar to Liverpool with general cargo.

CIVILIAN 7871 Grt. Blt. 1902
6.10.1917: Torpedoed and sunk in the Mediterranean 15 miles N. from Alexandria by the German submarine *UC 74* whilst on a voyage from Liverpool to Calcutta with general cargo. 2 lost.

COLLEGIAN 7520 Grt. Blt. 1899
20.10.1917: Torpedoed and sunk in the Mediterranean 100 miles N.W. by N. ¼N. from Alexandria in position 32.35N 28.41E by the German submarine *UB 48* whilst on a voyage from Liverpool to Calcutta with general cargo and coal.

MECHANICIAN 9044 Grt. Blt. 1900
20.1.1918: Torpedoed and sunk in the English Channel 8 miles W. from St. Catherine's Point by the German submarine *UB 35* whilst on a voyage from London to—with a cargo of Government stores. 13 lost.

INKOSI 3661 Grt. Blt. 1902
28.3.1918: Torpedoed and sunk in the North Channel 10 miles S.W. of Burrow Head, Luce Bay by the German submarine *U 96* whilst on a voyage from Liverpool to Pernambuco with general cargo and coal. 3 lost.

SCULPTOR ex *Saint Andrew* **4874 Grt. Blt. 1912**
17.5.1918: Torpedoed and damaged in the Mediterranean 60 miles N.W. by W. ¼W. from Oran by the German submarine *UB 50* whilst on a voyage from Swansea to Bizerta and Salonica with Government cargo. Subsequently beached but became a total loss. 7 lost including Master.

BARRISTER ex *Saint Hugo* **4952 Grt. Blt. 1916**
19.9.1918: Torpedoed and sunk in the Irish Sea 9 miles W. ½N. from Chicken Rock Lighthouse, S.W. of the Isle of Man by the German submarine *UB 64* whilst on a voyage from Glasgow and Liverpool to West Indies with general cargo and mails. 30 lost.

HARRISON'S (LONDON) LIMITED—LONDON

HARLYN 1794 Grt. Blt. 1915
9.12.1916: Struck a mine and sunk in the North Sea 4 miles S.W. from Shipwash Lightvessel laid by the German submarine *UC 11* whilst on a voyage from Tyne to London with a cargo of coal. 2 lost.

HARROWING, ROBERT & COMPANY—WHITBY

The Harrowing S.S. Co. Ltd.

ETHELBRYHTA 3084 Grt. Blt. 1898
30.7.1916: Captured and sunk by gunfire in the Mediterranean 11 miles W.S.W. from Pantellaria Island in position 36.43N 11.44E by the German submarine *U 35* whilst on a voyage from St. Louis du Rhone to Salonica with a cargo of hay.

WILBERFORCE 3074 Grt. Blt. 1899
7.7.1917: Torpedoed and sunk in the Mediterranean 25 miles S. from Cabo de Gata by the German submarine *U 34* whilst on a voyage from Algiers to Middlesbrough with a cargo of iron ore. 1 lost, Master and Chief Engineer taken prisoner.

ETHELINDA ex *Brooklet* *3257 Grt. Blt. 1911*
29.1.1918: Torpedoed and sunk in the Irish Sea 15 miles N.W. from the Skerries, Anglesey by the German submarine *U 103* whilst on a voyage from Bilbao to Barrow with a cargo of iron ore. 26 lost including Master.

HAY, J. & SONS—GLASGOW

***THE PRESIDENT* 647 Grt. Blt. 1904**
10.4.1915: Captured and sunk with bombs in the English Channel 14 miles S. by W. from Lizard by the German submarine *U 24* whilst on a voyage from Clyde to St. Malo with a cargo of coal tar pitch.

***THE QUEEN* 557 Grt. Blt. 1897**
17.8.1915: Captured and sunk by gunfire in the St. George's Channel 40 miles N.N.E. from the Smalls by the German submarine *U 38* whilst on a voyage from Ayr to Devonport with a cargo of coal.

***THE MARCHIONESS* 553 Grt. Blt. 1899**
20.10.1916: Captured and sunk by gunfire in the English Channel 30 miles N.W. from Fécamp by the German submarine *UB 18* whilst on a voyage from Clyde to Fécamp with a cargo of coal.

HEADLAM & ROWLAND—WHITBY

***GOATHLAND* 3044 Grt. Blt. 1906**
4.7.1917: Torpedoed and sunk in the Bay of Biscay 10 miles S. from Belle Ile in position 47.15N 03.15W by the German submarine *U 84* whilst on a voyage from St. Nazaire to the Gulf of Mexico in ballast. 21 lost including Master.

***JOHN H. BARRY* 3083 Grt. Blt. 1899**
18.3.1918: Torpedoed and sunk in the Mediterranean 104 miles N. by W. ¾W. from Cape Bourgaroni by the German submarine *UB 52* whilst on a voyage from La Goulette to the United Kingdom with a cargo of iron ore. 3 lost including Master.

Rowland & Marwood S.S. Co. Ltd.

***SNEATON* 3470 Grt. Blt. 1915**
3.4.1916: Captured and sunk with bombs in the Mediterranean 35 miles N.N.E. from Cape de Garde, Tunis in position 37.35N 07.57E by the German submarine *U 34* whilst on a voyage from Hull to Alexandria with a cargo of coal.

***KILDALE* 3830 Grt. Blt. 1906**
12.4.1917: Torpedoed and sunk in the Mediterranean 40 miles E. by S. from Pantellaria Island by the German submarine *U 32* whilst on a voyage from Barry to Malta with general cargo. 1 lost.

***BEEMAH* 4750 Grt. Blt. 1914**
27.4.1917: Torpedoed and sunk in the Atlantic 30 miles S.W. by S. from Bishop Rock by the German submarine *UB 32* whilst on a voyage from Cardiff to Montevideo with a cargo of coal. 3 lost.

INGLESIDE 3736 Grt. Blt. 1910
8.5.1918: Torpedoed and sunk in the Mediterranean 80 miles N. by E. from Algiers in position 38.08N 03.20E by the German submarine *U 38* whilst on a voyage from La Goulette to Barry with a cargo of iron ore. 11 lost.

HENDERSON, P. & COMPANY—GLASGOW

British & Burmese Steam Navigation Co. Ltd.

AVA 5076 Grt. Blt. 1906
26.1.1917: Torpedoed and sunk in the Atlantic off S.W. Ireland probably by the German submarine *U 45* whilst on a voyage from Liverpool to Dakar and Rangoon carrying passengers and general cargo. 92 lost including Master.

PEGU 6348 Grt. Blt. 1913
8.7.1917: Torpedoed and sunk in the Atlantic 7 miles S.E. from Galley Head by the German submarine *U 57* whilst on a voyage from Rangoon to Liverpool and Clyde with a cargo of rice and beans. 1 lost.

HENRY, H. C.—SEATTLE

H. C. HENRY 4219 Grt. Blt. 1909
28.9.1915: Captured and sunk by gunfire in the Mediterranean 59 miles S.½E. from Cape Matapan by the German submarine *U 39* whilst on a voyage from London and Alexandria to Mudros with a cargo of tar oil.

HEPBURN, WALTER & COMPANY—CARDIFF

Stella Shipping Co. Ltd.

SOMMEINA ex *Tanagra 3317 Grt. Blt. 1899*
15.9.1917: Struck a mine and sunk in the English Channel 4 miles S.E. from Manacle Rocks laid by the German submarine *UC 69* whilst on a voyage from Tyne to Leghorn with Admiralty cargo.

HERO STEAM SHIP CO. LTD.—HALIFAX, NOVA SCOTIA

SCOTTISH HERO 2205 Grt. Blt. 1895
10.6.1917: Captured and sunk by gunfire in the Atlantic 440 miles W. by S.½S. from the Fastnet Rock in position 46.59N 18.12W by the German submarine *U 155* whilst on a voyage from Sydney, (CB) to Le Havre with a cargo of steel goods. 1 lost.

HERRON, JOHN & COMPANY—LIVERPOOL

POLVENA ex *Trifels 4750 Grt. Blt. 1904*
17.10.1917: Torpedoed and sunk in the English Channel 25 miles N. by E.¼E. from Ushant in position 48.55N 05.10W by the German submarine *U 53* whilst on a voyage from Beira to London with general cargo. 3 lost.

HERSKIND & COMPANY—WEST HARTLEPOOL

ROWENA 3017 Grt. Blt. 1899
18.4.1917: Torpedoed and sunk in the Atlantic 95 miles W. by S.½S. from Bishop

Rock in position 49.03N 08.25W by the German submarine *U 84* whilst on a voyage from Alexandria to Hull with general cargo. 1 lost.

HORSA *2949 Grt. Blt. 1894*
30.4.1917: Torpedoed and sunk in the Atlantic 195 miles S.W. by W. from the Fastnet Rock in position 48.43N 12.35W by the German submarine *U 93* whilst on a voyage from Port Breira to Cardiff with a cargo of iron ore. Master, 11 Crew and 1 Gunner taken prisoner.

HESSLER & COMPANY—WEST HARTLEPOOL

The Hartlepools Seatonia S.S. Co. Ltd.

SEATONIA* ex *Mancunia 3533 Grt. Blt. 1898
1.11.1916: Captured and torpedoed in the Atlantic 80 miles N.W. ½N. from the Fastnet Rock in position 52.00N 11.30W by the German submarine *U 49* whilst on a voyage from Musgrave to Barry Roads with a cargo of pit props.

WEARSIDE 3560 Grt. Blt. 1899
25.10.1917: Struck a mine and sunk in the mouth of the River Thames 3 miles W. by S. from the Sunk Lightvessel laid by the German submarine *UC 11* whilst on a voyage from Tyne to Genoa with a cargo of coal.

HEYN, G. & SONS LIMITED—BELFAST

Head Line

ORLOCK HEAD 1945 Grt. Blt. 1913
12.4.1916: Captured and sunk by gunfire in the Mediterranean 65 miles S.E. from Barcelona by the German submarine *U 34* whilst on a voyage from Genoa and Valencia to Glasgow with general cargo.

INISHOWEN HEAD 3050 Grt. Blt. 1886
14.2.1917: Struck a mine and sunk in the St. George's Channel 1¼ miles S. from Skokham Island in position 51.40N 05.15W laid by the German submarine *UC 65* whilst on a voyage from Port Talbot to St. John (NB) in ballast. 1 lost.

BRAY HEAD 3077 Grt. Blt. 1894
14.3.1917: Captured and sunk by gunfire in the Atlantic 375 miles N.W. by W. from the Fastnet Rock in position 52.04N 18.50W by the German submarine *U 44* whilst on a voyage from St. John (NB) to Belfast with general cargo. 21 lost including Master.

HOWTH HEAD 4440 Grt. Blt 1906
19.4.1917: Torpedoed and sunk in the Atlantic 158 miles N.W. from the Fastnet Rock in position 52.20N 13.38W by the German submarine *U 60* whilst on a voyage from New Orleans and Norfolk (Va) to Dublin with general cargo. 2 lost.

TORR HEAD 5911 Grt. Blt. 1894
20.4.1917: Torpedoed and sunk in the Atlantic 160 miles N.W. by W. from the Fastnet Rock in position 52.10N 14.00W by the German submarine *U 60* whilst on a voyage from St. John (NB) to Dublin with general cargo.

DUNMORE HEAD 2293 Grt. Blt. 1889
27.4.1917: Torpedoed and sunk in the Atlantic 135 miles N.W. from Tory Island in position 56.12N 12.00W by the German submarine *U 62* whilst on a voyage from Manchester to Genoa with a cargo of coal and ammunition.

BENGORE HEAD 2490 Grt. Blt. 1884
20.6.1917: Captured and torpedoed in the Atlantic 150 miles N.W. from the Fastnet Rock in position 52.19N 13.39W by the German submarine *U 62* whilst on a voyage from Sydney (CB) to London with general cargo.

BLACK HEAD 1898 Grt. Blt. 1912
21.6.1917: Torpedoed and sunk in the North Sea 52 miles E.S.E. from Out Skerries, Shetland Islands in position 60.22N 01.00E by the German submarine *U 19* whilst on a voyage from Drammen to Lerwick with a cargo of wood pulp.

WHITE HEAD 1172 Grt. Blt. 1880
15.10.1917: Torpedoed and sunk in the Mediterranean 40 miles N.N.E. from Suda Bay by the German submarine *UC 74*. 23 lost.

GARRON HEAD 1933 Grt. Blt. 1913
16.11.1917: Torpedoed and sunk in the Bay of Biscay 40 miles N. by E. ½ E. from Bayonne by the German submarine *U 103* whilst on a voyage from Bilbao to Barrow and Maryport with a cargo of iron ore. 28 lost.

GLENARM HEAD 3908 Grt. Blt. 1897
5.1.1918: Torpedoed and sunk in the English Channel 5 miles S.W. by S. from Brighton Lightvessel in position 50.34N 00.12W by the German submarine *UB 30* whilst on a voyage from Southampton to Boulogne with a cargo of ammunition. 2 lost including Master.

TEELIN HEAD 1718 Grt. Blt. 1883
21.1.1918: Torpedoed and sunk in the English Channel 12 miles S.S.W. from Owers Lightvessel by the German submarine *UC 31* whilst on a voyage from Belfast to— with a cargo of potatoes. 13 lost including Master.

The Shipping Controller

HUNTSMOOR ex *Rostock* 4957 Grt. Blt. 1901
20.2.1918: Torpedoed and sunk in the English Channel 23 miles S. ½ W. from Owers Lightvessel by the German submarine *UB 40* whilst on a voyage from Le Havre to Southampton in ballast. 20 lost including Master.

HUNGERFORD ex *Lauterfels* 5811 Grt. Blt. 1913
16.4.1918: Torpedoed and sunk in the English Channel 9 miles S.S.E. from Owers Lightvessel by the German submarine *UC 75* whilst on a voyage from Le Havre to New York via St. Helens Roads in ballast. 8 lost.

HICK, THOMAS & COMPANY—LONDON

Cassar Ltd.

ANT CASSAR ex *Rio Sorocaba* ex *Yorkmoor* 3544 Grt. Blt. 1902
7.8.1918: Torpedoed and sunk in the St. George's Channel 30 miles N.N.W. from

Strumble Head in position 52.25N 05.45W by the German submarine *UB 118* whilst on a voyage from Clyde to Milford Haven with a cargo of coal.

HILL, CHARLES & SONS—BRISTOL

Bristol City Line

***NEW YORK CITY* 2970 Grt. Blt. 1907**
19.8.1915: Captured and sunk by gunfire in the Atlantic 44 miles S.S.E. from the Fastnet Rock in position 51.00N 08.50W by the German submarine *U 24* whilst on a voyage from Bristol and Swansea to New York with general cargo.

***BRISTOL CITY* 2511 Grt. Blt. 1899**
16.12.1917: Torpedoed and sunk in the Atlantic S.W. of Ireland by the German submarine *U 94* whilst on a voyage from Bristol to New York with general cargo. 30 lost including Master.

***BOSTON CITY* 2711 Grt. Blt. 1917**
2.1.1918: Torpedoed and sunk in St. George's Channel 11 miles W.½N. from St. Ann's Head, Milford Haven in position 51.40N 05.26W by the German submarine *U 91* whilst on a voyage from Bristol to New York with general cargo.

HINDE, W. E. & COMPANY—CARDIFF

Portloe S.S. Co. Ltd.

***PORTLOE* 3187 Grt. Blt. 1912**
20.4.1917: Torpedoed and sunk in the Atlantic 160 miles W.N.W. from the Fastnet Rock in position 51.13N 14.10W by the German submarine *U 67* whilst on a voyage from Bougie to Clyde with a cargo of phosphate. 24 lost including Master.

HOBBS, LINSLEY & COMPANY—GRIMSBY

Bargate S.S. Co. Ltd.

KATHLEEN LILY ex *Eidsvaag* ex *Alban* ex *Adelaer* ex *Bjorn* ex *Jemtland* ex *Brage* **521 Grt. Blt. 1872**
29.3.1917: Struck a mine and sunk in the North Sea 2 miles E. from North Cheek, Robin Hood Bay in position 54.27½N 00.28W laid by the German submarine *UC 31* whilst on a voyage from Tyne to Boulogne with a cargo of coke. 4 lost including Master.

HOGARTH, H. & SONS LIMITED (BARON LINE)—GLASGOW

Hogarth Shipping Co. Ltd.

BARON ERSKINE ex *Bedlington* **5585 Grt. Blt. 1911**
19.8.1915: Captured and torpedoed in the Atlantic 25 miles N.N.W. from Bishop Rock by the German submarine *U 38* whilst on a voyage from Avonmouth to New Orleans in ballast.

***SAINT CECILIA* 4411 Grt. Blt. 1913**
26.3.1916: Struck a mine and sunk in the Strait of Dover 4 miles from Folkestone laid by the German submarine *UC 6* whilst on a voyage from Portland (Me) to London with general cargo.

BARON TWEEDMOUTH ex *Belle of Scotland* **5007 Grt. Blt. 1907**
30.5.1916: Captured and sunk by gunfire in the Mediterranean 25 miles N.E. by N. from Cape Carbon in position 37.10N 05.15E by the German submarine *U 39* whilst on a voyage from Clyde to Alexandria with a cargo of coal.

BARON CAWDOR 4316 Grt. Blt. 1905
9.6.1917: Torpedoed and sunk in the Atlantic 150 miles S.W. by S.½S. from the Fastnet Rock in position 48.56N 10.09W by the German submarine *U 96* whilst on a voyage from Rangoon to Avonmouth with a cargo of rice and maize. 3 lost.

BARON OGILVY 4570 Grt. Blt. 1909
27.6.1917: Torpedoed and sunk in the Atlantic 172 miles N.W. from Tory Island in position 56.13N 13.40W by the German submarine *U 93* whilst on a voyage from Montreal to Liverpool with a cargo of wheat. 2 lost.

BARON BALFOUR 3991 Grt. Blt. 1901
28.10.1917: Torpedoed and sunk in the Arctic 8 miles N. from Seim Island, Murmansk by the German submarine *U 46* whilst on a voyage from Archangel to Lerwick with a cargo of pit props.

Kelvin Shipping Co. Ltd.

BARON VERNON 1779 Grt. Blt. 1912
29.5.1916: Captured and sunk by gunfire in the Mediterranean 56 miles N.E.½N. from Algiers in position 37.36N 03.37E by the German submarine *U 39* whilst on a voyage from Savona to Seville in ballast.

BARON YARBOROUGH 1784 Grt. Blt. 1913
1.9.1916: Captured and sunk with bombs in the Mediterranean 27 miles N.W. from Dragonera Island in position 39.48N 01.51E by the German submarine *U 34* whilst on a voyage from Glasgow to Savona with a cargo of coal.

BARON SEMPILL 1607 Grt. Blt. 1911
16.1.1917: Captured and sunk with bombs in the Atlantic 180 miles S.W. from the Fastnet Rock in position 48.49N 11.45W by the German submarine *U 44* whilst on a voyage from Clyde to Huelva with general cargo.

BARON WEMYSS 1605 Grt. Blt. 1912
7.3.1917: Captured and torpedoed in the Atlantic 73 miles N.W. by W. from the Fastnet Rock in position 51.40N 11.30W by the German submarine *UC 43* whilst on a voyage from Huelva and Lisbon to Clyde with general cargo. 2 lost including Master.

BARON BLANTYRE ex *Castle Eden* **1844 Grt. Blt. 1908**
3.10.1917: Torpedoed and sunk in the Atlantic 60 miles N.W.¾W. from Cape Finisterre in position 43.15N 10.30W by the German submarine *U 89* whilst on a voyage from Clyde to Huelva with a cargo of coal. 1 lost.

BARON GARIOCH ex *Kirkstall* **1831 Grt. Blt. 1895**
28.10.1917: Torpedoed and sunk in the English Channel 5 miles S.E. from Anvil Point by the German submarine *UC 63* whilst on a voyage from Calais to Liverpool in ballast. 2 lost.

BARON HERRIES 1610 Grt. Blt. 1907
22.4.1918: Torpedoed and sunk in the Atlantic 43 miles N. by W. ½ W. from Bishop Rock in position 50.27N 07.06W by the German submarine *U 91* whilst on a voyage from Huelva to Glasgow with a cargo of copper ore, cork and fishoil. 3 lost, 2nd Officer taken prisoner.

BARON AILSA 1836 Grt. Blt. 1912
9.5.1918: Torpedoed and sunk in the St. George's Channel 18 miles W.N.W. from the Smalls probably by the German submarine *UB 72* whilst on a voyage from Queenstown to Barry with a cargo of Government stores. 10 lost.

HOGG, SDYNEY & COMPANY—WEST HARTLEPOOL

BRIERTON 3255 Grt. Blt. 1911
22.11.1916: Torpedoed and sunk in the Bay of Biscay 32 miles S.W. from Ushant in position 48.00N 05.32W by the German submarine *UC 26* whilst on a voyage from Karachi to Manchester with a cargo of grain.

Bury Shipping Co. Ltd.

WELBURY 3591 Grt. Blt. 1907
1.7.1915: Captured and sunk by gunfire in the Atlantic 40 miles W. from the Fastnet Rock by the German submarine *U 24* whilst on a voyage from Kingston (Ja) to Queenstown with a cargo of sugar.

HOLLAND, ARTHUR & CO. LTD—LONDON

Buenoa Ayres Great Southern Railway Co. Ltd.

LOMAS 3048 Grt. Blt. 1898
30.6.1915: Captured and torpedoed in the Atlantic 65 miles W. from Bishop Rock in position 49.30N 08.15W by the German submarine *U 39* whilst on a voyage from La Plata to Belfast with a cargo of maize. 1 lost.

NEUQUEN 3583 Grt. Blt. 1913
20.1.1917: Captured and torpedoed in the Atlantic 20 miles N.W. by W. from the Skelligs in position 51.50N 10.52W by the German submarine *U 84* whilst on a voyage from Rosario to Belfast with a cargo of maize. 18 lost including Master.

AZUL 3074 Grt. Blt. 1898
5.2.1917: Torpedoed and sunk in the Atlantic 180 miles W. ½ N. from the Fastnet Rock in position 50.30N 14.15W by the German submarine *U 54* whilst on a voyage from Buenos Aires to Cherbourg with a cargo of wheat. 11 lost.

TANDIL 2897 Grt. Blt. 1900
12.3.1917: Torpedoed and sunk in the English Channel 20 miles W. by N. ½ N. from Portland in position 50.30N 03.00W by the German submarine *U 85* whilst on a voyage from Barry to Portland with a cargo of coal. 4 lost.

ALFALFA ex *Whitgift* ***2993 Grt. Blt. 1898***
27.4.1917: Torpedoed and sunk in the Atlantic 30 miles S.W. of the Scilly Isles in position 49.15N 06.20W by the German submarine *UB 32* whilst on a voyage from Newport, Mon. to Malta with a cargo of coal. 30 lost including Master.

HOLLAND, F. S.—LONDON

HOLLINGTON 4221 Grt. Blt. 1912
3.6.1917: Torpedoed and sunk in the Atlantic 14 miles S. from Faeroe Islands by the German submarine *U 95* whilst on a voyage from Liverpool to Archangel in ballast. 30 lost including Master.

HOLLICK, WILLIAM—LONDON

Frumentum S.S. Co. Ltd.

COTOVIA 4020 Grt. Blt. 1911
22.7.1917: Struck a mine and sunk in the North Sea 2 miles S.E. by E. from Auskerry, Orkney Islands in position 59.01N 02.37W laid by the German submarine *UC 49* whilst on a voyage from Archangel to Dundee with a cargo of flax.

SABIA 2807 Grt. Blt. 1903
24.11.1917: Torpedoed and sunk in the English Channel 6 miles S.S.E. from the Lizard by the German submarine *U 96* whilst on a voyage from Seville to Manchester with a cargo of copper ore and cork. 11 lost.

HOLT, ALFRED & COMPANY (BLUE FUNNEL LINE)—LIVERPOOL

China Mutual Steam Navigation Co. Ltd.

KINTUCK 4639 Grt. Blt. 1895
2.12.1917: Probably struck a mine and sunk in the Atlantic 8 miles N.W. by N.½N. from Godrevy Lighthouse laid by the German submarine *UC 17* whilst on a voyage from London to Barry Roads in ballast. 1 lost.

MOYUNE 4935 Grt. Blt. 1895
12.4.1918: Torpedoed and sunk in the Mediterranean 32 miles S.E. by E. from Cape de Palos in position 37.26N 00.60W by the German submarine *U 34* whilst on a voyage from Karachi to Liverpool with a cargo of maize.

OOPACK 3883 Grt. Blt. 1894
4.10.1918: Torpedoed and sunk in the Mediteranean 110 miles E. from Malta in position 35.56N 16.20E by the German submarine *UB 68* whilst on a voyage from Milo Island to Malta in ballast.

Ocean Steam Ship Co. Ltd.

DIOMED 4672 Grt. Blt. 1895
22.8.1915: Captured and sunk by gunfire in the Atlantic 57 miles W.N.W. from Scilly Isles by the German submarine *U 38* whilst on a voyage from Liverpool to Shanghai with general cargo. 10 lost including Master.

ACHILLES 7043 Grt. Blt. 1900
31.3.1916: Torpedoed and sunk in the Atlantic 90 miles W.N.W. from Ushant by the German submarine *U 44* whilst on a voyage from Sydney, NSW and Cape Town to London and Liverpool with a cargo of cereals and wool. 5 lost.

TROILUS 7625 Grt. Blt. 1916
2.5.1917: Torpedoed and sunk in the Atlantic 140 miles W.N.W. from Malin Head

in position 55.22N 15.52W by the German submarine *U 69* whilst on a voyage from Yokohama to Liverpool with general cargo.

CALCHAS 6748 Grt. Blt. 1899
11.5.1917: Torpedoed and sunk in the Atlantic 5 miles W. by S. from Tearaght Island in position 52.00N 10.45W by the German submarine *U 80* whilst on a voyage from New York to Liverpool with general cargo.

PHEMIUS 6699 Grt. Blt. 1913
4.6.1917: Torpedoed and sunk in the Atlantic 80 miles N.W.½N. from Eagle Island in position 54.56N 12.07W by the German submarine *UC 45* whilst on a voyage from Liverpool to Hong Kong with general cargo.

POLYXENA ex Nerine ex Helgoland ex Maria Rickmers 5737 Grt. Blt. 1896
12.6.1917: Torpedoed and sunk in the Atlantic 57 miles W. from the Fastnet Rock in position 51.06N 11.50W by the German submarine *U 95* whilst on a voyage from Australia to Queenstown with a cargo of wheat. 7 lost.

LAERTES 4541 Grt. Blt. 1904
1.8.1917: Torpedoed and sunk in the English Channel 1¼ miles S.S.W. from Prawle Point by the German submarine *UB 31* whilst on a voyage from Southampton to Montreal in ballast. 14 lost.

VEGHTSTROOM 1353 Grt. Blt. 1902
23.8.1917: Torpedoed and sunk in the Atlantic 7 miles N.W. from Godrevy Lighthouse by the German submarine *UC 47* whilst on a voyage from Penarth to Le Havre with a cargo of coal. 5 lost.

ELVE 899 Grt. Blt. 1904
12.10.1917: Torpedoed and sunk in the Atlantic in position 46.23N 11.19W by the German submarine *U 22* whilst on a voyage from Oporto to London with general cargo. 31 lost.

EUMAEUS 6696 Grt. Blt. 1913
26.2.1918: Torpedoed and sunk in the Atlantic 24 miles N.N.E. from Ile de Vierge, near Ushant in position 49.50N 04.26W by the German submarine *U 55* whilst on a voyage from Yokohama to London with general cargo.

MACHAON 6738 Grt. Blt. 1899
27.2.1918: Torpedoed and sunk in the Mediterranean 50 miles N.E¾N. from Cani Rocks in position 38.40N 10.35E by the German submarine UC 27 whilst on a voyage from Liverpool to Yokohama with general cargo.

AUTOLYCUS 5806 Grt. Blt. 1917
12.4.1918: Torpedoed and sunk in the Mediterranean 32 miles S.E. by E. from Cape de Palos in position 38.01N 00.23E by the German submarine *U 34* whilst on a voyage from Hong Kong to Liverpool with general cargo.

GLAUCUS 5295 Grt. Blt. 1896
3.6.1918: Torpedoed and sunk in the Mediterranean 20 miles W. from Cape Granitola, Sicily in position 37.33N 12.15E by the German submarine *UB 68* whilst on a voyage from Liverpool to Shanghai with general cargo. 2 lost.

DIOMED* 7523 Grt. Blt. *1917
21.8.1918: Captured and sunk by gunfire in the Atlantic 195 miles E.S.E. from Nantucket Island by the German submarine *U 140* whilst on a voyage from Liverpool to New York in ballast. 2 lost.

The Admiralty

STOLT NIELSEN* 5684 Grt. Blt. *1917
11.3.1918: Torpedoed and sunk in the Mediterranean 38 miles S.½E. from Dellimara Point in position 35.10N 14.40E by the Austro-Hungarian submarine *U 28* whilst on a voyage from Taranto to Malta with general cargo.

HOLT, J. & COMPANY—LIVERPOOL

USSA* 2066 Grt. Blt. *1913
3.5.1917: Struck a mine and sunk in the English Channel 2½ miles N.W. from the west entrance to Cherbourg harbour in position 49.41N 01.39W laid by the German submarine *UC 26* whilst on a voyage from Manchester to Cherbourg with a cargo of hay and wagons.

JONATHAN HOLT* 1522 Grt. Blt. *1910
7.6.1917: Torpedoed and sunk in the Atlantic 130 miles N.W. by W.½W. from the Fastnet Rock in position 51.42N 14.10W by the German submarine *U 54* whilst on a voyage from Sierra Leone to Liverpool with a cargo of palm oil and kernels.

HOOD, A. F.—LONDON

Minterne S.S. Co. Ltd.

MINTERNE* 3018 Grt. Blt. *1903
3.5.1915: Torpedoed and sunk in the Atlantic 50 miles S.W. from Wolf Rock by the German submarine *U 30* whilst on a voyage from Cardiff to Buenos Aires with a cargo of coal. 2 lost.

UPCERNE* 2984 Grt. Blt. *1906
28.4.1918: Torpedoed and sunk in the North Sea 4 miles S.E. by S. from Coquet Island by the German submarine *UC 40* whilst on a voyage from Narvik to Middlesbrough with a cargo of iron ore and wood. 16 lost.

HOULDER BROTHERS & CO. LTD.—LONDON

British Empire Steam Navigation Co. Ltd.

BRISBANE RIVER* 4989 Grt. Blt. *1914
17.4.1917: Captured and sunk with bombs in the Atlantic 140 miles W. from Gibraltar in position 35.30N 08.10W by the German submarine *U 35* whilst on a voyage from Malta to Baltimore in ballast. Master taken prisoner.

SWAN RIVER* 4724 Grt. Blt. *1915
27.9.1917: Torpedoed and sunk in the Mediterranean 27 miles N.N.W. from Oran by the German submarine *U 39* whilst on a voyage from Gibraltar to Benisaf in ballast.

Empire Transport Co. Ltd.

NATAL TRANSPORT 4107 Grt. Blt. 1910
4.9.1915: Captured and sunk by gunfire in the Mediterranean 40 miles W. from Gavdo Island by the German submarine *U 34* whilst on a voyage from Bombay to Liverpool with general cargo.

IMPERIAL TRANSPORT 4648 Grt. Blt. 1913
11.4.1917: Torpedoed and sunk in the Mediterranean 140 miles N.W. by N. ½N. from Alexandria in position 33.11N 28.30E by the German submarine *UC 34* whilst on a voyage from Port Said to Phillippeville, Algeria in ballast. Master taken prisoner.

NEW ZEALAND TRANSPORT 4481 Grt. Blt. 1913
14.6.1917: Torpedoed and sunk in the Aegean Sea 8 miles S.E. from Serphopulo Island by the German submarine *UC 23* whilst on a voyage from Port Talbot to Mudros with a cargo of coal. 3 lost.

AFRICAN TRANSPORT 4482 Grt. Blt. 1913
25.6.1918: Torpedoed and sunk in the North Sea 3 miles N. from Whitby by the German submarine *UB 88* whilst on a voyage from Tyne to Falmouth with a cargo of coal. 3 lost.

AUSTRALIAN TRANSPORT 4784 Grt. Blt. 1911
23.8.1918: Torpedoed and sunk in the Mediterranean 40 miles W.N.W. from Marittimo Island in position 38.08N 11.10E by the German submarine *UC 27* whilst on a voyage from Karachi to Bizerta with a cargo of wheat and onions. 1 lost.

Houlder Line, Ltd.

OLDFIELD GRANGE 4653 Grt. Blt. 1913
11.12.1917: Torpedoed and sunk in the Atlantic 30 miles N.E. from Tory Island in position 55.46N 07.56W by the German submarine *U 62* whilst on a voyage from New York to Cardiff with general cargo.

HOULDER, MIDDLETON & CO. LTD.—LONDON

ALMORA 4385 Grt. Blt. 1899
2.10.1917: Torpedoed and sunk in the Atlantic 100 miles W. ½N. from Cape Spartel in position 35.30N 08.00W by the German submarine *U 39* whilst on a voyage from Barry to Gibraltar with a cargo of coal.

GOOD HOPE 3618 Grt. Blt. 1903
19.10.1917: Torpedoed and sunk in the Mediterranean 125 miles E. by S. from Malta in position 35.53N 17.05E by the Austro-Hungarian submarine *U 14* whilst on a voyage from Siphnos Island to Middlesbrough with a cargo of iron ore.

Mitre Shipping Co. Ltd.

HEADLEY 4953 Grt. Blt. 1914
19.2.1917: Torpedoed and sunk in the English Channel 50 miles S.W. of the Lizard in position 49.09N 06.29W by the German submarine *U 67* whilst on a voyage from Portland (Me) to London with general cargo.

FARLEY 3692 Grt. Blt. 1916
14.5.1917: Torpedoed and sunk in the Atlantic 70 miles S.W.½W. from Bishop Rock in position 48.56N 07.22W by the German submarine *UC 17* whilst on a voyage from Cardiff to New York in ballast.

CASPIAN 3606 Grt. Blt. 1894
20.5.1917: Captured and torpedoed in the Mediterranean 3½ miles E. from Cape Cervera, near Alicante by the German submarine *U 34* whilst on a voyage from Antofagasta to Savona with a cargo of nitrate. 25 lost including Master. Chief Engineer, 2nd Officer and 1 Gunner taken prisoner.

PURLEY 4500 Grt. Blt. 1913
25.7.1917: Torpedoed and sunk in the Atlantic 210 miles S.W.¼S. from the Fastnet Rock in position 48.08N 11.35W by the German submarine *U 46* whilst on a voyage from Barry to Malta with general cargo and coal.

PROPHET 3230 Grt. Blt. 1912
14.11.1917: Torpedoed and sunk in the Mediterranean 3 miles S.E. from Antikithera Island in position 35.47N 23.22E by the German submarine *UC 74* whilst on a voyage from Barry and Malta to Mudros with a cargo of Government stores and coal.

MOORLANDS 3602 Grt. Blt. 1910
25.6.1918: Torpedoed and sunk in the North Sea 3 miles S.E. by E. from Whitby by the German submarine *UB 88* whilst on a voyage from La Goulette to Middlesbrough with a cargo of iron ore. 10 lost.

HOULT, JOSEPH & CO. LTD.—LIVERPOOL

Steam Transport Co. Ltd.

BENGROVE 3840 Grt. Blt. 1910
7.3.1915: Torpedoed and sunk in the Bristol Channel 5˙ miles N.N.E. from Illfracombe by the German submarine *U 20* whilst on a voyage from Barry to— with a cargo of coal.

BENHEATHER 4701 Grt. Blt. 1913
5.4.1917: Torpedoed and sunk in the Atlantic 110 miles W.N.W. from the Fastnet Rock in position 51.20N 12.30W by the German submarine *U 46* whilst on a voyage from Halifax, (NS) to Falmouth with a cargo of timber.

HOUSTON, R. P. & COMPANY—LIVERPOOL

British & South American Steam Navigation Co. Ltd.

HESIONE ex *Mamari* 3363 Grt. Blt. 1889
23.9.1915: Captured and sunk by gunfire in the Atlantic 86 miles S. by E. from the Fastnet Rock in position 50.15N 08.30W by the German submarine *U 41* whilst on a voyage from Clyde and Liverpool to Buenos Aires with general cargo.

HALIZONES 5093 Grt. Blt. 1902
7.10.1915: Captured and sunk by gunfire in the Mediterranean 122 miles S.S.E.½E. from Cape Martello in position 33.10N 26.26E by the German submarine *U 39*

whilst on a voyage from Bombay to Liverpool with a cargo of cotton and manganese ore.

HERMIONE ex *Yarrawonga* *4011 Grt. Blt. 1891*
14.4.1917: Struck a mine and sunk in the St. George's Channel 1½ miles S. from Coningbeg Lightvessel laid by the German submarine *UC 33* whilst on a voyage from Buenos Aires to Liverpool with general cargo and a consignment of horses.

HESPERIDES 3393 Grt. Blt. 1899
25.4.1917: Torpedoed and sunk in the Atlantic 130 miles N.W.½W. from the Fastnet Rock in position 52.00N 13.50W by the German submarine *U 69* whilst on a voyage from Buenos Aires to Liverpool with general cargo. 1 lost.

HYLAS 4240 Grt. Blt. 1899
15.8.1917: Torpedoed and sunk in the Atlantic 10 miles E. from Butt of Lewis by the German submarine *U 80* whilst on a voyage from Archangel to Belfast with a cargo of flax.

HYPERIA ex *Pinners Point* *3908 Grt. Blt. 1895*
28.7.1918: Torpedoed and sunk in the Mediterranean 84 miles N.W. by N. from Port Said by the German submarine *UB 51* whilst on a voyage from Marseilles to Port Said with military cargo. 7 lost including Master.

HUDSON, JOHN & CO. LTD.—LONDON

HORNCHURCH 2159 Grt. Blt. 1916
3.8.1917: Struck a mine and sunk in the North Sea 3½ miles E.N.E. from Coquet Island laid by the German submarine *UC 29* whilst on a voyage from Methil to London with a cargo of coal. 2 lost.

HUMPHRIES (CARDIFF) LIMITED—CARDIFF

Globe Shipping Co. Ltd.

PAIGNTON 2017 Grt. Blt. 1911
14.3.1917: Captured and sunk by gunfire in the Atlantic 40 miles N.W. from the Skelligs in position 52.01N 11.29W by the German submarine *U 81* whilst on a voyage from Gibraltar to Clyde with a cargo of magnesite. 1 lost.

RIBERA 3511 Grt. Blt. 1915
10.6.1917: Torpedoed and sunk in the Atlantic 70 miles N. from Cape Wrath by the German submarine *U 61* whilst on a voyage from Cardiff to Archangel with a cargo of coal.

GLOCLIFFE 2211 Grt. Blt. 1915
19.8.1917: Torpedoed and sunk in the English Channel 9 miles E.N.E. from Berry Head in position 50.29N 03.17W by the German submarine *UB 40* whilst on a voyage from Cardiff to Southampton with a cargo of coal. 2 lost.

MARS 3550 Grt. Blt. 1907
8.7.1918: Torpedoed and sunk in the Atlantic 74 miles W. by N. from Bishop Rock in position 49.44N 08.20W by the German submarine *U 92* whilst on a voyage from New York to Le Havre with general cargo.

HUMPHRIES (CARDIFF) LIMITED—SYDNEY, NEW SOUTH WALES

The Hazelwood Shipping Co. Ltd.

SOUTHBOROUGH ex *Anerley* *3709 Grt. Blt. 1910*
16.7.1918: Torpedoed and sunk in the North Sea 5 miles N. by E.½E. from Scarborough by the German submarine *UB 110* whilst on a voyage from La Goulette to Tees with a cargo of iron ore. 30 lost including Master.

HUNTING & SON—NEWCASTLE UPON TYNE

Hunting S.S. Co. Ltd.

CLEARFIELD *4229 Grt. Blt. 1909*
24.10.1916: Torpedoed and sunk in the Atlantic off the Flannan Islands, Outer Hebrides by the German submarine *U 55* whilst on a voyage from Invergordon to Hampton Roads in ballast. 36 lost including Master.

OILFIELD *4000 Grt. Blt. 1896*
16.3.1918: Torpedoed and damaged in the Atlantic 15 miles N.W. from Cape Wrath by the German submarine *U 90* whilst on a voyage from Grangemouth and Methil to New York in ballast. 3 lost. She was beached and refloated but became a total loss.

Northern Petroleum Tank S.S. Co. Ltd.

GARFIELD *3838 Grt. Blt. 1907*
15.1.1917: Torpedoed and sunk 60 miles N.E. by N.½N. from Alexandria by the German submarine *U 39* whilst on a voyage from Malta to Port Said with a cargo of coal. Master taken prisoner.

Saxoleine S.S. Co. Ltd.

ARTESIA ex *Energie* *2762 Grt. Blt. 1888*
8.2.1918: Captured and sunk with bombs in the Atlantic 190 miles E. by N. from Madeira in position 34.30N 13.41W by the German submarine *U 156* whilst on a voyage from Cette to New York in ballast. 1 lost.

HUTCHINSON, E. P.—HULL

TUMMEL *531 Grt. Blt. 1912*
24.2.1916: Struck a mine and sunk off the mouth of the River Thames 7 miles S. from Kentish Knock Lightvessel laid by the German submarine *UC 5* whilst on a voyage from Grimsby to Treport with a cargo of coal. 9 lost.

HUTCHINSON, J. & P. LIMITED—GLASGOW

FASTNET *2227 Grt. Blt. 1887*
24.2.1916: Captured and sunk by gunfire in the Mediterranean 55 miles S.W. from Planier Island by the German submarine *U 38* whilst on a voyage from Savona to Cartagena in ballast.

DEWSLAND *1993 Grt. Blt. 1883*
1.6.1916: Captured and sunk by gunfire in the Mediterranean 28 miles N.E. by

E. from Cape Carbon in position 37.07N 05.30E by the German submarine *U 39* whilst on a voyage from Philippeville to Penarth with a cargo of lead and shumac (dried leaves used in tanning).

PLUTUS 1189 Grt. Blt. 1910
24.4.1917: Torpedoed and sunk in the Atlantic 9 miles N.N.W. from Trevose Head by the German submarine *UC 47* whilst on a voyage from Rouen to Barry in ballast. 1 lost.

DARTMOOR 2870 Grt. Blt. 1892
27.5.1917: Torpedoed and sunk in the Atlantic 35 miles S.E. from the Fastnet Rock in position 51.09N 08.46W by the German submarine *UC 50* whilst on a voyage from Bona to Garston with a cargo of iron ore. 25 lost including Master.

ACHILLES 641 Grt. Blt. 1900
9.6.1917: Captured and sunk by gunfire in the Atlantic 75 miles W. by S. from the Fastnet Rock by the German submarines *U 55* and *U 95* whilst on a voyage from Cadiz to Liverpool and Clyde with general cargo. Master and 1 Gunner taken prisoner.

CHLORIS ex *Pegwell* ex *Mary Horton* **984 Grt. Blt. 1904**
27.7.1918: Torpedoed and sunk in the North Sea 17 miles S. by E. from Flamborough Head in position 53.52N 00.10E by the German submarine *UB 107*. 3 lost including Master.

INDIA RUBBER, GUTTA PERCHA & TELEGRAPH WORKS CO. LTD.—LONDON

DACIA 1856 Grt. Blt. 1867
3.12.1916: Torpedoed and sunk in the Atlantic in Funchal Roads, Madeira by the German submarine *U 38* whilst on a voyage from Gibraltar to Madeira with a cargo of cable.

INDIAN & PENINSULAR STEAM NAVIGATION CO. LTD.—BOMBAY

MONGOLIAN 4892 Grt. Blt. 1891
21.7.1918: Torpedoed and sunk in the North Sea 5 miles S.E. from Filey Brigg in position 54.10N 00.58W by the German submarine *UC 70* whilst on a voyage from Tees to London with general cargo. 36 lost.

INDO-CHINA STEAM NAVIGATION CO. LTD.—HONG KONG

KUT SANG 4895 Grt. Blt. 1905
29.4.1918: Torpedoed and sunk in the Mediterranean 40 miles E.S.E. from Cape de Palos by the German submarine *UB 105* whilst on a voyage from Genoa to Gibraltar in ballast. 59 lost including Master.

INGLIS, JAMES & COMPANY—GLASGOW

FAIREARN 592 Grt. Blt. 1915
24.3.1917: Captured and sunk with bombs in the Irish Sea 16 miles W.N.W. from South Stack Rock by the German submarine *UC 65* whilst on a voyage from Garston to Cork with a cargo of coal.

INSTONE, S. & CO. LTD.—LONDON

Woolston S.S. Co. Ltd.

***KNUTSFORD* ex *Gripwell* ex *Knutsford* 3842 Grt. Blt. 1903**
22.7.1916: Captured and sunk by gunfire in the Mediterranean 12 miles N.W. by N. from Cape Corbelin in position 37.30N 04.17E by the German submarine *U 39* whilst on a voyage from Tunis to Baltimore with a cargo of zinc ore.

***WOOLSTON* ex *White Wings* ex *Claverley* 2986 Grt. Blt. 1900**
14.5.1918: Torpedoed and sunk in the Mediterranean 1½ miles from Syracuse harbour in position 37.30N 12.20E by the German submarine *UC 52* whilst on a voyage from Syracuse to Messina with a cargo of sulphur. 19 lost including Master.

INTERNATIONAL NAVIGATION CO. LTD.—LONDON

American Line

***SOUTHLAND* ex *Vaderland* 11899 Grt. Blt. 1900**
4.6.1917: Torpedoed and sunk in the Atlantic 140 miles N.W.½W. from Tory Island in position 56.10N 12.14W by the German submarine *U 70* whilst on a voyage from Liverpool to Philadelphia with general cargo. 4 lost.

INTERNATIONAL PETROLEUM CO. LTD.—TORONTO

***LUZ BLANCA* 4868 Grt. Blt. 1913**
5.8.1918: Torpedoed and sunk in the Atlantic 35 miles S.W. from Outer Gas Buoy, Halifax, (NS) by the German submarine *U 156* whilst on a voyage from Halifax, (NS) to Tampico in ballast. 2 lost.

ISLE OF MAN STEAM PACKET CO. LTD.—DOUGLAS

***SNAEFELL* 1368 Grt. Blt. 1910**
5.6.1918: Torpedoed and sunk in the Mediterranean between Malta and Crete by the German submarine *UB 105*. Lost whilst on Government service employed as an Armed Boarding Steamer.

JACK, THOMAS—LARNE

Shamrock Shipping Co. Ltd.

***RALOO* 1012 Grt. Blt. 1898**
17.6.1917: Torpedoed and sunk in the St. George's Channel 6 miles S.E. by E. from Coningbeg Lightvessel by the German submarine *U 61* whilst on a voyage from Newport, Mon. to Cork with a cargo of coal. 3 lost including Master.

JACKSON BROTHERS & CORY—LONDON

Reindeer S.S. Co. Ltd.

***ARIES* 3071 Grt. Blt. 1895**
25.2.1917: Captured and sunk by gunfire in the Atlantic 190 miles N.W. by W. from the Fastnet Rock in position 51.55N 14.30W by the German submarine *U 50* whilst on a voyage from Melilla to Clyde with a cargo of iron ore. Master taken prisoner.

JACKSON, SIR JOHN, LIMITED—LONDON

Westminster Shipping Co. Ltd.

WHITGIFT 4397 Grt. Blt. 1901
20.4.1916: Torpedoed and sunk in the English Channel off Ushant by the German submarine *U 67* whilst on a voyage from Almeria to Tyne with a cargo of iron ore. 32 lost including Master.

WESTMINSTER 4342 Grt. Blt. 1905
14.12.1916: Torpedoed and sunk in the Mediterranean 196 miles E. by S. from Malta in position 35.35N 18.23E by the German submarine *UB 43* whilst on a voyage from Torre Annuziata, Bay of Naples to Aden in ballast. 15 lost including Master.

JACOBS, JOHN. I. & CO. LTD.—LONDON

Associated Oil Carriers Ltd.

BATOUM 4054 Grt. Blt. 1893
19.6.1917: Torpedoed and sunk in the Atlantic 6 miles S. from the Fastnet Rock by the German submarine *U 61* whilst on a voyage from New Orleans to Queenstown with a cargo of oil. 1 lost.

BAKU STANDARD 3708 Grt. Blt. 1893
11.2.1918: Torpedoed and sunk in the North Sea 5 miles S. by W. ½W. from Tod Head Point, 5¾ miles S. of Stonehaven by the German submarine *UC 58* whilst on a voyage from Greenock to Firth of Forth with a cargo of fueloil. 24 lost.

Oil & Molasses Tankers Ltd.

OAKWOOD 4279 Grt. Blt. 1903
11.8.1915: Captured and sunk by gunfire in the Atlantic 45 miles S.S.E. from Old Head of Kinsale by the German submarine *U 38* whilst on a voyage from Liverpool to Cienfuegos in ballast.

TEAKWOOD ex *Falls of Momess* ex *Indradeo* 5315 Grt. Blt. 1902
28.4.1917: Torpedoed and sunk in the Mediterranean 26 miles S.W. by W. from Sapienza Island in position 36.39N 21.10E by the Austro-Hungarian submarine *U 14* whilst on a voyage from Messina to Port Said in ballast.

Page Shipping Co. Ltd.

CORINTH 3669 Grt. Blt. 1904
13.11.1916: Captured and sunk with bombs in the North Sea 28 miles S.¾E. from Flamborough Head in position approximately 53.43N 00.14E by the German submarine *UB 39* whilst on a voyage from Blyth to Rochefort with a cargo of coal.

MARY BAIRD ex *Ulla Bovy* 1830 Grt. Blt. 1908
18.5.1917: Struck a mine and sunk in the Atlantic 2½ miles W.½N. from Pendeen Lighthouse laid by the German submarine *UC 47* whilst on a voyage from Rouen to Newport, Mon. in ballast. 7 lost.

CARMELITE ex *Clan Macrae* ex *Shatt-El-Arab* **2583 Grt. Blt. 1892**
2.3.1918: Torpedoed and sunk in the Irish Sea 10 miles S.W. by W. from the Calf of Man by the German submarine *U 105* whilst on a voyage from Bilbao to Clyde with a cargo of iron ore. 2 lost.

JAMES, H. R. & SONS—BRISTOL

HENRY R. JAMES 3146 Grt. Blt. 1909
16.7.1917: Torpedoed and sunk in the English Channel 10 miles E. by N. from Ile de Bas by the German submarine *UC 48* whilst on a voyage from Bilbao to Middlesbrough with a cargo of iron ore. 24 lost.

JAMES, MUERS & COMPANY—CARDIFF

Whitefield S.S. Co. Ltd.

WHITEFIELD 2422 Grt. Blt. 1891
1.9.1915: Captured and sunk by gunfire in the Atlantic 95 miles N. by W. from Cape Wrath in position 60.00N 06.40W by the German submarine *U 33* whilst on a voyage from Archangel to Tyne with a cargo of wheat.

LENA 2463 Grt. Blt. 1904
23.4.1917: Torpedoed and sunk in the Atlantic S.W. of Scilly Isles in position 48.45N 08.30W by the German submarine *U 61* whilst on a voyage from Huelva to Bristol with a cargo of Government stores. 25 lost including Master.

JAPP, HATCH & CO. LTD.—LONDON

SPITAL ex *Daldorch* **4718 Grt. Blt. 1907**
15.1.1918: Torpedoed and sunk in the English Channel 4 miles from St. Anthony's Point, near Falmouth by the German submarine *U 93* whilst on a voyage from Tyne to Savona with a cargo of coal.

JENKINS BROTHERS—CARDIFF

Cardigan S.S. Co. Ltd.

ANGLESEA 4534 Grt. Blt. 1914
24.4.1917: Torpedoed and sunk in the Atlantic 160 miles W. from Bishop Rock in position 48.56N 10.17W by the German submarine *U 53* whilst on a voyage from Boston, Mass. to Le Havre with a cargo of steel and oats.

Carmarthen S.S. Co. Ltd.

CARMARTHEN ex *Arlington* **4262 Grt. Blt. 1916**
26.7.1917: Torpedoed and sunk in the English Channel 2 miles S.E. from the Lizard in position 49.57N 05.08W by the German submarine *UC 50* whilst on a voyage from Genoa to the Tees in ballast.

Harrogate S.S. Co. Ltd.

MERIONETH 3004 Grt. Blt. 1916
3.6.1917: Captured and sunk by gunfire in the Greenland Sea 105 miles N. by W. from Tromso by the German submarine *U 28* whilst on a voyage from Cardiff to Archangel with a cargo of coal.

Italiana S.S. Co. Ltd.

ITALIANA* 2663 Grt. Blt. *1898
14.9.1916: Torpedoed and sunk in the Mediterranean 112 miles E. from Malta in position 36.00N 16.50E by the German submarine *UB 43* whilst on a voyage from Rocas Bay and Tarragona to Salonica with a cargo of hay.

JENKINS, E. & COMPANY—CARDIFF

Cornish Shipping Co. Ltd.

BOSCAWEN* 1936 Grt. Blt. *1909
21.8.1918: Torpedoed and sunk in the St. George's Channel 23 miles W.N.W. from Bardsey Island in position 52.46N 05.24W by the German submarine *UB 92* whilst on a voyage from Birkenhead to Barry Roads in ballast. 1 lost.

Hatfield S.S. Co. Ltd.

BOSCASTLE* 2346 Grt. Blt. *1912
7.4.1918: Torpedoed and sunk in the St. George's Channel 14 miles N.N.W. from Strumble Head by the German submarine *U 111* whilst on a voyage from Barry to Scapa Flow with a cargo of coal. 18 lost including Master.

JENKINS, RICHARDS & EVANS LIMITED—CARDIFF

Maindy Shipping Co. Ltd.

MAINDY BRIDGE* ex *Begonia* 3653 Grt. Blt. *1899
8.12.1917: Torpedoed and sunk in the North Sea 4 miles E.N.E. from Sunderland by the German submarine *UC 49* whilst on a voyage from Middlesbrough to Tyne in ballast. 2 lost.

JOHN, THOMAS D.—CARDIFF

Cleeve's Western Valleys Anthracite Collieries, Ltd.

BEATRICE* 712 Grt. Blt. *1890
20.7.1917: Torpedoed and sunk in the English Channel 10 miles E. by S. from the Lizard by the German submarine *UC 47* whilst on a voyage from Penarth to Honfleur with a cargo of coal. 11 lost.

WYNDHURST* 570 Grt. Blt. *1917
6.12.1917: Torpedoed and sunk in the English Channel 30 miles S. from St. Catherine's Point by the German submarine *UC 71* whilst on a voyage from Penarth to Rouen with a cargo of coal. 11 lost including Master.

JOHNSTON, SPROULE & COMPANY—LIVERPOOL

Liver Shipping Co. Ltd.

LYNORTA* 3684 Grt. Blt. *1902
12.8.1917: Torpedoed and sunk in the Atlantic 102 miles N.W. by N. from Tory Island in position 56.25N 10.30W by the German submarine *U 94* whilst on a voyage from Clyde to Leghorn with a cargo of coal. 2 lost.

JONES, EVAN & COMPANY—CARDIFF

Field Line (Cardiff) Ltd.

EASTFIELD 2145 Grt. Blt. 1901
27.11.1917: Torpedoed and sunk in the English Channel 7 miles E.S.E. from Dodman Point by the German submarine *UB 57* whilst on a voyage from Newport, Mon. to Dieppe with a cargo of coal. 1 lost.

WESTFIELD 3453 Grt. Blt. 1901
10.4.1918: Torpedoed and sunk in the Atlantic 45 miles S.W. by S. from Bishop Rock in position 49.10N 06.46W by the German submarine *U 82* whilst on a voyage from Aquilas to Clyde with a cargo of minerals.

JONES, H. REES—CARDIFF

BEGONA NO. 4 ex *Kardamila* ex *Forest Holme* **2407 Grt. Blt. 1890**
27.7.1917: Torpedoed and sunk in the Atlantic 70 miles W. by N.½N. from the Fastnet Rock in position 51.15N 11.45W by the German submarine *U 46* whilst on a voyage from Bona to Cork with a cargo of phosphates.

URD 3049 Grt. Blt. 1895
12.9.1917: Torpedoed and sunk in the Mediterranean 10 miles N. by E.½E. from Cape de Palos by the German submarine *U 64* whilst on a voyage from Cardiff to Civitavecchia with a cargo of coal. 3 lost.

JONES, HALLETT & COMPANY—CARDIFF

NORTHLANDS 2776 Grt. Blt. 1900
5.4.1915: Captured and torpedoed in the English Channel 24 miles S.W. from Beachy Head by the German submarine *U 33* whilst on a voyage from La Goulette to Tees with a cargo of iron ore.

JONES (HOWARD) & KING—CARDIFF

Tree S.S. Co. Ltd.

BEECHTREE 1277 Grt. Blt. 1912
10.2.1917: Torpedoed and sunk in the English Channel 11 miles S.E. from Start Point in position 50.08N 03.23W by the German submarine *UC 21* whilst on a voyage from Swansea to Rouen with a cargo of coal.

JONES, W. & C. T. CO. LTD.—CARDIFF

LLONGWEN 4683 Grt. Blt. 1907
18.7.1916: Captured and sunk by gunfire in the Mediterranean 90 miles N.E. from Algiers by the German submarine *U 39* whilst on a voyage from Naples to Barry. 14 lost.

BRONWEN 4250 Grt. Blt. 1913
24.9.1916: Captured and sunk by gunfire in the Mediterranean 25 miles N. by E. from Dragonera Island in position 40.21N 02.18E by the German submarine *U 35* whilst on a voyage from Barry to Marseilles with a cargo of coal. Master and 2 Gunners taken prisoner.

ADENWEN 3798 Grt. Blt. 1913
25.3.1917: Torpedoed and sunk in the St. George's Channel 6 miles S.E. by E. from North Arklow Lightvessel in position 52.36N 05.37W by the German submarine *UC 65* whilst on a voyage from Cienfuegos to Queenstown and Liverpool with a cargo of sugar. 10 lost.

RHYDWEN 4799 Grt. Blt. 1914
18.4.1917: Torpedoed and sunk in the Atlantic 170 miles N.W. by W. ½ W. from the Fastnet Rock in position 51.40N 14.00W by the German submarine *U 67* whilst on a voyage from Galveston to Cardiff with a cargo of wheat. 6 lost.

FREDERICK KNIGHT 3604 Grt. Blt. 1898
3.5.1917: Torpedoed and sunk in the Atlantic 115 miles N.W. by W. from the Fastnet Rock in position 51.43N 12.21W by the German submarine *U 62* whilst on a voyage from Norfolk (Va) to the United Kingdom with a cargo of sugar.

MILLICENT KNIGHT 3563 Grt. Blt. 1900
18.5.1917: Torpedoed and sunk in the Mediterranean 130 miles E. by S. ½ S. from Malta in position 35.37N 17.13E by the German submarine *UC 20* whilst on a voyage from Cardiff and Malta to Port Said with a cargo of Government stores. 1 lost.

ENIDWEN 3594 Grt. Blt. 1899
8.6.1917: Torpedoed and sunk in the Atlantic 170 miles N.W. from the Fastnet Rock by the German submarine *U 69* whilst on a voyage from Cuba to Queenstown with a cargo of sugar.

HAULWEN 4032 Grt. Blt. 1903
10.6.1917: Torpedoed and sunk in the Atlantic 250 miles N.W. from the Fastnet Rock in position 52.48N 16.00W by the German submarine *U 43* whilst on a voyage from Montreal to Manchester with a cargo of wheat. 4 lost.

VRONWEN ex *Universal* **5714 Grt. Blt. 1917**
29.8.1917: Torpedoed and sunk in the Mediterranean 20 miles N.W. by W. from Gozo Island in position 36.12N 13.56E by the German submarine *UC 38* whilst on a voyage from Tyne to Port Said with a cargo of coal. 1 lost.

JOSEPH CHAMBERLAIN 3709 Grt. Blt. 1910
18.9.1917: Torpedoed and sunk in the North Sea 50 miles N. by W. from Muckle Flugga by the German submarine *UB 62* whilst on a voyage from Archangel to Lerwick with a cargo of timber. 18 lost, Master and 1 Gunner taken prisoner.

SANWEN ex *Devian* **3689 Grt. Blt. 1915**
29.9.1917: Torpedoed and sunk in the Mediterranean in the Gulf of Lions by the German submarine *U 32* whilst on a voyage from Clyde to Genoa with a cargo of coal. 2 lost.

GROESWEN 3570 Grt. Blt. 1900
27.11.1917: Struck a mine and sunk off the mouth of the River Thames 3 miles N.E. ½ E. from the Sunk Lightvessel in position 51.55N 01.40E laid by the German submarine *UC 11* whilst on a voyage from Hull to—with a cargo of coal.

KARAM, GABRIEL TEWFIK—ALEXANDRIA, EGYPT

SYLVIE ex *Abdel-Kader* ex *Agios Georgios* ex *Martino* ex *Ecaterini Coupa* ex *Llandough* **1354 Grt. Blt. 1878**
15.7.1916: Captured and sunk by gunfire in the Mediterranean 15 miles from Cape Sigli by the German submarine *U 39* whilst on a voyage from Cartagena to Bona in ballast.

KAYE, SON & CO. LTD.—LONDON

The "K" S.S. Co. Ltd.

POLTAVA ex *George R* ex *Georg* **945 Grt. Blt. 1889**
19.4.1917: Struck a mine and sunk in the North Sea 3 miles E.N.E. from Souter Point Lighthouse, South Shields laid by the German submarine *UC 44* whilst on a voyage from Tyne to—with a cargo of coal.

POLYMNIA ex *Henriette Woermann* **2426 Grt. Blt. 1903**
15.5.1917: Torpedoed and sunk in the English Channel 15 miles W. from the Lizard in position 49.54N 05.34W by the German submarine *UC 75* whilst on a voyage from Huelva and Lisbon to Falmouth with a cargo of iron ore and fruit. 8 lost.

KEEP, HARRY—LONDON

NORTHFIELD 2099 Grt. Blt. 1901
3.3.1918: Torpedoed and sunk in the Bristol Channel 25 miles S.W. from Lundy Island by the German submarine *U 60* whilst on a voyage from Clyde to Devonport with a cargo of coal. 15 lost including Master.

KENNAUGH, W. S. & COMPANY—LIVERPOOL

West Coast Shipping Co. Ltd.

DALEGARTH FORCE 684 Grt. Blt. 1914
18.4.1918: Torpedoed and sunk in the Bristol Channel 12 miles S.W. from Hartland Point by the German submarines *UB 86* and *UB 73* whilst on a voyage from Treport to Barry Roads in ballast. 5 lost.

STOCKFORCE 732 Grt. Blt. 1917
30.7.1918: Torpedoed and sunk in the English Channel 25 miles W. of Start Point by the German submarine *UB 80*. Lost whilst on Government service employed as a Special Service Ship.

KESTELL BROTHERS—CARDIFF

Kestell S.S. Co. Ltd.

HOLMESBANK ex *Thirlwall* **3051 Grt. Blt. 1906**
26.5.1917: Captured and sunk by gunfire in the Mediterranean 90 miles N. by W. from Alexandria in position 32.26N 29.30E by the German submarine *U 38* whilst on a voyage from Swansea to Port Said with a cargo of coal.

KHEDIVAL MAIL STEAMSHIP & GRAVING DOCK CO. LTD.—LONDON

SAIDIEH 3303 Grt. Blt. 1878
1.6.1915: Torpedoed and sunk in the mouth of the River Thames 6 miles N.E. from Elbow Buoy by the German submarine *UB 6* whilst on a voyage from Alexandria to Hull with a cargo of cottonseed and onions. 8 lost.

BENHA ex *Naderi* **1878 Grt. Blt. 1891**
11.6.1917: Captured and sunk with bombs in the Mediterranean 50 miles N. by E. from Marsa Susa in position 33.45N 22.40E by the German submarine *UC 74* whilst on a voyage from Limassol to Leith with a cargo of carobs (edible seed pods).

OSMANIEH 4041 Grt. Blt. 1906
31.12.1917: Struck a mine and sunk in the Mediterranean at the entrance to Alexandria harbour laid by the German submarine *UC 34*. 24 lost including Master. Lost whilst on Government service employed as Fleet Messenger *No. 61*.

MISSIR ex *Argyll* **786 Grt. Blt. 1864**
29.5.1918: Torpedoed and sunk in the Mediterranean 80 miles W. by N. from Alexandria by the German submarine *UB 51* whilst on a voyage from Alexandria to Sollum with general cargo and Government stores. 34 lost.

MENZALEH ex *Abd-el-Monem* ex *Inanda* **1859 Grt. Blt. 1888**
6.6.1918: Torpedoed and sunk in the Mediterranean 230 miles E.S.E. from Malta by the German submarine *UB 105* whilst on a voyage from Alexandria to Bristol with a cargo of cottonseed. 10 lost, Master taken prisoner.

TEWFIKIEH ex *Rameses* **2490 Grt. Blt. 1893**
9.6.1918: Torpedoed and sunk in the Mediterranean 115 miles W.N.W. from Alexandria by the German submarine *UB 105* whilst on a voyage from Hull to Alexandria with general cargo and coal. 5 lost.

KOSSEIR ex *Vassilefs Gheorghios* ex *Victoria* ex *Esteban De Antunano* **1855 Grt. Blt. 1884**
20.7.1918: Torpedoed and sunk in the Mediterranean 40 miles N.E. by N.½N. from Alexandria by the German submarine *UB 51* whilst on a voyage from Alexandria to Port Said with general cargo. 39 lost including Master.

KITCHING, THOMAS—WEST HARTLEPOOL

DIXIANA ex *Putney Bridge* **3329 Grt. Blt. 1901**
29.5.1915: Captured and torpedoed in the English Channel 40 miles N. from Ushant by the German submarine *U 41* whilst on a voyage from Savannah to Le Havre with general cargo including pig iron and cotton.

LAMBERT BROTHERS LIMITED—LONDON

L.H. CARL 1916 Grt. Blt. 1898
20.7.1917: Torpedoed and sunk in the English Channel 14 miles W.½S. from Portland Bill in position 50.26N 02.48W by the German submarine *UB 40* whilst on a voyage from Barry to Rouen with a cargo of coal. 2 lost.

The Shipping Controller

ALGARVE 1274 Grt. Blt. 1899
20.10.1917: Torpedoed and sunk in the English Channel 15 miles W.S.W. from Portland Bill by the German submarine *UB 38* whilst on a voyage from Rouen to Swansea in ballast. 21 lost including Master.

LIVONIA 1879 Grt. Blt. 1904
3.12.1917: Torpedoed and sunk in the English Channel 4 miles E. by N.½N. from Start Point by the German submarine *UB 35* whilst on a voyage from Bilbao to Tyne with a cargo of iron ore. 23 lost including Master.

AVANTI 2128 Grt. Blt. 1912
2.2.1918: Torpedoed and sunk in the English Channel 4 miles S.E. by E. from St. Albans Head by the German submarine *UB 59* whilst on a voyage from Bilbao to West Hartlepool with a cargo of iron ore. 22 lost including Master.

ROMNY 1024 Grt. Blt. 1913
26.2.1918: Torpedoed and sunk in the English Channel 10 miles N.N.E. from Cape Barfleur by the German submarine *UB 74* whilst on a voyage from Rouen to Swansea in ballast. 9 lost.

EXCELLENCE PLESKE ex *Abeona* **2059 Grt. Blt. 1886**
31.3.1918: Torpedoed and sunk in the English Channel 2½ miles S.S.E. from Dungeness by the German submarine *UB 57* whilst on a voyage from Bilbao to Middlesbrough with a cargo of iron ore. 13 lost.

NORMANDIET ex *Kronprinsesse Louise* **1843 Grt. Blt. 1902**
21.4.1918: Torpedoed and sunk in the Irish Sea 34 miles S.W. by W. from the Calf on Man by the German submarine *U 91* whilst on a voyage from Bilbao to Clyde with a cargo of iron ore. 19 lost including Master.

KALO ex *Estonia* **1957 Grt. Blt. 1903**
13.6.1918: Torpedoed and sunk in the North Sea 18 miles S. by E.½E. from Flamborough Head by the German submarine *UB 107* whilst on a voyage from Tyne to Pauillac with a cargo of coal. 3 lost.

LAMBERT, F. H. BARNETT & COMPANY—CARDIFF

RANZA 2320 Grt. Blt. 1902
1.8.1915: Captured and torpedoed in the Atlantic 50 miles S.W. from Ushant by the German submarine *U 28* whilst on a voyage from Tyne to Gibraltar with a cargo of coal. 3 lost.

Pentwyn S.S. Co. Ltd.

PENTYRCH ex *Bardsey* **3312 Grt. Blt. 1899**
18.4.1918: Torpedoed and sunk in the English Channel 5 miles W.N.W. from Brighton Lightvessel by the German submarine *UB 40* whilst on a voyage from Tyne to Genoa with a cargo of coal. 1 lost.

PENTWYN 3587 Grt. Blt. 1910
16.10.1918: Torpedoed and sunk in the St. George's Channel 20 miles N.E. by

N.¼N. from the Smalls in position 52.30N 05.34W by the German submarine *U 90* whilst on a voyage from Lagos to Liverpool with a cargo of African produce. 1 lost.

West House S.S. Co. Ltd.

DENABY 2987 Grt. Blt. 1900
24.2.1916: Captured and sunk by gunfire in the Mediterranean 40 miles S.S.W. from Planier Island in position 42.32N 05.40E by the German submarine *U 38* whilst on a voyage from Huelva to St. Louis du Rhone with a cargo of iron ore. 1 lost.

LAMBROS, STEVEN. C.—GALATA, CONSTANTINOPLE

W. HARKNESS 1185 Grt. Blt. 1874
22.10.1916: Captured and sunk with bombs in the Mediterranean 17 miles W. from Cape Tenez by the German submarine *U 39* whilst on a voyage from Bona to Seville with a cargo of phosphate and empty barrels.

LAMING, A. & COMPANY—LONDON

Laming D'Ambrumenil S.S. Co. Ltd.

LEXIE 3778 Grt. Blt. 1911
10.9.1916: Captured and torpedoed in the Atlantic 42 miles S.W. from Ushant in position 47.51N 05.40W by the German submarine *UB 39* whilst on a voyage from Karachi to Barry with a cargo of wheat.

LAMPORT & HOLT LIMITED—LIVERPOOL

Liverpool, Brazil and River Plate Steam Navigation Co. Ltd.

PASCAL 5587 Grt. Blt. 1913
17.12.1916: Captured and torpedoed in the English Channel 12 miles N. from Casquets, 8 miles W. of Alderney in position 49.55N 02.27W by the German submarine *U 70* whilst on a voyage from Halifax, (NS) to Cherbourg with Government cargo. 2 lost, Master taken prisoner.

TERENCE 4309 Grt. Blt. 1902
28.4.1917: Captured and sunk by gunfire and torpedo in the Atlantic 150 miles N.W. by N. from the Fastnet Rock in position approximately 52.40N 12.55W by the German submarine *U 81* whilst on a voyage from Buenos Aires to Liverpool with general cargo, meat and wheat. 1 lost.

VERDI 7120 Grt. Blt. 1907
22.8.1917: Torpedoed and sunk in the Atlantic 115 miles N.W. by N. from Eagle Island by the German submarine *U 53* whilst on a voyage from New York to Liverpool with general cargo. 6 lost.

TITIAN 4170 Grt. Blt. 1902
26.8.1917: Torpedoed and sunk in the Mediterranean 170 miles S.E.½E. from Malta in position 34.20N 17.30E by the Austro-Hungarian submarine *U 14* whilst on a voyage from London to Alexandria with general cargo.

MEMLING 7307 Grt. Blt. 1917
3.10.1917: Torpedoed and damaged in the English Channel in L'Aberildat Channel, near Brest by the German submarine *UC 21* whilst on a voyage from Montreal to Bordeaux with a cargo of frozen meat. She was declared a constructive total loss and broken up.

CANOVA 4637 Grt. Blt. 1895
24.12.1917: Torpedoed and sunk in the Atlantic 15 miles S. from Mine Head by the German submarine *U 105* whilst on a voyage from Bahia Blanca to Liverpool with a cargo of wheat. 7 lost.

SPENSER ex *Tripoli* 4186 Grt. Blt. 1910
6.1.1918: Torpedoed and sunk in the St. George's Channel 35 miles N.E. of Tuskar Rock by the German submarine *U 61* whilst on a voyage from Buenos Aires to Liverpool with general cargo.

LANCASHIRE & YORKSHIRE RAILWAY COMPANY—GOOLE

DON 939 Grt. Blt. 1892
8.5.1915: Captured and torpedoed in the North Sea 7 miles E. from Coquet Island by the German submarine *U 9* whilst on a voyage from Cromarty to Blyth in ballast.

DUKE OF ALBANY 1997 Grt. Blt. 1907
25.8.1916: Torpedoed and sunk in the North Sea 20 miles E. from Pentland Skerries, Orkney in position 58.44N 02.28W by the German submarine *UB 27*. Lost whilst on Government service employed as an Armed Boarding Steamer.

HEBBLE 904 Grt. Blt. 1891
6.5.1917: Struck a mine and sunk in the North Sea 1½ miles E. from Roker Pier, Sunderland in position 54.55N 01.18E laid by the German submarine *UC 42* whilst on a voyage from Scapa Flow to Sunderland in ballast. 5 lost. Lost whilst on Government service employed as Store Carrier *No. 3*.

RYE 986 Grt. Blt. 1914
7.4.1918: Torpedoed and sunk in the English Channel 19 miles N. by W. ½ W. from Cape d'Antifer in position 49.57N 00.07W by the German submarine *UB 74* whilst on a voyage from Newhaven to Rouen with a cargo of military supplies. 4 lost.

UNITY 1091 Grt. Blt. 1902
2.5.1918: Torpedoed and sunk in the English Channel 3 miles W.S.W. from Varne Lightvessel, 9 miles S.E. of Folkestone by the German submarine *UB 57* whilst on a voyage from Newhaven to Calais with a cargo of ordnance. 12 lost.

LANE & MACANDREW LIMITED—LONDON

PALMLEAF 5489 Grt. Blt. 1916
4.2.1917: Torpedoed and sunk in the Atlantic 230 miles W. from the Fastnet Rock in position 51.00N 15.00W by the German submarine *U 54* whilst on a voyage from Devonport to Port Arthur, Texas in ballast. Master and Chief Engineer taken prisoner.

LUX ex *Le Lion* **2621 Grt. Blt. 1893**
5.2.1917: Torpedoed and sunk in the Atlantic S.W. of Ireland by the German submarine *U 60* whilst on a voyage from New York to Calais with a cargo of oil. 29 lost including Master.

ASHLEAF 5768 Grt. Blt. 1916
29.5.1917: Torpedoed and sunk in the Atlantic 150 miles W. from Bishop Rock in position 48.40N 09.30W by the German submarine *U 88* whilst on a voyage from Trinidad to Falmouth with a cargo of oil.

OAKLEAF ex *Montezuma* **8106 Grt. Blt. 1899**
25.7.1917: Torpedoed and sunk in the Atlantic 64 miles N.W.¼N. from Butt of Lewis in position 59.01N 07.26W by the German submarine *UC 41* whilst on a voyage from Invergordon to Port Arthur, Texas in ballast.

ORIFLAMME 3764 Grt. Blt. 1889
25.11.1917: Struck a mine and sunk in the English Channel 9 miles S. from Nab Lightvessel laid by the German submarine *UC 63* whilst on a voyage from New York to Le Havre and Rouen with a cargo of benzine.

Petroleum S.S. Co. Ltd.

CAUCASIAN 4656 Grt. Blt. 1899
1.7.1915: Captured and sunk by gunfire in the English Channel 80 miles S. from Lizard by the German submarine *U 39* whilst on a voyage from London to New Orleans with a cargo of creosote oil.

BALAKANI 3696 Grt. Blt. 1899
9.9.1915: Struck a mine and sunk at the mouth of the River Thames ½ mile S.W. from S. from Long Sand Buoy in position approximately 51.31N 01.22E laid by the German submarine *UC 1* whilst on a voyage from Port Arthur, Texas to London with a cargo of fueloil. 6 lost.

TEUTONIAN 4824 Grt. Blt. 1914
4.3.1916: Captured and torpedoed in the Atlantic 36 miles S.W. by W. from the Fastnet Rock by the German submarine *U 32* whilst on a voyage from Sabine to Avonmouth with a cargo of refined oil.

SAXONIAN 4855 Grt. Blt. 1914
7.2.1917: Captured and sunk by gunfire in the Atlantic 270 miles W. by N. from the Fastnet Rock in position 50.26N 16.26W by the German submarine *U 54* whilst on a voyage from Port Arthur, Texas to Dartmouth with a cargo of paraffin oil. 1 lost, Master taken prisoner.

LANGLANDS, M. & SONS—LIVERPOOL

PRINCESS VICTORIA 1108 Grt. Blt. 1894
9.3.1915: Torpedoed and sunk in the Irish Sea 16 miles N.W. by N. from Liverpool Bar Lightvessel by the German submarine *U 20* whilst on a voyage from Aberdeen to Liverpool with general cargo.

PRINCESS ALBERTA 1586 Grt. Blt. 1905
21.2.1917: Struck a mine and sunk in the Aegean Sea in Mudros Bay laid by the

German submarine *UC 23* whilst on a voyage from Styros Island to Mudros. Lost whilst on Government service employed as Fleet Messenger *No. 58*.

PRINCESS DAGMAR 913 Grt. Blt. 1907
8.5.1918: Torpedoed and sunk in the Bristol Channel by the German submarine *U 54* whilst on a voyage from Swansea to France with a cargo of coal. 24 lost including Master.

PRINCESS ROYAL 1986 Grt. Blt. 1912
26.5.1918: Torpedoed and sunk in the English Channel 3 miles W.N.W. from St. Agnes Head by the German submarine *U 101* whilst on a voyage from Swansea to Le Havre with general cargo. 19 lost.

PRINCESS MAUD 1566 Grt. Blt. 1902
10.6.1918: Torpedoed and sunk in the North Sea 5 miles N.E. by N. from Blyth probably by the German submarine *UB 34* whilst on a voyage from London to Leith with general cargo. 3 lost.

LARRINAGA & CO. LTD.—LIVERPOOL

Miguel de Larrinaga S.S. Co. Ltd.

JOSE DE LARRINAGA 5017 Grt. Blt. 1913
28.4.1917: Torpedoed and sunk in the Atlantic 150 miles W.N.W. from the Fastnet Rock in position 51.32N 13.20W by the German submarine *U 81* whilst on a voyage from Galveston to Manchester with general cargo. 12 lost including Master.

PILAR DE LARRINAGA 4136 Grt. Blt. 1902
4.5.1917: Torpedoed and sunk in the St. George's Channel 2 miles S.E. by S. from Tuskar Rock in position 52.10N 06.08W by the German submarine *UC 65* whilst on a voyage from Galveston to Manchester with general cargo and wheat. 20 lost including Master.

RICHARD DE LARRINAGA 5591 Grt. Blt. 1916
8.10.1917: Torpedoed and sunk in the Atlantic 15 miles S.E. ½S. from Ballycottin Island by the German submarine *U 57* whilst on a voyage from Manchester to Galveston in ballast. 35 lost including Master.

LAW, THOMAS & COMPANY—GLASGOW

Law Shipping Co. Ltd.

BERWICK LAW 4680 Grt. Blt. 1911
2.12.1917: Torpedoed and sunk in the Mediterranean 22 miles W. from Cape Tenez by the German submarine *U 34* whilst on a voyage from Port Said to Oran in ballast. 1 lost, Master taken prisoner.

LAWTHER, LATTA & COMPANY—LONDON

Nitrate Producers' S.S. Co. Ltd.

ANGLO-COLOMBIAN 4792 Grt. Blt. 1907
23.9.1915: Captured and sunk by gunfire in the Atlantic 79 miles S.E. from the

Fastnet Rock by the German submarine *U 41* whilst on a voyage from Quebec to Avonmouth with a consignment of horses.

ANGLO-PATAGONIAN 5017 Grt. Blt. 1910
11.7.1917: Torpedoed and sunk in the Bay of Biscay 20 miles W.S.W. from Les Sables d'Olonne, near La Rochelle in position 46.20N 02.15W by the German submarine *UC 72* whilst on a voyage from New York to Bordeaux with general cargo and a consignment of horses. 4 lost.

ANGLO-CANADIAN 4239 Grt. Blt. 1901
22.1.1918: Torpedoed and sunk in the Mediterranean 33 miles S.½E. from Malta in position 35.15N 15.05E by the Austro-Hungarian submarine *U 27* whilst on a voyage from Alexandria to Marseilles in ballast. 3 lost.

LE BOULANGER, F.—SWANSEA

The Shipping Controller.

BAMSE ex *Klondyke* ex *Syra* *958 Grt. Blt. 1875*
18.4.1918: Torpedoed and sunk in the English Channel 15 miles W. by N. from Portland Bill by the German submarine *UB 80* whilst on a voyage from Rouen to Swansea in ballast. 4 lost.

LEACH & CO. LTD.—LONDON

SEVEN SEAS 1194 Grt. Blt. 1888
1.4.1915: Torpedoed and sunk in the English Channel 6 miles S. from Beachy Head by the German submarine *U 37* whilst on a voyage from London to Liverpool in ballast. 9 lost including Master.

SEA SERPENT 902 Grt. Blt. 1898
23.3.1916: Struck a mine and sunk in the Strait of Dover off Folkestone Pier laid by the German submarine *UC 6* whilst on a voyage from Birkenhead to Dunkirk with a cargo of corrugated iron. 14 lost including Master.

SEA GULL 976 Grt. Blt. 1899
17.3.1918: Torpedoed and sunk in the Irish Sea 7 miles N.E. from Lynas Point by the German submarine *U 103* whilst on a voyage from Le Havre to Liverpool with general cargo. 20 lost including Master.

LETRICHEUX & DAVID LIMITED—SWANSEA

English S.S. Co. Ltd.

STANHOPE 2854 Grt. Blt. 1900
17.6.1917: Torpedoed and sunk in the English Channel 7 miles S.W. by W. from Start Point in position 50.08N 03.45W by the German submarine *UB 31* whilst on a voyage from Barrow to Dunkirk with a cargo of steel rails. 22 lost.

GIRDLENESS ex *Grelisle* ex *Rockabill* ex *Blacktor* *3018 Grt. Blt. 1905*
2.5.1918: Torpedoed and sunk in the Atlantic 1½ miles N.W. (mag) of Cambeck Point, 8 miles S.W. of Bude by the German submarine *U 60* whilst on a voyage from Swansea to—with a cargo of patent fuel. 2 lost.

ORFORDNESS ex *Blackfriargate **2790 Grt. Blt. 1906***
20.7.1918: Torpedoed and sunk in the Atlantic 2½ miles W. by N. from Newquay in position 50.25N 05.08W by the German submarine *U 60* whilst on a voyage from Rouen to Barry Roads in ballast. 2 lost.

Letricheux Line, Ltd.

GUILDHALL 2609 Grt. Blt. 1898
25.6.1917: Torpedoed and sunk in the Atlantic 40 miles S.W. by W.½W. from Bishop Rock by the German submarine *U 62* whilst on a voyage from Bougie and Valencia to Cardiff with a cargo of ore and oranges. 12 lost.

SARACEN 3272 Grt. Blt. 1911
26.12.1917: Struck a mine and sunk in the English Channel in Le Four Channel, near Ushant probably laid by the German submarine *UC 36* whilst on a voyage from Bilbao to Glasgow with a cargo of iron ore.

TARBETNESS ex *Kingtor **3018 Grt. Blt. 1904***
7.3.1918: Torpedoed and sunk in Caernarvon Bay 12 miles S.W. from Caernarvon Lightvessel by the German submarine *U 110* whilst on a voyage from Manchester to—with general cargo.

LEWIS, T. & COMPANY—CARDIFF

Lewis S.S. Co. Ltd.

RIO LAGES ex *Westmoor **3591 Grt. Blt. 1900***
26.4.1917: Torpedoed and sunk in the Atlantic 155 miles N.W. by W. from the Fastnet Rock in position 51.38N 12.52W by the German submarine *U 69* whilst on a voyage from Norfolk, (Va) to Queenstown with a cargo of sugar. 3 lost.

HANLEY 3331 Grt. Blt. 1902
30.5.1917: Torpedoed and sunk in the Atlantic 95 miles W. from Bishop Rock in position 49.23N 08.43W by the German submarine *U 87* whilst on a voyage from Bahia Blanca to Falmouth with a cargo of oats. 1 lost.

Lewis Trading Co. Ltd.

VAUXHALL 3629 Grt. Blt. 1900
26.4.1917: Torpedoed and sunk in the Atlantic 110 miles N.W. by W. from the Fastnet Rock in position 51.45N 12.30W by the German submarine *U 69* whilst on a voyage from Sfax to Dublin with a cargo of phosphate rock. 2 lost.

LEYLAND, FREDERICK & CO. LTD.—LIVERPOOL

Leyland Line.

ARMENIAN 8825 Grt. Blt. 1895
28.6.1915: Captured and torpedoed in the Atlantic 20 miles W. from Trevose Head by the German submarine *U 24* whilst on a voyage from Newport News to Avonmouth with a consignment of mules. 29 lost.

IBERIAN 5223 Grt. Blt. 1900
30.7.1915: Captured and torpedoed in the Atlantic 9 miles S. by W. from the

Fastnet Rock in position 51.15N 09.36W by the German submarine *U 28* whilst on a voyage from Manchester to Boston, Mass. with general cargo. 7 lost.

CALIFORNIAN 6223 Grt. Blt. 1902
9.11.1915: Torpedoed and sunk in the Mediterranean 61 miles S.S.W. from Cape Matapan in position 36.26N 22.40E by the German submarine *U 35* whilst on a voyage from Salonica to Marseilles in ballast. 1 lost.

RUSSIAN ex *Victorian* **8825 Grt. Blt. 1895**
14.12.1916: Torpedoed and sunk in the Mediterranean 210 miles E. by S. from Malta in position 35.30N 18.52E by the German submarine *UB 43* whilst on a voyage from Salonica to Newport, Mon. in ballast. 28 lost.

FLORIDIAN 4777 Grt. Blt. 1913
4.2.1917: Captured and torpedoed in the Atlantic 200 miles W. by N. from the Fastnet Rock in position 50.25N 15.00W by the German submarine *U 54* whilst on a voyage from Halifax, (NS) to Cherbourg with general cargo. 5 lost, Master, Chief Engineer and Wireless Operator taken prisoner.

GEORGIAN 5088 Grt. Blt. 1890
8.3.1917: Torpedoed and sunk in the Mediterranean 52 miles N. from Cape Sidero by the German submarine *UB 47*.

NORWEGIAN 6327 Grt. Blt. 1913
13.3.1917: Struck a mine and sunk in the Atlantic 4 miles S.W. from Seven Heads, near Clonakilty Bay by the German submarine *UC 43* whilst on a voyage from New York to Liverpool with general cargo and grain. 5 lost.

CANADIAN 9309 Grt. Blt. 1900
5.4.1917: Torpedoed and sunk in the Atlantic 47 miles N.W. from the Fastnet Rock in position 51.36N 10.48W by the German submarine *U 59* whilst on a voyage from Boston, Mass. to Liverpool with general cargo. Master lost.

BELGIAN 3657 Grt. Blt. 1900
24.5.1917: Torpedoed and sunk in the Atlantic 50 miles W.½S. from the Fastnet Rock in position 50.59N 10.42W by the German submarine *U 57* whilst on a voyage from New Orleans to Liverpool with general cargo. 2 lost.

CAMERONIAN ex *Kamerun* **5861 Grt. Blt. 1913**
2.6.1917: Torpedoed and sunk in the Mediterranean 50 miles N.W. by N.¼N. from Alexandria in position 31.53N 29.19E by the German submarine *UC 34* whilst on a voyage from Liverpool and Suda Bay to Alexandria with a consignment of mules. 11 lost including Master.

ANGLIAN ex *Megantic* **5532 Grt. Blt. 1896**
11.6.1917: Torpedoed and sunk in the Atlantic 43 miles S.W. by W.½W. from Bishop Rock in position 49.22N 07.12W by the German submarine *UC 75* whilst on a voyage from Boston, Mass. to London with general cargo. 1 lost.

SYLVANIAN 4858 Grt. Blt. 1914
24.6.1917: Torpedoed and sunk in the Atlantic 170 miles N.W. from Tory Island in position 56.27N 12.57W by the German submarine *U 94* whilst on a voyage from Liverpool to Kingston, (Ja) with general cargo. 2 lost.

CESTRIAN 8912 Grt. Blt. 1896
24.6.1917: Torpedoed and sunk in the Aegean Sea 4 miles S.E. from Skyros Island by the German submarine *UB 42* whilst on a voyage from Salonica to Alexandria with a consignment of horses. 3 lost.

ORUBIAN 3876 Grt. Blt. 1914
31.7.1917: Torpedoed and sunk in the Atlantic 160 miles N.W.½W. from Eagle Island in position 51.48N 14.35W by the German submarine *U 82* whilst on a voyage from Liverpool to Colon with general cargo. 1 lost.

DEVONIAN 10435 Grt. Blt. 1900
21.8.1917: Torpedoed and sunk in the Atlantic 20 miles N.E. from Tory Island by the German submarine *U 53* whilst on a voyage from Liverpool to Boston, Mass. with general cargo. 2 lost.

MEMPHIAN 6305 Grt. Blt. 1908
8.10.1917: Torpedoed and sunk in the St. George's Channel 7 miles E.N.E. from North Arklow Lightvessel by the German submarine *U 96* whilst on a voyage from Liverpool to Boston, Mass. in ballast. 32 lost.

BOSTONIAN ex *Cambrian* **5736 Grt. Blt. 1896**
10.10.1017: Torpedoed and sunk in the English Channel 34 miles S. by E.½E. from Start Point by the German submarine *U 53* whilst on a voyage from Philadelphia to London with general cargo. 4 lost.

PHILADELPHIAN 5165 Grt. Blt. 1891
19.2.1918: Torpedoed and sunk in the English Channel 47 miles S. by E.½E. from the Lizard by the German submarine *U 82* whilst on a voyage from New York to London with general cargo. 4 lost.

ETONIAN ex *Chicago* **6515 Grt. Blt. 1898**
23.3.1918: Torpedoed and sunk in the Atlantic 34 miles S. by E.½E. from Old Head of Kinsale by the German submarine *U 61* whilst on a voyage from Liverpool to Boston, Mass. with general cargo. 7 lost.

KINGSTONIAN 6564 Grt. Blt. 1901
11.4.1918: Torpedoed and damaged in the Mediterranean off Sardinia in position 39.20N 07.10E by the German submarine *UB 68* whilst on a voyage from Alexandria to Marseilles carrying troops and a cargo of equipment. 1 lost. She was beached in Carloforte Bay, Sardinia and on 29.4.1918 during salvage operations she was torpedoed by the German submarine *UB 48* and subsequently became a total loss.

ATLANTIAN 9399 Grt. Blt. 1899
26.6.1918: Torpedoed and sunk in the Atlantic 110 miles N. by W.½W. from Eagle Island in position 55.42N 12.57W by the German submarine *U 86* whilst on a voyage from Galveston to Liverpool with a cargo of cotton. Chief Officer and Wireless Operator taken prisoner.

ALMERIAN 3030 Grt. Blt. 1897
19.10.1918: Struck a mine and sunk in the Mediterranean 13 miles W. by S. from

Licata probably laid by the German submarine *UC 27* whilst on a voyage from Genoa and Licata to Liverpool with general cargo and sulphur.

LIM CHIN TSONG—RANGOON

SEANG CHOON ex *Cheshire* **5807 Grt. Blt. 1891**
10.7.1917: Torpedoed and sunk in the Atlantic 10 miles S.W. from the Fastnet Rock by the German submarine *U 87* whilst on a voyage from Sydney, NSW and Dakar to Liverpool with general cargo. 19 lost.

LIMERICK S.S. CO. LTD.—LIMERICK

OOLA ex *Highlander* **2494 Grt. Blt. 1891**
26.10.1916: Captured and sunk with bombs in the Arctic 22 miles N.E. by N. from North Cape in position 70.30N 26.24E by the German submarine *U 56* whilst on a voyage from Tyne to Archangel with a cargo of coal.

COONAGH ex *Almagro* **1412 Grt. Blt. 1904**
15.3.1917: Torpedoed and sunk in the Downs by the German submarine *UC 16* whilst on a voyage from Middlesbrough to Rouen with a cargo of pig iron. 10 lost including Master.

ISLANDMORE ex *Kylemhor* **3046 Grt. Blt. 1909**
3.6.1917: Captured and sunk by gunfire in the Mediterranean 20 miles N.W. from Cape Falcon by the German submarine *U 33* whilst on a voyage from Barry to Gibraltar and Malta with a cargo of coal. 2 lost, Master taken prisoner.

AYLEVARROO ex *Lillie* **908 Grt. Blt. 1903**
8.10.1917: Torpedoed and sunk in the Atlantic off the Ballycottin Islands by the German submarine *U 57* whilst on a voyage from Liverpool to Tralee and Limerick with general cargo. 20 lost including Master.

LITTLE, J. W.—BELFAST

COTTINGHAM **513 Grt. Blt. 1907**
26.12.1915: Captured and sunk by gunfire in the Bristol Channel 16 miles S.W. ½ W from Lundy Island by the German submarine *U 24* whilst on a voyage from Rouen to Swansea in ballast. 7 lost. The first British merchant ship to sink a U boat, the German minelaying submarine *UC 2* on the 2.7.1915 off Yarmouth.

LITTLEHALES, R. H.—MANCHESTER

LEUCTRA **3027 Grt. Blt. 1899**
12.6.1915: Torpedoed and sunk in the North Sea 1½ miles S.E. by S. from Shipwash Lightvessel by the German submarine *UB 16* whilst on a voyage from Rosario to Hull with a cargo of linseed.

MIDLOTHIAN **1321 Grt. Blt. 1871**
30.9.1917: Captured and sunk by gunfire in the Mediterranean 80 miles S. from Cape Greco by the German submarine *U 73* whilst on a voyage from Famagusta to Deir el Ballah with a cargo of firewood. Master and 2 Gunners taken prisoner.

LIVERPOOL & NORTH WALES S.S. CO. LTD.—LIVERPOOL

ST. SEIROL 928 Grt. Blt. 1914
25.4.1918: Struck a mine and sunk in the North Sea off Shipwash Lightvessel laid by the German submarine UC 4. Lost whilst on Government service employed as a Minesweeper.

LONDON & EDINBURGH SHIPPING CO. LTD.—LEITH

FINGAL 1562 Grt. Blt. 1894
15.3.1915: Torpedoed and sunk in the North Sea 6 miles E. by S. from Coquet Island by the German submarine U 23 whilst on a voyage from London to Leith with general cargo. 6 lost.

FARRALINE 1226 Grt. Blt. 1903
2.11.1917: Torpedoed and sunk in the English Channel 15 miles N.E.½E. from Ushant by the German submarine UC 69 whilst on a voyage from Bordeaux to Cardiff with a cargo of pit props. 1 lost.

MALVINA 1244 Grt. Blt. 1879
3.8.1918: Torpedoed and sunk in the North Sea 1 mile N.N.E. from Flamborough Head by the German submarine UB 104 whilst on a voyage from London to Leith with general cargo. 14 lost including Master.

LONDON & NORTH WESTERN RAILWAY COMPANY—LONDON

TARA ex Hibernia 1862 Grt. Blt. 1900
5.11.1915: Torpedoed and sunk in the Mediterranean off Bardia by the German submarine U 35. Lost whilst on Government service employed as an Armed Boarding Ship.

ANGLIA 1862 Grt. Blt. 1900
17.11.1915: Struck a mine and sunk in the Strait of Dover 1 mile E. from Folkestone Gate in position 51.02N 01.19E laid by the German submarine UC 5. 25 lost. Lost while on Government service employed as a Hospital Ship.

LONDON & SOUTH WESTERN RAILWAY COMPANY—SOUTHAMPTON

NORMANDY 618 Grt. Blt. 1910
25.1.1918: Torpedoed and sunk in the English Channel 8 miles E. by N. from Cape la Hague, near Cherbourg by the German submarine U 90 whilst on a voyage from Southampton to Cherbourg with general cargo and mails. 14 lost.

SOUTH-WESTERN 674 Grt. Blt. 1874
17.3.1918: Torpedoed and sunk in the English Channel 9 miles S.W. by S. from St. Catherine's Point by the German submarine UB 59 whilst on a voyage from Southampton to St. Malo with general cargo. 24 lost.

SARNIA 1498 Grt. Blt. 1910
12.9.1918: Torpedoed and sunk in the Mediterranean off Alexandria by the German submarine U 65. Lost whilst on Government service employed as an Armed Boarding Ship.

LONDONDERRY, MARQUESS OF—SEAHAM HARBOUR

LADY HELEN 811 Grt. Blt. 1909
27.10.1917: Torpedoed and sunk in the North Sea ½ mile E. from South Cheek, Robin Hood Bay by the German submarine *UB 34* whilst on a voyage from Yarmouth to Seaham Harbour in ballast. 7 lost including Master.

THE STEWART'S COURT 813 Grt. Blt. 1909
21.8.1918: Torpedoed and sunk in the North Sea 4 miles S.S.E. from Seaham Harbour by the German submarine *UB 112* whilst on a voyage from Seaham Harbour to London with a cargo of coal. 1 lost.

LORD STEWART 1445 Grt. Blt. 1905
16.9.1918: Torpedoed and sunk in the English Channel 6 miles E. ½ N. from Hope's Nose at the entrance to Tor Bay in position 50.30N 03.19W by the German submarine *UB 104* whilst on a voyage from Cherbourg to Barry Roads in ballast. 1 lost.

LOUGHER (LEWIS) & COMPANY—CARDIFF

POLDOWN ex *Pellworm* ex *Hank 1370 Grt. Blt. 1904*
9.10.1917: Struck a mine and sunk in the Atlantic 2 miles W.S.W. from Trevose Head in position 50.31N 05.04W laid by the German submarine *UC 51* whilst on a voyage from Penarth to Boulogne with a cargo of coal. 18 lost including Master.

Redcroft Steam Navigation Co. Ltd.

LADY NINIAN ex *Llanwern 4297 Grt. Blt. 1906*
28.5.1916: Captured and sunk by gunfire in the Mediterranean 106 miles N.E. ½ N. from Algiers in position 38.20N 04.08E by the German submarine *U 39* whilst on a voyage from Newport News to Leghorn with a cargo of steel rails and oats. 1 lost.

The Shipping Controller

RHEA 1308 Grt. Blt. 1917
22.6.1918: Struck a mine and sunk in the English Channel off Etaples laid by the German submarine *UC 49* whilst on a voyage from Tyne to Rouen with a cargo of coke.

LOWDEN, CONNELL & COMPANY—LIVERPOOL

British & Chilian S.S. Co. Ltd.

FERRONA 4591 Grt. Blt. 1914
28.10.1917: Captured and sunk with bombs in the Mediterranean 7 miles N.E. from Valencia by the German submarine *U 64* whilst on a voyage from Marseilles to Gibraltar in ballast. 1 lost.

LOWEN, GEORGE—MANCHESTER

HARE 774 Grt. Blt. 1886
14.12.1917: Torpedoed and sunk in the Irish Sea 7 miles E. from Kish Lightvessel by the German submarine *U 62* whilst on a voyage from Manchester to Dublin with general cargo. 12 lost.

LUCAS & COMPANY—BRISTOL

Dale S.S. Co. Ltd.

EDALE 3110 Grt. Blt. 1901
1.5.1915: Torpedoed and sunk in the Atlantic 45 miles N.W. by W. from Scilly Isles in position 50.09N 07.30W by the German submarine *U 30* whilst on a voyage from Rosario to Manchester with a cargo of wheat and linseed.

LUNN, J. T. & COMPANY—NEWCASTLE UPON TYNE

Dene S.S. Co. Ltd.

HEATHDENE 3541 Grt. Blt. 1901
7.9.1916: Captured and scuttled in the English Channel 38 miles S.S.W. from the Lizard in position 49.30N 05.30W by the German submarine *UB 39* whilst on a voyage from Benisaf to Tyne with a cargo of iron ore.

FERNDENE 3770 Grt. Blt. 1899
24.4.1917: Torpedoed and sunk in the Atlantic 150 miles W. from Bishop Rock in position 49.03N 10.00W by the German submarine *U 53* whilst on a voyage from Cape Town to London with a cargo of graphite and mealies (maize). 9 lost including Master.

LUNN & MACCOY—NEWCASTLE UPON TYNE

CRAGOSWALD 3235 Grt. Blt. 1899
18.4.1917: Torpedoed and sunk in the Atlantic 60 miles W. by S. from Bishop Rock by the German submarine *U 84* whilst on a voyage from Rosario to London with a cargo of maize. 2 lost.

BIRDOSWALD ex *Tropea* ***4013 Grt. Blt. 1892***
26.6.1917: Torpedoed and sunk in the Mediterranean 25 miles E.½S. from Tarragona by the German submarine *U 63* whilst on a voyage from Leghorn to Cartagena with a cargo of hemp. Master and Chief Engineer taken prisoner.

LYKIARDOPULO & COMPANY—LONDON

London & Piraeus S.S. Co. Ltd.

SAINT DIMITRIOS ex *Gwent* ex *Evangeline* ***3359 Grt. Blt. 1901***
20.3.1918: Torpedoed and sunk in the Mediterranean 50 miles N.¾E. from Port Said by the German submarine *U 33* whilst on a voyage from Karachi to Salonica with a cargo of grain.

LYLE SHIPPING CO. LTD. GLASGOW

CAPE FINISTERRE 4380 Grt. Blt. 1907
2.11.1917: Torpedoed and sunk in the English Channel 1 mile S.S.E. from Manacle Buoy by the German submarine *UC 17* whilst on a voyage from New York to Falmouth with a cargo of steel. 35 lost including Master.

MACANDREWS & CO. LTD.—LONDON

GRAVINA 1242 Grt. Blt. 1886
7.2.1917: Torpedoed and sunk in the Atlantic 85 miles W. from the Fastnet Rock in position 51.03N 11.30W by the German submarine *U 81* whilst on a voyage from Seville to London with a cargo of fruit. 7 lost, Master and 14 crew taken prisoner.

MACARTHY, LEONARD—NEWCASTLE UPON TYNE

Garth Shipping Co. Ltd.

AYSGARTH 3118 Grt. Blt. 1896
14.6.1917: Captured and sunk with bombs in the Atlantic 430 miles W.N.W. from Cape Finisterre by the German submarine *U 155* whilst on a voyage from Aquilas to Clyde with a cargo of iron ore. 3 lost.

ELMSGARTH ex *Juanita North* 3503 Grt. Blt. 1896
29.9.1917: Torpedoed and sunk in the Atlantic 50 miles N.W.½W. from Tory Island by the German submarine *U 61* whilst on a voyage from Kingston, (Ja) and Matanzas to Liverpool with a cargo of sugar. Master taken prisoner.

MACBETH & CO. LTD.—GLASGOW

CROSSHILL 5002 Grt. Blt. 1910
11.10.1916: Torpedoed and sunk in the Mediterranean 60 miles W. from Malta by the German submarine *UB 47* whilst on a voyage from Toulon to Salonica with a cargo of military stores. 4 lost.

CAIRNHILL 4981 Grt. Blt. 1912
17.4.1917: Captured and sunk with bombs in the Atlantic 160 miles N.W. from the Fastnet Rock in position 52.09N 13.16W by the German submarine *U 55* whilst on a voyage from New York to Le Havre with general cargo.

MACCALLUM P. and SONS. LIMITED—GREENOCK

Ard Coasters Ltd.

ARDGLASS 778 Grt. Blt. 1914
28.3.1917: Captured and sunk with bombs in the St. George's Channel 4 miles E. from South Arklow Lightvessel in position 52.41N 05.51W by the German submarine *UC 65* whilst on a voyage from Port Talbot to Belfast with a cargo of steel.

S.S. Ardgarry Co. Ltd.

ARDGASK 4542 Grt. Blt. 1917
3.4.1917: Torpedoed and sunk in the Mediterranean 15 miles S.W. from Cape Rosello, Sicily by the German submarine *U 35* whilst on a voyage from Bombay to Hull with general cargo. 1 lost.

ARDGLAMIS 4540 Grt. Blt. 1917
9.11.1917: Torpedoed and sunk in the Atlantic 125 miles W. from Cape Spartel by the German submarine *U 63* whilst on a voyage from Clyde to Naples with a cargo of coal.

***ARDGLASS** 4617 Grt. Blt. 1918*
1.4.1918: Torpedoed then captured and sunk with bombs in the North Channel 6 miles E. from the Maidens, 7 miles N.E. of Larne by the German submarine *UC 31* whilst on a voyage from Clyde to a Mediterranean port with a cargo of coal. 6 lost.

MACIVER, D. SONS & CO. LTD—LIVERPOOL

***BARBARY** 4185 Grt. Blt. 1901*
12.11.1917: Torpedoed and sunk in the Mediterranean 56 miles N.W. by N. from Port Said by the German submarine *UC 34* whilst on a voyage from Newport, Mon. and Milford Haven to a Mediterranean port. 3 lost including Master.

***GASCONY** 3133 Grt. Blt. 1908*
7.1.1918: Torpedoed and sunk in the English Channel 10 miles S.S.E. from Owers Lightvessel by the German submarine *UC 75* whilst on a voyage from Southampton to Calais with a cargo of Government stores.

***TARTARY** 4181 Grt. Blt. 1901*
16.5.1918: Torpedoed and sunk in the Irish Sea 8 miles E.N.E. from Skulmartin Lightvessel by the German submarine *U 86* whilst on a voyage from Liverpool to Buenos Aires with general cargo.

MACKAY, A. & COMPANY—GLASGOW

***SAINT NINIAN** 3026 Grt. Blt. 1894*
7.2.1917: Torpedoed and sunk in the North Sea 3 miles E. from Whitby by the German submarine *UB 34* whilst on a voyage from Port Kelah to Middlesbrough with a cargo of iron pyrites. 15 lost including Master.

MACKIE, R. & COMPANY—LEITH

New Line S.S. Co. Ltd.

***ROUMANIE** ex *Lucina* 2599 Grt. Blt. 1892*
2.9.1915: Captured and sunk with bombs in the Atlantic 40 miles N.N.W. from St. Kilda, Outer Hebrides by the German submarine *U 20* whilst on a voyage from Archangel to Clyde with a cargo of wood.

MACLAY & MCINTYRE—GLASGOW

***MANGARA** 1821 Grt. Blt. 1889*
28.7.1915: Torpedoed and sunk in the North Sea ¼ mile E. from Sizewell Buoy, Aldeburgh by the German submarine *UB 16* whilst on a voyage from Bilbao to Tees with a cargo of iron ore. 11 lost.

***SAMARA** 3172 Grt. Blt. 1906*
19.8.1915: Captured and sunk with gunfire in the Atlantic 35 miles W. from Bishop Rock by the German submarine *U 38* whilst on a voyage from Colombo to Bristol with a cargo of sugar.

***CRAIGENDORAN** ex *Loch Lintrathen* 2789 Grt. Blt. 1899*
3.3.1917: Torpedoed and sunk in the Mediterranean 6 miles E. from Cape Sigli

by the German submarine *UC 37* whilst on a voyage from Barry to Malta with a cargo of coal. 3 lost, Master and Chief Engineer taken prisoner.

VICTORIA 1620 Grt. Blt. 1887
29.4.1917: Torpedoed and sunk in the North Sea 5 miles N.E. by N. from Scarborough by the German submarine *UB 21* whilst on a voyage from Jarrow to Bayonne with a cargo of coal. 1 lost.

RUTHERGLEN 4214 Grt. Blt. 1906
24.7.1918: Torpedoed and sunk in the Mediterranean 50 miles E.S.E. from Port Mahon in position 39.43N 05.17E by the German submarine *UB 50* whilst on a voyage from Newport, Mon. to Genoa with a cargo of coal.

Glasgow Navigation Co. Ltd.

MEADOWFIELD 2750 Grt. Blt. 1904
9.7.1915: Captured and sunk by gunfire in the St. George's Channel 50 miles S.W. from Tuskar Rock by the German submarine *U 20* whilst on a voyage from Huelva to Clyde with a cargo of copper ore. 1 lost.

CAIRO 1671 Grt. Blt. 1882
13.8.1915: Captured and sunk by gunfire in the St. George's Channel 34 miles S.S.W. from Tuskar Rock by the German submarine *U 24* whilst on a voyage from Clyde to Huelva with general cargo.

MADURA 4484 Grt. Blt. 1901
18.10.1917: Torpedoed and sunk in the Atlantic 23 miles W.S.W. from Bishop Rock in position 49.36N 06.56W by the German submarine *U 62* whilst on a voyage from Montreal to France with general cargo. 3 lost.

NYASSA ex *Sceptre 2579 Grt. Blt. 1897*
24.11.1917: Torpedoed and sunk in the English Channel 3 miles E.S.E. from the Lizard by the German submarine *UB 57* whilst on a voyage from Cardiff to Rouen with a cargo of coal.

Glasgow United Shipping Co. Ltd.

MASUNDA 4952 Grt. Blt. 1909
28.2.1916: Captured and sunk by gunfire in the Mediterranean 106 miles S.W.½S. from Cape Matapan in position 34.54N 21.20E by the German submarine *U 35* whilst on a voyage from Bangkok to London with a cargo of rice.

S.S. Irthington Co. Ltd.

IRTHINGTON ex *Indianic 2845 Grt. Blt. 1897*
23.9.1917: Torpedoed and sunk in the Mediterranean 3 miles E.N.E. from Cape Vaticano, Gulf of Gioja by the German submarine *UC 53* whilst on a voyage from Naples to Messina in ballast.

S.S. Kassala Co. Ltd.

KASSANGA ex *John Coverdale 3015 Grt. Blt. 1899*
20.3.1918: Torpedoed and sunk in the St. George's Channel 23 miles S.E. by S.

from South Arklow Lightvessel in position 52.27N 05.26W by the German submarine *U 103* whilst on a voyage from Clyde to—with a cargo of coal.

S.S. Nyanza Co. Ltd.

NYANZA 4053 Grt. Blt. 1897
29.9.1918: Torpedoed and sunk in the North Channel 10 miles N.W. by W. from Corsewall Point Lighthouse by the German submarine *UB 95* whilst on a voyage from Cardiff to Archangel with a cargo of coal. 13 lost including Master.

MACLEAN, W. & COMPANY—WEST HARTLEPOOL

Maclean Shipping Co. Ltd.

DUART 3108 Grt. Blt. 1901
31.8.1916: Captured and sunk by gunfire in the Mediterranean 60 miles N.¾E. from Cape Shershel in position 37.39N 02.50E by the German submarine *U 38* whilst on a voyage from Cette to Newfoundland in ballast.

MACVICAR, MARSHALL & CO. LTD.—LIVERPOOL

Palace Shipping Co. Ltd.

FRANKLYN 4919 Grt. Blt. 1904
2.5.1918: Torpedoed and sunk in the Mediterranean 65 miles E. by N. from Port Mahon in position 40.24N 05.41E by the German submarine *UB 48* whilst on a voyage from Genoa to Montevideo in ballast.

MAIN COLLIERY CO. LTD.—BRISTOL

MAIN 715 Grt. Blt. 1914
9.10.1917: Captured and sunk by gunfire in the North Channel 1½ miles E. from Drummore, Luce Bay by the German submarine *UC 75* whilst on a voyage from Belfast to Liverpool in ballast. 12 lost.

MANCHESTER LINERS, LIMITED—MANCHESTER

MANCHESTER ENGINEER 4302 Grt. Blt. 1902
27.3.1916: Torpedoed and sunk in the St. George's Channel 20 miles W. by S. from Coningbeg Lightvessel by the German submarine *U 44* whilst on a voyage from Philadelphia to Manchester with general cargo.

MANCHESTER INVENTOR 4247 Grt. Blt. 1902
18.1.1917: Captured and sunk by gunfire in the Atlantic 50 miles N.W. by W.½W. from the Fastnet Rock in position 51.36N 10.56W by the German submarine *U 57* whilst on a voyage from St. John (NB) to Manchester with general cargo.

MANCHESTER CITIZEN 4251 Grt. Blt. 1912
27.4.1917: Torpedoed and sunk in the Atlantic 240 miles N.W. from the Fastnet Rock in position 52.30N 15.47W by the German submarine *U 70* whilst on a voyage from St. John (NB) to Manchester with general cargo. 1 lost.

MANCHESTER TRADER 3938 Grt. Blt. 1902
4.6.1917: Captured and sunk by gunfire in the Mediterranean 8 miles S.E. from Pantellaria Island by the German submarine *U 65* whilst on a voyage from Suda Bay to Algiers in ballast. 1 lost, 2nd Officer taken prisoner.

MANCHESTER MILLER 4234 Grt. Blt. 1903
5.6.1917: Torpedoed and sunk in the Atlantic 190 miles N.W.½N. from the Fastnet Rock by the German submarine *U 66* whilst on a voyage from Philadelphia to Manchester with general cargo. 8 lost.

MANCHESTER COMMERCE 4144 Grt. Blt. 1906
29.7.1917: Torpedoed and sunk in the Strait of Gibraltar 15 miles W. by N.½N. from Cape Spartel by the German submarine *U 39* whilst on a voyage from Cardiff to Gibraltar with a cargo of Government stores and coal. 1 lost.

MANCHESTER INVENTOR 4112 Grt. Blt. 1907
30.7.1917: Captured and sunk by gunfire in the North Sea 80 miles N.N.E. from Muckle Flugga in position 62.00N 00.45W by the German submarine *U 94* whilst on a voyage from Archangel to Belfast with a cargo of flax.

MANCHESTER ENGINEER 4465 Grt. Blt. 1905
16.8.1917: Torpedoed and sunk in the North Sea 4½ miles S.E. from Flamborough Head by the German submarine *UC 16* whilst on a voyage from Tyne to St. Nazaire with a cargo of coal.

MANCHESTER SPINNER 4247 Grt. Blt. 1903
22.1.1918: Torpedoed and sunk in the Atlantic 33 miles S.½E. from Malta in position 35.15N 15.05E by the Austro-Hungarian submarine *U 27* whilst on a voyage from Java to the United Kingdom with a cargo of sugar.

MANGO, J. A. & COMPANY—LONDON

FRINTON ex Freland 4194 Grt. Blt. 1912
19.3.1917: Torpedoed and sunk in the Atlantic 320 miles W. by N.½N. from Ushant in position 48.00N 13.00W by the German submarine *U 81* whilst on a voyage from Cartagena to Middlesbrough with a cargo of iron ore. 4 lost.

Lydford S.S. Co. Ltd.

EPTALOFOS ex Detmold 4413 Grt. Blt. 1911
23.3.1917: Torpedoed and sunk in the Mediterranean 47 miles N.W. from Malta by the German submarine *U 64* whilst on a voyage from Malta to Kingston, (Ja) in ballast. Master, 2 Officers, 4 Engineers and 1 Gunner taken prisoner.

Ognam Shipping Co. Ltd.

EPTAPYRGION ex Essex Baron 4307 Grt. Blt. 1914
23.4.1917: Torpedoed and sunk in the Atlantic 150 miles W. by S. from Scilly Isles in position 48.28N 09.40W by the German submarine *U 53* whilst on a voyage from Montevideo to Cherbourg with a cargo of oats and tinned meat.

MANN, MACNEAL & CO. LTD.—GLASGOW

Ford Shipping Co. Ltd.

BELFORD 516 Grt. Blt. 1904
20.12.1915: Torpedoed and sunk in the English Channel off Boulogne by the German submarine *UB 10* whilst on a voyage from Cardiff to Calais with a cargo of patent fuel.

SOUTHFORD ex *Sinbad* **963 Grt. Blt. 1883**
25.2.1916: Struck a mine and sunk in the North Sea 4 miles E.S.E. from Southwold laid by the German submarine *UC 10* whilst on a voyage from Tyne to Boulogne with a cargo of coke. 4 lost.

GOWER COAST ex *Sir George Bacon* ex *Prestonian* **804 Grt. Blt. 1899**
4.4.1917: Struck a mine and sunk in the English Channel off Treport laid by the German submarine *UC 71* whilst on a voyage from Tyne to Treport with a cargo of coal. 15 lost including Master.

MANN, MACNEAL & STEEVES LIMITED—LIVERPOOL

The Shipping Controller

BORGA 1046 Grt. Blt. 1907
1.3.1918: Torpedoed and sunk in the English Channel 9 miles S.E. by S. from Beer Head by the German submarine *U 55* whilst on a voyage from Swansea to Dieppe with a cargo of coal. 5 lost.

MARSHALL, C. & COMPANY—SUNDERLAND

The Shipping Controller

STEN ex *Jan Mayn* ex *Aarvak* ex *Neva* ex *Juana Mancy* **928 Grt. Blt. 1883**
18.10.1917: Torpedoed and sunk in the Atlantic 5 miles N. from Godrevy Lighthouse by the German submarine *UC 64* whilst on a voyage from Barry to St. Malo with a cargo of coal. 9 lost including Master.

MARTYN, MARTYN & CO. LTD.—CARDIFF

Mervyn S.S. Co. Ltd.

MADRYN 2244 Grt. Blt. 1916
16.9.1918: Torpedoed and sunk in the Atlantic 5 miles N.N.E. from Trevose Head by the German submarine *U 82* whilst on a voyage from Penarth to Devonport with a cargo of coal.

MARWOOD, GEORGE—WHITBY

International Line S.S. Co. Ltd.

VALENTIA 3242 Grt. Blt. 1898
16.7.1917: Torpedoed and sunk in the Atlantic 70 miles W.½S. from Bishop Rock by the German submarine *UC 41* whilst on a voyage from Cardiff to Dakar with general cargo and coal. 3 lost.

NUCERIA 4702 Grt. Blt. 1914
2.10.1917: Torpedoed and sunk in the Atlantic 120 miles W.½N. from Cape Spartel by the German submarine *U 39* whilst on a voyage from Barry to Italy with a cargo of coal. 2 lost.

MATHIAS, JOHN & SONS—CARDIFF

Cambrian Steam Navigation Co. Ltd.

HARROVIAN 4309 Grt. Blt. 1914
16.4.1916: Captured and sunk by gunfire in the Atlantic 60 miles W. from Bishop Rock by the German submarine *U 69* whilst on a voyage from New York to Le Havre with general cargo.

CLIFTONIAN 4303 Grt. Blt. 1911
6.2.1917: Torpedoed and sunk in the Atlantic 4½ miles S.¾E. from Galley Head in position 51.28N 08.55W by the German submarine *U 85* whilst on a voyage from Cardiff to Marseilles with a cargo of coal.

CHELTONIAN 4426 Grt. Blt. 1911
8.6.1917: Captured and sunk by gunfire in the Mediterranean 54 miles W. by S. from Planier Lighthouse by the German submarine *U 72* whilst on a voyage from Genoa to Oran in ballast. Master and 1 Gunner taken prisoner.

MCALLUM, WILLIAM & COMPANY—LONDON

Hendon S.S. Co. Ltd.

BUTETOWN ex *Langoe* **3789 Grt. Blt. 1905**
8.9.1916: Torpedoed and sunk in the Mediterranean 55 miles W.S.W. from Cape Matapan in position 36.00N 21.15E by the German submarine *UB 47* whilst on a voyage from Malta to Mudros with general cargo and coal.

MCGREGOR, GOW & CO. LTD.—LONDON

Glen Line Ltd.

GLENGYLE 9395 Grt. Blt. 1914
1.1.1916: Torpedoed and sunk in the Mediterranean 240 miles E. by S. from Malta by the German submarine *U 34* whilst on a voyage from Bombay to Genoa with a cargo of cotton and linseed. 10 lost.

GLENLOGAN ex *Denton Grange* **5838 Grt. Blt. 1896**
31.10.1916: Torpedoed and sunk in the Mediterranean 10 miles S.E. from Stromboli Island by the German submarine *U 21* whilst on a voyage from Yokohama to London and Hull with general cargo.

GLENOGLE 7682 Grt. Blt. 1916
27.3.1917: Torpedoed and sunk in the Atlantic 207 miles S.W. from the Fastnet Rock in position 48.20N 12.00W by the German submarine *U 24* whilst on a voyage from Tees and London to Yokohama with general cargo.

GLENSTRAE 4718 Grt. Blt. 1905
28.7.1917: Torpedoed and sunk in the Atlantic 66 miles S.W. by S.¼S. from Bishop Rock in position 48.40N 06.55W by the German submarine *UC 62* whilst on a voyage from Dakar to Dunkirk and London with general cargo. 1 lost.

GLENARTNEY ex *Montezuma 7263 Grt. Blt. 1915*
6.2.1918: Torpedoed and sunk in the Mediterranean 30 miles N.E. from Cape Bon by the German submarine *UC 54* whilst on a voyage from Singapore to London with general cargo. 2 lost.

MCLELLAND, REUBEN. A.—KINGSTON, ONTARIO

PORT DALHOUSIE ex *Tynemount 1744 Grt. Blt. 1913*
19.3.1916: Torpedoed and sunk off the mouth of the River Thames 2 miles S.½W. from Kentish Knock Lightvessel by the German submarine *UB 10* whilst on a voyage from Tees to Nantes with a cargo of steel billets. 12 lost including Master.

Forwarders Ltd.

W. H. DWYER 1770 Grt. Blt. 1913
26.8.1917: Torpedoed and sunk in the English Channel 15 miles E. by N. from Berry Head in position 50.18N 03.11W by the German submarine *UB 38* whilst on a voyage from Rouen to Newport. Mon. in ballast.

MERCANTILE S.S. CO. LTD.—LONDON

COQUET 4396 Grt. Blt. 1904
4.1.1916: Captured and sunk with bombs in the Mediterranean 200 miles E. from Malta by the German submarine *U 34* whilst on a voyage from Torrevieja to Rangoon with a cargo of salt. 17 lost and 10 taken prisoner by Arabs.

MEREVALE SHIPPING CO. LTD.—CARDIFF

CAMBANK ex *Raithmoor 3112 Grt. Blt. 1899*
20.2.1915: Torpedoed and sunk in the Irish Sea 10 miles E. from Point Lynas by the German submarine *U 30* whilst on a voyage from Huelva to Garston with a cargo of copper ore. 4 lost.

METCALF, SIMPSON & CO. LTD.—WEST HARTLEPOOL

MANCHURIA 2997 Grt. Blt. 1905
17.10.1917: Torpedoed and sunk in the Atlantic 60 miles N.W. from Ushant by the German submarine *U 53* whilst on a voyage from La Goulette to Hartlepool with a cargo of iron ore. 26 lost including Master.

MEXICO STEAM SHIP CO. LTD.—HONG KONG

MEXICO CITY 5078 Grt. Blt. 1896
5.2.1918: Torpedoed and sunk in the Irish Sea 15 miles W. by S.½S. from South Stack Rock by the German submarine *U 101* whilst on a voyage from Liverpool to Alexandria with general cargo. 29 lost including Master.

MIDLAND RAILWAY COMPANY—DERBY

DONEGAL 1885 Grt. Blt. 1904
17.4.1917: Torpedoed and sunk in the English Channel 19 miles S. from Dean Lightvessel off Spithead in position 50.26N 01.00W by the German submarine *UC 21* whilst on a voyage from Le Havre to Southampton. 11 lost. Lost whilst on Government service employed as a Hospital Ship.

MILLER, W. S. & COMPANY—GLASGOW

Ellaston S.S. Co. Ltd.

ELLASTON ex *Wearbeck* 3796 Grt. Blt. 1906
3.4.1916: Captured and torpedoed in the Mediterranean 65 miles N.W. by W. from Cape Serrat in position 37.40N 00.08E by the German submarine *U 34* whilst on a voyage from Immingham to Gibraltar and Alexandria with a cargo of coal.

LUCISTON 2948 Grt. Blt. 1910
29.11.1916: Torpedoed and sunk in the Mediterranean 4 miles E. from Dellamara Point by the German submarine *UC 22* whilst on a voyage from Cardiff to Gibraltar and Malta with a cargo of coal.

GRETASTON ex *Vauxhall Bridge* 3395 Grt. Blt. 1901
30.4.1917: Torpedoed and sunk in the Bay of Biscay S. of the mouth of the River Gironde in position 45.26N 01.37W by the German submarine *UC 72* whilst on a voyage from Huelva to Garston with a cargo of copper ore. 29 lost including Master.

MARISTON 2908 Grt. Blt. 1915
15.7.1917: Torpedoed and sunk in the Atlantic 82 miles W. from the Fastnet Rock in position 50.52N 11.38W by the German submarine *U 45* whilst on a voyage from Almeria to Clyde with a cargo of copper ore. 28 lost including Master.

PALATINE 2110 Grt. Blt. 1888
16.8.1917: Torpedoed and sunk in the Inner Hebrides 10 miles W.N.W. from Island of Canna by the German submarine *U 75* whilst on a voyage from Clyde to Bergen with a cargo of coal. Master taken prisoner.

IRISTON 3221 Grt. Blt. 1916
24.9.1917: Torpedoed and sunk in the Mediterranean 7 miles S.by W. from Cape Camerat, near Marseilles by the German submarine *U 32* whilst on a voyage from Clyde to Savona with a cargo of coal.

ELSISTON 2908 Grt. Blt. 1915
19.10.1917: Torpedoed and sunk in the Mediterranean 150 miles E. by S.½S. from Malta in position 35.40N 17.28E by the Austro-Hungarian submarine *U 14* whilst on a voyage from Malta to Suda Bay with a cargo of Government stores. 1 lost.

LUCISTON ex *Lucincita* ex *Red Cross* 2877 Grt. Blt. 1891
24.12.1917: Torpedoed and damaged in the English Channel 1½ miles W. by S. from Owers Lightvessel by the German submarine *UC 71* whilst on a voyage from Southampton to Boulogne with a cargo of Government stores. 1 lost. Beached and became a total loss.

ELLASTON ex *Rhodesian* ex *Matatua **3192 Grt. Blt. 1890***
16.3.1918: Torpedoed then captured and sunk with bombs 180 miles W. by S. (true) from Palma, Canary Islands in position 28.29N 21.00W by the German submarine *U 152* whilst on a voyage from Barry to Sierra Leone with a cargo of coal. Master taken prisoner.

FLORRIESTON ex *Battersea Bridge **3366 Grt. Blt. 1901***
20.4.1918: Torpedoed and sunk in the Irish Sea 6 miles E. ½N. from South Stack Rock in position 54.30N 05.11W by the German submarine *U 91* whilst on a voyage from Almeria to Clyde with a cargo of copper ore. 19 lost including Master.

WILEYSIKE 2501 Grt. Blt. 1888
10.5.1918: Torpedoed and sunk in the St. George's Channel 8 miles S.W. from St. Ann's Head by the German submarine *U 54* whilst on a voyage from Clyde to France with a cargo of coal. 4 lost.

MILLER & RICHARDS LIMITED—LONDON

Brook S.S. Co. Ltd.

CARISBROOK 2352 Grt. Blt. 1907
21.6.1915: Captured and sunk by gunfire in the North Sea 70 miles S. ¾W. from Start Point Lighthouse, Orkney by the German submarine *U 38* whilst on a voyage from Montreal to Leith with a cargo of wheat.

NEVISBROOK 3140 Grt. Blt. 1913
20.7.1917: Torpedoed and sunk in the Atlantic 90 miles W. ½S. from the Fastnet Rock in position 50.39N 11.42W by the German submarine *U 45* whilst on a voyage from La Goulette to Barrow with a cargo of iron ore.

S.S. Tregenna Co. Ltd.

MAVISBROOK 3152 Grt. Blt. 1912
17.5.1918: Torpedoed and sunk in the Mediterranean 50 miles S.E. by S. ½S. from Cabo de Gata in position 36.50N 01.35W by the German submarine *UB 50* whilst on a voyage from Cardiff to Malta with a cargo of coal. 18 lost including Master.

MITCHELL, JAMES & SONS—DUNDEE

DOLCOATH 1706 Grt. Blt. 1882
10.5.1916: Struck a mine and sunk in the Downs 3¼ miles N.N.E. from North Foreland laid by the German submarine *UC 7* whilst on a voyage from Tyne and Hull to Cette with a cargo of coal. 1 lost.

ISER ex *Lisl* ex *Iser **2160 Grt. Blt. 1888***
23.2.1917: Torpedoed and sunk in the Bay of Biscay 14 miles N.W. from Belle Ile in position 47.28N 03.35W by the German submarine *UC 17* whilst on a voyage from Newport, Mon. to Rochefort with a cargo of coal. 1 lost.

WARNOW ex *John Readhead **1593 Grt. Blt. 1883***
2.5.1917: Torpedoed and sunk in the Atlantic 6 miles W. from Trevose Head in position 50.30N 05.10W by the German submarine *UC 48* whilst on a voyage from Penarth to—with a cargo of railway material. 14 lost including Master.

***BRAMHAM** 1978 Grt. Blt. 1891*
20.7.1917: Struck a mine and sunk in the English Channel 10 miles E. by S. from the Lizard in position 50.01N 04.56W laid by the German submarine *UC 47* whilst on a voyage from Barry to Rouen with a cargo of coal. 1 lost.

ERIC CALVERT** ex Elmville **1862 Grt. Blt. 1889
22.4.1918: Torpedoed and sunk in the English Channel 4 miles S.S.W. from St. Anthony's Point by the German submarine *UB 103* whilst on a voyage from Penarth to Boulogne with a cargo of coal. 2 lost.

MOLLER & COMPANY—LONDON

Zodiac Shipping Co. Ltd.

***RIBSTON** 3372 Grt. Blt. 1894*
16.7.1917: Torpedoed and sunk in the Atlantic 85 miles W. from the Fastnet Rock in position 50.52N 11.38W by the German submarine *U 45* whilst on a voyage from Melilla to Clyde with a cargo of iron ore. 25 lost including Master.

***BLAKE** 3740 Grt. Blt. 1906*
24.7.1917: Torpedoed and sunk in the Atlantic 30 miles N. by W.½W. from Cape Wrath by the German submarine *UC 49* whilst on a voyage from Penarth to Archangel with a cargo of coal. 5 lost.

MOLLER & COMPANY—SHANGHAI

MORESBY** ex Jacob Christensen **1763 Grt. Blt. 1881
28.11.1916: Torpedoed and sunk in the Mediterranean 120 miles N.W. by N. from Alexandria in position 32.36N 28.38E by the German submarine *U 39* whilst on a voyage from Saigon to Dunkirk with a cargo of rice. 33 lost.

British China S.S. Co. Ltd.

GEMINI** ex Dingwall **2128 Grt. Blt. 1892
20.7.1918: Torpedoed and sunk in the Atlantic 7 miles N.W.½N. from Godrevy Lighthouse by the German submarine *U 60* whilst on a voyage from Belfast to St. Helens Roads with a cargo of hay, timber and felt. 2 lost.

MONROE BROTHERS—CARDIFF

***CORNELIA** 903 Grt. Blt. 1872*
6.3.1917: Captured and sunk by gunfire in the Atlantic 9 miles W.N.W. from the Skelligs in position 51.47N 10.43W by the German submarine *UC 43* whilst on a voyage from Oporto to Cardiff with a cargo of pitwood.

MOORGATE INVESTMENT & AGENCY CO. LTD. THE—LONDON

The Shipping Controller

HUNTSFALL** ex Goslar **4331 Grt. Blt. 1906
2.10.1916: Torpedoed and sunk in the Aegean Sea 12 miles S.S.E. from Skyro Island by the German submarine *UB 46* whilst on a voyage from St. Louis du Rhone to Salonica with a cargo of hay. Master taken prisoner.

MORDEY, JONES & COMPANY—NEWPORT, MON.

AUCKLAND CASTLE 1084 Grt. Blt. 1883
24.8.1918: Torpedoed and sunk in the North Sea 5 miles E. by S. ½ S. from Farne Island by the German submarine *UC 59* whilst on a voyage from Tyne to Moss with a cargo of coal. 12 lost including Master.

MOREL, R. E. & COMPANY—CARDIFF

CYFARTHFA 3014 Grt. Blt. 1904
11.4.1917: Torpedoed and sunk in the Mediterranean 32 miles W.S.W. from Cerigotto Island by the German submarine *UB 47* whilst on a voyage from Oran to Salonica with a cargo of hay and wine. Master taken prisoner.

DOWLAIS 3016 Grt. Blt. 1904
4.12.1917: Torpedoed and sunk in the Mediterranean off Cape de Fer, Algeria by the German submarine *UB 48* whilst on a voyage from Greece to Glasgow with a cargo of copper ore. 26 lost including Master.

St. Andrew's (Cardiff) Ltd.

ST. ANDREWS 3613 Grt. Blt. 1906
13.6.1917: Torpedoed and sunk in the Mediterranean 4 miles W. from Cape Spartivento, Italy by the German submarine *UC 38* whilst on a voyage from Karachi to Marseilles with a cargo of grain. 3 lost.

MORGAN & CADOGAN LIMITED—CARDIFF

NAILSEA COURT ex *Graphic* 3295 Grt. Blt. 1902
19.1.1917: Torpedoed and sunk in the Atlantic 32 miles W. from the Skelligs by the German submarine *U 48* whilst on a voyage from Bougie to Barrow with a cargo of iron ore.

BOYNTON 2578 Grt. Blt. 1892
25.9.1917: Torpedoed and sunk in the Atlantic 5 miles W.N.W. from Cape Cornwall, 4 miles N. of Lands End by the German submarine *UC 47* whilst on a voyage from Manchester to France with general cargo. 23 lost including Master.

Cambo Shipping Co. Ltd.

MARGA ex *Margaret* 674 Grt. Blt. 1908
9.11.1916: Captured and sunk by gunfire in the English Channel 16 miles N. by W. from Ushant by the German submarine *UC 18* whilst on a voyage from Cardiff to Lorient with a cargo of coal.

MORGAN, E. T.—CARDIFF

BARGANY 872 Grt. Blt. 1911
24.12.1916: Captured and sunk by gunfire in the English Channel 25 miles N. from Ushant in position 48.52N 05.19W by the German submarine *UC 17* whilst on a voyage from Cardiff to Lorient with a cargo of coal.

MORGAN, E. W. & CO. LTD.—LONDON

Gratitude S.S. Co. Ltd.

***GRANGEWOOD* 3422 Grt. Blt. 1902**
24.7.1915: Captured and torpedoed in the North Sea 20 miles E.N.E. from Flugga Lighthouse, Shetland by the German submarine *U 41* whilst on a voyage from Archangel to Le Havre with a cargo of wheat and flax.

MORRISON, JOHN M. & SON—NEWCASTLE UPON TYNE

Morrison Shipping Co. Ltd.

***BEN CRUACHAN* 3092 Grt. Blt. 1902**
30.1.1915: Captured and sunk with bombs in the Irish Sea 15 miles N.W. from Morecambe Bay Lightvessel in position 53.36N 03.51W by the German submarine *U 21* whilst on a voyage from Cardiff to Scapa Flow with a cargo of coal.

***BEN LOMOND* 2814 Grt. Blt. 1906**
8.7.1918: Torpedoed and sunk in the Atlantic 30 miles S.E. from Daunts Rock by the German submarine *U 92* whilst on a voyage from Seville to Ardrossan with a cargo of iron ore. 23 lost including Master.

MOSS, H. E. & COMPANY—LIVERPOOL

***LUMINA* 6219 Grt. Blt. 1915**
6.11.1915: Captured and sunk by gunfire in the Mediterranean 120 miles S. by E. from Cape Martello in position 33.40N 25.06E by the German submarine *U 35* whilst on a voyage from Tarakan to Malta with a cargo of fuel oil.

***MIRLO* 6978 Grt. Blt. 1917**
16.8.1918: Torpedoed and sunk in the Atlantic ½ mile S. by E. from Wimble Shoal Buoy, Cape Hatteras, North Carolina by the German submarine *U 117* whilst on a voyage from New Orleans to London with a cargo of gasolene and refined oil. 9 lost.

British Dyes Limited

***TURNBRIDGE* ex *Bala* ex *Ethel Radcliffe* 2874 Grt. Blt. 1894**
24.12.1917: Torpedoed and sunk in the Mediterranean 34 miles N.E. by N. from Cape Ivi, Algeria in position 36.37N 00.24E by the German submarine *U 35* whilst on a voyage from Cardiff to Malta with a cargo of coal. 1 lost.

Maritime Investment Limited

***REAPWELL* ex *Shirley* 3417 Grt. Blt. 1900**
27.11.1916: Torpedoed and sunk in the Mediterranean 148 miles N.W. by N. from Alexandria in position 33.37N 27.35E by the German submarine *U 39* whilst on a voyage from Cardiff to Malta and Port Said with general cargo and coal. Master taken prisoner.

Sefton S.S. Co. Ltd.

HEADLANDS 2988 Grt. Blt. 1982
12.3.1915: Torpedoed and sunk in the Atlantic 8 miles S. from Scilly Isles by the German submarine *U 29* whilst on a voyage from Marseilles to Swansea in ballast.

MOUNT CONISTON ex *Elmgrove* ex *Vortigem* 3018 Grt. Blt. 1892
5.8.1916: Captured and sunk with bombs in the Mediterranean 7 miles E. by S. from Medas Island, near Barcelona by the German submarine *U 35* whilst on a voyage from Port Talbot to Marseilles with a cargo of coal and machinery.

MOSS STEAM SHIP CO. LTD.—LIVERPOOL

VOSGES 1295 Grt. Blt. 1911
27.3.1915: Sunk by gunfire in the Atlantic 38 miles W. by N from Trevose Head in position 50.42N 05.35W by the German submarine *U 28* whilst on a voyage from Bordeaux to Liverpool with general cargo. 1 lost.

TANIS 3655 Grt. Blt. 1913
27.11.1915: Captured and sunk by gunfire in the Mediterranean 3 miles N. from Zembra Island, Tunis by the German submarine *U 33* whilst on a voyage from Liverpool to Alexandria with general cargo.

BUSIRIS 2705 Grt. Blt. 1904
9.12.1915: Captured and sunk by gunfire in the Mediterranean 190 miles W.N.W. from Alexandria in position 32.50N 26.20E by the German submarine *U 39* whilst on a voyage from Alexandria to Liverpool with general cargo.

MOERIS 3409 Grt. Blt. 1902
30.6.1916: Torpedoed and sunk in the Mediterranean 46 miles S.E. from Cape Sidero in position 34.50N 26.58E by the German submarine *UB 44* whilst on a voyage from Clyde to Malta and Alexandria with general cargo. 3 lost.

MEROE 3552 Grt. Blt. 1911
29.10.1916: Captured and torpedoed in the Atlantic 70 miles W.½N. from Cape Trafalgar in position 36.00N 07.35W by the German submarine *U 63* whilst on a voyage from Alexandria to Liverpool with general cargo.

KAPUNDA 3383 Grt. Blt. 1908
12.11.1916: Torpedoed and sunk in the Mediterranean 205 miles E.S.E. from Malta in position 35.00N 18.39E by the German submarine *UB 43* whilst on a voyage from Alexandria to Liverpool with general cargo.

SEBEK ex *Harpeake* 4601 Grt. Blt. 1909
21.4.1917: Torpedoed and sunk in the Atlantic 145 miles N.W. from Tory Island in position 56.12N 12.20W by the German submarine *U 70* whilst on a voyage from Liverpool to Alexandria with general cargo. 1 lost.

ESNEH 3247 Grt. Blt. 1909
31.5.1917: Torpedoed and sunk in the Atlantic 190 miles N.W. by W. from Tory Island in position 55.50N 13.50W by the German submarine *U 69* whilst on a voyage from Liverpool to Alexandria with general cargo.

VENDEE 1295 Grt. Blt. 1911
8.7.1917: Struck a mine and sunk in the Bay of Biscay at the mouth of the River Gironde in position 45.45N 01.20W laid by the German submarine *UC 71* whilst on a voyage from Bordeaux to Liverpool with general cargo.

KHEPHREN 2774 Grt. Blt. 1905
16.7.1917: Torpedoed and sunk in the Mediterranean 178 miles E. from Malta by the German submarine *U 32* whilst on a voyage from Liverpool to Alexandria with general cargo.

HATHOR 3823 Grt. Blt. 1914
27.8.1917: Torpedoed and sunk in the Mediterranean 3 miles N.W. from Cape Tedles, Algeria by the German submarine *UB 48* whilst on a voyage from Liverpool to Alexandria with general cargo. 1 lost, Master taken prisoner.

LUXOR 3571 Grt. Blt. 1918
19.3.1918: Torpedoed and sunk in the English Channel 27 miles S.W. by S. from St. Catherine's Point by the German submarine *UB 57* whilst on a voyage from Cherbourg to Barry Roads in ballast.

HATASU 3193 Grt. Blt. 1917
27.9.1918: Torpedoed and sunk in the Mediterranean 50 miles N.¾W. from Oran in position 36.32N 00.53W by the German submarine *UB 49* whilst on a voyage from Alexandria to Liverpool with a cargo of cotton, currants and onions. 2 lost.

LIBOURNE 1219 Grt. Blt. 1918
29.9.1918: Torpedoed and sunk in the English Channel 10 miles S. from the Lizard by the German submarine *U 54* whilst on a voyage from Bordeaux to Liverpool with general cargo. 3 lost.

MURPHY, M. LIMITED—DUBLIN

RHONA 640 Grt. Blt. 1909
27.11.1916: Captured and sunk with bombs in the English Channel 19 miles N.W. by N. from Guernsey by the German submarine *UB 18* whilst on a voyage from Cardiff to Servan with a cargo of coal.

FERGA 791 Grt. Blt. 1916
14.2.1917: Captured and sunk by gunfire in the St. George's Channel 15 miles S. from Bardsey Island in position 52.02N 05.04W by the German submarine *UC 65* whilst on a voyage from Swansea to Liverpool with general cargo.

MURPHY & SANDWITH—WORKINGTON

Stainburn S.S. Co. Ltd.

LYNBURN 587 Grt. Blt. 1917
29.8.1917: Struck a mine and sunk in the St. George's Channel ½ mile S.E. from North Arklow Lightvessel laid by the German submarine *UC 75* whilst on a voyage from Cork to Whitehaven with a cargo of pitwood. 8 lost.

MURRELL, JOSEPH E. & SON—WEST HARTLEPOOL

BRACONDALE ex *Chagford 2095 Grt. Blt. 1903*
5.8.1917: Torpedoed and damaged in the Atlantic 120 miles N.W. of Tory Island by the German submarine *U 44*. 1 lost. 6.8.1817 taken in tow by H.M. trawler *SAXON 239/07* but sunk on the 7.8.1917. Lost whilst on Government service employed as a Special Service Ship.

NELSON, DONKIN & CO. LTD.—LONDON

The Admiralty

MARQUIS BACQUEHEM 4396 Grt. Blt. 1893
30.10.1916: Torpedoed and sunk in the Atlantic 50 miles S. by E. from Cape St. Vincent in position 36.17N 08.30W by the German submarine *U 32* whilst on a voyage from Calcutta to Middlesbrough with a cargo of manganese ore.

NELSON, HUGH & WILLIAM LIMITED—LIVERPOOL

Nelson Line (Liverpool) Limited

HIGHLAND BRIGADE 5669 Grt. Blt. 1901
7.4.1918: Torpedoed and sunk in the English Channel 6 miles S. by E. from St. Catherine's Point in position 50.35N 01.14W by the German submarine *UC 71* whilst on a voyage from Liverpool to Buenos Aires with general cargo.

HIGHLAND HARRIS 6032 Grt. Blt. 1904
7.8.1918: Torpedoed and sunk in the Atlantic 82 miles N.¾W. from Eagle Island by the German submarine *U 96* whilst on a voyage from Liverpool to Rio de Janeiro with general cargo and carrying livestock. 24 lost.

Nelson Steam Navigation Co. Ltd.

HIGHLAND CORRIE 7583 Grt. Blt. 1910
16.5.1917: Torpedoed and sunk in the English Channel 4 miles S. from Owers Lightvessel in position 50.28N 00.38W by the German submarine *UB 40* whilst on a voyage from La Plata to London with a cargo of frozen meat. 5 lost.

NESS, JOHN—SUNDERLAND

DOROTHY 3806 Grt. Blt. 1902
24.2.1917: Torpedoed and sunk in the Mediterranean 25 miles S.E. by S.½S. from Pantellaria Island by the German submarine *U 35* whilst on a voyage from Tunis to Salonica. 6 lost.

NEW YORK & PACIFIC S.S. CO. LTD.—LONDON

CELIA 5004 Grt. Blt. 1904
2.2.1918: Torpedoed and sunk in the Mediterranean 44 miles E. by N.½N. from Cape Creus in position 42.39N 04.08E by the German submarine *UB 48* whilst on a voyage from Genoa to Gibraltar in ballast.

NEW ZEALAND SHIPPING CO. LTD.—LONDON

ROTORUA 11140 Grt. Blt. 1910
22.3.1917: Torpedoed and sunk in the English Channel 24 miles E. from Start Point in position 50.17N 03.07W by the German submarine *UC 17* whilst on a voyage from Wellington and Newport News to London with general cargo. 1 lost.

TURAKINA 9920 Grt. Blt. 1902
13.8.1917: Torpedoed and sunk in the Atlantic 120 miles W.S.W. from Bishop Rock in position 48.30N 08.34W by the German submarine *U 86* whilst on a voyage from London to New York and New Zealand with general cargo. 2 lost.

HURUNUI 10644 Grt. Blt. 1912
18.5.1918: Torpedoed and sunk in the English Channel 48 miles S. by W. from the Lizard in position 49.08N 05.00W by the German submarine *U 94* whilst on a voyage from Wellington and New York to London with general cargo. 1 lost.

NEWBIGIN, E. R. LIMITED—NEWCASTLE UPON TYNE

Newbigin Steam Shipping Co. Ltd.

GREAVESASH 1263 Grt. Blt. 1917
26.2.1918: Torpedoed and sunk in the English Channel 10 miles N.E. from Cape Barfleur by the German submarine *UB 74* whilst on a voyage from Le Havre to Barry Roads in ballast. 8 lost.

SUNNIVA 1913 Grt. Blt. 1917
28.6.1918: Torpedoed and sunk in the North Sea 4 miles E. from Sunderland by the German submarine *UC 17* whilst on a voyage from London to Tyne in ballast. 2 lost.

NICHOLL, E. & COMPANY—CARDIFF

SILKSWORTH HALL 4777 Grt. Blt. 1907
10.4.1916: Torpedoed and sunk in the North Sea 1¼ miles N.E. from Corton Lightvessel by the German submarine *UB 12* whilst on a voyage from Hull to Philadelphia in ballast. 3 lost.

HAIGH HALL 4809 Grt. Blt. 1908
30.6.1917: Torpedoed and sunk in the Mediterranean 40 miles E. from Malta in position 36.12N 15.24E by the Austro-Hungarian submarine *U 28* whilst on a voyage from Bombay to Naples with a cargo of wheat.

NICHOLLS, A. & COMPANY—NEWCASTLE UPON TYNE

PLANUDES 542 Grt. Blt. 1900
20.1.1917: Struck a mine and sunk in the North Sea off Whitby laid by the German submarine *UC 43* whilst on a voyage from Tyne to Trouville with a cargo of coal. 11 lost including Master.

NICHOLSON, R. & SONS—LIVERPOOL

Corinthian Shipping Co. Ltd.

CORFU* 3695 Grt. Blt. *1907
17.4.1917: Captured and sunk with bombs in the Atlantic 160 miles W. from Gibraltar in position 35.14N 18.25W by the German submarine *U 35* whilst on a voyage from Philadelphia to Genoa with a cargo of scrap iron. 3 lost.

NIELSEN, C. & SONS—WEST HARTLEPOOL

DULCIE* 2033 Grt. Blt. *1900
19.6.1915: Torpedoed and sunk in the North Sea 6 miles E. from Aldeburgh by the German submarine *UB 13* whilst on a voyage from Tyne to Le Havre with a cargo of coal, 1 lost.

JESSIE* 2256 Grt. Blt. *1891
16.6.1917: Torpedoed and sunk in the Atlantic 260 miles W.½S. from Bishop Rock by the German submarine *U 82* whilst on a voyage from Alexandria to Hull with a cargo of cottonseed.

LUIS* 4284 Grt. Blt. *1916
12.4.1918: Torpedoed and sunk in the English Channel 3½ miles S.S.E. from St. Catherine's Point by the German submarine *UC 71* whilst on a voyage from Halifax, (NS) to St. Helens Roads with a cargo of Government stores. 4 lost.

NISBET, EDWARD T.—NEWCASTLE UPON TYNE

Lambton & Hetton Collieries Limited.

LADY ANN* 1016 Grt. Blt. *1882
16.2.1917: Torpedoed and sunk in the North Sea 3 miles E. by S. from Scarborough by the German submarine *UB 21* whilst on a voyage from Sunderland to Rochester with a cargo of coal. 11 lost including Master.

HERRINGTON* 1258 Grt. Blt. *1905
4.5.1917: Struck a mine and sunk in the North Sea ¾ mile E.S.E. from Red Head, Forfar in position 56.37N 02.27W laid by the German submarine *UC 77* whilst on a voyage from Methil to—with a cargo of coal.

GREGYNOG* 1701 Grt. Blt. *1899
18.4.1918: Torpedoed and sunk in the Bristol Channel 16 miles S.W. from Hartland Point by the German submarine *UB 86* whilst on a voyage from Penarth to Portland with a cargo of coal. 3 lost.

NISBET, GEORGE & COMPANY—GLASGOW

Clydesdale Navigation Co. Ltd.

BLAIRHALL* ex *Heros* 2549 Grt. Blt. *1899
26.7.1918: Torpedoed and sunk in the North Sea 3½ miles E.N.E. from Sunderland by the German submarine *UC 40* whilst on a voyage from Middlesbrough to Tyne in ballast. 1 lost.

NORTH OF SCOTLAND & ORKNEY & SHETLAND STEAM NAVIGATION CO. LTD.—ABERDEEN

ST. MARGARET 943 Grt. Blt. 1913
12.9.1917: Torpedoed and sunk in the Atlantic 30 miles S.E. from Dimon Island, Faeroe Isles by the German submarine *U 103* whilst on a voyage from Leith to Reykjavik with general cargo. 5 lost.

ST. MAGNUS 809 Grt. Blt. 1912
12.2.1918: Torpedoed and sunk in the North Sea 3 miles N.N.E. from Peterhead by the German submarine *UC 58* whilst on a voyage from Lerwick to Aberdeen carrying passengers and general cargo. 5 lost.

NOURSE, JAMES LIMITED—LONDON

DEWA 3802 Grt. Blt. 1913
17.9.1916: Torpedeod and sunk in the Mediterranean 45 miles E.¾N. from Malta by the German submarine *UB 43* whilst on a voyage from Toulon to Port Said. 3 lost.

OCEAN SHIPPING CO. LTD.—ST. JOHN'S, NEWFOUNDLAND

CUPICA ex *Elfleda* ex *Gretchen* ex *Hartrod* ex *Cupica* 1240 Grt. Blt. 1888
19.10.1917: Captured and sunk by gunfire in the Atlantic 75 miles W. by S.½S. from Bishop Rock by the German submarines *U 107* and *UC 79* whilst on a voyage from Fowey to Savannah with a cargo of china clay.

OCEANIC STEAM NAVIGATION CO. LTD.—LONDON

White Star Line

ARABIC 15801 Grt. Blt. 1903
19.8.1915: Torpedoed and sunk in the Atlantic 50 miles S. by W.½W. from Old Head of Kinsale in position 50.50N 08.32W by the German submarine *U 24* whilst on a voyage from Liverpool to New York carrying passengers and general cargo including mails. 44 lost.

CYMRIC 13370 Grt. Blt. 1898
8.5.1916: Torpedoed and sunk in the Atlantic 140 miles W.N.W. from the Fastnet Rock by the German submarine *U 20* whilst on a voyage from New York to Liverpool with general cargo. 5 lost.

BRITANNIC 48758 Grt. Blt. 1915
21.11.1916: Struck a mine and sunk in the Aegean Sea in the Zea Channel laid by the German submarine *U 73* whilst on a voyage from Southampton and Naples to Mudros. 21 lost. Lost whilst on Government service employed as a Hospital Ship.

LAURENTIC 14892 Grt. Blt. 1908
25.1.1917: Struck a mine and sunk in the Atlantic off Malin Head laid by the German submarine *U 80*. Lost whilst on Government service employed as an Armed Merchant Cruiser.

AFRIC 11999 Grt. Blt. 1899
12.2.1917: Torpedoed and sunk in the English Channel 12 miles S.S.W. from the Eddystone Lighthouse in position 50.00N 04.25W by the German submarine *UC 66* whilst on a voyage from Liverpool via Devonport to Sydney, (NS) with general cargo. 5 lost.

DELPHIC 8273 Grt. Blt. 1897
16.8.1917: Torpedoed and sunk in the Atlantic 135 miles S.W.¾W. from Bishop Rock by the German submarine *UC 72* whilst on a voyage from Cardiff to Montevideo with a cargo of coal. 5 lost.

The Shipping Controller

JUSTICIA 32120 Grt. Blt. 1917
19.7.1918: Torpedoed and damaged in the Atlantic 20 miles W. by N.¾N. from Skerryvore Rock in position 55.38N 07.39W by the German submarine *UB 64* whilst on a voyage from Liverpool to New York in ballast. 10 lost. The following day whilst under tow 11 miles N.N.W. of Inishtrahull she was given the coup de grâce by the German submarine *UB 124*.

OLIVER & CO. LTD.—LONDON

Franco-British S.S. Co. Ltd.

ALGIERS ex *Lys* ex *Castle Eden* 2361 Grt. Blt. 1882
26.2.1917: Torpedoed and sunk in the Engish Channel 3 miles S. from Owers Lightvessel in position 50.35N 00.40W by the German submarine *UC 65* whilst on a voyage from Calais to Barry Roads in ballast. 8 lost.

RHODESIA 4313 Grt. Blt. 1900
11.10.1917: Torpedoed and sunk in the St. George's Channel 7 miles S.E. by S. from Coningbeg Lightvessel by the German submarine *U 61* whilst on a voyage from Puerto Mexico and Norfolk (Va) to London with a cargo of oil and bitumen. 4 lost.

WESTERGATE 1760 Grt. Blt. 1881
21.4.1918: Torpedoed and sunk in the English Channel 22 miles E.½S. from Start Point by the German submarine *UB 80* whilst on a voyage from Hartlepool to Cartagena. 24 lost including Master.

ORDERS & HANDFORD LIMITED—NEWPORT, MON.

Orders & Handford S.S. Co. Ltd.

REFUGIO 2642 Grt. Blt. 1905
12.5.1917: Captured and sunk by gunfire in the Atlantic 115 miles N.W.½W. from Tory Island in position 55.10N 11.35W by the German submarine *U 57* whilst on a voyage from Ardrossan to Huelva in ballast. 1 lost.

ROSARIO 1821 Grt. Blt. 1900
19.8.1917: Torpedoed and sunk in the Atlantic S.W. of Ireland by the German submarine *UC 55* whilst on a voyage from Huelva to Troon with a cargo of iron ore. 20 lost including Master, 1 Fireman taken prisoner.

***RUBIO** 2395 Grt. Blt. 1909*
25.2.1918: Struck a mine and sunk in the North Sea 4 miles N.½E. from Shipwash Lightvessel laid by the German submarine *UC 4* whilst on a voyage from Blyth to London with a cargo of coal.

***MURIEL** 1831 Grt. Blt. 1898*
17.9.1918: Torpedoed and sunk in the North Sea 3½ miles N.E. from Peterhead by the German submarine *UC 58* whilst on a voyage from Tyne to Scapa Flow with a cargo of coal.

ORIENT STEAM NAVIGATION COMPANY—LONDON

***OTWAY** 12077 Grt. Blt. 1909*
23.7.1917: Torpedoed and sunk in the Atlantic N. of the Butt of Lewis in position 58.54N 06.28W by the German submarine *UC 49*. Lost whilst on Government service employed as an Armed Merchant Cruiser.

***ORAMA** 12927 Grt. Blt. 1911*
19.10.1917: Torpedoed and sunk in the Atlantic in position 48.00N 09.20W by the German submarine *U 62*. Lost whilst on Government service employed as an Armed Merchant Cruiser.

***OMRAH** 8130 Grt. Blt. 1899*
12.5.1918: Torpedoed and sunk in the Mediterranean 40 miles S.W.¾S. from Cape Spartivento, Sicily by the German submarine *UB 52* whilst on a voyage from Marseilles to Alexandria with a cargo of mails. 1 lost.

OSBORN & WALLIS—CARDIFF

***EUTERPE** 1522 Grt. Blt. 1883*
7.1.1916: Struck a mine and sunk in the North Sea laid by unknown German submarine whilst on a voyage from Huelva to Tees with a cargo of pyrites. 19 lost including Master.

OWEN, DAVID—CARDIFF

Bont Shipping Co. Ltd.

***BONTNEWYDD** ex Kirriemoor 3296 Grt. Blt. 1897*
5.10.1917: Torpedoed and sunk in the Mediterranean 60 miles N.N.E. from Marsa Susa in position 33.53N 22.19E by the Austro-Hungarian submarine *U 28* whilst on a voyage from Marseilles to Karachi in ballast. 3 lost.

PACIFIC STEAM NAVIGATION COMPANY—LIVERPOOL

***BOGOTA** 4577 Grt. Blt. 1906*
10.11.1916: Torpedoed and sunk in the Atlantic 120 miles S.W.½W. from Ushant in position 46.51N 06.54W by the German submarine *U 50* whilst on a voyage from Coronel and Cristobal to London with general cargo.

***GALICIA** 5922 Grt. Blt. 1901*
12.5.1917: Struck a mine and sunk in the English Channel 3 miles E. from

Teignmouth in position 50.32N 03.24W laid by the German submarine *UC 17* whilst on a voyage from Liverpool and London to Valparaiso with general cargo.

CALIFORNIA 5629 Grt. Blt. 1902
17.10.1917: Torpedoed and sunk in the Atlantic 145 miles N.W. by N. ¾N. from Cape Villano in position 45.00N 11.26W by the German submarine *U 22* whilst on a voyage from Liverpool and Clyde to Callao with general cargo. 4 lost.

ORONSA 8075 Grt. Blt. 1906
28.4.1918: Torpedoed and sunk in the St. George's Channel 12 miles W. from Bardsey Island by the German submarine *U 91* whilst on a voyage from Talcaguano and New York to Liverpool with general cargo. 3 lost.

ORISSA 5358 Grt. Blt. 1895
25.6.1918: Torpedoed and sunk in the Atlantic 21 miles S.W. by W. ¼W. from Skerryvore Rock in position 56.20N 07.20W by the German submarine *UB 73* whilst on a voyage from Liverpool to Philadelphia in ballast. 6 lost.

MAGELLAN 3642 Grt. Blt. 1893
25.7.1918: Torpedoed and sunk in the Mediterranean 53 miles N. ½E. from Cape Serrat in position 38.06N 09.08E by the German submarine *UB 50* whilst on a voyage from Malta to Liverpool with general cargo. 1 lost.

PALGRAVE, MURPHY & COMPANY—DUBLIN

CITY OF BREMEN 1258 Grt. Blt. 1899
4.4.1915: Torpedoed and sunk in the Atlantic 20 miles S. ¾W. from Wolf Rock by the German submarine *U 24* whilst on a voyage from Port Talbot to Bordeaux with a cargo of coal. 4 lost.

CITY OF SWANSEA ex *Gwendoline* **1375 Grt. Blt. 1882**
25.9.1917: Torpedoed and sunk in the English Channel 15 miles E.N.E. from Berry Head by the German submarine *UB 40* whilst on a voyage from Tyne to France with a cargo of coal. 2 lost.

PARK, COLONEL J. SMITH—GLASGOW

NAIRN 3627 Grt. Blt. 1904
28.8.1917: Torpedoed and sunk in the Mediterranean 125 miles N. by W. ¼W. from Benghazi in position 34.05N 19.20E by the Austro-Hungarian submarine *U 14* whilst on a voyage from Malta to Port Said with a cargo of coal.

PATTERSON, G. N. & COMPANY—NEWCASTLE UPON TYNE

CARTERSWELL 4308 Grt. Blt. 1914
20.8.1915: Captured and sunk by gunfire in the English Channel 65 miles N.W. from Ushant by the German submarine *U 38* whilst on a voyage from Galveston and Newport News to Le Havre with a cargo of wheat.

PEKIN SYNDICATE LIMITED—LONDON

SIR RICHARD AWDRY 2234 Grt. Blt. 1912
8.11.1915: Captured and torpedoed in the Mediterranean 72 miles S. by E.½E. from Gavdo Island in position 31.25N 25.38E by the German submarine *U 35* whilst on a voyage from Saigon to Marseilles with a cargo of rice. 1 lost.

PELTON S.S. CO. LTD.—NEWCASTLE UPON TYNE

PRIMO 1366 Grt. Blt. 1898
26.11.1914: Captured and sunk by gunfire in the English Channel 6 miles N.W. by N. from Cape d'Antifer by the German submarine *U 21* whilst on a voyage from Tyne to Rouen with a cargo of coal.

ALTO 2266 Grt. Blt. 1916
16.7.1916: Struck a mine and sunk in the North Sea 4 miles off Kessingland laid by the German submarine *UC 1* whilst on a voyage from Rouen to Tyne in ballast.

PRESTO 1143 Grt. Blt. 1905
6.4.1917: Struck a mine and sunk in the North Sea 4 miles E. from Roker Point, Sunderland laid by the German submarine *UC 40* whilst on a voyage from London to Tyne in ballast. 6 lost.

LESTO 1940 Grt. Blt. 1916
23.5.1917: Torpedoed and sunk in the Bay of Biscay 8 miles W. from Ile du Pilier in position 46.57N 02.30W by the German submarine *UC 21* whilst on a voyage from Bilbao to Garston with a cargo of iron ore. 4 lost.

RAGNHILD ex *Carbonia* ex *Finland 1495 Grt. Blt. 1895*
3.9.1917: Torpedoed and sunk in the North Sea 14 miles S. by E.¼E. from Flamborough Head by the German submarine *UB 30* whilst on a voyage from Tyne to Rouen with a cargo of coal. 15 lost including Master.

AZIRA 1144 Grt. Blt. 1907
4.8.1917: Torpedoed and sunk in the North Sea 6 miles S.E. from Seaham Harbour by the German submarine *UB 22* whilst on a voyage from Tyne to Cherbourg with a cargo of coal. 1 lost.

LARGO 1764 Grt. Blt. 1910
27.2.1918: Torpedoed and sunk in the Irish Sea 12 miles W. from Calf of Man by the German submarine *UB 105* whilst on a voyage from Barry to Scapa Flow with a cargo of coal.

The Shipping Controller

DIANA 1119 Grt. Blt. 1899
7.6.1918: Torpedoed and sunk in the North Sea 10 miles S.S.E. from Flamborough Head by the German submarine *UB 108* whilst on a voyage from Tyne to Rouen with a cargo of coal.

PENINSULAR & ORIENTAL STEAM NAVIGATION CO. LTD.—LONDON

INDIA 7940 Grt. Blt. 1896
8.12.1915: Torpedoed and sunk in the Norwegian Sea off the Island of Helligvaer near Bodo in position 67.30N 13.20E by the German submarine *U 22*. 160 lost. Lost whilst on Government service employed as an Armed Merchant Cruiser.

PERSIA 7951 Grt. Blt. 1900
30.12.1915: Torpedoed and sunk in the Mediterranean 71 miles S.E. by S. from Cape Martello in position 34.10N 26.00E by the German submarine *U 38* whilst on a voyage from London to Marseilles and Bombay carrying passengers and general cargo. 334 lost including Master.

MALOJA 12431 Grt. Blt. 1911
27.2.1916: Struck a mine and sunk in the Strait of Dover 2 miles S.W. from Dover Pier laid by the German submarine *UC 6* whilst on a voyage from London to Bombay with general cargo. 122 lost.

SIMLA 5884 Grt. Blt. 1894
2.4.1916: Torpedoed and sunk in the Mediterranean 45 miles N.W.½W. from Gozo Island by the German submarine *U 39* whilst on a voyage from Marseilles to Egypt in ballast. 10 lost.

ARABIA 7903 Grt. Blt. 1898
6.11.1916: Torpedoed and sunk in the Mediterranean 112 miles W. by S. from Cape Matapan in position 36.00N 21.00E by the German submarine *UB 43* whilst on a voyage from Sydney, NSW to London with general cargo. 11 lost.

HARLINGTON ex *Figulina* 1089 Grt. Blt. 1913
9.12.1916: Struck a mine and sunk in the North Sea 4 miles S.W. from Shipwash Lightvessel laid by the German submarine *UC 11* whilst on a voyage from Tyne to London with a cargo of coal. 7 lost.

MEDINA 12350 Grt. Blt. 1911
28.4.1917: Torpedoed and sunk in the English Channel 3 miles E.N.E. from Start Point in position 50.15N 03.30W by the German submarine *UB 31* whilst on a voyage from Sydney, NSW and Indian ports to London via Plymouth carrying passengers and general cargo. 6 lost.

SALSETTE 5842 Grt. Blt. 1908
20.7.1917: Torpedoed and sunk in the English Channel 15 miles S.W. from Portland Bill by the German submarine *UB 40* whilst on a voyage from London to Bombay with general cargo. 15 lost.

MOOLTAN 9621 Grt. Blt. 1905
26.7.1917: Torpedoed and sunk in the Mediterranean 53 miles N.N.W.½W. from Cape Serrat in position 37.56N 08.34E by the German submarine *UC 27* whilst on a voyage from Sydney, NSW and Fremantle to London with general cargo, mails and meat. 2 lost.

CANDIA 6482 Grt. Blt. 1896
27.7.1917: Torpedoed and sunk in the English Channel 8 miles S. from Owers

Lightvessel in position 50.32N 00.26W by the German submarine *UC 65* whilst on a voyage from Sydney, NSW and Port Natal to London via Falmouth with a cargo of grain and foodstuffs. 1 lost.

PESHAWUR 7634 Grt. Blt. 1905
9.10.1917: Torpedoed and sunk in the Irish Sea 7 miles S.E. ¼ E. from Ballyquintin Point, co. Down by the German submarine *U 96* whilst on a voyage from Montreal and Sydney, (NS) to the United Kingdom and France with general cargo. 13 lost.

PERA 7635 Grt. Blt. 1903
19.10.1917: Torpedoed and sunk in the Mediterranean 105 miles E. ¾ N. from Marsa Susa in position 37.16N 24.00E by the German submarine *UB 48* whilst on a voyage from Liverpool to Port Said and Calcutta with general cargo and coal. 1 lost.

NAMUR 6694 Grt. Blt. 1906
29.10.1917: Torpedoed and sunk in the Mediterranean 55 miles E. by S. ½ S. from Gibraltar in position 36.00N 04.15W by the German submarine *U 35* whilst on a voyage from Shanghai to London with general cargo. 1 lost.

MOLDAVIA 9500 Grt. Blt. 1903
23.5.1918: Torpedoed and sunk in the English Channel off Beachy Head by the German submarine *UB 57*. 56 lost.

MARMORA 10509 Grt. Blt. 1903
23.7.1918: Torpedoed and sunk in the Atlantic S. of Ireland in position 50.24N 08.48W by the German submarine *UB 64* whilst on a voyage from Cardiff to Dakar. 10 lost.

P. & O. Branch Service

BALLARAT 11120 Grt. Blt. 1911
25.4.1917: Torpedoed and sunk in the Atlantic 24 miles S. by W. from Wolf Rock in position 49.33N 05.36W by the German submarine *UB 32* whilst on a voyage from Melbourne and Cape Town to London with general cargo including copper, antimony ore and bullion.

PETERSEN & CO. LTD.—LONDON

RIO TIETE ex *Pontop 3042 Grt. Blt. 1904*
28.3.1916: Captured and torpedoed in the Atlantic 140 miles W. from Ushant in position 47.30N 08.25W by the German submarine *U 28* whilst on a voyage from Barry to Alexandria with a cargo of coal.

Leander S.S. Co. Ltd.

RIO PARANA ex *Persiana 4015 Grt. Blt. 1902*
24.2.1915: Torpedoed and sunk in the English Channel 4 miles S.E. from Beachy Head by the German submarine *U 8* whilst on a voyage from Tyne to Portoferrajo with a cargo of coal.

RIVER FORTH 4421 Grt. Blt. 1907
3.3.1917: Torpedoed and sunk in the Mediterranean 60 miles S. by E. from Malta in position 34.54N 15.00E by the German submarine *UC 35* whilst on a voyage from Barry to Alexandria with general cargo and coal.

RIO SOROCABA ex Bramley 4307 Grt. Blt. 1906
21.3.1917: Captured and sunk with bombs in the English Channel 10 miles S. from Eddystone Lighthouse in position 50.04N 04.13W by the German submarine *UC 48* whilst on a voyage from Port Louis to Le Havre with a cargo of sugar.

RIO COLORADO ex Sheila 3565 Grt. Blt. 1903
22.3.1917: Struck a mine and sunk in the North Sea at the entrance to the River Tyne laid by the German submarine *UC 50* whilst on a voyage from La Plata to Tyne with a cargo of wheat. 10 lost including Master.

MARIE SUZANNE 3106 Grt. Blt. 1898
19.8.1918: Torpedoed and sunk in the Mediterranean 47 miles W. ¾ S. from Mudros Bay by the German submarine *UC 37* whilst on a voyage from Penarth to Mudros and Salonica with a cargo of coal.

London American Maritime Trading Co. Ltd.

MARIE ELSIE 2615 Grt. Blt. 1895
10.6.1917: Torpedoed and sunk in the Arctic 125 miles N. by W. from Cape Teriberski in position 71.21N 34.16E by the German submarine *U 28* whilst on a voyage from Penarth to Archangel with a cargo of coal. 3 lost.

CALLIOPE 2883 Grt. Blt. 1900
12.7.1917: Torpedoed and sunk in the Atlantic W. of Gibraltar by the German submarine *U 155* whilst on a voyage from Seville to Newport, Mon. with a cargo of pyrites. 27 lost including Master.

IOLANTHE 3081 Grt. Blt. 1904
5.1.1918: Torpedoed and sunk in the English Channel 10 miles S.E. by E. from Portland Bill in position 50.28N 02.12W by the German submarine *UC 75* whilst on a voyage from Clyde to St. Helens Roads with a cargo of hay and trucks.

RIO CLARO ex Elaine 3687 Grt. Blt. 1904
5.1.1918: Torpedoed and sunk in the Mediterranean in Rapallo Bay by the German submarine *U 63* whilst on a voyage from Leghorn to Cartagena in ballast.

RIO VERDE ex Austriana 4025 Grt. Blt. 1901
23.2.1918: Torpedoed and sunk in the North Channel 4 miles W. from Crammock Head, Mull of Galloway by the German submarine *U 86* whilst on a voyage from the Clyde to Milford Haven with a cargo of coal. 20 lost including Master.

PHILIPPS, PHILIPPS & CO. LTD.—LONDON

King Line

KING BLEDDYN 4387 Grt. Blt. 1905
1.12.1916: Captured and sunk with bombs in the Atlantic 30 miles S. by W. ½ W. from Ushant in position 47.54N 05.07W by the German submarine *UC 21* whilst on a voyage from New York to Le Havre with a cargo of machinery.

KING DAVID 3680 Grt. Blt. 1906
10.7.1917: Captured and sunk with gunfire in the Atlantic 360 miles N.W.½W. from the Fastnet Rock in position 52.53N 19.52W by the German submarine *U 49* whilst on a voyage from Brest to Archangel with munitions and aeroplanes. 2 lost.

KING IDWAL 3631 Grt. Blt. 1906
22.11.1917: Probably struck a mine and sunk in the North Sea 35 miles E. of Girdle Ness laid by the German submarine *U 75* whilst on a voyage from Archangel to Dunkirk with a cargo of wood. 1 lost.

Scottish S.S. Co. Ltd.

KING MALCOM 4351 Grt. Blt. 1906
28.11.1916: Torpedoed and sunk in the Mediterranean 144 miles N.W. by N. from Alexandria in position 33.14N 28.23E by the German submarine *U 39* whilst on a voyage from Marseilles to Mauritius in ballast. Master taken prisoner.

The Shipping Controller

WAR ARABIS 5183 Grt. Blt. 1918
9.9.1918: Torpedoed and sunk in the Mediterranean 88 miles N. by E.¼E. from Cape Sigli in position 38.08N 05.30E by the German submarine *U 34* whilst on a voyage from Bahia Blanca to Marseilles with a cargo of wheat.

PICKERING, W. & COMPANY—NEWCASTLE UPON TYNE

Gresham S.S. Co. Ltd.

LADY SALISBURY 1446 Grt. Blt. 1890
9.6.1915: Struck a mine and sunk off the mouth of the River Thames 1 mile N. from Sunk Lightvessel laid by the German submarine *UC 11* whilst on a voyage from Hartlepool to London with a cargo of coal. 3 lost.

PLISSON STEAM NAVIGATION CO. LTD.—CARDIFF

FRIMAIRE ex *Corso* **1778 Grt. Blt. 1900**
15.3.1917: Torpedoed and sunk in the Bay of Biscay 21 miles S.S.E. from Belle Ile in position 47.03N 02.26W by the German submarine *UC 21* whilst on a voyage from Glasgow to St. Nazaire in ballast. 12 lost including Master.

BRUMAIRE ex *Moldavia* ex *Delarne* **2324 Grt. Blt. 1901**
24.7.1917: Torpedoed and sunk in the Atlantic 265 miles W. by N. from Ushant in position 48.20N 11.41W by the German submarine *U 46* whilst on a voyage from Hartlepool to Spezia with a cargo of coal. 2 lost.

MESSIDOR ex *Claremont* **3883 Grt. Blt. 1904**
23.7.1918: Torpedoed and sunk in the Mediterranean 73 miles S.E. by S.¼S. from Port Mahon in position 38.59N 05.18E by the German submarine *UB 50* whilst on a voyage from Manchester to Civitavecchia with a cargo of coal. 1 lost.

PLYMOUTH MUTUAL CO-OPERATIVE INDUSTRIAL SOCIETY LTD.—PLYMOUTH

CHARLES GOODANEW ex *Levenwood* **791 Grt. Blt. 1911**
17.4.1917: Struck a mine and sunk in the North Sea 3½ miles E.N.E. from Rattray Head in position 57.39N 01.45W laid by the German submarine *UC 45* whilst on a voyage from Aberdeen to Scapa Flow with a cargo of Government stores. 13 lost including Master. Lost whilst on Government service employed as Store Carrier *No. 71*.

POST-MASTER, H.M. (TELEGRAPH DEPARTMENT)—LONDON

MONARCH **1122 Grt. Blt. 1883**
8.9.1915: Struck a mine and sunk in the Strait of Dover 2½ miles S. from Folkestone laid by the German submarine *UC 5*. 3 lost.

POWELL, BACON & HOUGH LINES LIMITED—LIVERPOOL

WESTERN COAST **1165 Grt. Blt. 1913**
24.2.1915: Torpedoed and sunk in the English Channel 8 miles S.E. by E.½E. from Beachy Head by the German submarine *U 8* whilst on a voyage from London to Liverpool with general cargo.

SUFFOLK COAST **780 Grt. Blt. 1913**
7.11.1916: Captured and sunk with bombs in the English Channel 14 miles E.S.E. from Cape Barfleur by the German submarine *UC 17* whilst on a voyage from Clyde to Fécamp with general cargo.

POWER, J. & COMPANY—LONDON

Power S.S. Co. Ltd.

PETRIDGE **1712 Grt. Blt. 1913**
8.4.1917: Torpedoed and sunk in the Atlantic 200 miles W.N.W. from Ushant in position 48.41N 10.10W by the German submarine *U 55* whilst on a voyage from Mogador to London with general cargo. Master and 1 Gunner taken prisoner.

PENSHURST **1191 Grt. Blt. 1906**
24.12.1917: Torpedoed and sunk in the Bristol Channel in position 51.31N 05.33W by the German submarine *U 110*. Lost whilst on Government service employed as Special Service Ship *Q7*.

PRATT, THOMAS & COMPANY—NEWCASTLE UPON TYNE

Brantingham S.S. Co. Ltd.

NORMA PRATT ex *Silvercedar* ex *Fitzpatrick* **4416 Grt. Blt. 1907**
16.3.1917: Captured and torpedoed in the Atlantic 150 miles W. from Bishop Rock in a position 48.53N 09.53W by the German submarine *U 70* whilst on a voyage from Le Havre to New York with a cargo of hides and wine. Chief Engineer and 3rd Engineer taken prisoner.

PRENTICE, SERVICE & HENDERSON—GLASGOW

Crown S.S. Co. Ltd.

CROWN OF CASTILE 4505 Grt. Blt. 1905
30.3.1915: Captured and sunk with bombs in the Atlantic 31 miles S.W. from Bishop Rock by the German submarine *U 28* whilst on a voyage from St. John (NB) to Le Havre with a cargo of cattle fodder.

CROWN OF ARRAGON 4550 Grt. Blt. 1905
24.6.1917: Torpedoed and sunk in the Atlantic 124 miles S.W.½W. from Bishop Rock in position 48.10N 08.14W by the German submarine *UC 17* whilst on a voyage from Cardiff and Penzance to Montreal with a cargo of Government stores. 1 lost.

PURDIE, GLEN & COMPANY—GLASGOW

Auchen S.S. Co. Ltd.

AUCHENCRAG 3916 Grt. Blt. 1903
12.1.1917: Captured and torpedoed in the English Channel 20 miles W. from Ushant in position 48.28N 05.35W by the German submarine *U 84* whilst on a voyage from La Plata to Cherbourg with a cargo of wheat. 4 lost.

PYMAN, BELL & CO. LTD.—NEWCASTLE UPON TYNE

EVELINE 2605 Grt. Blt. 1897
20.12.1917: Torpedoed and sunk in the English Channel 9½ miles S.½W. from Berry Head by the German submarine *UB 31* whilst on a voyage from Barry to Rouen with general cargo and coal.

MADELINE 2890 Grt. Blt. 1894
8.3.1918: Torpedoed and sunk in the Atlantic 14 miles E.N.E. from Pendeen Lighthouse by the German submarine *U 55* whilst on a voyage from Dieppe to Swansea in ballast. 3 lost.

PYMAN BROTHERS LIMITED—LONDON

London & Northern S.S. Co. Ltd.

DUNSLEY 4930 Grt. Blt. 1913
19.8.1915: Captured and sunk by gunfire in the Atlantic 48 miles S. by W. from Old Head of Kinsale in position 50.50N 08.30W by the German submarine *U 24* whilst on a voyage from Liverpool to Boston, Mass. with general cargo. 2 lost.

COBER 3060 Grt. Blt. 1904
21.8.1915: Captured and torpedoed in the Atlantic 45 miles S.S.W. from Scilly Isles in position 49.10N 06.30W by the German submarine *U 38* whilst on a voyage from Cardiff to Buenos Aires.

PYMAN, GEORGE & COMPANY—WEST HARTLEPOOL

Pyman S.S. Co. Ltd.

STANLEY 3987 Grt. Blt. 1914
21.3.1917: Torpedoed and sunk in the Atlantic 230 miles W. by N. from the Fastnet Rock in position 50.50N 16.00W by the German submarine *U 24* whilst on a voyage from Newport News to Cherbourg with a cargo of grain. 8 lost.

GEORGE PYMAN 3859 Grt. Blt. 1900
17.5.1917: Torpedoed and sunk in the Atlantic 130 miles N.W. from Tearaght Island in position 52.55N 13.56W by the German submarine *U 49* whilst on a voyage from Cuba to Queenstown with a cargo of sugar.

ROSEBANK 3837 Grt. Blt. 1901
31.5.1917: Torpedoed and sunk in the Mediterranean 120 miles N. from Benghazi in position 34.09N 19.35E by the German submarine *UC 73* whilst on a voyage from Port Said to Malta in ballast. 2 lost, Master taken prisoner.

MARMION 4066 Grt. Blt. 1912
26.8.1917: Torpedoed and sunk in the Atlantic 300 miles W.¾S. from Ushant in position 46.18N 11.40W by the German submarine *U 93* whilst on a voyage from New York to Bordeaux with a cargo of oats and steel. 17 lost.

SANDSEND 3814 Grt. Blt. 1899
16.9.1917: Torpedoed and sunk in the Atlantic 6 miles S.E. by E. from Mine Head by the German submarine *UC 48* whilst on a voyage from Barry to Queenstown with general cargo. 3 lost.

WAVERLEY 3853 Grt. Blt. 1901
20.12.1917: Torpedoed and sunk in the Mediterranean 33 miles N.E.½N. from Cape Ivi in position 36.37N 00.33E by the German submarine *U 35* whilst on a voyage from Newport, Mon. to Port Said with a cargo of coal, iron and wagons. 22 lost.

PYMAN, J. W.—CARDIFF

Raithwaite S.S. Co. Ltd.

NORTHWAITE 3626 Grt. Blt. 1905
13.3.1917: Torpedoed and sunk in the Atlantic 14 miles W.N.W. from the Blasket Islands, 12 miles W. of Dingle, co. Kerry in position 52.11N 11.07W by the German submarine *U 61* whilst on a voyage from Sfax and Bona to Dublin with a cargo of phosphate.

PYMAN, WATSON & CO. LTD.—CARDIFF

LONGHIRST 3053 Grt. Blt. 1904
23.2.1917: Torpedoed and sunk in the Mediterranean 20 miles E. from Cape Bon in position 57.08N 11.25E by the German submarine *U 35* whilst on a voyage from Philippeville to Salonica with a cargo of barley and hay. 2 lost.

RADCLIFFE, C. & COMPANY—CARDIFF

Snowdon S.S. Co. Ltd.

SNOWDON ex *Barnesmore* **3189 Grt. Blt. 1896**
19.5.1918: Torpedoed then captured and sunk by gunfire in the Mediterranean 84 miles S.½W. from Malta in position 34.26N 14.38E by the German submarine *U 63* whilst on a voyage from Cardiff to Milo Island with a cargo of coal. 2 lost, Master and 1st Officer taken prisoner.

RADCLIFFE, (EVAN THOMAS) & COMPANY—CARDIFF

WINDSOR **6055 Grt. Blt. 1911**
21.8.1915: Captured and sunk by gunfire in the Atlantic 70 miles S.W.½S. from Wolf Rock by the German submarine *U 38* whilst on a voyage from Barry to Leghorn with a cargo of coal.

LLANGORSE **3841 Grt. Blt. 1900**
8.9.1916: Torpedoed and sunk in the Mediterranean 48 miles W.S.W. from Cape Matapan by the German submarine *UB 47* whilst on a voyage from Montreal to Salonica with a cargo of oats.

FLIMSTON **5751 Grt. Blt. 1916**
18.12.1916: Captured and sunk with bombs in the English Channel 21 miles N. by E.½E. from Ushant in position 48.48N 05.08W by the German submarine *U 70* whilst on a voyage from Buenos Aires to London with a cargo of maize. Master and Chief Engineer taken prisoner.

WASHINGTON **5080 Grt. Blt. 1907**
3.5.1917: Torpedoed and sunk in the Mediterranean off Rapallo Bay by the German submarine *U 63* whilst on a voyage from New York to Naples with general cargo.

LLANDRINDOD **3841 Grt. Blt. 1900**
18.5.1917: Torpedoed and sunk in the Atlantic 165 miles N.W. by W. from the Fastnet Rock in position 51.45N 13.58W by the German submarine *U 46* whilst on a voyage from Port Natal to Clyde with a cargo of maize. Master taken prisoner.

LLANISHEN **3837 Grt. Blt. 1909**
8.8.1917: Torpedoed and damaged in the Mediterranean 8 miles N. by E. from Cape Creus by the German submarine *U 33* whilst on a voyage from Savona to Melilla in ballast. 2 lost. Beached but became a wreck.

JANE RADCLIFFE ex *Windsor* **4074 Grt. Blt. 1897**
28.11.1917: Struck a mine and sunk in the Mediterranean 2 miles S.W. from Antimilo Island, Greece laid by the German submarine *UC 74* whilst on a voyage from Barry to Port Said with a cargo of coal.

Douglas Hill S.S. Co. Ltd.

BONVILSTON ex *Anthony Radcliffe* **2865 Grt. Blt. 1893**
17.10.1918: Torpedoed and sunk in the North Channel 9½ miles N.W. by W. from Corsewall Point by the German submarine *UB 92* whilst on a voyage from Ayr to Barry Roads in ballast.

Dunraven S.S. Co. Ltd.

***DUNRAVEN* ex *Boverton* 3117 Grt. Blt. 1910**
8.8.1917: Severely damaged by gunfire in the Atlantic 130 miles W. of Ushant by the German submarine *UC 71* and foundered on the 10.8.1917 whilst under tow in the English Channel. Lost whilst on Government service employed as a Special Service Ship.

Euston S.S. Co. Ltd.

***EUSTON* 2841 Grt. Blt. 1910**
25.10.1917: Torpedoed and sunk in the Mediterranean 37 miles S.W. from Cape Matapan in position 34.53N 19.50E by the Austro-Hungarian submarine *U 14* whilst on a voyage from Cardiff and Malta to Mudros with a cargo of coal. 1 lost.

Iolo Morganwg S.S. Co. Ltd.

***IOLO* ex *Paddington* 3903 Grt. Blt. 1898**
11.10.1916: Captured and torpedoed in the Norwegian Sea 153 miles N. from Vardo by the German submarine *U 46* whilst on a voyage from Cardiff to Archangel with a cargo of coal.

***IOLO* ex *Paddington* ex *Llanover* 3840 Grt. Blt. 1899**
17.2.1917: Torpedoed and sunk in the Atlantic 40 miles S. by W. from the Fastnet Rock in position 50.43N 09.30W by the German submarine *U 60* whilst on a voyage from Cardiff to Spezia with a cargo of coal. 2 lost, Master, Chief Engineer and 2 Gunners taken prisoner.

Llandudno S.S. Co. Ltd.

***LLANDUDNO* 4187 Grt. Blt. 1910**
1.8.1917: Captured and sunk with bombs in the Mediterranean 110 miles S. by W. from Ile de Porquerolles in position 41.11N 06.12E by the German submarine *U 33* whilst on a voyage from Marseilles to Salonica with a cargo of stores. 1 lost.

Paddington S.S. Co. Ltd.

***PADDINGTON* ex *Swindon* ex *Patagonia* 5084 Grt. Blt. 1906**
21.7.1917: Torpedoed and sunk in the Atlantic 250 miles W. from the Fastnet Rock by the German submarine *U 96* whilst on a voyage from Cartagena to the United Kingdom. 29 lost including Master.

Patagonia S.S. Co. Ltd.

***PATAGONIA* 6011 Grt. Blt. 1913**
15.9.1915: Torpedoed and sunk in the Black Sea 10½ miles N.E. from Odessa by the German submarine *UB 7* whilst on a voyage from Odessa to Nicolaieff in ballast.

Sarah Radcliff S.S. Co. Ltd.

***SARAH RADCLIFFE* ex *Dunraven* 3333 Grt. Blt. 1896**
11.11.1916: Captured and torpedoed in the Atlantic 170 miles S.W. from Ushant in position 46.00N 07.00W by the German submarine *U 50* whilst on a voyage from Cardiff to St. Vincent, Cape Verde with general cargo and coal.

Walter Thomas S.S. Co. Ltd.

BADMINTON ex *Swindon* ***3847 Grt. Blt. 1899***
23.7.1916: Captured and sunk by gunfire in the Mediterranean 63 miles N.E. by N. from Cape Carbon by the German submarine *U 39* whilst on a voyage from Torre Annunziata to Algiers in ballast.

LLANCARVAN ex *W. I. Radcliffe* ***4749 Grt. Blt. 1904***
16.5.1918: Torpedoed and sunk in the Atlantic 370 miles E.½N. (true) from San Miguel, Azores in position 38.24N 17.18W by the German submarine *U 62* whilst on a voyage from New Orleans to Italy with a cargo of barley and steel billets.

RAEBURN & VEREL LIMITED—GLASGOW

POLITANIA ex *Aline Woermann* ***3133 Grt. Blt. 1910***
18.8.1917: Torpedoed and sunk in the Mediterranean 10 miles N.W. by W. from Cape Sigli in position 36.56N 04.38E by the German submarine *UC 67* whilst on a voyage from Tarragona to Salonica with a cargo of hay.

Monarch S.S. Co. Ltd.

SCOTTISH MONARCH 5043 Grt. Blt. 1906
29.6.1915: Captured and sunk by gunfire in the Atlantic 40 miles S. from Ballycottin Island in position 51.10N 08.00W by the German submarine *U 24* whilst on a voyage from New York to Manchester with general cargo. 15 lost.

ENGLISH MONARCH 4947 Grt. Blt. 1906
18.6.1917: Torpedoed and sunk in the Atlantic 300 miles N.W. by W. from the Fastnet Rock in position 52.60N 17.30W by the German submarine *U 24* whilst on a voyage from Clyde to Genoa with a cargo of coal. 3 lost.

SAXON MONARCH 4828 Grt. Blt. 1912
25.6.1917: Torpedoed and sunk in the Atlantic 140 miles S.W. by W. from Scilly Isles in position 48.24N 07.47W by the German submarine *UC 17* whilst on a voyage from Karachi and Cape Town to London with a cargo of grain. 2 lost.

BRITISH MONARCH 5749 Grt. Blt. 1913
4.8.1917: Struck a mine and sunk in the Mediterranean 2 miles S.S.W. from Ile de Porquerolles Lighthouse laid by the German submarine *U 72* whilst on a voyage from Hull to Genoa with a cargo of coal.

RANKIN, GILMORE & CO. LTD.—LIVERPOOL

British & Foreign S.S. Co. Ltd.

SAINT URSULA 5011 Grt. Blt. 1912
12.12.1916: Torpedoed and sunk in the Mediterranean 45 miles S.E. by S. from Malta in position 35.16N 15.08E by the German submarine *U 32* whilst on a voyage from Salonica to Newport News in ballast. 4 lost.

SAINT RONALD 4387 Grt. Blt. 1910
19.9.1917: Torpedoed and sunk in the Atlantic 95 miles N.N.W. from Tory Island in position 56.00N 12.00W by the German submarine *U 82* whilst on a voyage from Antofagasta and Norfolk, (Va) to Liverpool with a cargo of nitrate. 24 lost.

RANKINE LINE, LIMITED—GLASGOW

AMSTERDAM ex *Avon* *806 Grt. Blt. 1877*
24.2.1918: Torpedoed and sunk in the North Sea 3 miles S.E. by E. from Coquet Island by the German submarine *UC 49* whilst on a voyage from Leith to Rotterdam with general cargo and coal. 4 lost.

REA, R. &. J. H. LIMITED—LONDON

Rea Shipping Co. Ltd.

MONKSGARTH 1928 Grt. Blt. 1907
19.8.1917: Torpedoed and sunk in the English Channel 17 miles N. by E. ¼ E. from Ushant by the German submarine *UC 48* whilst on a voyage from Barry to Bordeaux with a cargo of coal.

BANGARTH 1872 Grt. Blt. 1906
13.12.1917: Torpedoed and sunk in the North Sea 13 miles N.N.E. from the River Tyne in position 55.14N 01.23W by the German submarine *UB 34* whilst on a voyage from Methil to Dunkirk with a cargo of coal. 2 lost.

KNIGHTSGARTH 2889 Grt. Blt. 1905
5.1.1918: Torpedoed and sunk in the North Channel 5 miles W.N.W. from Bull Point, Rathlin Island by the German submarine *U 91* whilst on a voyage from— to Barry Roads in ballast. 2 lost.

The Shipping Controller

KIELDRECHT 1284 Grt. Blt. 1916
15.6.1918: Torpedoed and sunk in the North Sea 21 miles E. by S. from Flamborough Head by the German submarine *UB 107* whilst on a voyage from Rouen to Tyne in ballast.

READHEAD, G. T. & COMPANY—NEWCASTLE UPON TYNE

Cliffe S.S. Co. Ltd.

ROCKCLIFFE 3073 Grt. Blt. 1904
2.7.1916: Torpedoed and sunk in the Black Sea by the German submarine *U 38*.

HIGHCLIFFE 3238 Grt. Blt. 1909
3.9.1918: Torpedoed and sunk in the St. George's Channel 13 miles S.E. from Tuskar Rock by the German submarine *UB 87* whilst on a voyage from Clyde to—with a cargo of coal. 1 lost.

RED FUNNEL SHIPPING CO. LTD.—LONDON

IMPERIAL 3818 Grt. Blt. 1902
8.8.1916: Captured and sunk by gunfire in the Mediterranean 38 miles S.W. by W. from Planier Island by the German submarine *U 35* whilst on a voyage from Marseilles to Montreal in ballast.

REES, T. BOWEN & CO. LTD.—LONDON

Egypt & Levant Steam Ship Co. Ltd.

ANTIOPE 2973 Grt. Blt. 1906
9.8.1916: Captured and sunk by gunfire in the Mediterranean 88 miles S.W. by W. from Marseilles in position 42.16N 04.03E by the German submarine *U 35* whilst on a voyage from Marseilles to Rosario in ballast.

ANTONIO 2652 Grt. Blt. 1905
7.3.1917: Torpedoed and sunk in the English Channel 7 miles from Dartmouth by the German submarine *U 48* whilst on a voyage from Barry to Cherbourg with a cargo of hay. 11 lost including Master.

ANTINOE 2396 Grt. Blt. 1907
28.5.1917: Torpedoed and sunk in the Atlantic 150 miles W.S.W. from Bishop Rock in position 48.50N 10.10W by the German submarine *U 86* whilst on a voyage from Seville to Newport, Mon. with a cargo of iron ore. 21 lost including Master.

ANTAEUS 3061 Grt. Blt. 1906
4.11.1917: Torpedoed and sunk in the Mediterranean 42 miles N. by W. ½W. from Cape Bon in position 37.44N 10.38E by the German submarine *UB 50* whilst on a voyage from Malta to Bizerta in ballast. Master taken prisoner.

ANTEROS 4241 Grt. Blt. 1917
24.3.1918: Torpedoed and sunk in the Irish Sea 16 miles W. by N. from South Stack Rock by the German submarine *UB 103* whilst on a voyage from Manchester to Port Talbot in ballast. 2 lost.

REID, J. & COMPANY—MONTREAL

Atlas Shipping Co. Ltd.

KILLELLAN 1971 Grt. Blt. 1915
8.11.1916: Captured and torpedoed in the English Channel 17 miles S.W. by S. ¼S. from Colbart Lightvessel, near Treport by the German submarine *UB 40* whilst on a voyage from Tyne to Rouen with a cargo of coal.

RENWICK, WILTON & CO. LTD.—DARTMOUTH

Wilton S.S. Co. Ltd.

CHURSTON 2470 Grt. Blt. 1914
3.9.1915: Struck a mine and sunk in the North Sea 2½ miles S. from Orfordness in position 52.01N 01.38E laid by the German submarine *UC 7* whilst on a voyage from Cardiff to—with a cargo of coal. 4 lost.

RICHARDS, TURPIN (SHIPPING) LIMITED—SWANSEA

Swansea Steamers Ltd.

ILSTON 2426 Grt. Blt. 1915
30.6.1917: Torpedoed and sunk in the English Channel 4 miles S.E. from the Lizard by the German submarine *UB 23* whilst on a voyage from Swansea to Falmouth and France with a cargo of railway material. 6 lost.

BISHOPSTON 2513 Grt. Blt. 1916
4.9.1917: Torpedoed and sunk in the English Channel 30 miles S. by E. from St. Catherine's Point in position 50.08N 00.57W by the German submarine *UC 16* whilst on a voyage from Le Havre to Portsmouth in ballast. 2 lost.

The Shipping Controller
THALIA 1308 Grt. Blt. 1916
8.10.1918: Torpedoed and sunk in the North Sea 4 miles E.S.E. from Filey Brigg by the German submarine *UC 17* whilst on a voyage from Rouen to Tyne in ballast. 3 lost.

RICHARDSON, P. WIGHAM & CO. LTD.—LONDON

Eftikhia S.S. Co. Ltd.

ENOSIS 3409 Grt. Blt. 1906
18.11.1915: Captured and torpedoed in the Mediterranean 150 miles E.S.E. from Malta by the German submarine *U 33* whilst on a voyage from Barry to Malta with a cargo of coal. Master lost.

RICKINSON, SONS & COMPANY—WEST HARTLEPOOL

ATLAS 3090 Grt. Blt. 1897
14.2.1918: Torpedoed and sunk in the North Sea 10 miles E.S.E. from Hartlepool by the German submarine *UC 71* whilst on a voyage from Narvik to Middlesbrough with a cargo of iron ore.

ARIEL 3428 Grt. Blt. 1902
3.10.1918: Torpedoed and sunk in the Mediterranean 54 miles N. from Cape Tenez in position 37.26N 01.08E by the German submarine *UB 105* whilst on a voyage from Sfax to the United Kingdom with a cargo of phosphates.

RIDLEY, (JOHN), SON & TULLY—NEWCASTLE UPON TYNE

ELEANOR 1980 Grt. Blt. 1888
12.2.1918: Torpedoed and sunk in the English Channel 9 miles W. by S.½S. from St. Catherine's Point in position 50.30N 01.30W by the German submarine *UB 57* whilst on a voyage from Immingham to Falmouth with a cargo of Government stores. 34 lost including Master.

Arctic S.S. Co. Ltd.

BELLE OF ENGLAND 3877 Grt. Blt. 1905
27.7.1917: Torpedoed and sunk in the Atlantic 155 miles W.N.W. from the Fastnet Rock by the German submarine *U 95* whilst on a voyage from Algiers to Barrow with a cargo of iron ore.

Screw Collier Co. Ltd.

BYWELL 1522 Grt. Blt. 1913
29.3.1917: Torpedoed and sunk in the North Sea 3 miles E. from Scarborough in position 54.17N 00.18W by the German submarine *UB 21* whilst on a voyage from Tyne to Rouen with a cargo of coal.

Tyneside Line, Ltd.

BLACKWOOD 1230 Grt. Blt. 1907
9.3.1915: Torpedoed and sunk in the English Channel 18 miles S.W. by S. from Dungeness by the German submarine *U 35* whilst on a voyage from Blyth to Le Havre with a cargo of coal.

BEAUFRONT 1720 Grt. Blt. 1915
6.1.1917: Captured and torpedoed in the English Channel 76 miles N.W. by W. from Ushant in position 48.40N 07.00W by the German submarine *U 82* whilst on a voyage from Bilbao to Tees with a cargo of iron ore.

RINGROSE, J. H. N.—HULL

Hull & Nethelands S.S. Co. Ltd.

RIEVAULX ABBEY 1166 Grt. Blt. 1908
3.9.1916: Struck a mine and sunk in the North Sea ¾ mile E.N.E. from Rosse Spit Buoy, River Humber in position 53.30N 00.17E laid by the German submarine *UC 10* whilst on a voyage from Rotterdam to Hull with general cargo. 2 lost.

KIRKHAM ABBEY 1166 Grt. Blt. 1908
27.7.1918: Torpedoed and sunk in the North Sea 2 miles N.E. by E. from Winterton in position 52.44N 01.42E by the German submarine *UB 40* whilst on a voyage from Rotterdam to Hull with general cargo. 8 lost.

RITSON, F. W.—SUNDERLAND

Nautilus S.S. Co. Ltd.

HOLLY BRANCH 3568 Grt. Blt. 1911
1.1.1917: Captured and sunk with bombs in the English Channel 14 miles N.E. by N. from Ile de Bas in position 48.59N 03.56W by the German submarine *UB 39* whilst on a voyage from La Plata to Le Havre with a cargo of oats.

VINE BRANCH ex *Clan Shaw* ex *Imperialist 3442 Grt. Blt. 1896*
6.4.1917: Torpedoed and sunk in the Atlantic S.W. of Ireland by the German submarine *U 55* whilst on a voyage from Valparaiso to Liverpool with a cargo of nitrate and frozen meat. 44 lost including Master.

OLIVE BRANCH ex *Bellorado 4649 Grt. Blt. 1912*
2.9.1917: Torpedoed and sunk in the Arctic 85 miles N. by E.½E. from North Cape in position 72.34N 27.56 E. by the German submarine *U 28* whilst on a voyage from Liverpool to Archangel with a cargo of munitions and stores. 1 lost.

ALMOND BRANCH ex *Ashmore 3461 Grt. Blt. 1896*
27.11.1917: Torpedoed and sunk in the English Channel 2 miles S.E. from Dodman Point by the German submarine *UB 57* whilst on a voyage from London and Port Talbot to South America with general cargo. 1 lost.

MYRTLE BRANCH ex *Isel Holme 3741 Grt. Blt. 1899*
11.4.1918: Torpedoed and sunk in the Atlantic 9 miles N.E. by N. from Inishtrahull

by the German submarine *UB 73* whilst on a voyage from Coronel and Newport News to the United Kingdom with general cargo. 15 lost including Master.

WILLOW BRANCH 3314 Grt. Blt. 1892
25.4.1918: Sunk by gunfire in the Atlantic off Cape Blanco, West Africa in position 20.00N 17.20W by the German submarines *U 153* and *U 154*. Lost whilst on Government Service employed as Special Service Ship *BOMBALA*.

ROBERTS, HUGH & SON—NEWCASTLE UPON TYNE

North Wales Shipping Co. Ltd.

NORTH WALES ex *Wakefield* 4072 Grt. Blt. 1909
26.10.1916: Torpedoed and sunk in the Atlantic off Scilly Isles by the German submarine *U 69* whilst on a voyage from Hull to Canada in ballast. 30 lost including Master.

ROBERTS, BRINING & CO. LTD.—LIVERPOOL

ARENDAL ex *Eastwood* 1387 Grt. Blt. 1885
18.9.1917: Captured and sunk by gunfire in the Atlantic 115 miles W.½N. from Cape Spartel by the German submarine *U 63* whilst on a voyage from Liverpool to Marseilles with a cargo of benzine and tar.

ROBERTSON, WILLIAM—GLASGOW

MALACHITE 718 Grt. Blt. 1902
23.11.1914: Captured and sunk by gunfire in the English Channel 4 miles N. by W. from Cape de la Heve, near Le Havre by the German submarine *U 21* whilst on a voyage from Liverpool to Le Havre with general cargo.

OLIVINE 634 Grt. Blt. 1902
4.4.1915: Captured and torpedoed in the English Channel 30 miles S. from St. Catherine's Point by the German submarine *U 33* whilst on a voyage from Guernsey to Calais with a cargo of granite.

SPHENE 740 Grt. Blt. 1902
3.8.1916: Captured and sunk with bombs in the English Channel 26 miles S.W. from St. Catherine's Point by the German submarine *UB 18* whilst on a voyage from Honfleur to Newport, Mon. in ballast.

OPAL 599 Grt. Blt. 1894
18.12.1916: Struck a mine and sunk in the Irish Sea off the Isle of Man laid by the German submarine *U 80* whilst on a voyage from Llandulas to Belfast and Clyde with a cargo of limestone. 12 lost including Master.

ESSONITE 589 Grt. Blt. 1904
1.2.1917: Torpedoed and sunk in the Atlantic 3 miles N.N.W. from Trevose Head in position 50.35N 05.04W by the German submarine *U 55* whilst on a voyage from Caernarvon to Rochester with a cargo of stone. 10 lost.

KYANITE 564 Grt. Blt. 1904
15.2.1917: Captured and sunk with bombs in the St. George's Channel 27 miles S.S.W. from Bardsey Island in position 52.18N 04.55W by the German submarine *UC 65* whilst on a voyage from Fleetwood to Bristol with a cargo of alkali.

TOPAZ 696 Grt. Blt. 1896
12.3.1917: Torpedoed and sunk in the English Channel 27 miles E. by N.½N. from Cape Barfleur in position 49.50N 00.40W by the German submarine *UB 18* whilst on a voyage from Honfleur to Port Talbot in ballast. 3 lost.

The Shipping Controller

HUNTSHOLM ex *Telde* **2073 Grt. Blt. 1914**
11.6.1917: Torpedoed and sunk in the English Channel 4 miles E. by S. from Owers Lightvessel by the German submarine *UB 40* whilst on a voyage from Dieppe to Southampton in ballast.

HUNSGROVE ex *Lorenzo* **3063 Grt. Blt. 1913**
8.6.1918: Torpedoed and sunk in the Atlantic 6 miles N.W. from Trevose Head by the German submarine *U 82* whilst on a voyage from Cardiff to France with a cargo of coal. 3 lost.

ROBINSON, BROWN & COMPANY—NEWCASTLE UPON TYNE

The Shipping Controller

SAGA 1143 Grt. Blt. 1901
14.2.1918: Torpedoed and sunk in the North Sea 4 miles E.N.E. from Sunderland by the German submarine *UB 64* whilst on a voyage from Sunderland to Rouen with a cargo of coal.

ROBINSON (JOSEPH) & SONS—NORTH SHIELDS

Stag Line

CLINTONIA 3830 Grt. Blt. 1907
1.8.1915: Captured and torpedoed in the Bay of Biscay 30 miles S.W. by W. from Ushant by the German submarine *U 28* whilst on a voyage from Marseilles to Tyne in ballast. 10 lost.

EUPHORBIA 3837 Grt. Blt. 1907
16.7.1916: Torpedoed and sunk in the Mediterranean 56 miles N.E. from Algiers by the German submarine *U 39* whilst on a voyage from Calcutta to London with general cargo. 11 lost.

EUPHORBIA 3109 Grt. Blt. 1917
1.12.1917: Torpedoed and sunk in the English Channel 14 miles E. by S. from the Royal Sovereign Lightvessel by the German submarine *UC 75* whilst on a voyage from Bassein to London with a cargo of rice. 14 lost.

BEGONIA 3070 Grt. Blt. 1918
21.3.1918: Torpedoed and sunk in the Atlantic 44 miles S. by W. from Wolf Rock by the German submarine *UB 55* whilst on a voyage from Tyne and Plymouth to Salonica with Admiralty cargo.

ROPNER, SIR R. & CO. LTD.—WEST HARTLEPOOL

OAKBY 1976 Grt. Blt. 1897
23.2.1915: Torpedoed and sunk in the English Channel 4 miles E. by N. from the Royal Sovereign Lightvessel by the German submarine *U 8* whilst on a voyage from London to Cardiff in ballast.

GADSBY 3497 Grt. Blt. 1899
1.7.1915: Captured and torpedoed in the Atlantic 33 miles S.S.W. from Wolf Rock by the German submarine *U 39* whilst on a voyage from Sydney (CB) to London with a cargo of wheat.

GLENBY 2196 Grt. Blt. 1900
17.8.1915: Captured and sunk by gunfire in the St. George's Channel 30 miles N. from the Smalls by the German submarine *U 38* whilst on a voyage from Cardiff to Archangel with a cargo of coal. 2 lost.

KIRKBY 3034 Grt. Blt. 1891
17.8.1915: Captured and torpedoed in the St. George's Channel 23 miles W. by S. from Bardsey Island by the German submarine *U 38* whilst on a voyage from Barry to—with a cargo of coal.

SCAWBY 3658 Grt. Blt. 1911
6.10.1915: Captured and sunk with bombs in the Mediterranean 220 miles E. from Malta by the German submarine *U 33* whilst on a voyage from Mudros to Malta in ballast.

THORNABY 1782 Grt. Blt. 1889
28.2.1916: Struck a mine and sunk in the North Sea 2 miles N.E. from Shipwash Lightvessel laid by the German submarine *UC 3* whilst on a voyage from Marbella to West Hartlepool with a cargo of iron ore. 19 lost including Master.

TRUNKBY 2635 Grt. Blt. 1896
27.5.1916: Captured and sunk by gunfire in the Mediterranean 50 miles S. by E. from Port Mahon in position 39.07N 04.45E by the German submarine *U 39* whilst on a voyage from Newport, Mon. to Cette with a cargo of coal.

WRAGBY 3641 Grt. Blt. 1901
4.1.1917: Captured and sunk by gunfire in the Atlantic 45 miles W. by N. from Cape Spartel by the German submarine *UC 37* whilst on a voyage from Barry to Gibraltar with a cargo of coal.

MARTIN 1904 Grt. Blt. 1895
14.1.1917: Captured and sunk by gunfire in the English Channel 8 miles N. by W. from Ushant in position 48.36N 05.08W by the German submarine *UC 18* whilst on a voyage from Bayonne to Barry with a cargo of pit props.

BURNBY 3665 Grt. Blt. 1905
26.2.1917: Torpedoed and sunk in the Mediterranean 20 miles N. from Cape Falcon by the German submarine *U 39* whilst on a voyage from Barry to Algiers with a cargo of coal. Master taken prisoner.

DALEBY 3628 Grt. Blt. 1900
29.4.1917: Torpedoed and sunk in the Atlantic 180 miles N.W. from the Fastnet Rock by the German submarine *U 70* whilst on a voyage from Huelva to Garston with a cargo of copper and silver ore. 25 lost including Master.

WESTONBY 3795 Grt. Blt. 1901
15.6.1917: Torpedoed and sunk in the Atlantic 195 miles S.W. by S. from the Fastnet Rock by the German submarine *U 82* whilst on a voyage from Huelva to London with a cargo of pyrites and lead.

BROOKBY 3679 Grt. Blt. 1905
19.6.1917: Captured and torpedoed in the Atlantic 155 miles S.½W. from the Fastnet Rock by the German submarine *U 60* whilst on a voyage from Sagunto to Middlesbrough with a cargo of iron ore.

THIRLBY 2009 Grt. Blt. 1898
2.7.1917: Torpedoed and sunk in the Atlantic 122 miles N.W. by W.¼W. from the Fastnet Rock in position 51.39N 12.52W by the German submarine *UC 31* whilst on a voyage from Bonanza to Garston with a cargo of copper and copper ore. 2 lost.

ROLLESBY 3955 Grt. Blt. 1906
15.9.1917: Captured and torpedoed in the North Sea 80 miles E.N.E. from Muckle Flugga by the German submarine *U 48* whilst on a voyage from Cardiff to Archangel with a cargo of coal.

MALTBY 3977 Grt. Blt. 1906
26.2.1918: Torpedoed and sunk in the Mediterranean 10 miles S.W. by S. from Pantellaria Island by the German submarine *UC 27* whilst on a voyage from Cardiff to Malta with a cargo of coal. 5 lost.

MOUNTBY 3263 Grt. Blt. 1898
10.6.1918: Torpedoed and sunk in the English Channel 8 miles E. by S. from the Lizard by the German submarine *UC 49* whilst on a voyage from Swansea to— with Admiralty cargo.

BALDERSBY 3613 Grt. Blt. 1913
28.9.1918: Torpedoed and sunk in the St. George's Channel 9 miles E.½S. from Codling Bank Lightvessel by the German submarine *UB 91* whilst on a voyage from Montreal to Avonmouth with a cargo of grain. 2 lost.

Pool Shipping Co. Ltd.

SALMONPOOL 4905 Grt. Blt. 1913
1.6.1916: Captured and torpedoed in the Mediterranean 30 miles N.E. by E. from Cape Carbon in position 37.10N 05.30E by the German submarine *U 39* whilst on a voyage from Naples to Baltimore in ballast.

ROCKPOOL 4502 Grt. Blt. 1912
2.3.1918: Torpedoed and sunk in the Atlantic 12 miles N.E. by N. from Eagle Island by the German submarine *U 94* whilst on a voyage from New Orleans to Dublin with a cargo of wheat and steel. Master taken prisoner.

ROWAT, R. J. & COMPANY—GLASGOW

Inverkip S.S. Co. Ltd.

INVERBERVIE 4309 Grt. Blt. 1913
14.9.1916: Torpedoed and sunk in the Mediterranean 17 miles S. by W. from Cape Rizzuto in position 38.55N 16.15E by the Austro-Hungarian submarine *U 4* whilst on a voyage from Cardiff to Messina and Taranto with a cargo of coal. 6 lost.

ROWLAND, A. & COMPANY—LIVERPOOL

West Lancashire S.S. Co. Ltd.

DINGLE 593 Grt. Blt. 1914
20.2.1916: Struck a mine and sunk off the mouth of the River Thames 10 miles S. by W. from Kentish Knock Lightvessel laid by the German submarine *UC 5* whilst on a voyage from Sunderland to Caen with a cargo of coal. 9 lost including Master.

AIGBURTH 824 Grt. Blt. 1917
5.12.1917: Torpedoed and sunk in the North Sea 2 miles N.E. by E. from South Cheek, Robin Hood Bay by the German submarine *UB 75* whilst on a voyage from Tyne to Treport with a cargo of coal. 11 lost including Master.

ROXBURGH, J. & A.—GLASGOW

Helmsdale Steam Ship Co. Ltd.

HALLAMSHIRE 4420 Grt. Blt. 1907
19.11.1915: Torpedoed and sunk in the Mediterranean 20 miles S.W. by S. from Cerigotto Island in position 35.38N 23.10E by the German submarine *U 34* whilst on a voyage from Cardiff to Malta and Milo Island with a cargo of coal.

LINCOLNSHIRE 3965 Grt. Blt. 1899
29.3.1917: Torpedoed and sunk in the Atlantic 8 miles S.W. by S. from Hook Point in position 52.00N 07.00W by the German submarine *U 57* whilst on a voyage from New York to Le Havre with general cargo.

ROYAL MAIL STEAM PACKET COMPANY—LONDON

CARONI 2652 Grt. Blt. 1904
7.9.1915: Captured and torpedoed in the Bay of Biscay 15 miles W. from Chassiron Point by the German submarine *U 20* whilst on a voyage from London to Bordeaux with a cargo of stores.

DRINA 11483 Grt. Blt. 1913
1.3.1917: Struck a mine and sunk in the St. George's Channel 2 miles W. from Skokham Island in position 51.41N 05.20W laid by the German submarine *UC 65* whilst on a voyage from Buenos Aires to Liverpool carrying passengers and a cargo of meat and coffee. 15 lost.

ARCADIAN ex *Ortona* *8939 Grt. Blt. 1899*
15.4.1917: Torpedoed and sunk in the Mediterranean 26 miles N.E. from Milo

Island by the German submarine *UC 74* whilst on a voyage from Salonica to France carrying troops. 35 lost.

TYNE 2909 Grt. Blt. *1900*
18.6.1917: Torpedoed and sunk in the English Channel 18 miles S.W. from the Lizard in position 49.42N 05.25W by the German submarine *UC 48* whilst on a voyage from Penarth to La Pallice with a cargo of coal and benzole.

ARAGON 9588 Grt. Blt. *1905*
30.12.1917: Torpedoed and sunk in the Mediterranean at the entrance to Alexandria harbour by the German submarine *UC 34* whilst on a voyage from Marseilles to Alexandria carrying troops. 19 lost including Master.

AMAZON 10037 Grt. Blt. *1906*
15.3.1918: Torpedoed and sunk in the Atlantic 30 miles N. by W. from Malin Head in position 55.49N 08.06W by the German submarine *U 110* whilst on a voyage from Liverpool to Buenos Aires.

MERIONETHSHIRE ex *Reptionian* **4308 Grt. Blt. *1913***
27.5.1918: Torpedoed and sunk in the Atlantic 120 miles N.½E. (true) from Flores, Azores by the German submarine *U 62* whilst on a voyage from London to Rio de Janeiro with general cargo.

The Shipping Controller
WAR HELMET 8184 Grt. Blt. *1917*
19.4.1918: Torpedoed and sunk in the English Channel 3 miles E. by N½N. from Owers Lightvessel by the German submarine *UC 75* whilst on a voyage from London to Barry Roads in ballast.

ROYDEN, THOMAS & SONS—LIVERPOOL

Santa Clara S.S. Co. Ltd.

SANTA ISABEL 2023 Grt. Blt. *1914*
14.4.1918: Captured and sunk by gunfire in the Atlantic 15 miles W. from Cape Verd, Senegal in position 14.40N 17.54 W by the German submarine *U 153* whilst on a voyage from Cardiff to Dakar and Sierra Leone with a cargo of coal. 1 lost.

The Admiralty
PROVIDENCE ex *Providentia* **2970 Grt. Blt. *1903***
22.3.1917: Struck a mine and sunk in the St. George's Channel 1¼ miles S. by W.½W. from Barrels Lightvessel laid by the German submarine *UC 48* whilst on a voyage from Cork to France with a cargo of hay.

RUNCIMAN, WALTER & CO. LTD.—NEWCASTLE UPON TYNE

Moor Line, Limited

SPENNYMOOR 2733 Grt. Blt. *1915*
28.5.1915: Captured and torpedoed in the English Channel 50 miles S.W.¼W. from Start Point by the German submarine *U 41* whilst on her maiden voyage from Sunderland to—. 5 lost including Master.

TULLOCHMOOR 3520 Grt. Blt. 1899
28.5.1915: Captured and sunk by gunfire in the English Channel 52 miles N. from Ushant in position 49.19N 05.21W by the German submarine *U 41* whilst on a voyage from Genoa to Tyne in ballast.

INGLEMOOR 4331 Grt. Blt. 1912
1.7.1915: Captured and torpedoed in the English Channel 75 miles S.W. by W. from the Lizard by the German submarine *U 39* whilst on a voyage from Barry to Malta with general cargo and coal.

LINKMOOR 4306 Grt. Blt. 1914
20.9.1915: Captured and sunk by gunfire in the Mediterranean 50 miles W. from Cape Matapan in position 36.16N 21.18E by the German submarine *U 35* whilst on a voyage from Lemnos Island to Malta with a cargo of coal.

GLENMOOR 3075 Grt. Blt. 1894
6.11.1915: Captured and torpedoed in the Mediterranean 5 miles N.E. from Cape de Fer by the German submarine *U 38* whilst on a voyage from Bombay to Tees with a cargo of manganese ore.

HOPEMOOR 3740 Grt. Blt. 1911
14.2.1917: Torpedoed and sunk in the Atlantic 20 miles N.W. from the Skelligs in position 51.53N 11.00W by the German submarine *U 60* whilst on a voyage from Baltimore to Hull with a cargo of wheat.

DUNBARMOOR 3651 Grt. Blt. 1903
8.3.1917: Captured and sunk by gunfire in the Atlantic 180 miles W.N.W. from the Fastnet Rock in position 51.22N 14.31W by the German submarine *U 44* whilst on a voyage from Rosario to Manchester with a cargo of wheat. 12 lost including Master.

FERNMOOR 3098 Grt. Blt. 1894
17.4.1917: Captured and sunk with bombs in the Atlantic 150 miles W. from Gibraltar in position 35.30N 08.18W by the German submarine *U 35* whilst on a voyage from Baltimore to Genoa with a cargo of iron and steel.

NENTMOOR 3535 Grt. Blt. 1903
20.4.1917: Captured and sunk by gunfire in the Atlantic 140 miles W. from Gibraltar in position 35.25N 08.02W by the German submarine *U 35* whilst on a voyage from Rosario to Gibraltar with a cargo of wheat.

CLODMOOR 3753 Grt. Blt. 1902
3.5.1917: Torpedoed and sunk in the English Channel 5 miles S.W. from Newhaven in position 50.43N on the Meridian by the German submarine *UB 48* whilst on a voyage from Bahia Blanca to Tyne with a cargo of wheat.

ELMMOOR 3744 Grt. Blt. 1910
23.5.1917: Torpedoed and sunk in the Mediterranean 36 miles E. by S. from Syracuse in position 37.00N 16.20E by the German submarine *UC 67* whilst on a voyage from Karachi to Leghorn with a cargo of wheat. Master taken prisoner.

***FORESTMOOR** 2844 Grt. Blt. 1910*
5.10.1917: Torpedoed and sunk in the Atlantic 54 miles W. by N.¾N. from Cape Spartel by the German submarine *UB 51* whilst on a voyage from Huelva to Dublin with a cargo of copper ore. 22 lost including Master.

***VENTMOOR** 3456 Grt. Blt. 1900*
14.2.1918: Torpedoed and sunk in the Aegean Sea 8 miles S.W. by W. from Skyro Island by the German submarine *UC 37* whilst on a voyage from Mudros to Sfax in ballast. 21 lost including Master.

***USKMOOR** 3189 Grt. Blt. 1912*
5.3.1918: Torpedoed and sunk in the English Channel 3 miles S.W. from Prawle Point by the German submarine *UB 80* whilst on a voyage from Dunkirk to Barry Roads in ballast.

***MARSTONMOOR** 2744 Grt. Blt. 1906*
14.4.1918: Torpedoed and sunk in the Atlantic 55 miles N.N.E. from Cape Wrath in position 59.34N 04.54W by the German submarine *U 107* whilst on a voyage from Barry to Archangel with general cargo and coal.

***WESTMOOR** 4329 Grt. Blt. 1911*
1.7.1918: Torpedoed and sunk in the Atlantic 210 miles N.W. by W.¾W. from Casablanca in position 34.10N 11.47W by the German submarine *U 91* whilst on a voyage from Gibraltar to La Plata in ballast. 2 lost, Master taken prisoner.

Novocastrian Shipping Co. Ltd.

***ROSEMOOR** 4303 Grt. Blt. 1914*
17.7.1916: Captured and sunk with bombs in the Mediterranean 80 miles N.E. by N. from Algiers by the German submarine *U 39* whilst on a voyage from Genoa to Hampton Roads in ballast.

***GRANGEMOOR** 3198 Grt. Blt. 1911*
20.7.1916: Captured and sunk by gunfire in the Mediterranean 75 miles N.W. by W. from Algiers in position 37.22N 02.20E by the German submarine *U 39* whilst on a voyage from Genoa to Baltimore in ballast.

RUSSELL, DAVID & CO. LTD.—EDINBURGH

Craigmhor S.S. Co. Ltd.

***CRAIGARD** 3286 Grt. Blt. 1901*
1.7.1915: Captured and torpedoed in the Atlantic 50 miles S.W. by S. from Wolf Rock in position 48.18N 06.10W by the German submarine *U 39* whilst on a voyage from Galveston to Le Havre with a cargo of cotton.

SALE & COMPANY—LONDON

***TUNG SHAN** ex Teodoro De Larrinaga 3999 Grt. Blt. 1899*
15.5.1917: Captured and sunk with bombs in the Mediterranean 7 miles N. from Cape San Antonio, Gulf of Valencia by the German submarine *U 34* whilst on a voyage from Tyne to Genoa with a cargo of coal. 1 lost, Master, Chief Engineer and 1 Gunner taken prisoner.

Bay Steam Ship Co. Ltd.

KILBRIDE 3712 Grt. Blt. 1901
1.3.1916: Captured and sunk by gunfire in the Mediterranean 30 miles E. from Galita Island by the German submarine *U 38* whilst on a voyage from Barry to Malta with a cargo of coal.

FELICIANA 4283 Grt. Blt. 1909
21.4.1916: Torpedoed and sunk in the Atlantic 67 miles W. by N.½N. from the Fastnet Rock by the German submarine *U 19* whilst on a voyage from London and Cardiff to New York in ballast.

BAYHALL ex *Brabandier* ex *Dinsdalehall 3898 Grt. Blt. 1906*
17.12.1916: Captured and sunk with bombs in the Atlantic 90 miles N. by E. from Cape Ortegal in position 45.16N 08.00W by the German submarine *U 46* whilst on a voyage from Port Louis to Bordeaux with a cargo of sugar. Master taken prisoner.

BAYCRAIG ex *Craigina* ex *Barra 3761 Grt. Blt. 1905*
1.1.1917: Torpedoed and sunk in the Mediterranean 84 miles E.S.E. from Malta in position 35.32N 16.10E by the German submarine *UC 22* whilst on a voyage from Port Louis to Marseilles with a cargo of sugar. Master taken prisoner.

BAYNESK ex *Glenesk 3286 Grt. Blt. 1906*
9.1.1917: Torpedoed and sunk in the Mediterranean 130 miles N. by W. from Alexandria by the German submarine *U 39* whilst on a voyage from Port Louis to Marseilles with a cargo of sugar. 7 lost.

BAYNAEN ex *Glenaen 3227 Grt. Blt. 1904*
25.3.1917: Torpedoed and sunk in the Bay of Biscay 20 miles N.W. by W. from Belle Ile in position 47.30N 03.41W by the German submarine *UC 36* whilst on a voyage from Tegal to Nantes with a cargo of sugar. 5 lost.

BAYSOTO ex *Cayo Soto 3082 Grt. Blt. 1905*
6.8.1917: Torpedoed and sunk in the North Sea 33 miles S.E. by E. from Girdle Ness in position 56.58N 01.50W by the German submarine *UC 42* whilst on a voyage from Archangel to Tyne and Le Havre with a cargo of flax.

BAYCHATTAN 3758 Grt. Blt. 1906
11.10.1917: Torpedoed and sunk in the English Channel ½ mile S.S.W. from Prawle Point by the German submarine *UC 50* whilst on a voyage from Le Havre to Cardiff in ballast.

BAYVOE ex *Wenvoe 2979 Grt. Blt. 1894*
9.1.1918: Torpedoed and sunk in the Bay of Biscay 10 miles S. from Iles de Glenan by the German submarine *U 84* whilst on a voyage from Portland (Me) to Bordeaux with a cargo of wheat. 4 lost.

BAYGITANO ex *Cayo Gitano 3073 Grt. Blt. 1905*
18.3.1918: Torpedoed and sunk in the English Channel 1½ miles S.W. from Lyme Regis by the German submarine *U 77* whilst on a voyage from Le Havre to Cardiff in ballast. 2 lost.

Hudson's Bay Company

***PRINCE ABBAS** 2030 Grt. Blt. 1892*
9.7.1917: Torpedoed and sunk in the North Sea 29 miles E. from Fair Island by the German submarine *U 52* whilst on a voyage from Tyne to Lerwick with a cargo of coal. 2 lost.

SALVESEN, CHRISTIAN & COMPANY—LEITH

***GLITRA** ex Saxon Prince 866 Grt. Blt. 1881*
20.10.1914: Captured and scuttled in the North Sea 14 miles W.S.W. from Skudesnes by the German submarine *U 17* whilst on a voyage from Grangemouth to Stavanger with a cargo of coal. The first British merchant ship to be sunk by a German U-boat in the First World War.

***AILSA** ex Twilight ex Emmanuel Scicluna 876 Grt. Blt. 1884*
18.6.1915: Captured and scuttled in the North Sea 30 miles E. by N. from Bell Rock, 12 miles S.E. of Arbroath by the German submarine *U 17* whilst on a voyage from Trondheim to Leith with a cargo of wood.

***CORONDA** ex Manica 2733 Grt. Blt. 1892*
13.3.1917: Torpedoed and sunk in the Atlantic 180 miles N.W. from Tory Island in position 56.11N 13.40W by the German submarine *U 81* whilst on a voyage from Clyde to South Georgia with general cargo. 9 lost.

***CADMUS** 1879 Grt. Blt. 1911*
18.10.1917: Torpedoed and sunk in the North Sea 20 miles S. by E.½E. from Flamborough Head by the German submarine *UC 47* whilst on a voyage from Dunkirk to Blyth with a cargo of empty shell cases.

***ARDANDEARG** 3237 Grt. Blt. 1895*
14.3.1918: Torpedoed and sunk in the Mediterranean 86 miles E.¼N. from Malta by the German submarine *UC 54* whilst on a voyage from Malta to—with a cargo of Government stores. 2 lost including Master.

***JOHN O. SCOTT** 1235 Grt. Blt. 1906*
18.9.1918: Torpedoed and sunk in the Atlantic 9 miles W. by N. from Trevose Head in position 50.32N 05.16W by the German submarine *UB 117* whilst on a voyage from Barry to Dover with a cargo of coal. 18 lost.

SALVESEN, J. T. & COMPANY—LEITH

***EMBLA** 1172 Grt. Blt. 1882*
24.12.1915: Struck a mine and sunk in the mouth of the River Thames 3 miles E.S.E. from the Tongue Lightvessel laid by the German submarine *UC 1* whilst on a voyage from London to Dunkirk with a cargo of jute, paper and oil.

***VESTRA** 1021 Grt. Blt. 1897*
5.2.1917: Torpedoed and sunk in the North Sea 5 miles N.E. from Hartlepool in position 54.46N 01.07W by the German submarine *UB 35* whilst on a voyage from Tyne to Rouen with a cargo of coal. 2 lost.

VALA 1016 Grt. Blt. 1894
20.8.1917: Torpedoed and sunk in the Atlantic 120 miles S.W. of the Scilly Isles in position 48.37N 09.28W by the German submarine *UB 54* whilst on a voyage from France to Queenstown. Lost whilst on Government service employed as a Special Service Ship.

SAMMAN, H. COMPANY—HULL

Deddington S.S. Co. Ltd.

ETTON 2831 Grt. Blt. 1905
20.9.1916: Struck a mine and sunk at the entrance to the White Sea in position 67.36N 41.20E laid by the German submarine *U 75* whilst on a voyage from Barry to Archangel with a cargo of coal. 1 lost.

The Shipping Controller

IDAHO ex *Ran* 3023 Grt. Blt. 1899
18.8.1918: Torpedoed and sunk in the Atlantic 120 miles N. by W.½W. from Cape Villano in position 44.40N 10.20W by the German submarine *U 107* whilst on a voyage from Clyde to—in ballast. 11 lost.

SAMUEL, MARCUS & COMPANY (SHELL LINE)—LONDON

Flower Motor Ship Co. Ltd.

ABELIA 3650 Grt. Blt. 1914
30.12.1915: Captured and sunk by gunfire in the Mediterranean 152 miles W. from Gavdo Island in position 34.30N 21.00E by the German submarine *U 34* whilst on a voyage from Bombay to Hull with a cargo of manganese ore and seed.

ARABIS 3928 Grt. Blt. 1914
16.9.1917: Torpedoed and sunk in the Atlantic 210 miles W. by S. from Ushant by the German submarine *U 54* whilst on a voyage from Sfax to Falmouth with a cargo of phosphate. 20 lost including Master.

Nella S.S. Co. Ltd.

CLIFTONDALE ex *Whindyke* ex *Ploughwell* ex *Selsdon* 3811 Grt. Blt. 1901
25.12.1917: Torpedoed and sunk in the Mediterranean 36 miles E. by N.½N. from Cape Tenez by the German submarine *U 35* whilst on a voyage from Cardiff to Algiers with general cargo and coal. 3 lost, Master taken prisoner.

Occidental & Oriental Steam Navigation Co. Ltd.

LORD DERBY 3757 Grt. Blt. 1905
28.12.1917: Torpedoed and sunk in the St. George's Channel 7 miles S.W. by S. from St. Ann's Head by the German submarine *U 105* whilst on a voyage from Cardiff to Milford Haven with a cargo of coal. 3 lost.

Universal Steam Navigation Co. Ltd.

KATHLEEN 3915 Grt. Blt. 1907
5.8.1917: Torpedoed and sunk in the Atlantic 90 miles W. from Skelligs by the German submarine *U 100* whilst on a voyage from Norfolk (Va) to Limerick with a cargo of wheat and maize. Master lost.

NORA 3933 Grt. Blt. 1908
3.6.1918: Torpedoed and sunk in the Mediterranean 205 miles S.E. from Malta in position 33.38N 17.42E by the German submarine *UB 105* whilst on a voyage from Port Said to Bizerta in ballast. 1 lost.

SARGEANT, R. & SONS—WEST HARTLEPOOL

RIBSTON 3048 Grt. Blt. 1906
23.4.1916: Captured and torpedoed in the Atlantic 66 miles W. by S. from Ushant in position 47.55N 06.32W by the German submarine *U 19* whilst on a voyage from Cardiff to a Mediterranean port with a cargo of coal.

SAVAGE, W. A. LIMITED—LIVERPOOL

Zillah Shipping & Carrying Co. Ltd.

SUMMERFIELD 687 Grt. Blt. 1913
13.8.1915: Struck a mine and sunk in the North Sea 2 miles E. from Lowestoft laid by the German submarine *UC 5* whilst on a voyage from Tyne to Dublin with a cargo of coal. 3 lost.

SCRUTTON, SONS & COMPANY—LONDON

SALYBIA 3352 Grt. Blt. 1904
24.3.1916: Torpedoed and sunk in the English Channel 4 miles S.W. by W. from Dungeness by the German submarine *UB 29* whilst on a voyage from Trinidad to London with general cargo.

SANTAREN 4256 Grt. Blt. 1912
15.9.1917: Torpedoed and sunk in the North Sea 40 miles N.E. from Muckle Flugga by the German submarine *UB 63* whilst on a voyage from Tyne to Archangel with a cargo of coke. Master and Chief Officer taken prisoner.

SERRANA 3677 Grt. Blt. 1905
22.1.1918: Torpedoed and sunk in the English Channel 10 miles W. from St. Catherine's Point by the German submarine *UB 35* whilst on a voyage from London to Barbados with general cargo. 5 lost.

SEAGER, W. H. & COMPANY—CARDIFF

POLBRAE ex *Marie Horn 1087 Grt. Blt. 1896*
4.5.1918: Torpedoed and sunk in the Atlantic 1¼ miles S.W. from Lower Sharpnose Point, 4½ miles N. of Bude by the German submarine *U 60* whilst on a voyage from Cardiff to St. Malo with a cargo of patent fuel. 1 lost.

Tempus Shipping Co. Ltd.

TEMPUS 2981 Grt. Blt. 1904
19.4.1917: Torpedoed and sunk in the Atlantic 130 miles N.W. by W. ½W. from the Fastnet Rock in position 51.45N 12.58W by the German submarine *U 53* whilst on a voyage from Cartagena to Garston with a cargo of iron ore. 1 lost.

DARIUS ex *Pennine Range* **3426 Grt. Blt. 1903**
13.6.1917: Torpedoed and sunk in the Atlantic 210 miles S.W. from the Fastnet Rock in position 48.08N 11.32W by the German submarine *U 54* whilst on a voyage from Villaricos to Tyne with a cargo of iron ore. 15 lost.

FISCUS 4782 Grt. Blt. 1917
20.12.1917: Torpedoed and sunk in the Mediterranean 10 miles N.N.E. from Cape Ivi by the German submarine *U 35* whilst on a voyage from Barry to Corfu with a cargo of coal. 1 lost.

SHARP & COMPANY—NEWCASTLE UPON TYNE

Sharp S.S. Co. Ltd.

ELFORD 1739 Grt. Blt. 1915
18.5.1917: Struck a mine and sunk in the English Channel 2 miles S. from the Nab Lightvessel laid by the German submarine *UC 36* whilst on a voyage from Chatham to Cherbourg with a cargo of Government stores.

SHAW, SAVILL & ALBION CO. LTD.—LONDON

TOKOMARU ex *Westmeath* **6084 Grt. Blt. 1893**
30.1.1915: Torpedoed and sunk in the English Channel 7 miles N.W. from Le Havre Lightvessel by the German submarine *U 20* whilst on a voyage from Dunedin to Le Havre and London with general cargo.

SHEPTON, G. C.—CARDIFF

West of England Shipping Co. Ltd.

RIO PIRAHY ex *Exmoor* **3561 Grt. Blt. 1901**
28.10.1916: Captured and sunk with bombs in the Atlantic 60 miles S. from Cape St. Vincent by the German submarine *U 63* whilst on a voyage from Leghorn to Barry Roads in ballast.

SHIPPING & COAL CO. LTD.—LONDON

FORELAND 1960 Grt. Blt. 1914
12.2.1917: Struck a mine and sunk in the North Sea 6 miles S.¾W. from Shipwash Lightvessel in position 51.56N 01.40E laid by the German submarine *UC 11* whilst on a voyage from Blyth to Devonport with a cargo of coal.

SLATER, JOHN LIMITED—LONDON

Thordis Shipping Co. Ltd.

LAURIUM 582 Grt. Blt. 1896
23.4.1918: Struck a mine and sunk in the North Sea near the Inner Dowsing Lightvessel, 15 miles E. from Skegness laid by the German submarine *UC 64* whilst on a voyage from Hull to Rouen with a cargo of coal. 1 lost.

SLIGO STEAM NAVIGATION CO. LTD.—SLIGO

LIVERPOOL 686 Grt. Blt. 1892
19.12.1916: Struck a mine and sunk in the Irish Sea 11 miles S.E. by S. from Chicken Rock in position 53.49N 04.23W laid by the German submarine *U 80* whilst on a voyage from Liverpool to Sligo with general cargo. 3 lost.

SLOAN, WILLIAM & CO. LTD.—GLASGOW

AFTON 1156 Grt. Blt. 1911
15.2.1917: Captured and sunk with bombs in the St. Georges Channel 23 miles N. by E. from Strumble Head in position 52.24N 05.09W by the German submarine *UC 65* whilst on a voyage from Bristol to Belfast and Glasgow with general cargo.

TWEED 1025 Grt. Blt. 1892
13.3.1918: Torpedoed and sunk in the English Channel 10 miles S. by W. ¼ W. from St. Catherine's Point by the German submarine *UB 59* whilst on a voyage from Newhaven to Cherbourg with general cargo. 7 lost.

SMAILES, T. & SON—WHITBY

Thomas Smailes & Son's S.S. Co. Ltd.

CONCORD 2861 Grt. Blt. 1902
22.3.1915: Torpedoed and sunk in the English Channel 9 miles S.E. by E. ½ E. from the Royal Sovereign Lightvessel by the German submarine *U 34* whilst on a voyage from Rosario to Leith with a cargo of grain.

BAGDALE 3045 Grt. Blt. 1904
1.5.1917: Torpedoed and sunk in the English Channel 13 miles N. by E. ½ E. from Creac'h Point, near Ushant in position 48.41N 05.08W by the German submarine *UC 66* whilst on a voyage from Clyde to Nantes with a cargo of coal. 23 lost including Master.

SMELLIE, WILLIAM—LIVERPOOL

British Sun Co. Ltd.

BRITISH SUN 5565 Grt. Blt. 1909
1.5.1917: Torpedoed and sunk in the Mediterranean 230 miles E.S.E. from Malta by the German submarine *UC 37* whilst on a voyage from Abadan to Malta with a cargo of fueloil.

SMITH, R. LAWRENCE, LIMITED—MONTREAL

FRESHFIELD ex *Clement* ex *La Plata* **3445 Grt. Blt. 1896**
5.8.1918: Torpedoed and sunk in the Mediterranean 4 miles N.E. by N. from Cape Colonne by the German submarine *UC 25* whilst on a voyage from Messina to Taranto in ballast. 3 lost.

SMITH, W. J.—LONDON

Tank Storage & Carriage Co. Ltd.

POWHATAN* ex *Tuscarora* 6117 Grt. Blt. *1898
6.4.1917: Torpedoed and sunk in the Atlantic 25 miles N. by W. from North Rona, Outer Hebrides in position 59.32N 06.30W by the German submarine *U 66* whilst on a voyage from Sabine to Kirkwall with a cargo of fueloil. 36 lost, Master taken prisoner.

SMITH, WILLIAM REARDON & SONS, LTD—CARDIFF

Instow S.S. Co. Ltd.

INDIAN CITY* 4645 Grt. Blt. *1915
12.3.1915: Captured and torpedoed in the Atlantic 10 miles S. from St. Mary's Scilly Isles by the German submarine *U 29* whilst on a voyage from Galveston and Newport News to Le Havre with a cargo of cotton and splelter.

St. Just S.S. Co. Ltd.

EASTERN CITY* 4341 Grt. Blt. *1913
9.4.1916: Captured and sunk by gunfire in the English Channel 18 miles N. by W. from Ushant by the German submarine *U 66* whilst on a voyage from St. Nazaire to Barry Roads in ballast.

JERSEY CITY* 4670 Grt. Blt. *1914
24.5.1917: Torpedoed and sunk in the Atlantic 35 miles N.W. from the Flannan Isles, Outer Hebrides in position 58.30N 08.36W by the German submarine *U 46* whilst on a voyage from Pensacola to Hull with a cargo of wheat. Master taken prisoner.

CONISTON WATER* 3738 Grt. Blt. *1908
21.7.1917: Torpedoed and sunk in the Atlantic 70 miles N. by W. from Butt of Lewis in position 59.29N 07.36W by the German submarine *U 87* whilst on a voyage from Newport, Mon. to Archangel with a cargo of coal.

BRADFORD CITY* 3683 Grt. Blt. *1910
16.8.1917: Torpedoed and sunk in the Mediterranean in the Strait of Messina in position 38.10N 15.36E by the Austro-Hungarian submarine *U 28*. Lost whilst on Government service employed as a Special Service Ship.

FALLODON* 3012 Grt. Blt. *1903
28.12.1917: Torpedoed and sunk in the English Channel 12 miles S.S.E. from St. Catherine's Point by the German submarine *UC 71* whilst on a voyage from Le Havre to Clyde in ballast. 1 lost.

RUNSWICK* 3060 Grt. Blt. *1904
18.4.1918: Torpedoed and sunk in the Atlantic 3 miles N. from Trevose Head by the German submarine *UB 109* whilst on a voyage from Newport, Mon. to— with a cargo of coal.

LEEDS CITY* 4298 Grt. Blt. *1908
6.5.1918: Torpedoed and sunk in the North Channel 5 miles E. by S.½S. from

Skulmartin Lightvessel by the German submarine *U 86* whilst on a voyage from Portland (Me) to Manchester with a cargo of flour and wheat.

ESCRICK 4151 Grt. Blt. 1910
17.8.1918: Torpedoed and sunk in the Atlantic 360 miles N.W. by N. from Cape Finisterre in position 46.42N 16.10W by the German submarine *U 90* whilst on a voyage from La Rochelle to Montreal in ballast. 1 lost, Master taken prisoner.

SOUTER, W. A. & COMPANY—NEWCASTLE UPON TYNE
Sheaf Steam Shipping Co. Ltd.
SHEAF BLADE ex *Mariner 2378 Grt. Blt. 1903*
25.10.1917: Torpedoed and sunk in the Mediterranean 13 miles S.E. by S. from Cabo de Gata by the German submarine *U 64* whilst on a voyage from Messina to Almeria in ballast. 2 lost including Master.

The Shipping Controller
DRONNING MAUD 2663 Grt. Blt. 1917
22.4.1918: Torpedoed and sunk in the Mediterranean 65 miles N. by E. ¾ E. from Cape Sigli in position 38.00N 04.56E by the German submarine *U 34* whilst on a voyage from Sunderland to Malta with a cargo of coal. 1 lost.

SOUTH METROPOLITAN GAS COMPANY—LONDON
RAMSGARTH 1553 Grt. Blt. 1910
28.11.1916: Captured and sunk with bombs in the English Channel 11 miles E. by S. from Owers Lightvessel by the German submarine *UB 39* whilst on a voyage from Cardiff to Tyne in ballast.

RAVENSBOURNE 1226 Grt. Blt. 1916
31.1.1917: Struck a mine and sunk in the North Sea 8 miles S.E. from the River Tyne laid by the German submarine *UC 31* whilst on a voyage from Tyne to London with a cargo of coal. 3 lost.

PONTYPRIDD 1556 Grt. Blt. 1883
12.3.1917: Struck a mine and sunk in the North Sea off Aldeburgh Napes in position 52.08N 01.46E laid by the German submarine *UC 4* whilst on a voyage from Tyne to London with a cargo of coal. 3 lost.

QUAGGY ex *Glenpark 993 Grt. Blt. 1904*
11.4.1917: Struck a mine and sunk in the North Sea 3 miles E. from North Cheek, Robin Hood Bay laid by the German submarine *UC 31* whilst on a voyage from London to Tyne in ballast. 2 lost.

DULWICH 1460 Grt. Blt. 1916
10.6.1917: Struck a mine and sunk in the North Sea 7 miles N. by E. ½ E. from Shipwash Lightvessel laid by the German submarine *UB 12* whilst on a voyage from Seaham Harbour to London with a cargo of coal. 5 lost.

AMSTELDAM 1233 Grt. Blt. 1907
18.10.1917: Torpedoed and sunk in the North Sea 6 miles N. from Flamborough

Head by the German submarine *UB 21* whilst on a voyage from Shields to London with a cargo of coal. 4 lost.

TOGSTON 1057 Grt. Blt. 1909
18.10.1917: Torpedoed and sunk in the North Sea 20 miles S. by E.½E. from Flamborough Head in position 53.40N 00.12E by the German submarine *UC 47* whilst on a voyage from Tyne to London with a cargo of coal. 5 lost.

KENNINGTON 1536 Grt. Blt. 1918
12.6.1918: Torpedoed and sunk in the North Sea 15 miles E. from Flamborough Head by the German submarine *UB 108* whilst on a voyage from London to Tyne in ballast.

GIRALDA 1100 Grt. Blt. 1887
28.8.1918: Torpedoed and damaged in the North Sea 5 miles N.N.W. from Whitby by the German submarine *UB 77* whilst on a voyage from London to Tyne in ballast. 6 lost. Later beached and became a total loss.

STAMP, MANN & COMPANY—NEWCASTLE UPON TYNE

Hopemount Shipping Co. Ltd.

HOPEMOUNT 3300 Grt. Blt. 1904
13.6.1915: Captured and sunk by gunfire in the Bristol Channel 70 miles W. by S. from Lundy Island by the German submarine *U 35* whilst on a voyage from Cardiff to Alexandria with a cargo of coal.

STANDARD TRANSPORTATION CO. LTD.—HONG KONG

WAPELLO ex *Clio* 5576 Grt. Blt. 1912
15.6.1917: Torpedoed and sunk in the English Channel 14 miles W.S.W. from Owers Lightvessel in position 50.30N 00.57W by the German submarine *UC 71* whilst on a voyage from Philadelphia to Thameshaven with a cargo of benzine. 2 lost.

SAMOSET ex *Cadillac* 5251 Grt. Blt. 1909
20.3.1918: Torpedoed and sunk in the Mediterranean 50 miles N. by E.¾E. from Port Said by the German submarine *U 33* whilst on a voyage from Port Said to Brindisi with a cargo of fueloil. 3 lost.

WANETA ex *Impoco* 1683 Grt. Blt. 1910
30.5.1918: Torpedoed and sunk in the Atlantic 42 miles S.S.E. from Kinsale Head by the German submarine *U 101* whilst on a voyage from Halifax, (NS) to Queenstown with a cargo of fueloil. 8 lost.

TATARRAX 6216 Grt. Blt. 1914
10.8.1918: Torpedoed and sunk in the Mediterranean off Rosetta in position 32.00N 30.45E by the German submarine *UC 34* whilst on a voyage from Port Said to Alexandria with a cargo of benzole.

STEEL, YOUNG & COMPANY—LONDON

CLUDEN 3166 Grt. Blt. 1896
22.10.1916: Torpedoed and sunk in the Mediterranean 11 miles W. from Cape Tenez by the German submarine *U 39* whilst on a voyage from Karachi to Cardiff with a cargo of wheat. 4 lost.

CAPENOR 2536 Grt. Blt. 1890
22.4.1917: Struck a mine and sunk in the Bay of Biscay at the entrance to La Pallice Roads in position 46.06N 01.17W laid by the German submarine *UC 21* whilst on a voyage from Nantes to Bilbao in ballast.

TEVIOTDALE 3847 Grt. Blt. 1894
11.6.1917: Torpedoed and sunk in the Atlantic 330 miles N.W. by W. from the Fastnet Rock in position 52.20N 18.27W by the German submarine *U 43* whilst on a voyage from Halifax, (NS) to Queenstown with a cargo of sugar. 1 lost.

Ilderton S.S. Co. Ltd.

EMBLETON 5377 Grt. Blt. 1917
11.9.1917: Captured and sunk by gunfire in the Atlantic 150 miles W. from Cape Spartel in position 35.20N 08.42W by the German submarine *U 63* whilst on a voyage from Tyne to Savona with a cargo of coal.

ILDERTON 3125 Grt. Blt. 1903
24.10.1917: Torpedoed and sunk in the Arctic 35 miles N.E. from Kildin Island in position 69.46N 35.32E by the German submarine *U 46* whilst on a voyage from Archangel to Lerwick with a cargo of timber.

STURTON 4406 Grt. Blt. 1912
7.2.1918: Torpedoed and sunk in the Mediterranean 15 miles S.E. by E¼E. from Ile de Porquerolles in position 42.54N 06.30E by the German submarine *UB 48* whilst on a voyage from Baltimore to Genoa with a cargo of steel and oats.

STEPHENS, SUTTON & STEPHENS LIMITED—NEWCASTLE UPON TYNE

Mira S.S. Co. Ltd.

MIRA 3700 Grt. Blt. 1901
11.10.1917: Struck a mine and sunk in the English Channel 4 miles S.W.½W. from Beachy Head in position 50.41N 00.09E laid by the German submarine *UC 50* whilst on a voyage from Port Arthur, Texas to Dover with a cargo of fueloil.

Red 'R' S.S. Co. Ltd.

RODDAM 3218 Grt. Blt. 1912
26.9.1916: Captured and sunk by gunfire in the Mediterranean 16 miles E.S.E. from Barcelona by the German submarine *U 35* whilst on a voyage from Savona to Barry Roads in ballast.

STEPHENSON, CLARKE & CO. LTD.—LONDON

CERNE 2579 Grt. Blt. 1915
26.3.1916: Struck a mine and sunk off the mouth of the River Thames 4 miles

N.E. from Elbow Buoy laid by the German submarine *UC 7* whilst on a voyage from Tyne to London with a cargo of coal.

JOHN MILES 687 Grt. Blt. 1908
22.2.1917: Torpedoed and sunk in the North Sea 11 miles S.E. from Hartlepool by the German submarine *UB 21* whilst on a voyage from Tyne to Shoreham with a cargo of coal. 10 lost including Master.

CORBET WOODALL 917 Grt. Blt. 1908
30.5.1917: Struck a mine and sunk in the English Channel 1½ miles E. from Nab Lightvessel laid by the German submarine *UC 36* whilst on a voyage from Tyne to Poole with a cargo of coal.

Normandy Shipping Co. Ltd.

SOMME 1828 Grt. Blt. 1916
30.3.1917: Torpedoed and sunk in the English Channel 20 miles E. by N. from Cape Barfleur in position 49.48N 00.41W by the German submarine *UB 40* whilst on a voyage from Newport, Mon. to Rouen with a cargo of coal. 5 lost.

AUBE 1837 Grt. Blt. 1916
4.8.1917: Torpedoed and sunk in the Bay of Biscay 3½ miles N. by W. from Ile d'Yeu, near St. Nazaire by the German submarine *UC 71* whilst on a voyage from Newport, Mon. to Bordeaux with a cargo of coal. 1 lost.

STEVEN THOMAS. C. & COMPANY—EDINBURGH

ARBONNE ex *Dorset Coast* **672 Grt. Blt. 1908**
26.2.1916: Torpedoed and sunk off the mouth of the River Thames near the Kentish Knock Lightvessel by the German submarine *UB 2* whilst on a voyage from Le Havre to Tyne in ballast. 14 lost including Master.

AURIAC ex *Adare* ex *Taff* **871 Grt. Blt. 1890**
23.4.1917: Captured and sunk by gunfire in the North Sea 5 miles E.S.E. from St. Abb's Head by the German submarine *UC 44* whilst on a voyage from Rouen to Leith in ballast. 1 lost.

STEWART, C. A. & COMPANY—LONDON

GARDEPEE 1633 Grt. Blt. 1882
10.10.1916: Captured and sunk with bombs in the Arctic 70 miles N.N.E. from North Cape by the German submarine *U 43* whilst on a voyage from Trondheim and Christiansand to Archangel with a cargo of spelter (zinc) and herrings.

STEWART & ESPLEN LIMITED—LIVERPOOL

Ince Shipping Co. Ltd.

PERTH ex *Brinio* **653 Grt. Blt. 1882**
1.4.1916: Torpedoed and sunk in the North Sea 1 mile S.E. by E. from Cross Sand Lightvessel, near Yarmouth by the German submarine *UB 16* whilst on a voyage from Fécamp to Hull in ballast. 6 lost.

STEWART & GRAY—GLASGOW

INVERGYLE 1794 Grt. Blt. 1907
13.3.1915: Torpedoed and sunk in the North Sea 12 miles N.N.E. from the Tyne by the German submarine *U 23* whilst on a voyage from Scapa Flow to Hartlepool in ballast.

ST. LAWRENCE SHIPPING CO. LTD.—SYDNEY, CAPE BRETON

MORWENNA ex *Ardeola* 1414 Grt. Blt. 1904
26.5.1915: Captured and torpedoed in the Atlantic 72 miles S. by E. from the Fastnet Rock in position 50.27N 08.44W by the German submarine *U 41* whilst on a voyage from Cardiff to Sydney (CB) in ballast. 1 lost.

STILLMAN, C. O.—SARNIA, ONTARIO

Imperial Oil Co. Ltd.

PALACINE ex *Khorazan* 3286 Grt. Blt. 1904
2.12.1916: Captured and sunk with bombs in the English Channel 18 miles E.N.E. from Ushant in position 48.40N 04.43W by the German submarine *UB 39* whilst on a voyage from New York to Le Havre and Rouen with a cargo of oil.

STONE & ROLFE—LLANELLY

ALLIE ex *Cachalote II* ex *Allie* 1127 Grt. Blt. 1899
5.1.1917: Captured and sunk with bombs in the Bay of Biscay 10 miles W. by N. from Ile de Re near La Rochelle in position 46.15N 01.48W by the German submarine *UB 39* whilst on a voyage from Swansea to Bordeaux with a cargo of sulphate of copper.

STRICK, FRANK C. & CO. LTD.—LONDON

Strick Line, Ltd.

TANGISTAN 3738 Grt. Blt. 1906
9.3.1915: Torpedoed and sunk in the North Sea 9 miles N. from Flamborough Head by the German submarine *U 12* whilst on a voyage from Benisaf to Tees with a cargo of iron ore. 38 lost including Master.

AVRISTAN ex *Imogen* 3818 Grt. Blt. 1901
7.12.1916: Torpedoed and sunk in the English Channel 14 miles S. by W.½W. from Ushant by the German submarine *UC 21* whilst on a voyage from Portland (Me) to London with general cargo.

SEISTAN ex *Headley* 4238 Grt. Blt. 1907
23.10.1917: Torpedoed and sunk in the North Sea 3½ miles N. by W.¼W. from Flamborough Head in position 54.09N 00.08W by the German submarine *UB 57* whilst on a voyage from Tyne to Falmouth (fo) with a cargo of coal. 5 lost.

KOHISTAN 4732 Grt. Blt. 1908
22.11.1917: Torpedoed and sunk in the Mediterranean 25 miles W.½S. from Marittimo Island by the German submarine *UC 35* whilst on a voyage from Rangoon to the United Kingdom with general cargo.

London & Paris S.S. Co. Ltd.

***KARA** 2338 Grt. Blt. 1889*
10.7.1916: Struck a mine and sunk in the North Sea near Pakefield Gat Buoy laid by the German submarine *UC 6* whilst on a voyage from Rouen to Tyne in ballast.

The Shipping Controller

***HUNTSTRICK** ex Belgier ex Mandasor ex Irak 8151 Grt. Blt. 1902*
8.6.1917: Torpedoed and sunk in the Atlantic 80 miles W.N.W. from Cape Spartel by the German submarine *U 39* whilst on a voyage from London to Salonica with a cargo of Government stores. 15 lost including Master.

SUTHERLAND, A. MUNRO—NEWCASTLE UPON TYNE

Sutherland S.S. Co. Ltd.

***DUMFRIES** ex Carthusian 4121 Grt. Blt. 1905*
19.5.1915: Torpedoed and sunk in the Atlantic 13 miles N. from Trevose Head by the German submarine *U 27* whilst on a voyage from Cardiff to Leghorn with a cargo of coal. 2 lost.

***RENFREW** ex Meridan 3488 Grt. Blt. 1898*
3.7.1915: Captured and sunk by gunfire in the Atlantic 85 miles S.W. by S. from the Wolf Rock by the German submarine *U 39* whilst on a voyage from Marseilles to Barry Roads in ballast.

***SUTHERLAND** 3542 Grt. Blt. 1901*
17.1.1916: Captured and sunk by gunfire in the Mediterranean 192 miles S.E. by E. from Malta in position 34.43N 18.08E by the German submarine *U 35* whilst on a voyage from Bombay to Hull with a cargo of manganese ore and seeds. 1 lost.

***KINCARDINE** ex Countess Warwick 4108 Grt. Blt. 1906*
3.3.1917: Torpedoed and sunk in the Atlantic 20 miles N.E. from Tearaght Island in position 52.22N 10.26W by the German submarine *U 70* whilst on a voyage from Cardiff to Genoa with a cargo of coal.

***ARGYLL** 3547 Grt. Blt. 1901*
13.4.1917: Torpedoed and sunk in the Atlantic 110 miles W. from Bishop Rock in position 49.23N 09.07W by the German submarine *U 84* whilst on a voyage from Port Kelah to Middlesbrough with a cargo of iron ore. 22 lost.

***CAITHNESS** 3500 Grt. Blt. 1898*
20.4.1917: Torpedoed and sunk in the Atlantic 130 miles N.W. by N. from Cape Ortegal in position approximately 44.00N 10.00W by the German submarine *U 52* whilst on a voyage from Tyne to—with a cargo of coal. 47 lost including Master.

***KINROSS** 4120 Grt. Blt. 1911*
7.5.1917: Torpedoed and sunk in the Atlantic 10 miles E. from the Wolf Rock in position 49.59N 05.35W by the German submarine *UC 48* whilst on a voyage from Fremantle to London with a cargo of wheat.

CLAVERLEY 3829 Grt. Blt. 1907
20.8.1917: Torpedoed and sunk in the English Channel 4 miles S.E. from the Eddystone Lighthouse by the German submarine *UB 38* whilst on a voyage from Tyne to Genoa with a cargo of coal. 10 lost.

PEEBLES 4284 Grt. Blt. 1911
12.10.1917: Torpedoed and sunk in the North Sea 14 miles S. by E.½E. from Flamborough Head by the German submarine *UB 18* whilst on a voyage from Tyne to Genoa with a cargo of coal and firebricks.

DUNROBIN 3617 Grt. Blt. 1903
24.11.1917: Torpedoed and sunk in the English Channel 49 miles S.W. by S.½S. from the Lizard by the German submarine *U 53* whilst on a voyage from Almeria to Tyne with a cargo of iron ore and grapes. 31 lost including Master.

FORFAR 3827 Grt. Blt. 1907
4.12.1917: Torpedoed and sunk in the English Channel 115 miles S.W. by W. from the Lizard by the German submarine *UC 17* whilst on a voyage from Blyth to Gibraltar with Admiralty cargo. 3 lost.

ROXBURGH ex *Drumeldre* **4630 Grt. Blt. 1906**
5.3.1918: Torpedoed and sunk in the Mediterranean 15 miles E. by N.½N. from Cape St. John by the German submarine *UC 74* whilst on a voyage from Karachi to Salonica with a cargo of barley. 6 lost.

ARCHBANK 3767 Grt. Blt. 1905
6.6.1918: Torpedoed and sunk in the Mediterranean 240 miles E.S.E. from Malta by the German submarine *UB 105* whilst on a voyage from Alexandria to Bizerta with a cargo of naval stores. 1 lost.

FLORENTIA 3688 Grt. Blt. 1912
29.6.1918: Torpedoed and sunk in the North Sea 2 miles E. by N. from South Cheek. Robin Hood Bay by the German submarine *UB 88* whilst on a voyage from Tyne to—with a cargo of coal. 3 lost.

SUTHERLAND, B. J. & CO. LTD.—NEWCASTLE UPON TYNE

Irismere S.S. Co. Ltd.

LOTUSMERE 3911 Grt. Blt. 1908
2.10.1916: Captured and torpedoed in the Arctic 48 miles N.N.E. from Teriberski Lighthouse in position 69.58N 35.50E by the German submarine *U 48* whilst on a voyage from Barry to Archangel with a cargo of coal.

RENFREW ex *Galavale* **3830 Grt. Blt. 1907**
24.2.1918: Torpedoed and sunk in the St. George's Channel 8 miles W. by N. from St. Ann's Head by the German submarine *U 91* whilst on a voyage from Bilbao to Barrow with a cargo of iron ore. 40 lost including Master.

Isles S.S. Co. Ltd.

ISLE OF JURA ex *Elloe* **3809 Grt. Blt. 1906**
8.6.1917: Captured and sunk with bombs in the Atlantic 15 miles W.S.W. from

Cape Spartel by the German submarine *U 39* whilst on a voyage from Middlesbrough to Savona with a cargo of munitions and coal. 2 lost.

SWAN, HUNTER & WIGHAM RICHARDSON LIMITED—WALLSEND-ON-TYNE

ARUM 3681 Grt. Blt. 1914
4.9.1918: Torpedoed and sunk in the Mediterranean 40 miles E. from Pantellaria Island in position 36.50N 12.50E by the German submarine *UC 54* whilst on a voyage from Cardiff to Malta with a cargo of coal.

TAN KAH KEE—SINGAPORE

TONG HONG ex *Cametense* ex *Carlo Berio* **2184 Grt. Blt. 1891**
27.6.1917: Captured and torpedoed in the Mediterranean 75 miles S.W. from Cape Sicie, Gulf of Lions by the German submarine *U 63* whilst on a voyage from Marseilles to Saigon with a cargo of empty oil drums. Master taken prisoner.

TATEM, W. J. LIMITED—CARDIFF

Atlantic Shipping & Trading Co. Ltd.

CHULMLEIGH 4911 Grt. Blt. 1916
14.9.1917: Torpedoed and sunk in the Mediterranean 10 miles S.W. by W. from Cape Salou near Tarragona by the German submarine *U 64* whilst on a voyage from Newcastle to Genoa with a cargo of coal, coke and iron.

WELLINGTON 5600 Grt. Blt. 1905
16.9.1918: Torpedoed and sunk in the Atlantic 175 miles N. by W. from Cape Villano in position 45.48N 10.58W by the German submarine *U 118* whilst on a voyage from Newport, Mon. to Naples with a cargo of coal. 5 lost including Master.

Tatem Steam Navigation Co. Ltd.

HONITON 4914 Grt. Blt. 1916
30.8.1915: Struck a mine and was damaged in the mouth of the River Thames ½ mile E. from Long Sand Lightvessel laid by the German submarine *UC 5* whilst on a voyage from Buenos Aires to Hull with a cargo of linseed and maize. Later beached at Shoeburyness, Essex and declared a total loss.

BRAUNTON 4575 Grt. Blt. 1911
7.4.1916: Torpedoed and sunk in the English Channel 4½ miles S. by W. from Beachy Head by the German submarine *UB 29* whilst on a voyage from Boulogne to Newport, Mon. with a cargo of Government stores.

TORRIDGE 5036 Grt. Blt. 1912
6.9.1916: Captured and sunk with bombs in the English Channel 40 miles S.S.E. from Start Point by the German submarine *UB 29* whilst on a voyage from Genoa to Tyne in ballast.

***TORRINGTON** 5597 Grt. Blt. 1905*
8.4.1917: Torpedoed and sunk in the Atlantic 150 miles S.W. of the Scilly Isles in position 49.11N 09.58W by the German submarine *U 55* whilst on a voyage from Savona to Barry Roads in ballast. 34 lost, Master taken prisoner.

***APPLEDORE** 3843 Grt. Blt. 1901*
9.6.1917: Torpedoed and sunk in the Atlantic 165 miles S. by W. from the Fastnet Rock in position 48.42N 08 56W by the German submarine *U 70* whilst on a voyage from Sagunto to Middlesbrough with a cargo of iron ore.

***EXFORD** 5886 Grt. Blt. 1914*
14.7.1917: Torpedoed and sunk in the Atlantic 180 miles W. by S.½S. from Ushant in position 46.48N 08.50W by the German submarine *U 48* whilst on a voyage from New York to Cherbourg with a cargo of steel and oats. 6 lost.

***ASHLEIGH** 6985 Grt. Blt. 1917*
23.7.1917: Torpedoed and sunk in the Atlantic 290 miles S.W. from the Fastnet Rock in position 47.10N 12.35W by the German submarine *U 54* whilst on a voyage from Tyne to Port Said with a cargo of coal.

TAYLOR (JENNESON) & COMPANY—SUNDERLAND

***HAYDN** 3923 Grt. Blt. 1906*
29.9.1915: Captured and sunk with bombs in the Mediterranean 80 miles S. by E.½E. from Gavdo Island by the German submarine *U 39* whilst on a voyage from Karachi to Glasgow with a cargo of barley.

TEDCASTLE, McCORMICK & CO. LTD.—DUBLIN

***ADELA** 685 Grt. Blt. 1878*
27.12.1917: Torpedoed and sunk in the Irish Sea 12 miles N.W. from the Skerries, Anglesey by the German submarine *U 100* whilst on a voyage from Dublin to Liverpool with general cargo. 24 lost.

TEMPERLEY, J. & COMPANY—LONDON

Temperley Steam Shipping Co. Ltd.

***TROWBRIDGE** 3712 Grt. Blt. 1904*
14.11.1917: Torpedoed and sunk in the Mediterranean 12 miles S.E. from Cabo de Gata by the German submarine *U 63* whilst on a voyage from Blyth to Alexandria with a cargo of coal.

TEMPLE, THOMSON & CLARK—LONDON

***NEWBY** 2168 Grt. Blt. 1890*
26.9.1916: Captured and sunk by gunfire in the Mediterranean 53 miles E. from Barcelona by the German submarine *U 35* whilst on a voyage from St. Raphael near Nice to Clyde.

THOMAS & APPLETON—CARDIFF

Thomas & Appleton Shipping Co. Ltd.

MASTON 3881 Grt. Blt. 1912
13.8.1917: Torpedoed and sunk in the Mediterranean 35 miles E.N.E. from Cape Spartivento, Italy in position 38.25N 16.43E by the Austro-Hungarian submarine *U 28* whilst on a voyage from Cardiff and Malta to Taranto with a cargo of coal and stores. 2 lost.

THOMAS, J. J. & COMPANY—CARDIFF

The Shipping Controller

PRIMO ex *Remus* ex *Falstad 1037 Grt. Blt. 1908*
18.9.1918: Torpedoed and sunk in the Atlantic 3½ miles N.N.W. from Godrevy Lighthouse by the German submarine *UB 117* whilst on a voyage from Penarth to Rouen with a cargo of coal.

THOMAS, STEPHENS & WILSON—CARDIFF

Porthcawl S.S. Co. Ltd.

PORTHKERRY 1920 Grt. Blt. 1911
20.5.1917: Torpedoed and sunk in the English Channel 16 miles W. by S. from Beachy Head in position approximately 50.38N 00.08W by the German submarine *UB 40* whilst on a voyage from Cardiff to Sheerness with a cargo of coal. 7 lost including Master.

THOMAS, WILLIAM & SONS (TIMBER IMPORTERS) LIMITED—SWANSEA

HAILEYBURY 2888 Grt. Blt. 1902
22.2.1918: Torpedoed and sunk in the North Channel 15 miles S.E. by E.¾E. from The Maidens by the German submarine *U 91* whilst on a voyage from Clyde to Nantes with a cargo of coal. 2 lost including Master.

THOMPSON, R. C.—SUNDERLAND

RIVERSDALE 2805 Grt. Blt. 1906
18.12.1917: Torpedoed and sunk in the English Channel 1 mile S. from Prawle Point by the German submarine *UB 31* whilst on a voyage from Tyne to Savona with a cargo of coal. 1 lost.

THOMPSON, S. & J.—LONDON

St. Helen's S.S. Co. (1912) Ltd.

SILVERASH ex *Farringford 3753 Grt. Blt. 1904*
6.10.1915: Captured and sunk by gunfire in the Mediterranean 184 miles E. from Malta in position 35.30N 18.20E by the German submarine *U 33* whilst on a voyage from Barry to Malta in ballast.

THOMPSON, V. T. & COMPANY—SUNDERLAND

Thompson S.S. Co. Ltd.

PELHAM 3534 Grt. Blt. 1906
13.6.1915: Captured and sunk with bombs in the Atlantic 30 miles N.W. from the Scilly Isles by the German submarine *U 35* whilst on a voyage from Malta to Barry Roads in ballast.

FARNHAM 3102 Grt. Blt. 1898
19.5.1917: Torpedoed and sunk in the Atlantic 10 miles W. from Brow Head, near Mizen Head, Dunmanus Bay, co. Cork in position aproximately 51.23N 09.58W by the German submarine *U 57* whilst on a voyage from Bizerta to Clyde with a cargo of iron ore. 17 lost including Master.

GRESHAM 3774 Grt. Blt. 1905
27.4.1918: Torpedoed and sunk in the St. George's Channel 18 miles N.W. by N.½N. from Strumble Head in position 52.14N 05.25W by the German submarine *U 91* whilst on a voyage from Clyde to Barry Roads in ballast.

THOMSON, WILLIAM & COMPANY—LEITH

Ben Line

BENVORLICH 3381 Grt. Blt. 1896
1.8.1915: Captured and torpedoed in the Atlantic 50 miles S.W. from Ushant by the German submarine *U 28* whilst on a voyage from Manila to London with general cargo.

The Shipping Controller

LADOGA 1917 Grt. Blt. 1914
16.4.1918: Torpedoed and sunk in the St. George's Channel 15 miles S.E. from South Arklow Lightvessel by the German submarine *UB 73* whilst on a voyage from Bilbao to Maryport with a cargo of iron ore. 29 lost including Master.

THOMSON, WILLIAM & COMPANY—ST. JOHN, NEW BRUNSWICK

S.S. Eretria Co. Ltd.

ERETRIA 3464 Grt. Blt. 1901
13.5.1916: Struck a mine and sunk in the Bay of Biscay 15 miles S.S.W. from Ile d'Yeu laid by unknown German submarine whilst on a voyage from Tampa to La Pallice with a cargo of phosphate rock.

TILLETT, W. J. & COMPANY—CARDIFF

W. J. Tillett S.S. Co. Ltd.

ROSEHILL ex Minster 2788 Grt. Blt. 1911
23.9.1917: Torpedoed and sunk in the English Channel 5 miles S.W. by S. from Fowey by the German submarine *UB 40* whilst on a voyage from Cardiff to Devonport with a cargo of coal.

CASTLEFORD ex *Chantenay 1741 Grt. Blt. 1897*
14.3.1918: Torpedoed and sunk in the North Sea 2 miles E. by N. from South Cheek, Robin Hood Bay by the German submarine *UC 40* whilst on a voyage from Hull to Leith in ballast.

TRECHMANN BROTHERS—WEST HARTLEPOOL

Trechmann S.S. Co. Ltd.

HARTDALE ex *Benbrook 3839 Grt. Blt. 1910*
13.3.1915: Torpedoed and sunk in the Irish Sea 7 miles S.E. by E. from South Rock by the German submarine *U 27* whilst on a voyage from Clyde to Alexandria with a cargo of stone. 2 lost.

HUDWORTH 3966 Grt. Blt. 1916
6.1.1917: Torpedoed and sunk in the Mediterranean 94 miles E.S.E. from Malta in position 35.31N 16.24E by the German submarine *U 35* whilst on a voyage from Karachi to Hull with a cargo of barley and seed.

TRINDER, ANDERSON & COMPANY—LONDON

Australind S.S. Co. Ltd.

ASHBURTON 4445 Grt. Blt. 1905
1.4.1916: Captured and torpedoed in the English Channel 80 miles W.N.W. from Ushant by the German submarine *U 44* whilst on a voyage from Wellington and Montevideo to London with general cargo and wool.

ARMADALE 6153 Grt. Blt. 1909
27.6.1917: Torpedoed and sunk in the Atlantic 160 miles N.W. from Tory Island in position 56.00N 12.00W by the German submarine *U 60* whilst on a voyage from Manchester to Salonica with a cargo of Government stores. 3 lost.

ARRINO 4484 Grt. Blt. 1906
1.2.1918: Torpedoed and sunk in the English Channel 14 miles N.W. by W. from Ile de Vierge by the German submarine *U 90* whilst on a voyage from Brest to—in ballast.

TULLEY, W. & COMPANY—HULL

Amyl S.S. Co. Ltd.

FLAWYL 3592 Grt. Blt. 1906
2.5.1918: Torpedoed and sunk in the Mediterranean 30 miles E.S.E. from Pantallaria Island in position 36.41N 12.42E by the German submarine *UB 52* whilst on a voyage from Malta to Bizerta with a cargo of metals. 1 lost.

TURNBULL BROTHERS—CARDIFF

Turnbull Brothers Shipping Co. Ltd.

RUEL 4029 Grt. Blt. 1913
21.8.1915: Captured and sunk by gunfire in the Atlantic 45 miles S.W. from Bishop Rock by the German submarine *U 38* whilst on a voyage from Malta to Barry Roads in ballast. 1 lost.

***OLIVE** 3678 Grt. Blt. 1900*
22.7.1916: Captured and sunk by gunfire in the Mediterranean 10 miles N.W. by N. from Cape Corbelin by the German submarine *U 39* whilst on a voyage from Algiers to Salonica with a cargo of fodder.

***EMMA** 2520 Grt. Blt. 1898*
20.4.1917: Torpedoed and sunk in the Atlantic 200 miles S.W. by S. from the Fastnet Rock in position 49.55N 14.40W by the German submarine *U 50* whilst on a voyage from Baltimore, Mass. to Clyde with a cargo of maize. 2 lost.

***BERNARD** 3682 Grt. Blt. 1900*
15.12.1917: Torpedoed and sunk in the Atlantic 180 miles W.S.W. from Bishop Rock in position 48.40N 09.58W by the German submarine *U 94* whilst on a voyage from Barry to Malta with a cargo of coal. 1 lost.

***BERTRAND** 3613 Grt. Blt. 1913*
6.7.1918: Torpedoed and sunk in the Mediterranean 28 miles E.S.E. from Cap Bon in position 36.58N 11.36E by the German submarine *UC 67* whilst on a voyage from Oran and Bizerta to Salonica with a cargo of straw.

TURNBULL, SCOTT & COMPANY—LONDON

***PARKGATE** 3232 Grt. Blt. 1906*
4.4.1917: Captured and sunk with bombs in the Mediterranean 80 miles N.E. from Cap de Fer in position 38.12N 08.10E by the German submarine *U 35* whilst on a voyage from Malta to Gibraltar in ballast. 16 lost, Master taken prisoner.

***TRONGATE** 2553 Grt. Blt. 1897*
22.9.1917: Torpedoed and sunk in the North Sea 5 miles N. from Flamborough Head by the German submarine *U 71* whilst on a voyage from Tyne to France with a cargo of coal. 2 lost.

The Shipping Controller.

***VICTORIA** 974 Grt. Blt. 1896*
17.11.1917: Torpedoed and sunk in the English Channel 14 miles W.½N. from Eddystone Lighthouse probably by the German submarine *U 103* whilst on a voyage from Penarth to Dieppe with a cargo of coal. 2 lost.

TURNBULL, THOMAS & SON—WHITBY

Thos. Turnbull & Son Shipping Co. Ltd.

***WARRIOR** 3674 Grt. Blt. 1901*
21.4.1917: Struck a mine and sunk in the Mediterranean 7 miles N. from Fratelli Rocks, Tunis laid by the German submarine *UC 37* whilst on a voyage from Cardiff to Algiers and Alexandria with a cargo of coal. 1 lost.

TURNER, BRIGHTMAN & COMPANY—LONDON

***ZOROASTER** 3803 Grt. Blt. 1900*
29.12.1916: Struck a mine and sunk off the mouth of the River Thames 1¾ miles E.N.E. from Sunk Lightvessel in position 51.53N 01.38E laid by the German submarine *UC 11* whilst on a voyage from Tyne to St. Nazaire with a cargo of coal. 3 lost.

ZAMBESI 3759 Grt. Blt. 1901
1.4.1917: Torpedoed and sunk in the Mediterranean 15 miles N. by W. from Alexandria by the German submarine U 63 whilst on a voyage from Tyne to Port Said with a cargo of coal. 3 lost.

ZANONI 3851 Grt. Blt. 1907
12.5.1917: Captured and torpedoed in the Mediterranean 12 miles N.E. by E. from Cape Oropesa by the German submarine *U 34* whilst on a voyage from Tyne to Genoa with a cargo of coal. 1 lost.

ZYLPHA 2917 Grt. Blt. 1894
11.6.1917: Torpedoed and damaged in the Atlantic S.W. of Ireland in position 51.20N 11.00W by the German submarine *U 82* taken in tow on the 14.6.1917 by H.M. sloop *DAFFODIL 1200/15* on the 15.6.1917 she sank at 11.20pm near the Great Skelligs Rocks near Bolus Head, co. Kerry. 1 lost. Lost whilst on Government service employed as a Special Service Ship.

ZERMATT 3767 Grt. Blt. 1901
24.7.1917: Torpedoed and sunk in the Atlantic 355 miles W. by N. from Ushant in position 47.40N 13.38W by the German submarine *U 46* whilst on a voyage from Barry to Campana with general cargo and coal. 3 lost.

ZETA 2269 Grt. Blt. 1888
14.9.1917: Torpedoed and sunk in the Atlantic 8 miles S. by W. from Mine Head by the German submarine *UC 51* whilst on a voyage from Barry to Zarate with a cargo of coal.

ZILLAH 3788 Grt. Blt. 1900
22.10.1917: Torpedoed and sunk in the Arctic 25 miles N.E. from Kildin Island by the German submarine *U 46* whilst on a voyage from Archangel to Lerwick with a cargo of wood. 18 lost.

ZONE 3914 Grt. Blt. 1903
30.12.1917: Torpedoed and sunk in the Atlantic 4 miles N. from St. Ives by the German submarine *U 110* whilst on a voyage from Boulogne to Barry with a cargo of frozen offal.

ZENO 2890 Grt. Blt. 1893
20.2.1918: Torpedoed and sunk in the Mediterranean 48 miles S.W.½S. from Dellimara Point by the German submarine *UB 52* whilst on a voyage from Alexandria to La Goulette in ballast.

ZINAL 4037 Grt. Blt. 1912
19.8.1918: Torpedoed and sunk in the Atlantic 360 miles N. by E. (true) from Terceira, Azores by the German submarine *UB 109* whilst on a voyage from Barry to Campana with general cargo. 2 lost.

The Shipping Controller

PAROS ex *Richmond Castle* **3596 Grt. Blt. 1898**
17.8.1915: Captured and torpedoed in the St. George's Channel 30 miles W. by N. from Bardsey Island by the German submarine *U 38* whilst on a voyage from Karachi to Manchester with a cargo of wheat.

TYNE-TEES S.S. CO. LTD.—NEWCASTLE UPON TYNE

SIR WILLIAM STEPHENSON 1540 Grt. Blt. 1906
29.8.1915: Struck a mine and was badly damaged in the North Sea off Cockle Lightvessel at the entrance to Yarmouth laid by the German submarine *UC 6* whilst on a voyage from Tyne to London with general cargo. 2 lost. She was taken in tow to Yarmouth Roads where she sank.

NOVOCASTRIAN 1151 Grt. Blt. 1915
5.10.1915: Struck a mine and sunk in the North Sea 3½ miles S.E. by E. from Lowestoft laid by the German submarine *UC 7* whilst on a voyage from London to Tyne with general cargo.

CLAUDIA 1144 Grt. Blt. 1897
30.7.1916: Struck a mine and sunk in the North Sea 8½ miles S.E. by S. ½ S. from Lowestoft laid by the German submarine *UC 1* whilst on a voyage from Middlesbrough to London with general cargo and iron. 3 lost.

GRENADIER 1004 Grt. Blt. 1895
23.2.1917: Struck a mine and sunk in the North Sea 6 miles E.N.E. from Shipwash Lightvessel in position 52.06N 01.42E laid by the German submarine *UC 4* whilst on a voyage from Rotterdam to Tyne with general cargo. 8 lost including Master.

STEPHEN FURNESS 1712 Grt. Blt. 1910
13.12.1917: Torpedoed and sunk in the Irish Sea W. off the Isle of Man by the German submarine *UB 64*. Lost whilst on Government service employed as an Armed Boarding Steamer.

TYZACK & BRANFOOT—NEWCASTLE UPON TYNE

SPRINGWELL 5593 Grt. Blt. 1914
9.2.1916: Torpedoed and sunk in the Mediterranean 64 miles S.W. by W. from Gavdo Island in position 34.10N 23.00E by the German submarine *U 38* whilst on a voyage from Tees and London to Calcutta with general cargo.

UNION CASTLE MAIL STEAMSHIP CO. LTD.—LONDON

GALEKA 6772 Grt. Blt. 1899
28.10.1916: Struck a mine and was damaged in the English Channel 5 miles N.W. from Cape la Hague in position 49.34N 00.05E laid by the German submarine *UC 26* whilst on a voyage from England to Le Havre, she was beached at Cape la Hague and became a total loss. 19 lost. Lost whilst on Government service employed as a Hospital Ship.

ALNWICK CASTLE 5900 Grt. Blt. 1901
19.3.1917: Torpedoed and sunk in the Atlantic 310 miles W. ½ S. from Bishop Rock in position 47.38N 13.24W by the German submarine *U 81* whilst on a voyage from London to Cape Town. 40 lost.

DOVER CASTLE 8271 Grt. Blt. 1904
26.5.1917: Torpedoed and sunk in the Mediterranean 50 miles N. from Bona in position 37.54N 07.36E by the German submarine *UC 67* whilst on a voyage from

Malta to Gibraltar. 7 lost. Lost whilst on Government service employed as a Hospital Ship.

AROS CASTLE 4460 Grt. Blt. 1901
21.11.1917: Torpedoed and sunk in the Atlantic 300 miles W. by S.¼S. from Bishop Rock in position 47.19N 12.45W by the German submarine *U 90* whilst on a voyage from London to Baltimore, Mass. in ballast. 2 lost.

CARLISLE CASTLE ex *Holtye* 4325 Grt. Blt. 1913
14.2.1918: Torpedoed and sunk in the English Channel 8 miles E. by N. from the Royal Sovereign Lightvessel by the German submarine *UB 57* whilst on a voyage from Portland (Me) to London with general cargo and grain. 1 lost.

GLENART CASTLE ex *Galician* 6824 Grt. Blt. 1900
26.2.1918: Torpedoed and sunk in the Bristol Channel 10 miles W. from Lundy Island by the German submarine *UC 56* whilst on a voyage from Newport, Mon. to Brest. 168 lost including Master. Lost whilst on Government service employed as a Hospital Ship.

LEASOWE CASTLE 9737 Grt. Blt. 1916
27.5.1918: Torpedoed and sunk in the Mediterranean 104 miles W. by N.½N. from Alexandria by the German submarine *UB 51* whilst on a voyage from Alexandria to Marseilles. 92 lost including Master.

LLANDOVERY CASTLE 11423 Grt. Blt. 1914
27.6.1918: Torpedoed and sunk in the Atlantic 116 miles W. from the Fastnet Rock by the German submarine *U 86* whilst on a voyage from Halifax (NS) to Liverpool. 234 lost. Lost whilst on Government service employed as a Hospital Ship.

GALWAY CASTLE 7988 Grt. Blt. 1911
12.9.1918: Torpedoed and sunk in the Atlantic 160 miles S.W.½S. from the Fastnet Rock in position 48.50N 10.40W by the German submarine *U 82* whilst on a voyage from Plymouth to Port Natal with general cargo. 143 lost.

UNION STEAM SHIP COMPANY OF NEW ZEALAND LIMITED—LONDON

LIMERICK ex *Rippingham Grange* 6827 Grt. Blt. 1898
28.5.1917: Torpedoed and sunk in the Atlantic 140 miles W.½S. from Bishop Rock in position 48.53N 09.45W by the German submarine *U 86* whilst on a voyage from Sydney, NSW to London with general cargo and frozen meat. 8 lost.

AVENGER ex *Aotearoa* 13441 Grt. Blt. 1916
14.6.1917: Torpedoed and sunk in the Atlantic W. of the Shetland Islands in position 61.03N 03.57E by the German submarine *U 69*. Lost whilst on Government service employed as an Armed Merchant Cruiser.

ROSCOMMON ex *Oswestry Grange* 8238 Grt. Blt. 1902
21.8.1917: Torpedoed and sunk in the Atlantic 20 miles N.E. from Tory Island in position 55.27N 08.00W by the German submarine *U 53* whilst on a voyage from Manchester to Australia with general cargo.

WAIKAWA ex *Maritime* ex *Schlesieu* ***5666 Grt. Blt. 1907***
19.10.1917: Torpedoed and sunk in the English Channel 4 miles E.N.E. from Start Point by the German submarine *UB 31* whilst on a voyage from Rouen to Barry Roads in ballast.

APARIMA 5704 Grt. Blt. 1902
19.11.1917: Torpedoed and sunk in the English Channel 6 miles S.W. ¾ W. from Anvil Point by the German submarine *UB 40* whilst on a voyage from London to Barry Roads in ballast. 56 lost.

WAIHEMO ex *Canada Cape* ***4283 Grt. Blt. 1904***
17.3.1918: Torpedoed and sunk in the Aegean Sea 3 miles S.W. from Pleval Light, Piraeus in the Gulf of Athens by the German submarine *UC 37* whilst on a voyage from Port Natal to Piraeus with a cargo of maize.

WAITEMATA 5432 Grt. Blt. 1908
14.7.1918: Torpedoed and sunk in the Mediterranean 100 miles E. ¾ N. from Marsa Susa in position 33.21N 24.10E by the German submarine *UB 105* whilst on a voyage from Barry and Bizerta to Alexandria with a cargo of coal and carbide of calcium.

VERNALL, W. H. & COMPANY—LONDON

ARGO 3071 Grt. Blt. 1895
25.12.1917: Torpedoed and sunk in the Mediterranean 18 miles N.W. from Cape Tenez by the German submarine *U 35* whilst on a voyage from Penarth to Alexandria with general cargo and coal.

WADSWORTH, G. B.—GOOLE

REMUS 1079 Grt. Blt. 1908
23.2.1918: Torpedoed and sunk in the Atlantic 6 miles S.S.W. from Copinsay, Orkney in position 58.50N 02.42W probably by the German submarine *UC 59* whilst on a voyage from Longhope, Orkney to—. 5 lost.

WAIT & DODDS—NEWCASTLE ON TYNE

Admiral Nelson S.S. Co. Ltd.

BENDEW 3681 Grt. Blt. 1909
4.4.1916: Struck a mine and sunk off the mouth of the River Thames 9 miles S. ½ E. from Kentish Knock Lightvessel laid by the German submarine *UC 1* whilst on a voyage Port Breira to Tyne with a cargo of iron ore. 1 lost.

WALFORD, LEOPOLD (LONDON) LIMITED—LONDON

Bolivian General Enterprise Ltd.

GLENCOE 2560 Grt. Blt. 1900
14.12.1916: Captured and torpedoed in the Bay of Biscay 14 miles N.N.W. from Ile d'Yeu in position 46.54N 02.38W by the German submarine *UC 18* whilst on a voyage from Clyde to Bordeaux with a cargo of coal.

DAUNTLESS 2157 Grt. Blt. 1897
4.2.1917: Captured and sunk with bombs in the Bay of Biscay 10 miles from La Coubre Point at the mouth of the River Gironde by the German submarine *UB 39* whilst on a voyage from Tyne to Bayonne with a cargo of coal. 15 lost.

TASSO 1859 Grt. Blt. 1904
17.3.1917: Probably struck a mine and sunk in the Bay of Biscay 5 miles S. from Ile de Groix near Lorient laid by the German submarine *UC 70* whilst on a voyage from Manchester to La Pallice with a cargo of war materials. 19 lost including Master.

ALHAMA ex *Axinite* **1744 Grt. Blt. 1899**
26.4.1917: Struck a mine and sunk in the English Channel 1½ miles N. from Calais laid by the German submarine *UB 12* whilst on a voyage from Bayonne to Dunkirk with a cargo of pit props.

Entente S.S. Co. Ltd.

SAXON 1595 Grt. Blt. 1881
7.5.1918: Torpedoed and sunk in the North Sea 83 miles E.S.E. from Fair Isle by the German submarine *U 105* whilst on a voyage from Odde to Leith with a cargo of carbide. 22 lost.

Equinox S.S. Co. Ltd.

YONNE ex *Kastalia* **4039 Grt. Blt. 1897**
6.4.1916: Torpedoed and sunk in the Mediterranean 18 miles N.N.W. from Cape Shershel in position 36.52N 02.00E by the German submarine *U 34* whilst on a voyage from Clyde to Alexandria with a cargo of coal.

Gascony S.S. Co. Ltd.

COUNTESS OF MAR 2234 Grt. Blt. 1916
4.8.1917: Torpedoed and sunk in the Bay of Biscay 55 miles N.¼E. from Bayonne in position 44.27N 01.48W by the German submarine *U 61* whilst on a voyage from Bilbao to Cardiff with a cargo of iron ore. 20 lost including Master.

HAZELWOOD 3120 Grt. Blt. 1904
19.10.1917: Struck a mine and sunk in the English Channel 8 miles S. by E. ½E. from Anvil Point laid by the German submarine *UC 62* whilst on a voyage from Tyne to—with a cargo of coal. 32 lost including Master.

GASCONIA ex *Pennar River* **3801 Grt. Blt. 1915**
16.11.1917: Torpedoed and sunk in the Mediterranean 12 miles N.E.½E. from Cape Shershel by the German submarine *U 63* whilst on a voyage from Barry to Malta with a cargo of coal and Government stores. 3 lost.

LANDONIA 2504 Grt. Blt. 1917
21.4.1918: Torpedoed and sunk in the St. George's Channel 27 miles N. by W.½W. from Strumble Head by the German submarine *U 91* whilst on a voyage from Bilbao to Glasgow with a cargo of iron ore. 21 lost, Master taken prisoner.

Laurium Transport Co. Ltd.

GARTNESS ex *Charles T. Jones* **2422 Grt. Blt. 1890**
19.8.1917: Torpedoed and sunk in the Mediterranean 180 miles S.E. by E. ¾ E. from Malta in position 34.52N 18.14E by the Austro-Hungarian submarine *U 40* whilst on a voyage from Ergasteria to Middlesbrough with a cargo of manganese ore, lead and arsenic. 13 lost including Master.

WALKER & BAIN—GRANGEMOUTH

Kerse S.S. Co. Ltd.

SAXON BRITON **1337 Grt. Blt. 1883**
6.2.1917: Torpedoed and sunk in the Atlantic 3 miles N.N.E from Gurnards Head by the German submarine *U 55* whilst on a voyage from Portishead to Calais with a cargo of petrol. 2 lost.

WALTON, SAMUEL—LONDON

Kent. S.S. Co. Ltd.

WOLF **2443 Grt. Blt. 1894**
21.7.1916: Captured and sunk by gunfire in the Mediterranean 75 miles N.N.W. from Algiers by the German submarine *U 39* whilst on a voyage from Tyne to Genoa with a cargo of coal.

BARBARA **3740 Grt. Blt. 1897**
20.10.1916: Captured and sunk by gunfire in the English Channel 25 miles S. from the Isle of Wight by the German submarine *UB 40* whilst on a voyage from Philadelphia to West Hartlepool with a cargo of sugar.

COMMONWEALTH **3353 Grt. Blt. 1896**
19.2.1918: Torpedoed and sunk in the North Sea 5 miles N.E. from Flamborough Head by the German submarine *UC 71* whilst on a voyage from Bizerta to Middlesbrough with a cargo of iron ore. 14 lost.

WANDSWORTH & DISTRICT GAS COMPANY—LONDON

LIGHTFOOT **1873 Grt. Blt. 1916**
16.3.1918: Torpedoed and sunk in the English Channel 2 miles S. from Owers Lightvessel by the German submarine *UB 30* whilst on a voyage from London to Barry Roads in ballast.

WATSON BROTHERS—GLASGOW

Watson Brothers Shipping Co. Ltd.

BEN VRACKIE **3908 Grt. Blt. 1905**
18.8.1915: Captured and sunk by gunfire in the Atlantic 55 miles N.W. by N. from Scilly Isles in position 50.30N 07.30W by the German submarine *U 27* whilst on a voyage from Cardiff to Malta with a cargo of coal and stores.

WATSON, HERBERT & COMPANY—MANCHESTER

Watson S.S. Co. Ltd.

ELLESMERE 1170 Grt. Blt. 1906
9.7.1915: Captured and torpedoed in the St. George's Channel 48 miles S.W. from the Smalls by the German submarine *U 20* whilst on a voyage from Valencia to Manchester with a cargo of fruit. 1 lost.

WATSON, MUNRO, CORNFORTH & COMPANY—LONDON

Lodore S.S. Co. Ltd.

LODANER ex *Ancroft* **3291 Grt. Blt. 1905**
16.4.1918: Torpedoed and sunk in the Irish Sea by the German submarine *UB 73* whilst on a voyage from Bilbao to Glasgow with a cargo of iron ore. 32 lost.

WATSON, WILLIAM A.—SUNDERLAND

ROCHESTER CITY 1239 Grt. Blt. 1910
2.5.1916: Struck a mine and sunk in the North Sea 3 miles E. from Southwold laid by the German submarine *UC 10* whilst on a voyage from Seaham Harbour to Rochester with a cargo of coal. 1 lost.

WATSON, WILLIAM W.—GLASGOW

ST. GOTHARD 2788 Grt. Blt. 1903
26.9.1916: Captured and torpedoed in the North Sea 12 miles N. by W. from Fair Isle in position 59.41N 01.45W by the German submarine *U 52* whilst on a voyage from Shetland to the Forth River in ballast.

WATTS, WATTS & CO. LTD.—LONDON

Britain S.S. Co. Ltd.

DULWICH 3289 Grt. Blt. 1893
15.2.1915: Torpedoed and sunk in the English Channel 6 miles N. of Cape d'Antifer by the German submarine *U 16* whilst on a voyage from Hull to Rouen with a cargo of coal. 2 lost.

RICHMOND 3214 Grt. Blt. 1904
1.7.1915: Captured and sunk by gunfire in the Atlantic about 54 miles S.W. by S. from Wolf Rock in position 49.11N 06.10W by the German submarine *U 39* whilst on a voyage from Gulfport to Boulogne with a cargo of sleepers.

WOOLWICH ex *Electrician* **2936 Grt. Blt. 1887**
3.11.1915: Captured and sunk by gunfire in the Mediterranean 104 miles S. from Cape Sidero in position 33.35N 26.30E by the German submarine *U 35* whilst on a voyage from Safaga Island to Plymouth and Ayr with a cargo of phosphate.

TOTTENHAM ex *Harewood* **3106 Grt. Blt. 1906**
4.8.1916: Captured and sunk by gunfire in the Mediterranean 22 miles S.W. of Planier Island Lightvessel by the German submarine *U 35* whilst on a voyage from Oneglia to Gibraltar in ballast.

CHERTSEY ex *Reynolds* **3264 Grt. Blt. 1898**
26.4.1917: Torpedoed and sunk in the Mediterranean 4 miles N. from Algiers by the German submarine *UC 67* whilst on a voyage from Tyne to Port Said with a cargo of coal.

LEWISHAM 2810 Grt. Blt. 1898
17.5.1917: Torpedoed and sunk in the Atlantic W. of Ireland in position 53.25N 13.30W by the German submarine *U 46* whilst on a voyage from New York to Le Havre with a cargo of wheat. 24 lost, Master and 2 Gunners taken prisoner.

HIGHBURY 4831 Grt. Blt. 1912
14.6.1917: Torpedoed and sunk in the Atlantic W.S.W. from Bishop Rock by the German submarine *U 82* whilst on a voyage from Antofagasta and Halifax, (NS) to Liverpool with a cargo of nitrate. 39 lost.

MOLESEY ex *Salamanca* **3218 Grt. Blt. 1912**
30.11.1917: Torpedoed and sunk in the English Channel 9 miles S.W. by W. from Brighton Lightvessel by the German submarine *UB 81* whilst on a voyage from Sfax to the United Kingdom with a cargo of phosphate.

GREENWICH 2938 Grt. Blt. 1899
5.12.1917: Torpedoed and sunk in the Mediterranean 9 miles S. from Planier Island by the German submarine *UC 67* whilst on a voyage from Saigon to Marseilles with a cargo of rice, alcohol and pepper.

ROMFORD 3035 Grt. Blt. 1898
10.2.1918: Probably struck a mine and sunk in the Mediterranean 2½ miles E. from Cape Carthage, Tunis in position 36.54N 10.24E laid by the German submarine *UC 54* whilst on a voyage from Tunis and Bizerta to the United Kingdom with a cargo of phosphate. 28 lost including Master.

HENLEY ex *Janeta* **3249 Grt. Blt. 1894**
10.4.1918: Torpedoed and sunk in the English Channel 25 miles S.W. ½ W. from the Lizard by the German submarine *UB 109* whilst on a voyage from Barry to St. Nazaire with a cargo of coal. 6 lost.

ISLEWORTH ex *Eversley* **2871 Grt. Blt. 1896**
30.4.1918: Torpedoed and sunk in the English Channel 3 miles S.W. from Ventnor Pier, Isle of Wight by the German submarine *UC 17* whilst on a voyage from Bilbao to Middlesbrough with a cargo of iron ore. 29 lost.

SANDHURST ex *Inca* ex *Craigneuk* **3034 Grt. Blt. 1897**
6.5.1918: Torpedoed and sunk in the North Channel 6 miles N.W. by W. ¼ W. from Corsewall Point in position 54.58N 05.25W by the German submarine *UB 72* whilst on a voyage from Bilbao to Ardrossan with a cargo of iron ore. 20 lost.

CHATHAM ex *Clifton* **3592 Grt. Blt. 1904**
21.5.1918: Torpedoed and sunk in the Mediterranean 80 miles S.W. ¼ S. from Cape Matapan in position 34.51N 21.34E by the Austro-Hungarian submarine *U 32* whilst on a voyage from Karachi to Marseilles with a cargo of grain and onions.

ALDERSHOT 2177 Grt. Blt. 1897
23.9.1918: Torpedoed and sunk in the English Channel 5 miles E.S.E. from Dartmouth by the German submarine *UB 113* whilst on a voyage from Glasgow to Nantes with a cargo of machinery and coal. 1 lost.

WEARDALE S.S. CO. LTD.—SUNDERLAND

SILVERDALE 3835 Grt. Blt. 1906
9.3.1918: Torpedoed and sunk in the Mediterranean 28 miles E. by N.½N. from Cani Rocks by the German submarine *U 35*.

WEBSTER & BARRACLOUGH LIMITED—WEST HARTLEPOOL

DALTON 3486 Grt. Blt. 1904
10.4.1917: Torpedoed and sunk in the Mediterranean 25 miles S. by W. from Cape Matapan in position 36.00N 22.40E by the Austro-Hungarian submarine *U 29* whilst on a voyage from Salonica to Malta in ballast. 3 lost, Master taken prisoner.

WEIDNER, HOPKINS & COMPANY—NEWCASTLE UPON TYNE

Elswick S.S. Co. Ltd.

ELSWICK MANOR 3943 Grt. Blt. 1901
19.4.1917: Torpedoed and sunk in the Atlantic 180 miles W. from Ushant in position 47.36N 09.32W by the German submarine *U 84* whilst on a voyage from Tyne to Naples with a cargo of coal.

ELSWICK LODGE 3558 Grt. Blt. 1900
20.8.1917: Torpedoed and sunk in the Atlantic 260 miles W. by S. from Ushant in position 46.15N 10.30W by the German submarine *U 93* whilst on a voyage from Buenos Aires to Falmouth with a cargo of maize. 4 lost.

WEIR, ANDREW & COMPANY—LONDON

Bank Line

DESABLA 6047 Grt. Blt. 1913
12.6.1915: Captured and torpedoed in the North Sea 15 miles E. from Tod Head Point by the German submarine *U 17* whilst on a voyage from Port Arthur, Texas to the United Kingdom with a cargo of oil.

ORTERIC 6535 Grt. Blt. 1911
9.12.1915: Captured and torpedoed in the Mediterranean 140 miles S. by E.½E. from Gavdo Island in position 32.30N 25.30E by the German submarine *U 39* whilst on a voyage from Antofagasta to Alexandria with a cargo of nitrate. 2 lost.

YEDDO 4563 Grt. Blt. 1901
24.12.1915: Captured and sunk with bombs in the Mediterranean 122 miles S.W. by S. from Cape Matapan in position 34.36N 21.21E by the German submarine *U 34* whilst on a voyage from Calcutta to New York with general cargo.

AYMERIC 4363 Grt. Blt. 1905
30.5.1918: Torpedoed and sunk in the Mediterranean 145 miles S.W. by W. from

Cape Matapan by the German submarine *U 63* whilst on a voyage from Clyde to Port Said with a cargo of coal.

WEISS, THOMAS L. & COMPANY—NEWCASTLE UPON TYNE

DUCKBRIDGE 1491 Grt. Blt. 1914
22.2.1916: Struck a mine and sunk in the Atlantic 6 miles N.E. from Strathy Point near Thurso laid by unknown German submarine whilst on a voyage from Cardiff to—with a cargo of coal. 19 lost, including Master.

WELSFORD, J. H. & CO. LTD.—LIVERPOOL

INDUSTRY ex *Idar 4044 Grt. Blt. 1888*
27.4.1916: Captured and torpedoed in the Atlantic 120 miles W. by N. from the Fastnet Rock in position 51.11N 12.46W by the German submarine *U 45* whilst on a voyage from Barry to Newport News.

IKEDA 6311 Grt. Blt. 1917
21.3.1918: Torpedoed and sunk in the English Channel 7 miles W. from Brighton Lightvessel by the German submarine *UB 40* whilst on a voyage from London to Galveston in ballast.

The Gulf Transport Co. (Liverpool) Limited

INKUM 4747 Grt. Blt. 1901
4.6.1915: Torpedoed and sunk in the English Channel 40 miles S.W. from Lizard in position 49.25N 06.35W by the German submarine *U 34* whilst on a voyage from New York to London with general cargo.

Leyland Shipping Co. Ltd.

IKARIA ex *Planet Mars 4335 Grt. Blt. 1900*
30.1.1915: Torpedoed and sunk in the English Channel 25 miles N.W. from Le Havre by the German submarine *U 20* whilst on a voyage from Buenos Aires to Le Havre, London and Liverpool with general cargo including coffee and sugar.

IKALIS ex *Planet Venus 4329 Grt. Blt. 1900*
7.6.1917: Torpedoed and sunk in the Atlantic 170 miles N.W.½W. from the Fastnet Rock in position 52.19N 13.57W by the German submarine *U 66* whilst on a voyage from New York to Liverpool with a cargo of wheat.

WEST HARTLEPOOL STEAM NAVIGATION CO. LTD.—WEST HARTLEPOOL

HENDONHALL 3994 Grt. Blt. 1901
1.5.1916: Struck a mine and sunk in the North Sea 2 miles S.½E. from Inner Gabbard Buoy laid by the German submarine *UC 10* whilst on a voyage from Portland (Me) to Rotterdam with a cargo of grain.

HEIGHINGTON 2800 Grt. Blt. 1891
1.8.1916: Captured and torpedoed in the Mediterranean 40 miles N.E. from Cape Serrat by the German submarine *U 35* whilst on a voyage from Naples to Oran in ballast.

APSLEYHALL 3882 Grt. Blt. 1911
30.12.1916: Torpedoed and sunk in the Mediterranean 28 miles W. by N. from Gozo Island by the German submarine *UC 22* whilst on a voyage from Karachi to Cardiff with a cargo of wheat. Master taken prisoner.

POLAMHALL 4010 Grt. Blt. 1901
7.5.1917: Torpedoed and sunk in the Atlantic 80 miles W.S.W. from Bishop Rock in position 49.02N 08.00W by the German submarine *U 62* whilst on a voyage from Alexandria to Hull with general cargo.

GRANTLEYHALL 4008 Grt. Blt. 1902
23.12.1917: Struck a mine and sunk in the North Sea 5 miles E. from Orfordness laid by the German submarine *UC 4* whilst on a voyage from Villaricos to Middlesbrough with a cargo of iron ore.

BOLTONHALL 3595 Grt. Blt. 1900
20.8.1918: Torpedoed and sunk in the St. George's Channel 34 miles S.W. by W.¼W. from Bardsey Island by the German submarine *UB 92* whilst on a voyage from Manchester to Gibraltar with a cargo of coal. 5 lost.

The Shipping Controller

WAR CROCUS 5296 Grt. Blt. 1918
8.7.1918: Torpedoed and sunk in the North Sea 2½ miles E. by N. from Flamborough Head by the German submarine *UB 107* whilst on her maiden voyage from Hartlepool to—with a cargo of coal.

WESTOLL, JAMES—SUNDERLAND

Westoll Line

FULGENT 2008 Grt. Blt. 1910
30.4.1915: Torpedoed then captured and sunk with bombs in the Atlantic 45 miles N.W. of the Skelligs by the German submarine *U 30* whilst on a voyage from Cardiff to Scapa Flow with a cargo of coal. 2 lost including Master.

LAVINIA WESTOLL 3131 Grt. Blt. 1895
28.3.1916: Struck a mine and sunk in the North Sea 33 miles S.E. by S. from Spurn Lightvessel laid by the German submarine *UC 6* whilst on a voyage from Almeria to Tees with a cargo of iron ore.

ROBERT ADAMSON 2978 Grt. Blt. 1895
10.4.1916: Torpedoed and sunk in the North Sea 3 miles N. by E. from Shipwash Lightvessel by the German submarine *UB 16* whilst on a voyage from Dundee to Le Havre with a cargo of pit props.

J. Y. SHORT 2193 Grt. Blt. 1887
3.10.1916: Captured and sunk by gunfire in the Arctic 80 miles E. from Vardo in position 70.14N 35.30E by the German submarine *U 43* whilst on a voyage from Penarth to Archangel with a cargo of coal.

EXCELLENT 1944 Grt. Blt. 1907
9.1.1917: Captured and sunk by gunfire in the Atlantic 40 miles N.E. from Noup

Head, Orkney Islands in position 59.37N 04.18W by the German submarine *U 70* whilst on a voyage from Penarth to Lerwick with a cargo of coal. Master taken prisoner.

***LUCENT** 1409 Grt. Blt. 1879*
12.2.1917: Captured and sunk by gunfire in the English Channel 20 miles E. of the Lizard in position 50.20N 04.43W by the German submarine *UC 66* whilst on a voyage from Cardiff to St. Malo with a cargo of coal.

***F. D. LAMBERT** 2195 Grt. Blt. 1892*
13.2.1917: Struck a mine and sunk in the English Channel 1 mile E. from the Royal Sovereign Lightvessel laid by the German submarine *UC 47* whilst on a voyage from Tyne to Savona with a cargo of gas coal.

***OKEMENT** 4349 Grt. Blt. 1915*
17.2.1917: Torpedoed and sunk in the Mediterranean 140 miles S.E. by S. from Malta by the German submarine *U 64* whilst on a voyage from Barry to—with general cargo and coal. 11 lost including Master.

***BENEFICENT** 1963 Grt. Blt. 1881*
24.2.1917: Torpedoed and sunk in the North Sea 5 miles E.N.E. from Hartlepool Heugh in position 54.44½N 01.04W by the German submarine *UC 31* whilst on a voyage from Tyne to Le Havre with a cargo of coal. 3 lost.

***MUNIFICENT** 3270 Grt. Blt. 1892*
1.3.1917: Torpedoed and sunk in the English Channel 3½ miles N.N.W. from Cape Gris Nez in position 50.55N 01.32E by unknown German submarine whilst on a voyage from Tyne to Boulogne with a cargo of coal. 3 lost.

***WESTWICK** 5694 Grt. Blt. 1916*
7.3.1917: Struck a mine and sunk in the Atlantic 1 mile S. from Roche's Point, Queenstown laid by the German submarine *UC 44* whilst on a voyage from Baltimore, Mass. to Hull with a cargo of maize.

***AMBIENT** 1517 Grt. Blt. 1904*
12.3.1917: Struck a mine and sunk in the North Sea 7 miles N. from Shipwash Lightvessel in position 52.08½N 01.46E laid by the German submarine *UC 4* whilst on a voyage from Sunderland to Dunkirk with a cargo of coal.

***LIZZIE WESTOLL** 2855 Grt. Blt. 1895*
17.6.1917: Torpedoed and sunk in the Atlantic 120 miles N.W. by W. from the Fastnet Rock in position 51.39N 12.44W by the German submarine *UC 42* whilst on a voyage from Port Signa to Garston with a cargo of magnesite ore and volonea.

***FLUENT** 3660 Grt. Blt. 1911*
20.7.1917: Torpedoed and sunk in the English Channel 15 miles S.W. from Portland Bill in position 50.26N 01.52½W by the German submarine *UC 65* whilst on a voyage from New York to London with a cargo of steel and oats.

***NASCENT** 4969 Grt. Blt. 1915*
25.8.1917: Torpedoed and sunk in the Atlantic 35 miles S.W. from Wolf Rock by the German submarine *UC 49* whilst on a voyage from Tegal and Dakar to Hull with general cargo. 6 lost.

ROBERT EGGLETON 2274 Grt. Blt. 1890
28.12.1917: Torpedoed and sunk in the St. George's Channel 10 miles S.W. from Bardsey Island by the German submarine *U 91* whilst on a voyage from Clyde to Leghorn with a cargo of coal. 1 lost.

INTENT 1564 Grt. Blt. 1911
8.3.1918: Torpedoed and sunk in the North Sea 4 miles E. by N. from Seaham Harbour by the German submarine *UC 40*. 1 lost.

T. R. THOMPSON 3538 Grt. Blt. 1897
29.3.1918: Torpedoed and sunk in the English Channel 7 miles S. from Newhaven by the German submarine *UB 57* whilst on a voyage from Benisaf to Middlesbrough with a cargo of iron ore. 33 lost including Master.

VIRENT 3771 Grt. Blt. 1902
24.8.1918: Torpedoed and sunk in the St. George's Channel 38 miles W. by S. from the Smalls by the German submarine *UB 92* whilst on a voyage from Cartagena to Clyde with a cargo of iron ore.

WETHERALL, J. H. & CO. LTD.—GOOLE

Wetherall S.S. Co. Ltd.

PEARL 613 Grt. Blt. 1904
23.9.1916: Captured and sunk with bombs in the English Channel 41 miles S.¼E. from the Nab Lighthouse by the German submarine *UB 37* whilst on a voyage from Llanelly to Treport with a cargo of coal.

WHIMSTER & COMPANY—GLASGOW

Gart S.S. Co. Ltd.

GARTLAND ex *Trewidden* 2613 Grt. Blt. 1892
3.1.1918: Torpedoed and sunk in the English Channel 5 miles E.S.E. from Owers Lightvessel by the German submarine *UB 30* whilst on a voyage from Tyne to Gibraltar with a cargo of coal. 2 lost.

WILLIAMS & MORDEY—CARDIFF

LORD TREDEGAR 3856 Grt. Blt. 1914
17.9.1916: Torpedoed and sunk in the Mediterranean 51 miles S.E. by E. from Malta in position 35.31N 15.26E by the German submarine *UB 43* whilst on a voyage from New York to Bombay with general cargo. 4 lost.

Carrington S.S. Co. Ltd.

LADY CARRINGTON ex *Kilnsea* 3269 Grt. Blt. 1907
12.11.1916: Torpedoed and sunk in the Atlantic 98 miles N. by W. from Cape Ortegal in position 44.15N 08.50W by the German submarine *U 49* whilst on a voyage from Barry to Malta with a cargo of coal.

LUDGATE 3708 Grt. Blt. 1906
26.7.1917: Struck a mine and sunk in the Atlantic 2 miles S. from Galley Head laid by the German submarine *UC 51* whilst on a voyage from Huelva to Garston with a cargo of iron ore. 24 lost including Master.

Margam Abbey S.S. Co. Ltd.

MARGAM ABBEY 4471 Grt. Blt. 1907
10.4.1916: Captured and sunk by gunfire in the English Channel 55 miles S.W.¼S. from the Lizard by the German submarine *U 66* whilst on a voyage from Bordeaux to Barry Roads in ballast.

MARGAM ABBEY ex *Barrington Court 4367 Grt. Blt. 1906*
1.11.1917: Torpedoed and damaged in the Mediterranean near Collo, Algeria by the German submarine *UB 50* whilst on a voyage from Cardiff to Alexandria. 2 lost. She was beached at Collo and became a constructive total loss.

The Shipping Controller

GEFION 1123 Grt. Blt. 1914
25.10.1917: Torpedoed and sunk in the English Channel 10 miles N.E. from Berry Head by the German submarine *UB 40* whilst on a voyage from Penarth to Rouen with a cargo of coal. 2 lost including Master.

WILLIAMS, W. J.—CARDIFF

RUYSDAEL 3478 Grt. Blt. 1912
7.9.1918: Torpedoed and sunk in the Atlantic 228 miles W.¾S. from Ushant in position 46.53N 10.07W by the German submarine *U 105* whilst on a voyage from Barry to Taranto with a cargo of coal. 12 lost including Master.

WILLIAMS (OWEN & WATKIN) & COMPANY—CARDIFF

Canganian S.S. Co. Ltd.

CANGANIAN 1143 Grt. Blt. 1900
17.11.1916: Struck a mine and sunk in the North Sea S.E. of Montrose laid by the German submarine *UC 29* whilst on a voyage from Methil to Scapa Flow with a cargo of coal. 18 lost.

S.S. Demetian & Ordovician Co. Ltd.

EDERNIAN 3588 Grt. Blt. 1906
20.8.1917: Torpedoed and sunk in the North Sea 6 miles S. by E. from Southwold in position 52.13N 01.45E by unknown German submarine whilst on a voyage from Middlesbrough to Dieppe with a cargo of steel. 14 lost.

S.S. Goidelian & Coranian Co. Ltd.

SNOWDONIAN 3870 Grt. Blt. 1907
31.7.1917: Captured and sunk with bombs in the Atlantic 245 miles S. by E. from Sta. Maria, Azores in position 33.44N 22.22W by the German submarine *U 155* whilst on a voyage from Barry to Freetown with a cargo of coal.

Golden Cross Line, Ltd.

CYMRIAN ex *Kingwood* **1014 Grt. Blt. 1905**
25.8.1917: Torpedoed and sunk in the St. George's Channel 134 miles S.E. by S. from Tuskar Rock by the German submarine *UC 75* whilst on a voyage from Newport, Mon. to Dublin with general cargo. 10 lost.

WILLIS, THOMAS W.—WEST HARTLEPOOL

***HILDAWELL* 2494 Grt. Blt. 1892**
20.12.1916: Struck a mine and sunk in the North Sea off Sunderland laid by the German submarine *UC 32* whilst on a voyage from Bilbao to Middlesbrough with a cargo of iron ore. 22 lost including Master.

***LONGSCAR* 2777 Grt. Blt. 1903**
14.2.1917: Captured and sunk with bombs in the Bay of Biscay 15 miles S.W. from the River Gironde in position 45.25N 01.55W by the German submarine *UC 21* whilst on a voyage from Nantes to Bilbao in ballast. 2 Gunners taken prisoner.

WILLS, G. H. & CORY LIMITED—CARDIFF

Empire Shipping Co. Ltd.

CORSO ex *Caradoc* ex *Reptonian* ex *Warfield* **3242 Grt. Blt. 1899**
19.2.1917: Torpedoed and sunk in the Mediterranean 110 miles S. by W. from Malta by the German submarine *U 64* whilst on a voyage from Bombay to Hull with general cargo. Master, Chief Engineer and 2 Gunners taken prisoner.

WILSON, JOSEPH F. & COMPANY—WEST HARTLEPOOL

Wilson Shipping Co. Ltd.

***WESTLANDS* 3112 Grt. Blt. 1905**
23.11.1917: Torpedoed and sunk in the English Channel 10 miles N. from Ile de Vierge by the German submarine *U 53* whilst on a voyage from Leith to Nantes with a cargo of coal.

***EASTLANDS* 3113 Grt. Blt. 1905**
25.1.1918: Torpedoed and sunk in the English Channel 13 miles N.W. from Ile de Vierge by the German submarine *UB 55* whilst on a voyage from Bordeaux to Dunkirk with a cargo of Government stores. 1 lost.

***BYLANDS* 3309 Grt. Blt. 1899**
1.10.1918: Captured and sunk by gunfire in the Atlantic 150 miles N.N.W. from Cape Villano by the German submarine *U 139* whilst on a voyage from Bona to Dublin with a cargo of phosphates.

WITHERINGTON & EVERETT—NEWCASTLE UPON TYNE

John George Hill S.S. Co. Ltd.

***SWIFTSURE* 823 Grt. Blt. 1894**
9.9.1917: Struck a mine and sunk in the North Sea in Shapinsay Sound, Orkney Islands laid by the German submarine *UC 40* whilst on a voyage from Arendal to Sunderland with a cargo of deal and battens. 1 lost.

TWEED* 1777 Grt. Blt. *1907
14.3.1918: Torpedoed and sunk in the St. George's Channel 15 miles S.S.E. from Tuskar Rock by the German submarine *UC 75* whilst on a voyage from Clyde to Devonport with a cargo of coal.

The Shipping Controller

SAIMA* 1147 Grt. Blt. *1914
8.6.1918: Torpedoed and sunk in the Atlantic 10 miles W. from Trevose Head by the German submarine *U 82* whilst on a voyage from Rouen to Barry Roads in ballast. 16 lost including Master.

WOODS, TYLOR & BROWN—LONDON

BURRSFIELD* 4037 Grt. Blt. *1902
5.10.1915: Captured and sunk by gunfire in the Mediterranean 70 miles W. from Cape Matapan by the German submarine *U 33* whilst on a voyage from Barry and Malta to Salonica with a cargo of Government stores. 4 lost including Master.

Woodfield S.S. Co. Ltd.

WOODFIELD* 3584 Grt. Blt. *1905
3.11.1915: Captured and sunk by gunfire in the Mediterranean 40 miles E.S.E. from Ceuta by the German submarine *U 38*. 8 lost.

FRAMFIELD* 2510 Grt. Blt. *1894
24.10.1916: Struck a mine and sunk in the mouth of the River Thames 3 miles N.E. from the Sunk Lightvessel laid by the German submarine *UC 11* whilst on a voyage from Port Kelah to Tees with a cargo of iron ore. 6 lost including Master.

WORKMAN, ARBUCKLE & MACKINNION—GLASGOW

BALGRAY* ex *Osceola* 3603 Grt. Blt. *1903
20.2.1918: Torpedoed and sunk in the Mediterranean 38 miles S.W. by W. from Dellimara Point by the German submarine *UB 52* whilst on a voyage from Malta to Sfax in ballast.

WORKMAN, CLARK & CO. LTD.—BELFAST

SAN RITO* 3310 Grt. Blt. *1916
15.2.1918: Torpedoed and sunk in the Aegean Sea 23 miles S.W. by W.½W. from Cape Mastiko, Khios Island in position 37.51N 33.00E by the German submarine *UC 37* whilst on a voyage from Salonica to Port Said in ballast. 3 lost.

YEOMAN, F. & SONS—CARDIFF

CHATBURN* 1942 Grt. Blt. *1894
1.3.1917: Torpedoed and sunk in the English Channel 22 miles N.E.½E. from Cape Barfleur in position 50.00N 00.55W by the German submarine *UB 18* whilst on a voyage from Sunderland to Rouen with a cargo of coal.

CHELFORD 2995 Grt. Blt. 1906
14.4.1918: Torpedoed and sunk in the St. George's Channel 10 miles N.W. by W. from Bardsey Island by the German submarine *UB 73* whilst on a voyage from Clyde to Barry Roads in ballast.

HASLINGDEN 1934 Grt. Blt. 1895
12.5.1918: Torpedoed and sunk in the North Sea 7 miles E. from Seaham Harbour by the German submarine *UB 21* whilst on a voyage from Rouen to Tyne in ballast. 11 lost including Master.

YEOWARD BROTHERS—LIVERPOOL

AGUILA 2114 Grt. Blt. 1909
27.3.1915: Captured and torpedoed in the St. George's Channel 47 miles S.W. from the Smalls by the German submarine *U 28* whilst on a voyage from Liverpool to Las Palmas with general cargo. 8 lost.

AVOCET 1219 Grt. Blt. 1885
19.4.1917: Captured and torpedoed in the Atlantic 100 miles W.N.W. from the Fastnet Rock in position 51.19N 12.30W by the German submarine *U 50* whilst on a voyage from Lisbon to Liverpool with general cargo and cork wood.

Avetoro S.S. Co. Ltd.

VALDES 2233 Grt. Blt. 1914
18.2.1917: Torpedoed and sunk in the English Channel 7 miles S. from Portland Bill by the German submarine *U 84* whilst on a voyage from Manchester to Cherbourg with a cargo of flour and hay. 11 lost.

INDEX OF SHIPS' NAMES

Name	Page	Name	Page	Name	Page
AARO	81	AMSTERDAM	192	ARMENIAN	152
ABELIA	206	ANATOLIA	77	ARMONIA	36
ABOSSO	71	ANDALUSIAN	78	ARNEWOOD	91
ABOUKIR	106	ANDANIA	61	AROS CASTLE	226
ABURI	71	ANDONI	73	ARRINO	222
ACADIAN	36	ANGLESEA	140	ARTESIA	136
ACHAIA	107	ANGLIA	156	ARTIST	121
ACHILLES 641	137	ANGLIAN	153	ARUM	218
ACHILLES 7043	130	ANGLO-CANADIAN	151	ASABA	71
ADALIA	77	ANGLO-COLOMBIAN	150	ASHBURTON	222
ADAMS	9	ANGLO-PATAGONIAN	151	ASHLEAF	149
ADAMTON	57	ANGUS	30	ASHLEIGH	219
ADANSI	72	ANHUI	44	ASHMORE	9
ADDAH	72	ANNAPOLIS	93	ASIATIC PRINCE	99
ADELA	219	ANNA SOFIE	92	ASSYRIA	30
ADENWEN	143	ANTAEUS	193	ASTORIA	85
AFRIC	178	ANT CASSAR	126	ASTROLOGER	105
AFRICA	21	ANTEROS	193	ATHENIA	67
AFRICAN PRINCE	99	ANTIGUA	117	ATLANTIAN	154
AFRICAN TRANSPORT	133	ANTINOE	193	ATLAS 989	58
AFTON	209	ANTIOPE	193	ATLAS 3090	194
AGBERI	72	ANTONIO	193	AUBE	214
AGNETE	64	ANTONY	24	AUCHENCRAG	187
AGUILA	240	ANTWERPEN	91	AUCKLAND CASTLE	170
AIGBURTH	200	APAPA	71	AUDAX	39
AILSA	205	APARIMA	227	AULTON	9
AILSA CRAIG	58	APOLLO	31	AURANIA	61
AISLABY	58	APPLEDORE	219	AURIAC	214
AKASSA	73	APSLEYHALL	234	AUSONIA	61
ALACRITY	118	ARAB	32	AUSTRALBUSH	50
ALAUNIA	60	ARABIA	182	AUSTRALDALE	50
ALAVI	23	ARABIAN	75	AUSTRALIAN TRANSPORT	133
ALDERSHOT	232	ARABIC	177	AUSTRALIER	31
ALERT	54	ARABIS	206	AUTOLYCUS	131
ALFALFA	129	ARAGON	201	AVA	124
ALGARVE	146	ARANMORE	46	AVANTI	146
ALGERIAN	78	ARBONNE	214	AVENGER	226
ALGIERS	178	ARCA	14	AVOCET	240
ALHAMA	228.	ARCADIAN	200	AVON	39
ALICE MARIE	101	ARCHBANK	217	AVRISTAN	215
ALLANTON	66	ARDANDEARG	205	AXMINSTER	38
ALLENDALE	94	ARDENS	102	AXWELL	48
ALMERIAN	154	ARDGASK	159	AYLEVARROO	155
ALMOND BRANCH	195	ARDGLAMIS	159	AYMERIC	232
ALMORA	133	ARDGLASS 778	159	AYR	115
ALLIE	215	ARDGLASS 4617	160	AYSGARTH	159
ALNWICK CASTLE	225	ARDMORE	45	AZIRA	181
ALSTER	63	ARENDAL	196	AZUL	129
ALTO	181	ARGALIA	67		
AMAKURA	24	ARGO 1720	26		
AMAZON	201	ARGO 3071	227	BADAGRI	73
AMBIENT	235	ARGYLL	216	BADMINTON	191
AMPLEFORTH	59	ARIEL	194	BAGDALE	209
AMPLEGARTH	10	ARIES	138	BAKU STANDARD	139
AMSTELDAM	211	ARMADALE	222	BALAKANI	149

BALDERSBY	199	BELGIAN PRINCE	99	BRANKSOME CHINE	118
BALGOWNIE	103	BELGIER	31	BRANKSOME HALL	78
BALGRAY	239	BELLBANK	20	BRANTINGHAM	53
BALLARAT	183	BELLE OF ENGLAND	194	BRAUNTON	218
BALLOCHBUIE	9	BELLE OF FRANCE	21	BRAY HEAD	125
BALLOGIE	65	BELLUCIA	20	BREMA	86
BAMSE 958	151	BELLVIEW	20	BRENTWOOD	54
BAMSE 1001	23	BEN CRUACHAN	171	BRETWALDA	115
BANDON	44	BENDEW	227	BRIARDENE	66
BANGARTH	192	BENEFICENT	235	BRIERLEY HILL	109
BARBARA	229	BENGALI	30	BRIERTON	129
BARBARY	160	BENGORE HEAD	126	BRIGHTON QUEEN	35
BARGANY	170	BENGROVE	134	BRIGITTA	49
BARNTON	106	BENHA	145	BRIKA	25
BARON AILSA	129	BENHEATHER	134	BRISBANE RIVER	132
BARON BALFOUR	128	BENITO	73	BRISTOL CITY	127
BARON BLANTYRE	128	BEN LOMOND	171	BRITANNIA 765	63
BARON CAWDOR	128	BENVORLICH	221	BRITANNIA 1814	116
BARON ERSKINE	127	BEN VRACKIE	229	BRITANNIA 3129	79
BARON GARIOCH	128	BERBERA	28	BRITANNIC 3487	48
BARON HERRIES	129	BERNARD	223	BRITANNIC 48758	177
BARON OGILVY	128	BERNICIA	63	BRITISH MONARCH	191
BARON SEMPILL	128	BERTRAND	223	BRITISH SUN	209
BARON TWEEDMOUTH	128	BERWICK LAW	150	BRITISH VISCOUNT	29
BARON VERNON	128	BILSWOOD	51	BRODERICK	23
BARON WEMYSS	128	BIRCHGROVE	11	BRODMORE	23
BARON YARBOROUGH	128	BIRCHWOOD	51	BRODNESS	23
BARRISTER 3679	121	BIRDOSWALD	158	BRODSTONE	23
BARRISTER 4952	122	BIRKHALL	63	BRONWEN	142
BARROWMORE	97	BIRTLEY	33	BROOKBY	199
BARUNGA	50	BIRUTA	84	BROOKWOOD	51
BASUTA	18	BISHOPSTON	194	BROOMHILL	48
BATHURST	72	BITTERN	52	BRUMAIRE	185
BATOUM	139	BLACK HEAD	126	BRUNHILDA	38
BAYANO	74	BLACKWOOD	195	BUFFALO	82
BAYCHATTAN	204	BLAGDON	117	BULGARIAN	79
BAYCRAIG	204	BLAIRHALL	176	BULLMOUTH	14
BAYGITANO	204	BLAKE	169	BULYSSES	14
BAYHALL	204	BLEAMOOR	23	BURCOMBE	32
BAYNAEN	204	BOGOTA	179	BURESK	32
BAYNESK	204	BOLDWELL	84	BURMA	21
BAYSOTO	204	BOLTONHALL	234	BURNBY	198
BAYVOE	204	BOMA	73	BURNHOPE	33
BAY STATE	100	BONIFACE	24	BURNSTONE	11
BEACHY	46	BONNY	72	BURRSFIELD	239
BEACON LIGHT	25	BONTNEWYDD	179	BUSIRIS	172
BEATRICE	141	BONVILSTON	189	BUTETOWN 1829	120
BEAUFRONT	195	BORDER KNIGHT	79	BUTETOWN 3789	165
BEAUMARIS	94	BORG	35	BYLANDS	238
BEDALE	94	BORGA	164	BYWELL	194
BEECHPARK	65	BOSCASTLE	141		
BEECHTREE	142	BOSCAWEN	141		
BEEMAH	123	BOSTON CITY	127		
BEGONA NO.4	142	BOSTONIAN	154	CABOTIA	67
BEGONIA	197	BOYNTON	170	CADEBY	22
BEGUM	15	BRACONDALE	174	CADMUS	205
BELFORD	164	BRADFORD CITY	210	CAIRNDHU	34
BELGIAN	153	BRAMHAM	169	CAIRNGOWAN	34

242

CAIRNHILL	159	CHAGRES	74	CLAN SHAW	40
CAIRNROSS	35	CHANCELLOR	120	CLANGULA	53
CAIRNSTRATH	38	CHANTALA	27	CLARA	32
CAIRNTORR	34	CHARING CROSS	56	CLAUDIA	225
CAIRO	161	CHARLES GOODANEW	186	CLAVERLEY	217
CAITHNESS	216	CHARLESTON	94	CLEARFIELD	136
C. A. JACQUES	36	CHARTERHOUSE	19	CLIFTONDALE	206
CALCHAS	131	CHATBURN	239	CLIFTONIAN	165
CALDERGROVE	117	CHATHAM	231	CLINTONIA	197
CALEDONIA 9223	12	CHELFORD	240	CLODMOOR	202
CALIFORNIA 8669	12	CHELTONIAN	165	CLUDEN	213
CALIFORNIA 5629	180	CHERBURY	68	COALGAS	103
CALIFORNIAN	153	CHERTSEY	231	COATH	19
CALGARIAN	37	CHESTERFIELD	110	COBER	187
CALLIOPE 3829	106	CHEVIOT RANGE	97	COILA	21
CALLIOPE 2883	184	CHIC	19	COLEMERE	111
CALYPSO	81	CHICAGO	83	COLENSO	80
CAMBANK	166	CHIRRIPO	74	COLLEGIAN	122
CAMBERWELL	30	CHLORIS	137	COLORADO	82
CAMBRIC	48	CHORLEY	31	COMEDIAN	121
CAMERONIA	12	CHULMLEIGH	218	COMMODORE	120
CAMERONIAN	153	CHURSTON	193	COMMONWEALTH	229
CANADIAN	153	CILURNUM	115	CONARGO	50
CANDIA	182	CITY OF ADELAIDE	78	CONCH	13
CANDIDATE	120	CITY OF BARODA	77	CONCORD	209
CANFORD CHINE	118	CITY OF BIRMINGHAM	76	CONDESA	95
CANGANIAN	237	CITY OF BREMEN	180	CONINGBEG	47
CANNIZARO	81	CITY OF BRISBANE	78	CONISTON WATER	210
CANOVA	148	CITY OF CAMBRIDGE	76	CONNAUGHT	45
CAPE FINISTERRE	158	CITY OF CORINTH	77	CONSOLS	90
CAPENOR	213	CITY OF FLORENCE	77	CONSTANTIA	103
CARIA	60	CITY OF GLASGOW	76	CONWAY	95
CARISBROOK	168	CITY OF LUCKNOW 3669	76	COONAGH	155
CARLISLE CASTLE	226	CITY OF LUCKNOW 8293	77	COPELAND	47
CARLO	82	CITY OF PARIS	76	COPENHAGEN	110
CARLTON	42	CITY OF PERTH	76	COPSEWOOD	51
CARMARTHEN	140	CITY OF SWANSEA	180	COQUET	166
CARMELITE	140	CIVILIAN	122	CORBET WOODALL	214
CARONI	200	CLACTON	110	CORFU	176
CARPATHIA	61	CLAN ALPINE	41	CORINTH	139
CARTERSWELL	180	CLAN CAMERON	41	CORK	45
CARTHAGINIAN	37	CLAN CAMPBELL	40	CORNELIA	169
CASPIAN	134	CLAN DAVIDSON	41	CORNUBIA	43
CASTILIAN	79	CLAN FARQUHAR	40	CORONDA	205
CASTLE EDEN	94	CLAN FERGUSON	41	CORSHAM	55
CASTLEFORD	222	CLAN FORBES	41	CORSICAN PRINCE	98
CASTLETON	85	CLAN LESLIE	40	CORSO	238
CATERHAM	120	CLAN MACALISTER	40	COSTELLO	107
CATTARO	82	CLAN MACCORQUODALE	41	COTOVIA	130
CAUCASIAN	149	CLAN MACDOUGALL	41	COTTINGHAM	155
CAVALLO	83	CLAN MACFARLANE	40	COUNSELLOR	121
CAVINA	74	CLAN MACLEOD	40	COUNTESS OF MAR	228
CAYO BONITO	31	CLAN MACMILLAN	41	CRAGOSWALD	158
CEDARWOOD	50	CLAN MACNAB	42	CRAIGARD	203
CELIA	174	CLAN MACNEIL	42	CRAIGENDORAN	160
CENTURION	120	CLAN MACPHERSON	41	CRAIGSTON	57
CERNE	213	CLAN MACVEY	42	CRAYFORD	55
CESTRIAN	154	CLAN MURRAY	41	CRESSWELL	94

Name	Page	Name	Page	Name	Page
CRISPIN	24	DOURO	78	ELLESMERE	230
CROSSHILL	159	DOVER CASTLE	225	ELMGROVE	11
CROWN OF ARRAGON	187	DOWLAIS	170	ELMMOOR	202
CROWN OF CASTILE	187	DRAKE	104	ELMSGARTH	159
CROWN POINT	97	DRESDEN	63	ELOBY	72
CUPICA	177	DRINA	200	ELSISTON	167
CUYAHOGA	13	DROMORE	96	ELSWICK LODGE	232
CYFARTHFA	170	DRONNING MAUD	211	ELSWICK MANOR	232
CYMBELINE	24	DRUMCREE	42	ELVE	131
CYMRIAN	238	DUART	162	EMBLA	205
CYMRIC	177	DUCHESS OF CORNWALL	43	EMBLETON	213
CYRENE	58	DUCHESS OF HAMILTON	35	EMLYNVERNE	84
		DUCKBRIDGE	233	EMMA	223
DACIA	137	DUKE OF ALBANY	148	EMPRESS	58
DAFILA	53	DULCIE	176	EMPRESS OF FORT	
D. A. GORDON	36	DULWICH 1460	211	WILLIAM	85
DALEBY	199	DULWICH 3289	230	EMPRESS OF MIDLAND	35
DALEGARTH	14	DUMFRIES	216	ENGLAND	68
DALEGARTH		DUNBARMOOR	202	ENGLISHMAN	27
FORCE	144	DUNDALK	48	ENGLISH MONARCH	191
DALEWOOD	92	DUNDEE 2187	69	ENIDWEN	143
DALTON	232	DUNDEE 2290	35	ENNISMORE	54
DARIUS	208	DUNMORE HEAD	126	ENNISTOWN	120
DART	114	DUNRAVEN	190	ENOSIS	194
DARTMOOR	137	DUNROBIN	217	EPTALOFOS	163
DAUNTLESS	228	DUNSLEY	187	EPTAPYRGION	163
DAYBREAK	84	DURANGO	94	ERA	17
DELAMERE	111	DURWARD	105	ERATO	82
DELPHIC	178	DUX	87	ERETRIA	221
DENABY	147	DWINSK	62	ERIC CALVERT	169
DENBIGH HALL	77	DYKLAND	68	ERIK	17
DENEBOLA	87			ERNA BOLT	86
DENEWOOD	54	EAGLE POINT	97	ERMINE	33
DEN OF CROMBIE	19	EARL OF ELGIN	13	EROS	90
DERBENT	10	EAST POINT	98	ESCRICK	211
DESABLA	232	EASTERN CITY	210	ESKMERE	111
DESTRO	83	EASTERN PRINCE	99	ESNEH	172
DEVONIAN	154	EASTFIELD	142	ESSONITE	196
DEWA	177	EASTLANDS	238	ESTRELLA	74
DEWSLAND	136	EAST WALES	105	ESTRELLANO	79
DIADEM 3752	115	EAVESTONE	93	ETAL MANOR	88
DIADEM 4307	115	ECCLESIA	112	ETHEL	32
DIANA	181	ECHUNGA	10	ETHELBRYHTA	122
DICTATOR	120	EDALE	158	ETHEL DUNCAN	69
DIDO	80	EDERNIAN	237	ETHELINDA	123
DINGLE	200	EDLINGTON	65	ETHIOPE	73
DIOMED 4672	130	EGYPTIANA	93	ETONIAN	154
DIOMED 7523	132	EGYPTIAN PRINCE	99	ETTON	206
DIXIANA	145	EL ARGENTINO	95	EUMAEUS	131
DJERV	15	EL ZORRO	26	EUPHORBIA 3837	197
DOLCOATH	168	ELAX	13	EUPHORBIA 3109	197
DON	148	ELBA	64	EUPION	29
DON ARTURO	66	ELEANOR	194	EUSTON	190
DON DIEGO	66	ELELE	72	EUTERPE	179
DON EMILIO	66	ELFORD	208	EVELINE	187
DONEGAL	167	ELLA SAYER	90	EXCELLENCE PLESKE	146
DOROTHY	174	ELLASTON 3796	167	EXCELLENT	234
DOTTEREL	53	ELLASTON 3192	168	EXFORD	219

Name	No.	Name	No.	Name	No.
FABIAN	79	GAFSA 3922	25	GLOCLIFFE	135
FAIREARN	137	GAFSA 3974	25	GLOW	102
FAIRPORT	57	GALEKA	225	GLYNYMEL	118
FALABA	73	GALICIA 5922	179	GOATHLAND	123
FALCON	44	GALICIA 1400	116	GOLCONDA	27
FALLODON	210	GALLIER	31	GOLD COAST	73
FARLEY	134	GALWAY CASTLE	226	GOLDMOUTH	13
FARN	88	GANGES	114	GOOD HOPE	133
FARNHAM	221	GANNET	104	GOODWOOD	51
FARRALINE	156	GARDEPEE	214	GORSEMORE	97
FASTNET	136	GARFIELD	136	GOWER COAST	164
FAUVETTE	104	GARMOYLE	46	GOWRIE	69
FAVONIAN	78	GARRON HEAD	126	GRANGEMOOR	203
F. D. LAMBERT	235	GARTHCLYDE	101	GRANGEWOOD	171
FELICIANA	204	GARTHWAITE	101	GRANTLEYHALL	234
FELTRIA	61	GARTLAND	236	GRAVINA	159
FENAY BRIDGE	48	GARTNESS	229	GREATHAM	52
FENAY LODGE	48	GASCONIA	228	GREAVESASH	175
FERGA	173	GASCONY	160	GREENBANK	117
FERNDENE	158	GAUPEN	92	GREENLAND	62
FERNMOOR	202	GEFION	237	GREENWICH	231
FERRONA	157	GEMINI	169	GREGYNOG	176
FINGAL	156	GEMMA	86	GRELDON	108
FIRELIGHT	102	GEO	19	GRELEEN	108
FIRFIELD	68	GEORGE PYMAN	188	GRELHAME	108
FISCUS	208	GEORGIAN	153	GRELTORIA	108
FLAMINIAN	78	GEORGIOS ANTIPPA	35	GRENADIER	225
FLAVIA	61	GHAZEE	103	GRESHAM	221
FLAWYL	222	GIBEL HANAM	22	GRETASTON	167
FLIMSTON	189	GIBEL YEDID	22	GRIVE	105
FLORAZAN	89	GIBRALTAR	106	GRODNO	80
FLORENTIA	217	GIRALDA	212	GROESWEN	143
FLORIDIAN	153	GIRDLENESS	151	GRONINGEN	103
FLORRIESTON	168	GISELLA	11	GRYFEVALE	18
FLUENT	235	GLADIATOR	120	GUIDO	80
F. MATARAZZO	59	GLAUCUS	131	GUILDHALL	152
FOLIA	60	GLENALMOND	100		
FORELAND	208	GLENARM HEAD	126	HADLEY	54
FORESTMOOR	203	GLENART CASTLE	226	HAIGH HALL	175
FORFAR	217	GLENARTNEY 5201	101	HAILEYBURY	220
FORMBY	47	GLENARTNEY 7263	166	HALBERDIER	90
FORNEBO	65	GLENBY	198	HALCYON	104
FORTH	39	GLENCARRON	99	HALIZONES	134
FOYLEMORE	97	GLENCLIFFE	89	HALLAMSHIRE	200
FRAMFIELD	239	GLENCLUNY	101	HANLEY	152
FRANCONIA	60	GLENCOE	227	HANNA LARSEN	86
FRANKLYN	162	GLENFOYLE	111	HARBERTON	55
FREDERICK KNIGHT	143	GLENFRUIN	70	HARBURY	119
FREMONA	34	GLENGYLE	165	HARE	157
FRESHFIELD	209	GLENLEE 4140	101	HAREWOOD	119
FRIMAIRE	185	GLENLEE 4915	99	HARFLETE	119
FRINTON	163	GLENLOGAN	165	HARLINGTON	182
F. STOBART	48	GLENMOOR	202	HARLYN	122
FULGENS	102	GLENOGLE	165	HARMATRIS	119
FULGENT	234	GLENRAVEL	14	HARMATTAN	119
FULMAR	53	GLENSTRAE	166	HARPAGUS	119
		GLEN TANAR	52	HARPALION	119
GADSBY	198	GLITRA	205	HARPALUS	88

245

HARPALYCE	119	HOPEMOOR	202	INVERBERVIE	200
HARPATHIAN	119	HOPEMOUNT	212	INVERGYLE	215
HARROVIAN	165	HORDEN	32	IOLANTHE	184
HARROW	55	HORNCHURCH	135	IOLO 3903	190
HARTBURN	38	HORNSUND	86	IOLO 3840	190
HARTDALE	222	HORSA	125	IONA	34
HARTLEY	73	HOWTH HEAD	125	IONIAN	37
HASLINGDEN	240	HUDWORTH	222	IRAN	30
HATASU	173	HUELVA	25	IRENE	54
HATHOR	173	HUGUENOT	16	IRISTON	167
HAULWEN	143	HUNGERFORD	126	IRTHINGTON	161
HAWORTH	64	HUNSBRIDGE	88	ISER	168
HAYDN	219	HUNSDON	74	ISLANDMORE	155
HAZELPARK	65	HUNSGROVE	197	ISLE OF HASTINGS	38
HAZELWOOD	228	HUNSTANTON	110	ISLE OF JURA	217
H. C. HENRY	124	HUNTLY	10	ISLEWORTH	231
HEADLANDS	172	HUNTSFALL	169	ISTRAR	29
HEADLEY	133	HUNTSHOLM	197	ITALIANA	141
HEATHDENE	158	HUNTSLAND	100	ITINDA	29
HEATHPARK	65	HUNTSMAN	121	ITONUS	28
HEATHERSIDE	43	HUNTSMOOR	126	IVERNIA	60
HEBBLE	148	HUNTSTRICK	216	IVYDENE	20
HEBBURN	33	HUNTSVALE	90		
HEIGHINGTON	233	HURST	47	JAFFA	83
HELMSMUIR	68	HURSTSIDE	43	JANE RADCLIFFE	189
HENDONHALL	233	HURSTWOOD	55	JAPANESE PRINCE	98
HENLEY	231	HURUNUI	175	JERSEY CITY	210
HENRY R. JAMES	140	HYLAS	135	JESSIE	176
HERCULES 1095	87	HYPERIA	135	JESSMORE	96
HERCULES 1295	58			JEVINGTON	20
HERDIS	15	IBERIAN	152	JOHN HARDIE	117
HERMIONE	135	ICELAND	62	JOHN H. BARRY	123
HERON	104	IDAHO	206	JOHN MILES	214
HERON BRIDGE	85	IGNIS	102	JOHN O. SCOTT	205
HERRINGTON	176	IKALIS	233	JONATHAN HOLT	132
HESIONE	134	IKARIA	233	JOSE DE LARRINAGA	150
HESPERIAN	37	IKBAL	71	JOSEPH CHAMBERLAIN	143
HESPERIDES	135	IKEDA	233	JOSHUA NICHOLSON	80
HIDALGO	82	ILARO	71	JULIA PARK	57
HIGHBURY	231	ILDERTON	213	JUNO	27
HIGHCLIFFE	192	ILSTON	193	JUPITER	26
HIGHGATE	55	ILVINGTON COURT	115	JUSTICIA	178
HIGHLAND BRIGADE	174	IMATAKA	23	JUTLAND	13
HIGHLAND CORRIE	174	IMPERIAL	192	J. Y. SHORT	234
HIGHLAND HARRIS	174	IMPERIAL TRANSPORT	133		
HIGHLAND PRINCE	99	INCEMORE	96	KAFUE	75
HILARY	24	INDIA	182	KALGAN	44
HILDA LEA	54	INDIAN CITY	210	KALIBIA	47
HILDAWELL	238	INDRANI	67	KALLUNDBORG	112
HINDUSTAN	49	INDUSTRY	233	KALO	146
HIRONDELLE	104	INGLEMOOR	202	KAPUNDA	172
HOGARTH	9	INGLESIDE	124	KARA	216
HOLGATE	117	INISHOWEN HEAD	125	KAREMA	75
HOLLINGTON	130	INKOSI	122	KARIBA	108
HOLLINSIDE	43	INKUM	233	KARINA	71
HOLLY BRANCH	195	INNISCARRA	45	KARMA	108
HOLMESBANK	144	INNISFALLEN	45	KARONGA	75
HONITON	218	INTENT	236	KARUMA	108

KASENGA	75	LADY ANN	176	LLWYNGWAIR	118
KASSANGA	161	LADY CARRINGTON	236	LOCHWOOD	50
KATHLEEN	206	LADY CORY WRIGHT	55	LOCKSLEY HALL	76
KATHLEEN LILY	127	LADY HELEN	157	LODANER	230
KEELUNG	76	LADY NINIAN	157	LOFOTEN	58
KEEPER	18	LADY OLIVE	27	LOMAS	129
KELSO	82	LADY PATRICIA	27	LONDON	69
KELVINBANK 4209	21	LADY SALISBURY	185	LONGBENTON	118
KELVINBANK 4072	22	LADYWOOD	91	LONGHIRST	188
KELVINHEAD	22	LAERTES	131	LONGSCAR	238
KELVINIA	22	LAKE MICHIGAN	37	LORCA	25
KENDAL CASTLE	42	LAMPADA	102	LORD CHARLEMONT	57
KENILWORTH	64	LANDONIA	228	LORD DERBY	206
KENMARE	45	LANFRANC	24	LORD ROBERTS	66
KENMORE	97	LANGTON HALL	76	LORD STEWART	157
KENNETT	53	LANTERNA	102	LORD TREDEGAR	236
KENNINGTON	212	LANTHORN	102	LORLE	39
KHEPHREN	173	LAPWING	105	LOTUSMERE	217
KIELDRECHT	192	LARCHMORE	96	LOUVAIN	111
KILBRIDE	204	LARGO	181	LOWDALE	59
KILDALE	123	LARISTAN	49	LOWLANDS	59
KILDONAN	57	LAURENTIC	177	LOWMOUNT	38
KILLELLAN	193	LAURIUM	208	LOWTHER RANGE	97
KILMAHO	57	LAVINIA WESTOLL	234	LOWTYNE	59
KILWINNING	17	LAVERNOCK	9	LUCENT	235
KINCARDINE	216	LEASOWE CASTLE	226	LUCISTON 2877	167
KING BLEDDYN	184	LEDBURY	39	LUCISTON 2948	167
KING DAVID	185	LEEDS CITY	210	LUCY ANDERSON	109
KING IDWAL	185	LEEUWARDEN	103	LUDGATE	237
KING MALCOM	185	LEICESTER	110	LUGANO	95
KINGSDYKE	59	LEINSTER	45	LUIS	176
KINGSTONIAN	154	LENA	140	LULLINGTON	20
KINGSWAY	85	LEONATUS	46	LUMINA	171
KINROSS	216	LESBIAN	78	LUSITANIA 30396	60
KINTUCK	130	LESTO	181	LUSITANIA 1834	116
KIOTO	75	LEUCTRA	155	LUX	149
KIRKBY	198	LEWISHAM	231	LUXEMBOURG	63
KIRKHAM ABBEY	195	LEXIE	147	LUXOR	173
KISH	46	L. H. CARL	145	LUZ BLANCA	138
KITTIWAKE	53	LIBOURNE	173	LYCIA	60
KNARSDALE	106	LIGHTFOOT	229	LYDIE	32
KNIGHTSGARTH	192	LIMERICK	226	LYNBURN	173
KNUTSFORD	138	LINCAIRN	43	LYNFIELD	15
KOHINUR	14	LINCOLNSHIRE	200	LYNORTA	141
KOHISTAN	215	LINKMOOR	202		
KOSSEIR	145	LISBON	79	MABEL BAIRD	17
KUL	52	LISETTE	87	MACHAON	131
KURDISTAN	49	LISMORE	44	MADAME RENEE	19
KUT SANG	137	LIVERPOOL	209	MADAME MIDAS	19
KWASIND	21	LIVONIA	146	MADELINE	187
KYANITE	197	LIZZIE WESTOLL	235	MADRYN	164
KYARRA	17	LLANCARVAN	191	MADURA	161
KYNO	83	LLANDOVERY CASTLE	226	MAGELLAN	180
		LLANDRINDOD	189	MAIN	162
LA BLANCA	95	LLANDUDNO	190	MAINDY BRIDGE	141
LA NEGRA	95	LLANGORSE	189	MAINE	16
LACONIA	60	LLANISHEN	189	MAIZAR	30
LADOGA	221	LLONGWEN	142	MALACHITE	196

MALAKAND	30	MEDORA	37	MORA	25
MALDA	28	MELANIE	11	MORAZAN	89
MALINCHE	100	MELDON	65	MORDENWOOD	51
MALOJA	182	MELFORD HALL	77	MORESBY	169
MALTBY	199	MEMLING	148	MORWENNA	215
MALVINA	156	MEMNON	73	MOUNTBY	199
MANCHESTER CITIZEN	162	MEMPHIAN	154	MOUNT CONISTON	172
MANCHESTER COMMERCE	163	MENZALEH	145	MOYUNE	130
		MERGANSER	52	MUIRFIELD	68
MANCHESTER ENGINEER 4302	162	MERIONETH	140	MUNIFICENT	235
		MERIONETHSHIRE	201	MURCIA	26
MANCHESTER ENGINEER 4465	163	MEROE	172	MUREX	13
		MERSARIO	112	MURIEL	179
MANCHESTER INVENTOR 4247	162	MERTON HALL	77	MYRTLE BRANCH	195
		MESABA	16		
MANCHESTER INVENTOR 4112	163	MESSIDOR	185	NAILSEA COURT	170
		MEXICO CITY	166	NAIRN	180
MANCHESTER MILLER	163	MIAMI	74	NAMUR	183
MANCHESTER SPINNER	163	MIDDLESEX	88	NANTES	26
MANCHESTER TRADER	163	MIDDLETON	38	NARRAGANSETT	13
MANCHURIA	166	MIDLAND	68	NASCENT	235
MANGARA	160	MIDLAND QUEEN	36	NATAL TRANSPORT	133
MANISTEE	74	MIDLOTHIAN	155	NEEPAWAH	36
MANTOLA	28	MILLICENT KNIGHT	143	NENTMOOR	202
MAPLEWOOD	51	MILLY	11	NEOTSFIELD	20
MARDINIAN	79	MILWAUKEE	37	NESS	114
MARERE	49	MIMOSA	13	NETHERLEE	111
MARGA	170	MINIOTA	37	NEUQUEN	129
MARGAM ABBEY 4471	237	MINNEAPOLIS	16	NEVISBROOK	168
MARGAM ABBEY 4367	237	MINNEHAHA	16	NEWBURN	91
MARGIT	11	MINNETONKA	16	NEWBY	219
MARIE ELSIE	184	MINNEWASKA	16	NEWCASTLE	91
MARIE LEONHARDT	86	MINORCA	63	NEWHOLM	91
MARIE SUZANNE	184	MINTERNE	132	NEWLYN	91
MARINA	67	MIRA	213	NEWMARKET	110
MARION DAWSON	65	MIRLO	171	NEWMINSTER ABBEY	90
MARISTON	167	MISSANABIE	38	NEWSTEAD	92
MARMION	188	MISSIR	145	NEW YORK CITY	127
MARMORA	183	M. J. CRAIG	59	NEW ZEALAND TRANSPORT	133
MARQUETTE	16	MOBILE	92		
MARQUIS BACQUEHEM	174	MOERIS	172	NIGEL	105
MARS	135	MOHACSFIELD	67	NIRPURA	28
MARSTONMOOR	203	MOIDART	54	NORA	207
MARTIN	198	MOLDAVIA	183	NORFOLK COAST	47
MARY BAIRD	139	MOLESEY	231	NORHILDA	56
MASCOTTE	106	MOMBASSA	27	NORMANDIET	146
MASHOBRA	28	MONARCH	186	NORMANDY	156
MASTON	220	MONGARA	28	NORMANTON	89
MASUNDA	161	MONGOLIAN	137	NORMA PRATT	186
MATADOR	121	MONITORIA	85	NORTHFIELD	144
MATIANA	29	MONKSGARTH	192	NORTHLANDS	142
MAUDE LARSSEN	35	MONKSTONE	84	NORTH SEA	54
MAVISBROOK	168	MONTEBELLO	83	NORTHVILLE	59
MAXTON	94	MONTFORT	38	NORTHWAITE	188
MAYWOOD	68	MOOLTAN	182	NORTH WALES	196
MEADOWFIELD	161	MOORINA	50	NORWEGIAN	153
MECHANICIAN	122	MOORLANDS	134	NORWOOD	58
MEDINA	182	MOPSA	21	NOVOCASTRIAN	225

Name	Page	Name	Page	Name	Page
NOYA	25	PASHA	15	PONTIAC 1698	107
NUCERIA	165	PATAGONIA	190	PONTIAC 3345	39
NYANZA	162	PATIA	75	PONTYPRIDD	211
NYASSA	161	PATAGONIER	31	PORT ADELAIDE	49
		PEARL	236	PORT CAMPBELL	50
OAKBY	198	PEEBLES	217	PORT CURTIS	49
OAKLEAF	149	PEERLESS	115	PORT DALHOUSIE	166
OAKWOOD	139	PEGU	124	PORT HARDY	50
OBUASI	72	PELHAM	221	PORT NICHOLSON	49
OCEAN	55	PENHALE	43	PORTHKERRY	220
OILFIELD	136	PENHALLOW	44	PORTLOE	127
OKEMENT	235	PENINSULA	116	POWHATAN	210
OLDFIELD GRANGE	133	PENISTONE	109	PRESTO	181
OLIVE	223	PENSHURST	186	PRIMO 1366	181
OLIVE BRANCH	195	PENTWYN	146	PRIMO 1037	220
OLIVINE	196	PENTYRCH	146	PRINCE ABBAS	205
OMRAH	179	PENVEARN	44	PRINCESS ALBERTA	149
OOLA	155	PENYLAN	116	PRINCESS DAGMAR	150
OOPACK	130	PERA	183	PRINCESS MAUD	150
OPAL	196	PERLA	110	PRINCESS ROYAL	150
ORAMA	179	PERSIA	182	PRINCESS VICTORIA	149
ORANGE PRINCE	98	PERSIER	31	PROPHET	134
ORATOR	121	PERTH	214	PROVIDENCE	201
ORFORDNESS	152	PERUGIA	12	PRUNELLE	87
ORIFLAMME	149	PESHAWUR	183	PTARMIGAN	103
ORIGEN	24	PETRIDGE	186	PUNDIT	15
ORIOLE	103	PETUNIA	54	PURLEY	134
ORISSA	180	PEVERIL	106		
ORLOCK HEAD	125	PHARE	102	QUAGGY	211
ORONSA	180	PHEMIUS	131	QUEEN	90
ORONSAY	101	PHILADELPHIAN	154	QUEEN ADELAIDE	69
ORTERIC	232	PHILOMEL	105	QUEEN AMELIE	69
ORTOLAN	104	PILAR DE LARRINAGA	150	QUEEN EUGENIE	69
ORTONA	95	PINEGROVE	11	QUEEN MARY	69
ORUBIAN	154	PINEWOOD	91	QUEEN OF THE NORTH	22
OSLO	82	PLANUDES	175	QUEEN WILHELMINA	93
OSMANIEH	145	PLAWSWORTH	64	QUEENSWOOD	51
OSTPREUSSEN	86	PLUTO	27	QUERNMORE	96
OSWALD	24	PLUTUS	137		
OSWEGO	82	POLA	25	RAGNHILD	181
OTIS TETRAX	16	POLAMHALL	234	RALOO	138
OTWAY	179	POLANNA	47	RALLUS	53
OVID	107	POLAR PRINCE	87	RAMAZAN	89
		POLBRAE	207	RAMILLIES	56
PADDINGTON	190	POLDOWN	157	RAMSGARTH	211
PAGENTURM	110	POLESLEY	88	RANZA	146
PAIGNTON	135	POLITANIA	191	RAPALLO	96
PALACINE	215	POLJAMES	45	RAPPAHANNOCK	93
PALATINE	167	POLLEON	87	RAVENSBOURNE	211
PALMELLA	79	POLO	83	REAPWELL	171
PALMGROVE	10	POLPEDN	87	REDBREAST	33
PALMLEAF	148	POLTAVA	144	REDESMERE	111
PARISIANA	93	POLVARTH	17	REMEMBRANCE	84
PARKGATE	223	POLVENA	124	REFUGIO	178
PARKMILL	112	POLWELL	47	REMUS	227
PAROS	224	POLYMNIA	144	RENFREW 3488	216
PARTHENIA	67	POLYXENA	131	RENFREW 3830	217
PASCAL	147	POMERANIAN	37	REPTON	100

RESTORMEL	56	ROWENA	124	SARAH RADCLIFFE	190
REVENTAZON	75	ROXBURGH	217	SARDINIA	62
REWA	28	ROYAL EDWARD	36	SARNIA	156
RHEA	157	RUABON	56	SAVONA	62
RHINELAND	62	RUBIO	179	SAXON	228
RHODESIA	178	RUEL	222	SAXON BRITON	229
RHONA	173	RUNSWICK	210	SAXONIAN	149
RHYDWEN	143	RUPERRA	56	SAXON MONARCH	191
RIBERA	135	RUSSIAN	153	SCALPA	63
RIBSTON 3048	207	RUSTINGTON	20	SCAWBY	198
RIBSTON 3372	169	RUTHERGLEN	161	SCHOLAR	107
RICHARD DE		RUYSDAEL	237	SCOTTISH HERO	124
LARRINAGA	150	RYDAL HALL	77	SCOTTISH MONARCH	191
RICHMOND	230	RYE	148	SCULPTOR 3846	121
RIEVAULX ABBEY	195	RYTONHALL	112	SCULPTOR 4874	122
RINALDO	81			SEA GULL	151
RIO CLARO	184	SABBIA	86	SEANG CHOON	155
RIO COLORADO	184	SABIA	130	SEA SERPENT	151
RIO LAGES	152	SAGA	197	SEATONIA	125
RIO PALLARESA	21	SAGAMORE	99	SEBEK	172
RIO PARANA	183	SAIDIEH	145	SECONDO	89
RIO PIRAHY	208	SAILOR PRINCE	98	SEISTAN	215
RIO SOROCABA	184	SAIMA	239	SEMANTHA	19
RIO TIETE	183	ST. ANDREWS	170	SERAPIS	59
RIO VERDE	184	SAINT CECILIA	127	SERBINO	80
RIVER FORTH	184	SAINT DIMITRIOS	158	SERRANA	207
RIVERSDALE	220	ST. GOTHARD	230	SERULA	53
ROANOKE	94	ST. MAGNUS	177	SETTER	33
ROBERT ADAMSON	234	ST. MARGARET	177	SEVEN SEAS	151
ROBERT EGGLETON	236	SAINT NINIAN	160	SHEAF BLADE	211
ROCHESTER CITY	230	SAINT RONALD	191	SHELDRAKE	104
ROCKCLIFFE	192	ST. SEIROL	156	SHENANDOAH	93
ROCKPOOL	199	SAINT URSULA	191	SHIMOSA	18
RODDAM	213	SALDANHA	75	SHIRALA	29
ROLLESBY	199	SALERNO	80	SIDMOUTH	112
ROMANY	14	SALMO	81	SILKSWORTH HALL	175
ROMEO	83	SALMONPOOL	199	SILVERASH	220
ROMFORD	231	SALSETTE	182	SILVERDALE	232
ROMNY	146	SALTA	10	SILVERTON	34
ROMSDALEN	117	SALYBIA	207	SILVIA	26
RONA	63	SAMARA	160	SIMLA	182
ROSALIND	26	SAMOSET	212	SIR FRANCIS	55
ROSALIE 4237	57	SAN ANDRES	45	SIRIUS	103
ROSALIE 4243	56	SAN BERNARDO	71	SIR RICHARD AWDRY	181
ROSARIO	178	SANDHURST	231	SIR WILLIAM	
ROSCOMMON	226	SANDON HALL	77	STEPHENSON	225
ROSE LEA	116	SANDSEND	188	SJAELLAND	64
ROSE MARIE	101	SAN HILARIO	70	SKARAAS	85
ROSEBANK	188	SAN ONOFRE	70	SKERRIES	46
ROSEHILL	221	SAN RITO	239	SNAEFELL	138
ROSEMOOR	203	SANTA AMALIA	70	SNEATON	123
ROSEMOUNT	57	SANTA ISABEL	201	SNOWDON	189
ROSS	56	SANTAREN	207	SNOWDONIAN	237
ROTA	93	SAN URBANO	70	SNOWDON RANGE	97
ROTHESAY	56	SANWEN	143	SOMERSET	88
ROTORUA	175	SAPELE	72	SOMME	214
ROUMANIE	160	SARACEN	152	SOMMEINA	124
ROWANMORE	96	SARAGOSSA	118	SONNIE	118

250

SOUTHBOROUGH	136	SYLVIE	144	TORRIDGE	218
SOUTHFORD	164	SZECHUEN	44	TORRINGTON	219
SOUTHGARTH	17			TORTUGUERO	75
SOUTHINA	70	TABASCO	93	TOTTENHAM	230
SOUTHLAND	138	TAGONA	36	TOWARD	46
SOUTH POINT 3837	92	TAGUS	78	TOWERGATE	31
SOUTH POINT 4258	98	TAMELE	72	TOWNELEY	33
SOUTH WALES	105	TANDIL	129	T. R. THOMPSON	236
SOUTH-WESTERN	156	TANGISTAN	215	TRAFALGAR	106
SOWWELL	100	TANIS	172	TRANSYLVANIA	12
SPECTATOR	121	TARA	156	TRAQUAIR	105
SPENNYMOOR	201	TRABETNESS	152	TREDEGAR HALL	116
SPENSER	148	TARPEIA	39	TREFUSIS	113
SPERO	81	TARQUAH	71	TREGANTLE	113
SPHENE	196	TARTARY	160	TREGENNA	114
SPIRAL	40	TASMAN	88	TREKIEVE	114
SPITAL	140	TASSO	228	TRELISSICK	114
SPITHEAD	46	TATARRAX	212	TRELOSKE	114
SPRAY	84	TEAKWOOD	139	TRELYON	114
SPRINGHILL	90	TEAL	104	TREMATON	113
SPRINGWELL	225	TEANO	80	TREMEADOW	113
STAMFORDHAM	118	TEELIN HEAD	126	TREMORVAH	113
STANDISH HALL	117	TELA	45	TRENEGLOS	113
STANHOPE	151	TELENA	14	TREVARRACK	113
STANLEY	188	TEMPUS	207	TREVEAL	114
STATESMAN	121	TERGESTEA	86	TREVEAN	113
STATHE	89	TERENCE	147	TREVERBYN	114
STEELVILLE	18	TEUTONIAN	149	TREVOSE	113
STEN	164	TEVIOTDALE	213	TRIDENT	115
STEPHEN FURNESS	225	TEWFIKIEH	145	TRINGA	52
STEPHANO	26	THALIA	194	TRINIDAD	36
STEPHANOTIS	30	THAMES	40	TRITONIA	67
STOCKFORCE	144	THELMA	107	TROCAS	14
STOLT NIELSEN	132	THE MARCHIONESS	123	TROILUS	130
STRATHALBYN	34	THE PRESIDENT	123	TROJAN PRINCE	98
STRATHALLAN	89	THE QUEEN	123	TRONGATE	223
STRATHCARRON	33	THE STEWART'S COURT	157	TROWBRIDGE	219
STRATHCONA	36	THIRLBY	199	TRUNKBY	198
STRATHDENE	34	THISTLEARD	12	TRURO	80
STRATHNAIRN	33	THISTLEBAN	11	TULLOCHMOOR	202
STRATHTAY	34	THISTLEDHU	12	TUMMEL	136
STRYN	52	THORNABY	198	TUNG SHAN	203
STUART PRINCE	99	THORPWOOD	50	TUNISIANA	93
STURTON	213	THORSA	64	TURAKINA	175
SUBADAR	15	THRACIA	60	TURINO	95
SUFFOLD COAST	186	THURSO	81	TURNBRIDGE	171
SUMMERFIELD	207	TIBERIA	12	TUSCANIA	12
SUNNIVA	175	TITIAN	147	TUSKAR	47
SUNTRAP	102	TITHONUS	10	TWEED 1025	209
SURADA	29	TOFTWOOD	51	TWEED 1777	239
SUTHERLAND	216	TOGSTON	212	TYCHO	82
SWANMORE	96	TOKOMARU	208	TYNE	201
SWAN RIVER	132	TONG HONG	218	TYRHAUG	107
SWEDISH PRINCE	98	TOPAZ	197		
SWIFTSURE	238	TORCELLO	82	UGANDA 4315	18
SWIFT WINGS	116	TORINO	107	UGANDA 5431	29
SYCAMORE	96	TORO	81	ULTONIA	61
SYLVANIAN	153	TORR HEAD	125	UMARIA	28

Name	Page	Name	Page	Name	Page
UMBA	83	WAR MONARCH	62	WOLF	229
UMBALLA	28	WAR PATROL	42	WOODFIELD	239
UMETA	27	WAR SONG	92	WOOLSTON	138
UMVOTI	32	WAR SWALLOW	43	WOOLWICH	230
UNITY	148	WAR TUNE	92	WRAGBY	198
UPCERNE	132	WARILDA	10	WREATHIER	9
URBINO	80	WARLEY PICKERING	51	WYCHWOOD	91
URD	142	WARNER	46	WYNDHURST	141
USKMOOR	203	WARNOW	168		
USSA	132	WARREN	17	YEDDO	232
		WARRIOR	223	YOCHOW	44
VALA	206	WARSAW	63	YONNE	228
VALDES	240	WARTENFELS	110	YZER	30
VALENTIA	164	WASHINGTON	189		
VALETTA	109	WATHFIELD	67	ZAFRA	25
VAN STIRUM	10	WAVERLEY	188	ZAMBESI	224
VANDALIA	61	WEARSIDE	125	ZANONI	224
VANELLUS	53	WEGA	86	ZARA	81
VASCO	81	WELBECK HALL	117	ZENO	224
VAUXHALL	152	WELBURY	129	ZENT	74
VEDAMORE	96	WELLINGTON	218	ZERMATT	224
VEGHTSTROOM	131	WELSH PRINCE	98	ZETA	224
VELLORE	109	WENTWORTH	64	ZILLAH	224
VENDEE	173	WESTBURY	39	ZINAL	224
VENETIA	109	WESTERGATE	178	ZONE	224
VENTMOOR	203	WESTERN COAST 1165	186	ZOROASTER	223
VERDI	147	WESTERN COAST 1394	47	ZYLPHA	224
VERIA	60	WESTFIELD	142		
VERNON	55	WESTLANDS	238		
VESTRA	205	WESTMINSTER	139		
VESUVIO	104	WESTMOOR	203		
VICTORIA 974	223	WESTONBY	199		
VICTORIA 1620	161	WESTPHALIA	63		
VIENNA	109	WEST POINT	97		
VIMEIRA	109	WESTVILLE	18		
VINE BRANCH	195	WEST WALES	105		
VINOVIA	61	WESTWICK	235		
VIRENT	236	WESTWOOD	95		
VIRGINIA	111	W. HARKNESS	147		
VOLNAY	109	W. H. DWYER	166		
VOLODIA	61	WHITE HEAD	126		
VOSGES	172	WHITECOURT	23		
VRONWEN	143	WHITEFIELD	140		
		WHITEHALL	22		
WAIHEMO	227	WHITGIFT	139		
WAIKAWA	227	WHORLTON	94		
WAITEMATA	227	WILBERFORCE	122		
WALLSEND	33	WILEYSIKE	168		
WANETA	212	WILLINGTONIA	85		
WAPELLO	212	WILLOW BRANCH	196		
WAR ARABIS	185	WILTONHALL	112		
WAR BARON	62	WINDERMERE	52		
WAR CLOVER	66	WINDSOR	189		
WAR COUNCIL	100	WINSDOR HALL	116		
WAR CROCUS	234	WINLATON	108		
WAR FIRTH	42	WIRRAL	70		
WAR HELMET	201	WISBECH	15		
WAR KNIGHT	100	W. M. BARKLEY	112		

INDEX OF PLACES

Alboran Island, Morocco
Anvil Point, 10 miles S. of Poole, Dorset

Ballycottin Islands, 11¼ miles S.E. of Middleton, co. Cork
Bardsey Island, Cardigan Bay, Wales
Beachy Head, 3 miles S.W. of Eastbourne, Susssex
Belle Ile near Lorient, France
Berry Head, Torbay, Devon
Bishop Rock, Scilly Islands, Cornwall
Black Head, Belfast Lough, co. Antrim
Black Head, 6 miles N.E. of the Lizard Point, Cornwall
Bull Point, co. Antrim
Bull Rock, 3 miles W. from Dursey Island, co. Cork
Butt of Lewis, Hebrides

Cabo Blanco, Majorca, Spain
Cabo de Gata near Almeria, Spain
Cabo de las Huertas near Alicante, Spain
Caldy Island, Bristol Channel
Calf of Man, Isle of Man
Canet Point near Valencia, Spain
Cani Rocks, Tunis
Cape Barfleur near Cherbourg, France
Cape Bengut, Algeria
Cape Bon, Tunis
Cape Bougaroni, Tunis
Cape Camerat near Marseilles, France
Cape Carbon, Algeria
Cape Carbonara, Sardinia
Cape Carthage, Tunis
Cape Caxine, Algeria
Cape Cervera near Alicante, Spain
Cape Corbelin, Algeria
Cape Colonne, Gulf of Taranto, Italy
Cape Creus, Gulf of Lions
Cape d'Antibes near Nice, France
Cape d'Antifer near Fécamp, France
Cape de Fer, Algeria
Cape de Garde, Tunis
Cape de Palos near Cartagena, Spain
Cape de la Heve near Le Havre, France
Cape de las Huertas near Alicante, Spain
Cape Doro, Greece
Cape Drepano, Crete
Cape Falcon, Algeria
Cape Ferrat, Algeria
Cape Finisterre near Corunna, Spain
Cape Granitola, Sicily
Cape Greco, Cyprus

Cape Griz Nez near Calais, France
Cape Ivi, Algeria
Cape la Hague near Cherbourg, France
Cape Martello, Crete
Cape Matapan, Greece
Cape Mele, Gulf of Genoa, Italy
Cape Oropesa near Castellon, Spain
Cape Ortegal near Corunna, Spain
Cape Papas, Greece
Cape Passaro, Sicily
Cape Peloro, Sicily
Cape Pula, Sardinia
Cape Rosello, Sicily
Cape St. John, Crete
Cape St. Vincent, Portugal
Cape Salon near Tarronga, Spain
Cape San Antonia, Gulf of Valencia, Spain
Cape Scala, Gulf of Ploicastro, Italy
Cape Serrat, Tunis
Cape Shershel, Algeria
Cape Sicie, Gulf of Lions
Cape Sidero, Crete
Cape Sigli, Algeria
Cape Sines near Sines, Portugal
Cape Spartel, Morocco
Cape Spartivento, Italy
Cape Spartivento, Sicily
Cape Sperone, Sardinia
Cape Tedles, Algeria
Cape Tenez, Algeria
Cape Terberski, Murmansk
Cape Trafalgar near Cadiz, Spain
Cape Vado, Gulf of Genoa, Italy
Cape Villano near Corunna, Spain
Cape Vaticano, Gulf of Gioja, Italy
Cape Verd, Senegal
Cape Wrath, Sutherland
Cape da Roca near Lisbon, Portugal
Capo delle Mele, Gulf of Genoa
Cerigo Island, Greece
Cerigotto Island, Greece
Chassion Point near Rochefort, France
Codling Bank Lightvessel, 10, miles N.E. of Wicklow Head, co. Wicklow
Coningbeg Lightvessel, Saltee Islands, co. Wexford
Corsewall Point, 9 miles N.W. of Stranraer, Wigtownshire
Coquet Island, Northumberland

Daunts Rock, co. Cork
Dellimara Point, Malta
Dodman Point, 8½ miles S. of St. Austell, Cornwall
Dragonera Island, Balearic Islands, Spain

Eagle Island, 3 miles S.W. of Erris Head, co. Mayo
Eddystone Lighthouse, English Channel. 14 miles S.W. of Plymouth, Devon

Fair Isle midway between Orkney and Shetland Islands
Farne Islands, Northumberland
Fastnet Rock, 4 miles S.W. of Cape Clear, co. Cork
Flamborough Head, Yorkshire
Filey Brigg, 9½ miles S.E. of Scarborough, Yorkshire
Formentera Island, Balearic Islands, Spain

Galita Island, Tunis
Galley Head near Rosscarbery Bay, co. Cork
Gavdo Island, Crete
Girdle Ness near Aberdeen, Aberdeenshire
Godrevy Lighthouse, St. Ives Bay, Cornwall
Gorgona Island near Leghorn, Italy
Gozo Island near Malta
Gurnards Head, 5½ miles S.W. of St. Ives, Cornwall

Hartland Point, Devon
Hook Point, 3 miles S. of Fethard, co. Wexford

Ile d'Oleron near Rochefort, France
Ile d'Yeu near St. Nazaire, France
Ile de Bas near Ushant, France
Ile de Groix near Lorient, France
Ile de Porquerolles near Toulon, France
Ile de Re near La Rochelle, France
Ile de Sein near Brest, France
Ile de Vierge near Ushant, France
Ile du Pilier near St. Nazaire, France
Iles de Glenan near Lorient, France
Inishtrahull, 9 miles N.E. of Malin Head, co. Donegal

Jidjelli, Algeria

Kentish Knock Lightvessel at the mouth of the River Thames
Kinnaird Head N. of Fraserburgh, Aberdeenshire
Kingsdown 2½ miles S. of Deal, Kent
Kinsale Head, 17¼ miles S. of Cork, co. Cork
Kirkabister Lighthouse, 2½ miles S.E. of Lerwick, Shetland Islands

Lampedusa Island midway between Malta and Tunis
Les Sables d'Olonne near La Rochelle, France
Linosa Island midway between Malta and Tunis
Lizard Point, 12 miles S. of Helston, Cornwall
Longstone, Farne Islands, Northumberland
Loop Head, mouth of the River Shannon, co. Clare
Lundy Island, Bristol Channel
Lynas Point, Anglesey

Maidens, 7 miles N.E. of Larne, co. Antrim

Malin Head, 7 miles N.W. of Malin, co. Donegal
Malta, Mediterranean Sea
Manacle Rocks, 7½ miles S. of Falmouth, Cornwall
Marittimo Island, W.C. Italy
Marsa Susa, Libya
May Island, Firth of Forth, Fifeshire
Milo Island, Greece
Mine Head 5 miles S.W. of the entrance to Dungarvan harbour, co. Wexford
Muckle Flugga, Shetland Islands
Mudros, Aegean Sea
Mull of Galloway, 5 miles S.E. of Drummore, Wigtownshire
Melilla, Morocco

North Arklow Lightvessel 3¼ miles from N. buoy of Arlow Bank, Irish Sea, co. Wicklow
North Cheek, 1½ miles N. of Robin Hood's Bay, Yorkshire
North Foreland, 2½ miles S.E. of Margate, Kent
Noss Head, 3½ miles N.E. of Wick, Caithness
Noup Head, Orkney Islands

Old Head of Kinsale, co. Cork
Ovo Island, Crete
Owers Lightvessel in the English Channel 7 miles S.E. of Selsey Bill, Sussex

Pantellaria Island, Mediterranean Sea
Pendeen Lighthouse near St. Just, Cornwall
Planier Island, Gulf of Lions
Pointe de Penmarch near Lorient, France
Pointe de Pontusval near Ushant, France
Port Kelah, Algeria
Port Mahon, Minorca
Portland Bill, 4 miles S.W. of Weymouth, Dorset
Prawle Point, 7 miles S.E. of Kingsbridge, Devon

Queenstown (Cobh) 13 miles S.E. of Cork, Co. Cork

Ram Head near Youghal, co. Waterford
Rathlin Island 5 miles N. of Ballycastle, co. Antrim
Rattray Head 7½ miles N.W. of Peterhead, Aberdeenshire
Rockabill Lighthouse near the Skerries, Irish Sea, co. Dublin
Royal Sovereign Lightvessel in the English Channel 10 miles S.W. of Hastings, Sussex
Rundle Stone, Mounts Bay, Cornwall

St. Abb's Head 4 miles N.W. of Eyemouth, Berwickshire
St. Anns Head near Milford Haven, Pembrokeshire
St. Anthony's Point near Falmouth, Cornwall
St. Catherine's Point, Isle of Wight
St. Govan's Head near Pembroke
St. Helens Roads, Isle of Wight
St. Kilda Island, Outer Hebrides
St. Mathieu Point near Finisterre, France

Sept Isles near Roscoff, France
Skelligs Rocks, 7 miles W. of Bolus Head, co. Kerry
Skerries rocky islands in the Irish Sea off N.W. coast of Anglesey
Skerries Islands, co. Dublin
Skerryvoe Lighthouse, 10 miles S.W. from Tiree Island
Skokham Island in the St. George's Channel off the coast of Pembrokeshire
Shipwash Lightvessel in the North Sea, 15 miles E. of Harwich, Essex
Skulmartin Lightvessel in the North Channel, 9 miles S.E. from Donaghadee, co. Down
Skyro Lighthouse, Aegean Sea
Smalls Lighthouse in the St. George's Channel near St. David's Head, Pembrokeshire
South Arklow Lightvessel in the Irish Sea at the mouth of the River Avoca, co. Wicklow
South Bishop Rock Lighthouse, 5½ miles S.W. from St. David's Head, Pembrokeshire
South Cheek, Robin Hood Bay, 5 miles S.E. of Whitby, Yorkshire
South Foreland, 3 miles N.E. of Dover, Kent
South Rock Lightvessel in the Irish Sea 5 miles N.E. of Ballyquintin, co. Down
South Stack Rock, Holyhead Island, Anglesey
Spurn Point at the mouth of the River Humber, Yorkshire
Start Point, 9½ miles S.S.W. of Dartmouth, Devon
Strangford Light Buoy in the Irish Sea, co. Down
Strumble Head, 5 miles N.W. of Fishguard, Pembrokeshire
Suda Bay, Crete
Sunk Lightvessel at the mouth of the River Thames

Tabarka Island, Algeria
Tearaght Island, Blasket Islands, co. Kerry
Tintagel Head, 5 miles N.W. from Camelford, Cornwall
Tod Head Point 5¾ miles S. of Stonehaven, Kincardineshire
Tongue Lightvessel at the mouth of the River Thames
Tory Island 9 miles N.W. of Dunfanaghy, co. Donegal
Trevose Head, 4½ miles W. of Padstow, Cornwall
Tuskar Rock 7 miles N.E. of Carnsore Point, co. Wexford

Ushant Island near Brest, France
Ustica Island N. of Sicily

Wolf Rock 8 miles S.W. of Land's End, Cornwall

Zembra Island, Tunis

BIBLIOGRAPHY

Lloyd's Marine Collection at Guildhall Library.
Lloyd's Register of Shipping—Registers 1914-1918.
British Vessels Lost at Sea 1914-1918—His Majesty's Stationery Office, 1919.
Der Handelskrieg mit U-Booten, 1914-1918, Vols 1-5—Spindler, Rear Admiral—Mittler & Sohn, 1932-1966.
British Warships 1914-1919—Dittmar & Colledge—Ian Allen, 1972
Q Ships and their story—E. Keble Chatterton—Conway Maritime Press, 1972.